ADVANCE PRAISE FOR *THE HARDHAT RIOT*

"David Paul Kuhn has written perhaps the best book ever on how Democrats lost the white working class. *The Hardhat Riot* is a great read, but also a must-read to understand the voters that Democrats neglected at their own peril."
—**James Carville**, former Chief Strategist for President Bill Clinton

"Riveting . . ."
—**Jill Lepore**, *The New Yorker*

"A gripping history of a moment when two visions of America clashed—with fists flying—throughout the Wall Street district. *The Hard-Hat Riot* excavates conflicts over protest politics, American military power, and the party loyalties of the white working class that remain with us half a century later."
—**Beverly Gage**, Professor of History and American Studies, Yale University

"David Paul Kuhn's *The Hardhat Riot* captures a seminal but long-neglected turning point in the steady erosion of Democratic support among the core of the New Deal Coalition. The May 8, 1970, confrontation—AKA, 'Bloody Friday'—between anti-war protestors, mostly students, and tough, unionized construction workers determined to demonstrate their support of American troops in Vietnam, marked the start of the split between a well-educated elite and an increasingly discontented working class, a split that over time produced the election of Donald Trump. This book is crucial for anyone seeking to understand the politics of 2020 and beyond."
—**Thomas B. Edsall**, Contributing Opinion Writer, *The New York Times*, and author of *Building Red America*

"David Paul Kuhn has breathed new life into an uproarious seminal event in modern political history, skillfully tracing fault lines running from the late 1960s up to the present. A timely, smart, adrenalin-fueled account conveyed with you-are-there immediacy."
—**Laurence Bergreen**, author of *Over the Edge of the World*

"This is red-meat history with a hot splash of tabasco. David Paul Kuhn brings to life a period that is not only fascinating in itself but also illuminates the age of Donald Trump. If you want to understand how blue-collar Americans came to feel so disparaged and deplored, *The Hardhat Riot* is a great place to start. A truly captivating read."

—**Robert Guest**, Foreign Editor, *The Economist*

"Sometimes events that are long forgotten have reverberations that dominate our times. In *The Hardhat Riot*, David Paul Kuhn skillfully shows how the split between traditionally Democratic constituencies—blue-collar workers and militant students—eerily foreshadows the bitter political splits of our time."

—**Michael Barone**, author of *The Almanac of American Politics* and Emeritus Fellow, American Enterprise Institute

"*The Hardhat Riot* is an arresting and often chilling narrative of the events that drove a wedge between white working-class voters and the Democratic Party, setting America on the road to today's right-wing populism. I couldn't stop reading it. If you want to understand why cultural issues became central to our politics, read this book."

—**William Galston**, former policy advisor to President Clinton and Senior Fellow, the Brookings Institution

"Trenchant. . . . A welcome resurrection of a forgotten riot with relevance for our current fragmented political landscape."

—*Kirkus*

"David Paul Kuhn details, with much new research, the changing political conditions before and after the spring of 1970, when Nixon saw the opportunity after the May 8 Hardhat Riot. No previous book has so convincingly documented how important this single event was in changing the class base of both the Republican and Democratic parties."

—**Joan Hoff**, former president of the Center for the Study of the Presidency

"I picked up David Paul Kuhn's *The Hardhat Riot* with the intention of skimming and found myself engrossed, reading every page. Well-written, painstakingly researched, this is an important book that gives life to history and explains the divorce between working-class whites and the Democratic Party, and yet rarer still, is also a real pleasure to read."

—**Charlie Cook**, Editor and Publisher of The Cook Political Report

"Largely through the microcosm of New York City, David Paul Kuhn's *The Hardhat Riot* delves deeply into the estrangement of the Democratic Party from America's blue-collar workers. For all of its fascinating detail of the travails of America's metropolis, *The Hardhat Riot* also offers a broad and rich panorama of American politics of the past 50 years and the most persuasive explanation for the rise of Donald Trump that has yet appeared."

—**Ross K. Baker**, Professor of American Government, Rutgers University

The Hardhat Riot

*Nixon, New York City,
and the Dawn of the
White Working-Class
Revolution*

DAVID
PAUL KUHN

OXFORD
UNIVERSITY PRESS

OXFORD
UNIVERSITY PRESS

Oxford University Press is a department of the University of Oxford. It furthers
the University's objective of excellence in research, scholarship, and education
by publishing worldwide. Oxford is a registered trade mark of Oxford University
Press in the UK and certain other countries.

Published in the United States of America by Oxford University Press
198 Madison Avenue, New York, NY 10016, United States of America.

Library of Congress Cataloging-in-Publication Data
Names: Kuhn, David Paul, author.
Title: The hardhat riot : Nixon, New York City, and the dawn of the white
working-class revolution / David Paul Kuhn.
Description: New York, NY : Oxford University Press, [2020] |
Includes bibliographical references and index. |
Identifiers: LCCN 2019058321 (print) | LCCN 2019058322 (ebook) |
ISBN 9780190064716 (hardback) | ISBN 9780190064730 (epub)
Subjects: LCSH: Riots—New York (State)—New York—History—20th century. |
Anti-war demonstrations—New York (State)—New York—History—20th century. |
Student protesters—Violence against—New York (State)—New York—History—20th century. |
Construction workers—New York (State)—New York—History—20th century. |
Social conflict—New York (State)—New York—History—20th century. |
United States—Social conditions—1960–1980. | United States—History—1969–
Classification: LCC HV6483.N7 K84 2020 (print) | LCC HV6483.N7 (ebook) |
DDC 363.32/309747109047—dc23
LC record available at https://lccn.loc.gov/2019058321
LC ebook record available at https://lccn.loc.gov/2019058322

9 8 7 6 5 4 3

Printed by LSC Communications, United States of America

CONTENTS

Introduction

I am seeking to rescue the poor stockinger, the Luddite cropper, the "obsolete" hand-loom weaver, the "utopian" artisan, and even the deluded . . . from the enormous condescension of posterity. Their crafts and traditions may have been dying. Their hostility to the new industrialism may have been backward-looking. Their communitarian ideals may have been fantasies. Their insurrectionary conspiracies may have been foolhardy. But they lived through these times of acute social disturbance, and we did not. Their aspirations were valid in terms of their own experience.

—E. P. Thompson, *The Making of the English Working Class*[1]

They arrived in waves, in colored hard hats and worn steel-toed boots, shouldering American flags, thundering, "U—S—A. All the way," intent on confronting antiwar demonstrators on Wall Street. Police rushed to form a human chain and separate the two factions. Hippies chanted, "Peace now!" Hardhats shot back, "Love it or leave it!" The protestors pushed forward and shouted their opposition to the "fucking war." They expected it to be a matter of words. They had been told "the police are here to protect us." Then, in the same place where George Washington was inaugurated, the construction workers charged and the police did not protect them.

The hardhats plowed through thousands, swinging their fists wildly, fighting to raise American flags. Students tripped and screamed and flailed for escape. For hours, they ran for their lives "like a cattle stampede." Young people were pulled from melees by their hair. Others were found unconscious and prone in the dirty streets. By the time the police realized the scope of the riot, the mob was too large and the cops were too few. City Hall was now under siege.

Two liberalisms collided that day, presaging the long Democratic civil war ahead, and revealing a rupture expanding across the American landscape, a divide that had grown so vast it seemed unbridgeable by the time elites noticed. That is, unless one looked back to understand how it all began.

An earthquake only feels like an aberration. We know otherwise, of course. It's the consequence of vast plates that move with glacial time, mere millimeters a year, yet build mountains and carve oceans. Normally, these plates pass one another with friction so minimal it doesn't register in our lives. But sometimes too much subterranean stress amasses and the plates get stuck, frequently where the strain has long collected—that is, a fault line. Then the pressure rises. The force exceeds what bonds the plates together. Blocks of crust collide and some fall. The fault line ruptures and the land shakes.

◆

In 2016, the Democratic nominee performed worse with working-class whites than any other nominee, of either party, since the Second World War. Yet before that fateful campaign, we had arrived at a place where the party of the workingman relied most on the allegiance of educated whites, and the party of big business depended on working-class whites. Years later, even well-informed Americans still struggled to consider all Donald Trump exposed—the fragility of our norms, the degradation of blue-collar America, aloof elites, the corrosion of our common ground. What revealed that corrosion, and shook American life afterward, was not detached from history. It was the consequence of a tectonic break a half-century ago.

May 1970 was a tumultuous month in a tumultuous era. After Cambodia and Kent State, the antiwar movement revived and radicalized as never before. Even after Watergate, Richard Nixon recalled these weeks as some of the most traumatic of his presidency. His expansion of the war into Cambodia caused a cascade of events that brought much of the nation to the brink, and Nixon with it—until, as William Safire put it, the hardhats helped "turn the tide."[2]

Those who raged most against the war were not only college students, they also tended to hail from suburban affluence. They were the educated youth who ushered in the counterculture, who believed in men by the name of Gene McCarthy, John Lindsay, and George McGovern. They were also a class apart from most soldiers over there. Most Vietnam veterans were blue-collar whites. They were usually boys of the lower middle class and poorer backgrounds. Vietnam, unlike any war since at least the Civil War, asked the most of those who came from less.

New York was still a blue-collar city at the dawn of the 1970s. The deindustrialization of America had hit it early and hard. The consequences for the city forecasted those for America. For a time, New York staved off the worst. There was a roaring national economy, a stock market bubble, a "Second Skyscraper Age" remaking downtown. Thousands of tradesmen and laborers crowded into Lower Manhattan for the work, including to build two colossal towers.

It was a cold rainy morning when hundreds descended those towers and other worksites between Battery Park and the Bowery. There was talk of it being their turn now, of reaching their "boiling point." Some solely wanted to "break heads."

It was the era when FDR's everyman first turned against the liberalism that once had championed him. When Richard Nixon, more than any other, moved the Republican Party from blue bloods to blue collars and wrote the strategic playbook for GOP campaigns thereafter. It was when the New Left won popular culture, then the Democratic Party, but lost blue-collar whites along the way. And that conflict never burned brighter and more brutal than during the Hardhat Riot, when two archetypes of liberalism clashed, and the Democratic Party proved one of its casualties.

The hardhats won the day but lost the long fight. Blue-collar whites' societal clout withered before their wages did, but that too was near. This book brings us back to when the middle class reached its apex in American life, and working-class whites began their long march to less. The Hardhat Riot, and what it inspired, was not *the* turning point in the story of America's conservative party winning the working class (a peculiar tale when seen beside other developed nations in the second half of the twentieth century). Few historic moments are without precedent. Few people change tides. But sometimes episodes capture an era and steer the current. Sometimes, the contemporary can best be understood by the lessons of history, including one story that shifted history.

We rarely recall the past linearly. Our memories feature the events that struck us, for good and for ill. This is a book, in part, about the issues and episodic dramas that drove the hardhats to the streets, these men who became stand-ins for Nixon's Silent Majority, in the same year that *Time* magazine named "Middle Americans" its person of the year.

This is also the story of a city, a mayor, a president, a people, and an era when the nation diverged—living different cultures, different wars, different economies, until the American experience became so fragmented that the singular became an anachronism. It was not even a year after Americans had landed on the moon. It was a time of big things. At the dawn of the seventies, however, those big things that had helped unite these states already felt like vestiges of a fading nation.

It's unclear why the Hardhat Riot's story has gone untold until now. The thousands of pages of never-before-seen records, which served as the foundation of the riot's story, could have been accessed sooner by an industrious researcher. Histories of the era tend to note the riot as a flare of backlash, if they mention it at all. At the most contentious level, perhaps that stems from what all freshmen history students learn: that winners write history. We think of that axiom in terms of the wars between nations. But it also applies to cultural conflicts within nations.

There are other riots we associate with the era, whose stories have been told. The Detroit Riot, Attica, and Stonewall were fundamentally significant for what they symbolized. And, as Stonewall reminds us, their full meaning is not always recognized in their time. Yet the Hardhat Riot resonates with the significance of presidents by the name of Reagan and W. and Trump. Modern liberalism, and the innumerable books and films born of it, capably depict the "root causes" that shaped contemporary Democratic constituencies. Here is a book—not *the* book, just a book—that reaches back to Democrats' old constituency. This is a book about some of our history, of stories not yet fully told, that shaped American politics for more than a half-century after. Many of the seminal Vietnam marches of the era, such as the march on the Pentagon immortalized by Norman Mailer, had fewer attendees than the hardhats' largest rally, the "Workers' Woodstock" recounted in this book. Or maybe this story is only now being told for simpler reasons. Episodes of the past sometimes require the present. Or is it, rather, that a difficult present compels a better understanding of what made it?

The first day after the Hardhat Riot, it was front-page news and network evening news. But it faded into footnotes and anecdote thereafter. Perhaps, however, some early tremors' importance is only appreciable after the quake. And it's the aftermath—whether it has come to pass or has only just begun— that highlights the need to go back, back to the time when Manhattan sank as the World Trade Center rose, to when regular people had to answer for their convictions, and to a day that captured it all, when two liberalisms battled and the era's festering divisions first exploded on the streets of New York.

PART 1 | Backdrop

CHAPTER 1 | **"Out for Blood"**
May 8, 1970

PROTESTS HAD BECOME common within the Financial District's main plaza, where Wall Street and Broad Street cross beneath the New York Stock Exchange, the House of Morgan, the Bankers Trust tower, and Federal Hall, the site of the first US Congress and George Washington's inauguration. "Wall Street, like other streets across the nation, has been rent by antiwar protests," the *Wall Street Journal* fumed in an editorial that morning.

It was one of those cold, wet mornings common to the city in early May, when the temperature feels closer to winter than summer. Still, by 7:30 students emerged from subway tunnels at Broadway and Wall Street, at Chase Manhattan Plaza, and weaved their way through commuters and an avenue crowded with yellow taxis that tinged neon in the rain, their tailpipe vapor drifting into Manhattan's interminable smog. The students gathered to the south, midblock. They had white armbands and held placards that read, NOW BEFORE IT'S NEVER. More than 48,000 Americans were already lost to the war.

Demonstrators rotated two abreast before the Stock Exchange's marble colonnade. They were kids just south and north of twenty years, soft-looking, pale, shaggy. Boys, serious but subdued, with cherubic faces hidden behind overgrown beards. Girls with little makeup and often center-parted long hair. The clothing was loose, worn, wooly, velveteen. They wore bell-bottoms, antiwar buttons on big lapels, a lot of glasses. There was a girl in a baby blue poncho, her black hair halfway down her small back. A boy with circular eyeglasses and a faded green military coat, muttering, "Death is war." A girl in a striped serape. Her antiwar placard hung off her neck. A longhaired boy played his harmonica. At least one black boy, natural hair, dark clothes. A white boy with an afro.

Activists planned to "close down Wall Street today," once reinforcements arrived. For now, they were mellow. Many held their arms aloft, fingering peace signs, chanting, "Peace now!" Some sang "Dow Jones is falling down" to the tune of "London Bridge." A young man with an unkempt beard and beaked nose wore an inverted stainless-steel pot on his head. Still, antipathy accompanied the sparse lightheartedness. At one point, two businessmen in beige raincoats hurried by the picketers. A young protestor heckled: "Hey, how's the war profiting? Pretty good this week, huh?"

A student leader looked "fearful," police reported. He had heard construction workers planned to attack them. He reminded the cops that he had phoned them twice last night. The students would learn later that there had been other warnings.

About seventy-five policemen were assigned to the area for today's rally. Deputy Chief Inspector Valentine Pfaffmann told subordinates to "be alert" for clashes between hardhats and hippies.

It was Friday, May 8, 1970. Four days earlier, at Kent State in Ohio, four student protestors had been shot dead. One of the deceased hailed from a New York City suburb.

The antiwar movement had dragged on for years. Still, the body bags came home. Still, young people were drafted. Still, powerful men told America, *We're winning*. Still, the Vietnam War slogged on—and more boys died in a faraway land for a stalemate. Yet protestors believed Kent State was a turning point. That it clarified the stakes, that it was life or death for them too. That Americans would surely now champion their cause. That the war could finally end.

Mayor John Lindsay believed that too. He was certain that the antiwar movement's opportunity was his own. Lindsay had closed the public schools for the day to encourage New Yorkers to "reflect solemnly on the numbing events at Kent State" and the "fate of America," giving more than a million students the day off. The Roman Catholic schools, heavily blue-collar and ethnic, remained open. Advisors had urged Lindsay to also lower American flags citywide. "Who could complain?" mayoral aide Sid Davidoff thought. "Nonviolent kids were shot by National Guardsmen!"

In recent days, however, there had been scattered confrontations south of City Hall. The antiwar movement's resurgence had riled local workmen. Thousands of construction workers were downtown. The city was experiencing its skyscraper renaissance. At one location, near Wall Street, hardhats were erecting the tallest towers in the world—the World Trade Center.

Meanwhile, by half past eight, as Mayor Lindsay played tennis uptown and protestors swelled to five hundred downtown, a workman phoned the police. He said hardhats "are out for blood today."

CHAPTER 2 | The Revolutionaries of Grand
Central and Columbia
Spring 1968

I N THE CANYONS of downtown Manhattan, the Democratic Party's future
would be bludgeoned by its past. It would have been unthinkable only one
generation before: the New Deal "forgotten man" siding with the "party of
big business and privilege," as Richard Nixon once rued the label. The nation was more divided than any time since the Civil War. But even a couple
of years back, no one imagined that workers would attack students. That
family men, long demanding "law and order," would create anarchy. That the
old Democratic Party would attack the new and Richard Nixon would seize
the breach. That the Silent Majority would riot. At the time, few people of
influence were troubled by class conflict; fewer still expected it to boil over
into mass violence. The chattering class worried about race wars. Would the
president further escalate the real war? The media was obsessed with hippies.
But the average American was neither impressed by the counterculture nor
especially bothered about it. Hippies were considered apart from activism.
The antiwar movement, in its early years, had echoed protests of earlier eras.
People seemed to be always marching about something. What was changing
happened gradually, until it seemed that everything had changed, on television at least. There was no singular beginning. But in March 1968, all that
did change, seemed to still be beginning.[1]

◆

Yippies plied newsmen with free coffee and Danish. Allen Ginsberg played a small one-octave organ and chanted, "Hari Krishna, Hari Krishna, Krishnaaaaaaa, Rama Krishna, Hari Krishna, Hari Rama." The yippies' spokesman appeared "distressed." It was an introduction. Newsmen, meet the new Youth International Party. No flower children they. Yippies were radicalized hippies, it was suggested. Theatrical rabble-rousers, it was already clear. As one speaker tittered, "A yippie is what happens to a hippie when a cop hits him." The police would soon oblige.

The yippies were in midtown Manhattan, inside the nation's tallest hotel, courting publicity like admen. They explained their plans for the 1968 Democratic convention in Chicago. There was Allen Ginsberg, the bespectacled and black-bearded poet, coffeehouse famous, but also singers Judy Collins and Phil Ochs, and the revolutionary vanguard, Jerry Rubin, et al. Camera flashes flickered. Judy Collins said that Chicago would be a "testimonial for life." Lest elders mock, the *Washington Post* noted that these were the people who "set the tone" in popular culture. The popular kids now promised political action—a quarter-million youths would storm Chicago and "a hundred thousand people may burn draft cards." As one yippie put it, "We're going to Chicago not to drop out of society but to claim it as rightfully ours."[2]

But first this Friday, they promoted a "yip-in" at Grand Central Station, the city's transportation hub. The flyer promised a "spring mating service celebrating the Equinox." Mostly boys showed up. It was America's mutinous bourgeois youth, college-bred, proudly *not* uptight. By midnight, three thousand youths crowded the main concourse. Long hair, sideburns, mop-tops, turtlenecks, rectangular coats, jeans, beaded necklaces, floppy hats, striped and corduroy slacks. A fraction came in face paint and costume—velvet capes, gowns, top hats, keffiyehs. Students spoke of ending the war. They also snake-danced, formed conga lines, hummed "ommm," reveled beside radios. Hundreds of colored balloons floated up to the zodiac constellations of the vast domed cerulean ceiling. Atop one of the grand marble staircases, hippies unfurled a banner that read, LIBERTY, EQUALITY, FRATERNITY. Commuters dodged these Jacobins. Men in fedoras and skinny ties tarried for the spectacle. Clean-shaven cops, in blue caps and long buttoned coats, kept back.

Mayor Lindsay's staff had been warned. A few aides showed up. Their liaison was yippie leader Abbie Hoffman, a New Left gadfly with a nasal New England accent, a thick nose, and curly hair that ran long "like a female," to quote his FBI file. Hoffman's childhood had been upper-middle-class and "idyllic," and he had been rebelling ever since. The year before, Hoffman and others rained cash down on the Stock Exchange trading floor.

Brokers leapt to snatch the drifting dollar bills. Two months later—about when the Stock Exchange erected a bulletproof glass barrier to prevent sequels—Hoffman, Ginsberg, and Rubin joined tens of thousands of others in Washington. They marched for immediate withdrawal from Vietnam. It was "for the most part orderly," narrated one newsreel. A turtlenecked boy placed carnations in soldiers' rifle barrels, which became the day's iconic image. Norman Mailer, reporting in his celebrated book *Armies of the Night*, had words with a neo-Nazi. A US marshal slammed the Nazi against a wall: "You're nothing but a rat fart who makes my job harder, and gives the scum around me room to breathe, cause they look at you and feel righteous." There were omens that extremists could eat the movement. The *New York Times*'s James Reston described the march as "taken over by the militant minority." He added, "It is difficult to report publicly the ugly and vulgar provocation of many of the militants. They spat on some of the soldiers in the front line at the Pentagon and goaded them with the most vicious personal slander." Other young people sought to "exorcise" the Pentagon. Protestors incanted, "Out! . . . Out! . . . Out!" Abbie Hoffman had pledged "to raise the Pentagon three hundred feet." Mailer caught himself whispering along, "Out, demons, out!"[3]

At Grand Central, on the milky glass-and-brass clock, the little hand struck one. A "mating" celebration, it was not. Boys wrote "fuck you" on station walls. They puffed joints beside the Tactical Patrol Force. Youths shouted, "Peace now! Peace now!" At the center of the station, more than a dozen boys scaled the famed gazebolike information booth. Railroad officials bellowed angrily. A boy broke a hand off the landmark clock. Cops tried to seize him. Forty kids swarmed the gazebo's rooftop. One student raised his fist into the air and unfolded a banner, UP AGAINST THE WALL, MOTHER FUCKER. Cops were "physically restraining" their own men. Boys spray-painted the glass opals of the four faces of the clock. Cherry bombs exploded overhead. Students chanted, "Burn, baby, burn! Burn, baby, burn!" More firecrackers. Young people held small plastic transistor radios to their ears. WBAI's Bob Fass, a popular disc jockey, was heard waxing, "As H. Rap Brown said, 'Violence is as American as apple pie and cherry bombs.'"

Abbie Hoffman, costumed as a Native American, stood on the sidelines. Hoffman begged a Lindsay aide for a bullhorn.

"Abbie, you blew it," said the aide, Barry Gottehrer. "Why didn't you bring your own damn megaphone and clear this place an hour ago? Look at this mess. This thing is so fucked up now."

Cops were told to empty the station. "At first they were pretty nice," noted a reporter, "but then something happened." Cops wedged in swinging.

Batons clapped off heads and backs. Students fell and fled and shouted, "Fascist! . . . Pig!" A *Village Voice* reporter was shoved into a glass door and cut on the forehead. The reporter saw a captain approach a hunched-over boy and crack his head against an iron-grated door, only for the boy to be charged with assault. Hundreds of young people gave Hitler salutes to the cops and shouted, "Sieg heil!" Abbie Hoffman was struck by police batons and cowered into a fetal position. Yippies appropriated an antiwar chant to their circumstance: "Hell no, we won't go!" Most were driven to the street like a "cattle-run." Jerry Rubin paced one corridor, stopping students fleeing the cops, asking if they thought the violence would impact plans for Chicago. In the main concourse, the marble floor was left littered and bloodstained. Balloons, stenciled with YIPPIE, still floated at the celestial ceiling. Said one observer, "A helluva way to run a railroad."

POLITICAL ACTIVISM NEW HIPPIE 'THING,' headlined the *Times*. The paper of record pondered whether the yip-in signaled a "new turn in the hippie movement toward activism." The *Washington Post* quoted one on-looker, "This is a preview of what Chicago is going to look like." Or as Abbie Hoffman later wrote, "The Grand Central Station Massacre knocked out the hippie image of Chicago and let the whole world know there would be blood on the streets of Chicago." The next day, Hoffman flew to Illinois to join Movement leaders—Tom Hayden, Jerry Rubin, Dave Dellinger, Rennie Davis—at a YMCA camp near Chicago, where they planned for the Democratic convention.[4]

◆

One month later, on a cool gray spring day in 1968, activists seized the headquarters of Columbia College. Columbia stood atop high ground that George Washington's army had once defended. Beside the campus, a rock escarpment loomed over Harlem. There, in a park, Columbia planned to build a gymnasium. To show civic solidarity, it offered Harlemites their own free facilities. Local activists still considered it a "land grab." Once more, elite Columbia had encroached on the black and poor. The architect's rendering didn't help. A lavish entrance faced the campus. A plain door faced Harlem, on the lower level. Separate and unequal. Ivy League activists rallied to "Gym Crow must go!"

It was students radicalized by Vietnam, the draft, the school's affiliation with a military research consortium, civil rights, the tin ear of authority, distrust of authority. Counterculture zealotry had swept over campuses worldwide. "Take your desires for reality," read Paris graffiti. By April '68, Columbia's activists wanted a fight.

Their leader knew how to pick it. Mark Rudd was the son of suburban strivers, thin with wavy blond hair that did not run long. He looked like a college square. He felt like Che. He had recently returned from a sojourn to Castro's Cuba (an "extremely humanistic society," he explained). Rudd was the campus leader of Students for a Democratic Society. And he came to Columbia's sundial that day, the center of campus, to rouse.

But activists wanted action, not oratory. They marched to the gym work-site off campus. Among them, another SDS leader, Ted Gold. They tore down some fencing. Rudd chased the police sirens, yelling, "Tear down the fucking fence!" A cop wrestled one student to the ground. Others "jumped the cop, beating and kicking him." Rudd arrived. A student was in handcuffs. Rudd stood on his soapbox, a mound of dirt, and threatened, "You have fifteen minutes to get that guy unbusted." More sirens. More cop lights. The kids realized they were not on safe turf. Their confederation was a few hundred strong—white student radicals, some black collegians, and Harlem activists. The group retreated behind Columbia's iron gate. A runner said, "Hamilton Hall is open." Someone yelled, "Seize Hamilton!"

Dean Henry S. Coleman, crewcut and square-jawed, awaited them in the lobby. He was conciliatory. He proffered the gym. The activists gained a foothold and took a mile. Inside the inspiring neoclassical hall, before a college dean fidgeting with his tobacco pipe, Rudd thought, "This [is] war— or something very close to it." They took the dean and two other officials hostage, and the hall with them. Rudd yelled, "We've got the Man!" For SDS, which had its national office in Manhattan for several years, Columbia marked the beginning of its shift from organizing to direct action. There had been smaller occupations elsewhere. But Columbia's experience was transformative. College radicals had "the Man." Student activists had discovered their power, and how easily administrators and faculty were cowed by it.

"During the first night the white students discovered something else: black power," as historian William Manchester wrote. "Despite all our talk about revolution, most of the whites, myself included, were scared," Rudd recalled of that first night. "We were still really middle-class kids." At first, the two bands harmonized. Blacks put up their posters (Malcolm X and Stokely Carmichael). Whites put up their posters (Che and Lenin). The black students soon wanted to barricade the building. The white radicals thought that would irritate other students. The groups separated. The SDS kids held a typical symposium—Russian Revolution, Vietnam, campus politics. It lasted hours. Before dawn, the blacks broke the news: "It would be better if you left." Rudd was "stunned speechless." SDS leaders, Rudd and Ted Gold and kindred, woke their soldiers (students sleeping on pillows and blankets). Three hundred white kids filed nicely out the door. Rudd had tears in his eyes.[5]

About half of the kids trailed off. The remainder broke into Low Library, a grand building modeled after Rome's Pantheon. The radicals overran security and crowded the marble rotunda, beneath statues of Sophocles, Demosthenes, Augustus, and Euripides (who had once advised, "Impudence is the worst of all human diseases").

Rudd was "amazed" by "what we had just done." The library housed the school president's office. The radicals broke in. They read his files, smoked his cigars, sipped his sherry, urinated into his wastebasket, admired his Rembrandt and Ming vases and "seemingly miles" of books. "None" of the school president's books, Rudd claimed, "showed signs of having been read." And the Ivy League revolutionary concluded, unread books proved Columbia's president was a "phony."

The black activists released the hostages after a day. White students occupied more halls. Radicals hung a sign outside the president's office window: LIBERATED AREA, BE FREE TO JOIN US. And a hero came from the west. Tom Hayden was working across the river in Newark. He had a plump nose and pockmarked cheeks and showed up trim, clean-shaven, short-haired, his collared shirt tucked in, a narrow tie finely knotted. Hayden was fresh from mainstream activism. He was in his late twenties now, the old man of the young radicals. Hayden was a former SDS national president and the Jefferson of its founding statement. "I had never seen anything quite like this," Hayden remembered. "Students, at last, had taken power in their own hands." Hayden led the Mathematics Hall occupation. In two days, the students "liberated" five halls. Abbie Hoffman and Jerry Rubin showed up.

The police were dispatched to campus for the first time in years. "Previously," the *Times* clarified, "the police have gone to the Columbia vicinity during panty raids." Thirty of Columbia's junior faculty massed in front of Low Library's high columns. The faculty intended to block police from entering. But the NYPD was not ordered in, not yet. Columbia's president, scholarly and aloof Grayson Kirk, sought Mayor Lindsay's intervention. Lindsay's best and brightest were already there. They met with a group of professors. The left-leaning aides were startled by the instructors' ignorance of realpolitik. "They were literally crazy," aide Barry Gottehrer recalled. Lindsay's bullish streetwise aide, Sid Davidoff, challenged one professor, "What are you going to do when the radical right starts taking buildings?"

The gym project was suspended. It didn't pacify. Columbia's administration asked police to evict the white students but leave the black activists
alone. They feared Harlem's wrath. They hoped Lindsay would make the hard
call. Lindsay's base included blacks, the avant-garde, counterculture youth,
bookish liberals. He wisely kept clear. Columbia's leadership dithered.[6]

Inside one occupied hall, in large print across a door, someone wrote:

LENIN WON

FIDEL WON

WE WILL

WIN[7]

The white radicals began asking supporters for Vaseline to shield their skin
from Mace. They chatted all day in their "communes" and bonded over their
common "struggle." "We shared everything. We shared our oranges, our cokes,
our sandwiches," said one female occupier. "People are living here," said another
young woman. "It's a home. I've never been so comfortable on this campus."
Students danced, played drums, burned draft cards, participated in rap ses-
sions at all hours. "We talked endlessly of issues and strategies," recalled Abbie
Hoffman. But, Hoffman added, they also "laughed, made love, smoked dope,
sang, argued, and waited." One couple wed in a hall and called it "holy ground."
They were pronounced not husband and wife but "children of the new age,"
which elicited wild applause. There was a fixation on winning amnesty, little
sleep, much discussion about what to do when the cops came. Sirens cried at
all hours. Graffiti expressed yippies' outlook: UP AGAINST THE WALL MOTHER
FUCKER. They chanted, "Hell no, we won't go!" In this era, radicals were
investing in an idea—repression riles revolutionaries (the converse was ignored).
They favored Albert Camus, C. Wright Mills, Herbert Marcuse. One popular
New Left slogan: "Heighten the contradictions."

For help "rattling the pigs," female students were recruited. "What we
are dealing with is a certain kind of Irish Catholic prudity," a Columbia student leader instructed. "Pick up your shirt. . . . Tell 'em their mother sucks
black cocks or takes black cocks in the ass. . . . I know that can be tough. We
aren't all completely liberated. But if we use words like 'sucks' about their
mother, these fuckin' cops will blow like a balloon. And when they blow," he
added, "the whole country will see the naked face, the naked ass, of fascism."[8]

Indeed, "a Barnard woman was more likely than a Columbia man to
'curse a cop' during a riot," a Columbia psychologist said. Or as a reform
Democratic pol from the area put it, "Coeds would use enormously provocative language and would spray the cops with hair spray and do everything
they could to incite them." There seemed to be a presumption that the police

were less likely to rough up girls for insults, and maybe so, but not always so. One cop told a female student to move aside. She refused. She yelled, "Your sister sucks off your mother!" The cop struck her.

"The revolutionary students spat at people they disliked, including senior faculty members," wrote Diana Trilling, one of the "New York intellectuals" (an esteemed group of the city's older intelligentsia); her renowned husband, Lionel Trilling, was a Columbia professor. "An old couple crossing the campus was shouted at: 'Go home and die, you old people, go home and die.' A law professor . . . walking with his wife near the campus gates, was gratuitously punched in the stomach by a passing student wearing the red armband of his militancy."

The prestige press breathlessly covered the occupation. But as Diana Trilling noted, bourgeois proprieties prevented them from detailing the obscene.[9]

About a week into the siege, a Lindsay aide warned Rudd and Gold that the cops were coming. Columbia's President Kirk made "the most painful" decision of his life. With black lawyers and black cops assisting, all the black activists surrendered and left peaceably. White radicals refused to go. A faculty emissary passed along a final warning to each "commune." In the Mathematics Hall (where Tom Hayden and Abbie Hoffman were), students barricaded doors with steel desks and cabinets and tied them together with hoses. They crisscrossed windows with nailed plywood boards and soaped the stairs to fell cops. Police squadrons assembled with civilian observers, including Columbia faculty. The police were ordered in. Some cops intended to make it hurt. Inside President Kirk's office, students sang out, "We shall not be moved." They were moved. Police whacked numerous resisters and reporters with their clubs, often needlessly. Some activists were shoved down concrete stairways. There was teargas. Students shouted "obscenities," along with, "Pig . . . pig . . . pig!" Some students hurled bottles, office supplies, and furniture at the cops. Others kicked and scratched and flailed. Many police were spat on. Numerous activists linked arms or went limp, forcing patrolmen to carry them out (one girl bit a cop in the stomach as he did). There were some "faked cries of pain" before newsmen. One doctor saw four handcuffed male students dragged down stone steps, and as their heads collided, he yelled, "You don't have to be that rough." "Get out of the way," a cop responded, rather typically. On the street, bloody and dazed students were shoved inside police wagons. Some students chanted, "More police! More police!"[10]

Before dawn, exhausted cops milled in the darkness on the green campus quad. Radicals yelled more insults. They had called cops swine for days. One cop charged. Soon many. They clubbed radical and regular students alike, chasing some kids into their dorms. One taciturn local cop admitted the overnight violence was "uncalled for."

"It's some joke, ain't it, a rich kid calling a police officer 'pig,'" said a stocky black Irish cop chain-smoking over a beer, the same man who struck the female student for telling him "your sister sucks off your mother." "Everything I got I worked for. It gets me sore when I see these kids, who been handed everything, pissing it away, talking like bums." The police had seethed for days. The common New York cop was either of Irish or Italian descent, from a blue-collar Catholic family, many living in ethnic enclaves of Queens or Brooklyn. (One poll found that a majority of white Catholic Brooklynites had kin or a close friend in the NYPD.) Many saw spoiled brats protesting—kids dismissing advantages they never had, while scorning them for doing their job. Lionel Trilling grew up in a working-class home, like most of the elder New York intellectuals. He saw cops stoked by "animosity, jealousy, of the white students who could so easily throw away their educational advantages, treat them so lightly." Todd Gitlin, a future Columbia professor and former SDS national leader, noted: "In the iconography of the underground press, they were uptight, uniformed, helmeted goons; we were loose, free, loving freaks. They harrumphed about law and order; we desecrated their temples." Looking back decades later, in his book *The Sixties,* Gitlin recognized that his fellow SDS activists were often "children of privilege" who "had not reckoned" with, or perhaps even noticed, the "class war." But few did, back then.[11]

Afterward, activists recalled the occupation as paradise lost. Students had built communes, made a stand, fought police. It was all very exciting. As one male occupier said while socializing with students before the cops came in: "Our struggle" is an "electric awakening."

There were 696 arrests (about seven in ten were Columbia students). Tom Hayden, Abbie Hoffman, and Jerry Rubin were charged with second-degree trespassing. Seventy-seven students sustained injuries ranging from "heavy bruises and scalp lacerations" to "sprains and severe fright," and there were two fractures. Fourteen cops were hurt, some seriously. After one cop was reportedly kicked, he had a heart attack. On May Day, with the large-scale clashes over, bands of students still scuffled with cops. A student knocked a policeman's cap off his head. The cop bent over to retrieve it. A boy leapt from a second-floor window onto his back. The cop would endure three spinal operations in three years. His attacker ran away. As the *Times* reported, the cop never ran again.[12]

"It is the biggest year for students since 1848—a year of student-led revolution in Europe," *Time* reported. Students were protesting worldwide. In the United States, from January to June '68, there were major demonstrations on about a hundred campuses. But no campus roused American radicals like Columbia. In the Mathematics Hall, CHE was found written across one wall, below CREATE TWO, THREE, . . . MANY COLUMBIAS, a rally cry Tom Hayden repeated afterward (it was based off a Che Guevara anthem: "Create two, three, many Vietnams"). Ted Gold told reporters, "We are working, not just for a revolutionary Columbia, but for a revolutionary America." Columbia "confirmed" Abbie Hoffman's belief that "young people were on the brink of an explosion and that police violence would radicalize them," wrote biographer Marty Jezer. Jerry Rubin said, "We're now in the business of wholesale disruption" and the "dislocation of the American society." Columbia's renowned anthropologist Margaret Mead said the student occupation marked "the end of an epoch" in campus culture. *Time* noted, "Columbia seemed contagious, as minirevolutions broke out on other campuses."[13]

But the people were not with the revolutionaries. Even at Columbia, a citadel of liberalism, two-thirds of students and three-fourths of faculty opposed the occupation, despite a narrow majority of both groups supporting their goals. The greater New York City area—still left of America's center—blamed student radicals for the violence and unrest. One-tenth blamed the administration. Columbia offered an early lesson. A fulcrum of New Left activism, the Students for a Democratic Society had estranged itself from the public. But collegian leftists were not ready to heed that lesson. A *Times* editorial cautioned, "In society, as in physics, actions tend to produce reactions."[14]

◆

Conservatives were a small faction at Columbia. The radicals saw them as retrograde, "jocks," "isolated and pathetic," in Rudd's words. Rightists called leftists "pukes." But one conservative student group framed their criticism a different way, a most Nixonian way. It turned class against the admirers of Lenin and Che. They contended it was working class versus tony greenbelt: "We're Staten Island. They're Scarsdale."[15]

In midtown Manhattan, at Richard Nixon's new campaign headquarters, staff watched Columbia and found their inner Staten Islander. Pat Buchanan, Nixon's young conservative aide, shot off a missive about the Ivy "national disgrace." Both parties' presidential primaries were at full bore. A few weeks after the occupation, while contesting the 1968 Oregon primary, Nixon read of a lightning rod he could wield. Columbia's seizure was "the first major skirmish in a revolutionary struggle to seize the universities of this country and transform them into sanctuaries for radicals and vehicles for [the] revolutionary," Nixon preached at one stop. If "student violence is either rewarded or goes unpunished," he added, it would "invite" worse.[16]

Chicago cops also followed events in New York. Some officers worried that Manhattan's troubles could preview their own. The two police departments conferred. Said one Chicago cop after Columbia, "I hope that doesn't happen here."[17]

| Chicago '68

E ACH NIGHT THE conflict reran like a play, capturing the drama of the era or the tragedy of it, as the media broadcasted the performances—pigs against peaceniks—and the big lights turned on and teargas guns went *putt-putt-putt* and canisters sailed through the sky and smoke consumed the land. Demonstrators screamed and hurled rocks and fled as the cops marched forward, slapping nightsticks against their palms, battling youths once more in that familiar haze.

It began on Sunday night. Chicago mayor Richard Daley glad-handed donors and delegates, welcoming them to the 1968 Democratic convention, beneath a large portrait of himself. A short drive away, hundreds of police collected along the edge of Lincoln Park. Inside the park, activists hoped to camp for the night. Chicago parks closed at eleven. The cops were ordered to enforce the curfew. In recent months, radicals had threatened to poison the city's water with LSD or flood the sewers with gasoline. They had promised hundreds of thousands rallying to their standard. But only five thousand young people arrived from out of town, with the most coming from New York. An equal number of local youths joined the protestors. There were more police and guardsmen than demonstrators. Organizers were deflated by the turnout. Still, by Sunday night in the park, the ingredients were there—riot-ready cops, radicals, and wristwatches ticking toward an ultimatum.[1]

Police ordered protestors out. Inside the park, Allen Ginsberg's flock chanted "ommm." Abbie Hoffman approached the blue helmets and mocked, "Where's the law and order?" He told a commander, "We're going to test our legal right to be in this park." The commander assured him that arrests would follow. "Groovy," Hoffman replied.

Protestors piled picnic tables and trash bins into a barricade. Their standards flapped in the blinking city lights. The red and black flags, the Vietcong flag, the North Vietnamese flag. Chants of "Ho, Ho, Ho Chi Minh!"

Cones of bright television light punctured the darkness, and for August, the air was cold off the lakefront. At half past ten, police announced their "final warning." The curfew passed. A thousand activists amassed inside the park. A demonstrator urged retreat. "Daley gives us orders," one radical shot back. "Don't give us orders, you fascist!" "This is suicide!" yelled one protest marshal. "Authoritarian!" yippies shouted back, as some attempted to rip the microphones from marshals' hands.

Teargas guns fired. The air clouded orange and white. Police marched forward, cinematically silhouetted with Fresnel light, a faceless skirmish line of gas masks and nightsticks and rifles advancing into the radiant haze. Cops clubbed peaceniks and reporters. Some protestors came back for more. They shouted "Police brutality!" in front of newsmen. Young men dared cops, "Do it again!" Cops did it again.[2]

Richard Daley was brash, round, double-chinned, his hair slicked back and streaking gray by now. A descendant of Irish refugees, he was raised working class, attended a Catholic high school known as the "poor boys' college," worked the stockyards, and attended law school at night (slogging through over eleven years). He ran for office and gradually rose through Chicago's political bowels to rule the city. He was one of the last big bosses of politics, a Midwest potentate who helped choose presidents, an alpha predator who did not realize he was a dying breed. An old joke went: Daley, JFK, and Nikita Khrushchev are in a sinking lifeboat with only one life preserver. JFK says he should have it. Khrushchev demands he have it. Daley calls for a vote and wins, eight to two. It was that Chicago boss who vowed, "No thousands will come to our city and take over our streets, our city, our convention."[3]

Of course, they did. Americans sat in their living rooms, adjusting their TVs' rabbit-ear antennas, stunned by the footage. A fraction of the street violence was broadcasted. But it amplified the discord inside the convention—delegates shoving each other and burning their passes, cops in sky-blue helmets dragging delegates off the convention floor. The dramatics earned a historic television audience. And as the disarray escalated, so did the sense of Democratic dysfunction.

By Tuesday night, LBJ's birthday, fuses were short. On NBC, after an advertising break—"have a party" with six varieties of Planters peanuts—David Brinkley told America of the latest convention "disorder, that is to say, some kind of unusual disorder beyond the normal and familiar disorder." ABC News spoke of "pitched battles" and "youths hurling bottles" and cops' "ruthless attitude" toward activists and media "without the slightest provocation," as footage showed cops whirling in the dark with demonstrators.

Later that evening, on a hill inside Lincoln Park, Black Panther Bobby Seale and yippie Jerry Rubin rallied about fifteen hundred. Seale said they must "remove" the "pigs and hogs" who were "terrorizing" them. Rubin urged a "new white revolution."[4]

Protestors pressed their ears to transistor radios for news from the convention. As the hour neared eleven, they gathered outside the Hilton, the den of the powerful. Helmeted cops formed a demarcation line along the avenue, between the hotel and Grant Park. In the park, activists shouted, sang, burned draft cards. Small bonfires flickered orange in the darkness.

Richard Nixon had deployed firebrand Pat Buchanan to monitor events in Chicago. Buchanan had a room at the Hilton. Nixon called late. "What's going on now?" the candidate asked. "Listen," Buchanan said. He held the phone out the window. From nineteen floors above, Nixon heard it: "Dump the Hump! . . . Fuck Daley!" Buchanan knew how to make the "old man" smile.[5]

Back at Lincoln Park, midnight came and Wednesday with it. The protestors swelled to three thousand. They chanted and clutched sticks and rocks. Garbage fires burned. The cops gave a five-minute warning. Clergy urged the protestors, "Sit or split." Floodlights cut into the darkness. Sirens flashed. Faces loomed in the light and receded into the black. Literati clustered—Allen Ginsberg, Jean Genet, William Burroughs, Terry Southern. At one point that week, Burroughs and Genet and Southern were overheard debating apposite aspersions for police—were they more like "vicious dogs" or "mad dogs" or "swine"? The debate went unsettled, reportedly. In the park, Ginsberg chanted again. Soon the teargas. The screaming, the coughing. The cops pushing in, swinging. Protestors tossed rocks and brickbats. Policemen caged bloody activists inside paddy wagons. Blue cop lights revolved in the white mist.[6]

To the south, along the lakefront, cops kept their cool. Inside the Hilton, overlooking the park, were the political and media elites. Outside, activists bombarded these cops with soda cans filled with urine and sand, ceramic tile chips, and ping-pong balls with nails driven through them. One demonstrator goaded some patrolmen, "We're fucking your wives and daughters while you guys are protecting your city." A spectator saw a girl throw feces at a cop. Local officials tried to negotiate. One protestor screamed in an official's face, "Your wife sucks cock." The official walked away. At about half past one in the morning, the police announced the kids could stay in the park overnight. Some protestors shouted, "Yip, yip, hooray!"

Seven hundred cops were stationed at the hotel. They had worked twelve-hour shifts for at least the past three days. Many cops were pushing their fifteenth hour. A *Washington Post* reporter later said that "up to this point" the police had been "fairly calm but now they were showing visible signs of strain," and "the kids knew this full well." Yet barring periodic skirmishes, calm prevailed outside the Hilton. The band Peter, Paul and Mary sang. Military trucks with barbed-wire gratings rumbled in. Guardsmen, boys in khaki uniforms and big helmets, quickstepped with M-1 rifles. Some guardsmen had been called back to the city from their jobs in other states, including Cazzie Russell. The New York Knick was ordered to patrol Chicago rooftops for snipers. There were no snipers.

Demonstrators sang "This Land Is Your Land." Some radicals gave Nazi salutes to a Guard commander and shouted "Sieg heil!" One activist prodded a Guard skirmish line, spitting, flicking his cigarette. He read nameplates and called a Jewish guardsman a "kike." At half past four, Tom Hayden showed. He spoke to the crowd about being "underground." (He had been arrested Monday and his bail money came from a highborn activist named Diana Oughton.) Hayden was now spotlit. The tie and collared shirt, seen at Columbia, were gone. He calmly explained they would march tomorrow to the convention by "any means necessary," and then he disappeared. Dawn came and a thin haze with it. Campfires crackled.[7]

Dayside, thousands of young people rallied in Grant Park. A young man tried to lower the American flag. Police arrested him. There was yelling. Stones were thrown. A cop shouted at a cameraman: "Get a picture of them throwing the rocks at us!" Pacifist leader David Dellinger pleaded with protestors to sit down. Police lowered their Plexiglas visors. Protestors piled benches into a barricade and hurled branches, rocks, plastic bags of cow's blood, paint, feces. Some activists wielded sticks with pointed nails (sanitation workers gave them to young people to help clean up the park). Cops drove forward, beating protestors vengefully. White collegians were shocked by the police brutality. Activists aided their injured, including the clean-shaven son of a Truman advisor, organizer Rennie Davis, who was bleeding on a stretcher. David Dellinger sought to calm the crowd. Tom Hayden grabbed the microphone away from Dellinger and yelled, "Let us make sure that if blood flows, it flows all over the city."[8]

Dellinger tried to shepherd thousands with a peaceful march toward the convention. The police blocked it. Protestors scattered.

In Chicago's streets, more police phalanxes assembled beneath skyscrapers. More gas-masked guardsmen with bayonets. Hippies chanted. More Hitler salutes. Teargas popped. Smoke billowed. Again they clashed.[9]

"They were young men who were not going to Vietnam," Norman Mailer wrote. "So they would show . . . that the reason they did not go was not for lack of the courage to fight." It was not war. No gunshots. No Molotov cocktails even. Plenty of convention attendees conducted business as usual. A senator's son and Harvard student, Al Gore, kept to his hotel room and the amphitheater, avoiding the activists, assisting his father. Among the protestors, there were pacifists, clergy, a poor people's march. But as Todd Gitlin wrote, "The proportion bent on fighting and fighting back was high—high enough to provoke the easily provoked police." They were mostly boys furious with rebellion, late teens to young twenties. In Chicago, unlike most antiwar demonstrations, males outnumbered females by a ratio of at least eight to one. Nearly nine in ten of those arrested were male (668 were booked in total). Plenty of women also protested, including Ellen Willis, an emerging feminist social critic. During the "tense precurfew hours," Willis recalled, the protest organizers urging deescalation inside Lincoln Park "received almost universal hostility." She recounted one drum circle around a firepit, and the Greek chorus that stirred:

"If one of us dies, how many pigs will die?"
"Ten!"
"Twenty!"
"They got the guns but we got the numbers."

"I remember watching, amazed, as kids a year or two younger than me threw rocks and slabs of sidewalks at the police, hoping to provoke reprisal," *Village Voice* reporter Paul Cowan later recalled. He killed his story on the rock throwing after the police brutality. "The police riot seemed to me a far greater evil than the fact that some kids had wanted to provoke it," he said. A Los Angeles police inspector, deployed as an observer, concluded, "The restraint of the police, both as individual members and as an organization, was beyond reason." But by Wednesday night, "many officers acted without restraint." The punditocracy fixated on the generation gap. But as with earlier events in New York, class lingered in the subtext. "The Chicago policemen who were in the streets of Chicago were from blue-collar families. They didn't have any opportunities to go to college," David Stahl, the city's deputy mayor at the time, said years later. "And I think those Chicago police officers didn't understand why these kids, the sons and daughters of the affluent, were out in the streets trying to wreck the system."[10]

Later that night, the competing narratives famously converged at the Democratic convention. Senator Abraham Ribicoff railed on the rostrum against the "Gestapo tactics on the streets of Chicago." Daley soon stood, batting away a white balloon and swinging an arm furiously, as he cupped his hands around his mouth and shouted up at the senator: Fuck you! You Jew son of a bitch! You lousy motherfucker! Go home! Or so lip-readers later surmised for the media. No one knows Daley's actual words. It was too clamorous. Ribicoff nodded from the rostrum and said, "How hard it is to accept the truth."[11]

"No political event since 1860 has mirrored the harsh specifics of national tribulation as dramatically," *Life* magazine wrote. As *Time* reported, the protest leaders' strategy was "calculated provocation" and "they left Chicago more as victors than as victims." At one point, leaders Tom Hayden and John Froines were seen standing on a doorstep "balefully looking on the scene as if watching an electrical storm. 'Beautiful, beautiful,' one muttered." Or as Mailer reported: "Demonstrators were afterward delighted to have been manhandled before the public eye," certain their victimization would inspire the Movement and reveal their virtue. Protest organizer Rennie Davis said the goal was "to force the police state to become more and more visible, yet somehow survive in it." Todd Gitlin would later recall that when he left a 1967 antiwar conference with Tom Hayden at the University of Chicago, Hayden told him their strategy was to "arouse the sleeping dogs on the Right." Gitlin wrote, "It would take confrontation, disruption, Tom went on. If and only if the country polarized sharply enough, the war would have to end." Added Gitlin, "If Dean Rusk thought Vietnam was Munich, much of the movement thought Chicago was Mississippi—or the early days of Nazi Germany."

News stories led with the police brutality. The grandson of Winston Churchill, a reporter, said he was clubbed and described "horrifying scenes." A cop inadvertently provided a feminist upside as he whacked *Playboy*'s Hugh Hefner in the backside. A young CBS newsman, Dan Rather, was knocked to the convention floor. About one in five reporters were assaulted, arrested, or had their equipment destroyed. They left Chicago fuming. News executives telegrammed Daley that journalists had been "singled out by policemen and deliberately beaten" to "prevent reporting."[12]

Protestor Bill Ayers, a future Weatherman, thought radicals had won with martyrdom. "We were their sons and daughters," Ayers said. *Times* man Tom Wicker wrote, "These were our children in the streets, and the Chicago police beat them up." "If Blacks got whipped nobody would pay attention. It would just be history," Jesse Jackson had advised Rennie Davis. "But if whites got whipped, it would make the newspapers." It did. But the reaction was not as expected.[13]

America did not see itself in *these* white kids. Two-thirds of adults believed Mayor Daley "used police against demonstrators" in the "right" way, and two-thirds of Democrats agreed. A majority also approved of the cops' conduct—the "way the Chicago police dealt with the young people." Blue-collar whites were even more likely to back the cops than affluent whites.[14]

Reporters quickly realized they had misread the big story. At CBS stations, the mail ran about eleven to one in favor of Daley and the police. Of the 8,500 letters to NBC about the convention, only around 1,000 supported the protestors. The era had seen exponential surges in crime, hundreds of urban riots, relentless campus upheaval. Between 1964 and 1968, 257 cities were rocked by 329 riots—fires, looting, the sort of sudden mass disturbance that shakes residents' basic sense of safety. In recent months, Martin Luther King Jr. and Robert Kennedy had been murdered. The public watched Chicago amid that anarchic backdrop. As Garry Wills wrote, "There was a sense everywhere, in 1968, that things were giving, that man had not merely lost control of his history, but might never regain it."

Americans concluded that activists stoked that turmoil. They saw privileged kids venting rage on working-class guys trying to maintain order.[15]

Still, Chicago's impact would be exaggerated. Democratic nominee Hubert Humphrey's support remained statistically unchanged after the convention. The convention earned historic ratings for its dramatics, but it was still political dramatics. A slim majority of Americans said they only paid some or no attention to Chicago '68. The unrest was important, instead, for how it underlined a public impression. Rather than show a way out, Democrats seemed to amplify the era's disarray.[16]

Days after the convention, Nixon came to Chicago. His motorcade navigated the same streets. Tickertape drifted down. Hundreds of thousands cheered him. Nixon later spoke of "law and order," but he already had his coup. The media showed peaceful Chicago under Nixon, so soon after Democratic chaos.[17]

◆

Hubert Humphrey had flashes of hope. As Pennsylvania put him over the top at the convention and the nomination was his, he grinned and blew kisses at the cameras. Later, back inside the Hilton's Waldorf Room, he jigged before newsmen and young ladies in white boaters. He assured them the party would unite and "climb to new heights." But Humphrey had arrived in Chicago to bagpipes but no crowd. All week, the acrid teargas stalked him. It even spoiled his shower. Too much else had gone too wrong. Humphrey was a onetime mayor who had decreased crime and reformed a police force—but he surrendered the "law and order" issue to Nixon. Humphrey realized early that Vietnam was a lost cause—but he let LBJ muzzle him on the war, rather than risk LBJ's support. He was a civil rights trailblazer—but he failed to convince activists to respect him. In Chicago, one activist told him, "You used to be our hero." Humphrey later wrote, "I felt robbed of my personal history." And rob they did. After the worst street troubles had subsided and Humphrey was the Democrats' nominee, liberal hero Eugene McCarthy spoke to a crowd of peaceniks still in Chicago. McCarthy said of Nixon *and* Humphrey, "I do not endorse either one of them." The young people shouted delight. "We want peace!" they chanted. And they would attack Humphrey to express it. New Left youth booed Humphrey into the general election. It was a historic act of electoral immolation. After Chicago, Abbie Hoffman exaggerated radicals' impact and betrayed one aim: "Because of our actions in Chicago, Richard Nixon will be elected President." "Heighten the contradictions," went that mantra. And the FDR coalition fractured.[18]

On election night in Manhattan, Richard Nixon sat alone in his bathrobe on the thirty-fifth floor of the Waldorf-Astoria. He didn't want a television in his room. Aides updated him. He had placed his family in a separate suite. He didn't want to compel them to "keep up a cheerful front." He had come from little to become vice president by age 40. Then Ike belittled him. Then he lost a nail-biter to JFK. Then he lost the California governorship. "You won't have Nixon to kick around anymore, because gentlemen, this is my last press conference," he told reporters afterward. But this awkward man knew of no other life but the public life.

Nixon anxiously smoked five cigars election night. Illinois seemed his, and with it the presidency. Chicago's Mayor Daley held back returns. The hours ticked toward dawn. Nixon conferred with staff. Still no concession. He thought about 1960. The presidency had seemed to be his then too. And Daley had been mixed up in that too. Old nightmares stirred. The orange light pierced the horizon of Manhattan's skyline. The networks finally called Illinois. An aide burst into his room: "You've won!" Nixon hurried into another room with staff. He put his hand on his campaign manager's shoulder and said they should "get this thing planned out."[19]

Humphrey had recognized it could end this way. "There may be a tendency to conservatism in the country right now," Humphrey conceded after Chicago. "If you let the country move that way, it will." It did. Liberals had failed to translate a historically electrified base into electoral force. The New Left was bitterly lovelorn and in no mood for a marriage of convenience (otherwise known as the two-party system). And if these activists could not have love, they would have Nixon.[20]

| Two Moratorium Days
October 1969

MONTHS INTO RICHARD Nixon's presidency, the Movement seemed wiser for Chicago, for all America had lost that awful year. Radicals persisted. But most Democrats refused to be taken over more cliffs. And on October 15, 1969, a popular movement seemed possible. Two million marched nationwide. It was the Moratorium to End the War in Vietnam. To date, the largest demonstration in American history.

A quarter-million Americans demonstrated in Washington. Martin Luther King's widow, Coretta Scott King, wearing black and pearls, stood atop a maple podium and said, "The war is destroying the very fabric and fiber of this society." White candles were circulated for a nighttime march. At midday, government workers flooded the Capitol steps for a silent vigil. Above another crowd, the patriarch of the antiwar movement, Dr. Benjamin Spock, rumbled gutturally into the microphone, "We certainly are entitled to dissent." Nearby, twenty radicals tried to rush the White House grounds with a coffin and a Vietcong flag, but were repulsed. It was a rare flash of violence on a day of solemnity, tolled bells, teach-ins, oratory, and song— "We Shall Overcome," "Get Together," "Let the Sunshine In." NBC noted a middle-class presence amid DC's throng—"the un-young, the un-poor, and the un-black"—demonstrating alongside "rowdy youngsters."

It was mostly matriculating youngsters who blanketed historic Boston Common. But there were also professors, high schoolers, some office workers. One hundred thousand people in all. Nearby, Senator Ted Kennedy said President Nixon must make the "irrevocable decision" to withdraw all troops within two years. In affluent Boston suburbs—such as Wellesley,

Peace protesters gathered on the Washington Monument grounds on October 15, 1969, before a planned candlelit walk to the White House after nightfall. Nationwide, two million marched against the Vietnam War on this date, known as Moratorium Day. It was, to date, the largest demonstration in US history. (AP)

Winchester, and Milton—there were vigils attended by housewives and merchants. Prominent academics, from J. K. Galbraith to George Wald to Howard Zinn, spoke at rallies across Boston. At the main demonstration, students held black balloons, drank cider and wine, smoked weed. Senator George McGovern said ending the war was now "the most urgent and responsible act of American citizenship," that demonstrating exhibits the "highest patriotism," and "this is not a day of destruction or of violence" but "of reconciliation."

The moratorium's backdrop was another, though far smaller, rampage in Chicago. By autumn of 1969, Mark Rudd and his fellow travelers led a fringe faction of SDS. They sought an army for "days of rage" in "pig city" to "bring the war home." Three hundred showed. They were clad in helmets. They gripped clubs, sticks, rolls of pennies. They smashed windows and charged police. "Off the pigs! Off the pigs!" It was America's introduction to the Weathermen. The moratorium, occurring soon after, benefited by contrast. Its national turnout was 10,000-fold larger, peaceful, and far more impactful. If the diseased limb was amputated, the Movement's body seemed to have hope.

There were twenty-five thousand demonstrating at the University of Michigan, where SDS had been founded, and no gas masks were needed. Fifteen thousand jammed Detroit's Kennedy Square. The same number rallied in Philadelphia's Kennedy Plaza. Ten thousand marched in Minneapolis, and only half were from the state university. A similarly sized crowd jammed a parking lot in Los Angeles, near UCLA. Civil rights leader Ralph Abernathy urged America to "come home" and "redeem your soul." At a veterans cemetery in LA, five hundred housewives placed flowers on gravestones. Elsewhere in California, at Nixon's alma mater, Whittier College, a brazier was lit. It would burn until the war ended. At a rally in downtown Cincinnati, the crowd included New York Knicks starters Bill Bradley and Dave DeBusschere (they had a game nearby). In Lewiston, Maine, Senator Ed Muskie said that President Nixon should implement a "standstill ceasefire."

In suburban Chicago, three hundred housewives marched; it was the first time most had ever marched. Thirty thousand rallied at Chicago's Civic Center. Along the lakefront, at Loyola University, students read the names of the nearly forty thousand Americans who had died in Vietnam by then, a service repeated nationwide. In Houston, someone read names and paused when he recognized a friend's. At Bethel College in Kansas, students tolled an old Mennonite church bell every four seconds. They did it for four days. Each clang symbolized a dead American. Across the Atlantic in London, a Rhodes Scholar named Bill Clinton helped organize a small rally outside the American embassy. Clinton had volunteered the past summer for the moratorium's organizational committee, headquartered in Manhattan.

In New York, tens of thousands of demonstrators shut down Times Square for the moratorium. One hundred thousand people rallied in nearby Bryant Park, including Mayor John Lindsay, New York's two senators, and bold-faced names from Woody Allen to Lauren Bacall. The political headliner was Senator Eugene McCarthy. Earlier that day, McCarthy said, "If Richard Nixon did preside over the first military defeat of this country," it would exhibit "great statesmanship." The political "guru of the peace movement" in 1969, as *Newsweek* titled him, was poking Nixon and extending an olive branch at the same time.

Yet it was New York's liberal Republican mayor, John Lindsay, who proved the most visible figure of the day. He gave half a dozen speeches throughout the city. "People have returned to their strongest heritage," Lindsay said. "The heritage of independent judgment." He rallied crowds against the "self-defeating" war. He said America's "greatness comes from our right to speak out." He also criticized the South Vietnamese government (America's ally), but not the North Vietnamese or the Vietcong (America's foe). At Washington Square Park, beside NYU in the Village, Lindsay spoke at a rally with New York senator Jacob Javits. Javits said the United States "must at the earliest possible time disengage" from Vietnam. But Javits added that he was "not joining the draft card burners or flag destroyers." The audience hissed and hollered and shouted him down.

Lindsay told the crowd, "This form of dissent is the highest form of patriotism." The youthful crowd swooned.

At Wall Street's plaza, some twenty thousand rallied amid peace signs and chants of "Peace now!" "A sea of humanity," reported CBS News. "It was one of the largest crowds ever to jam the area."

Afterward, a thousand crowded inside historic Trinity Church. The bell tolled. Judy Collins sang. A former LBJ spokesman, Bill Moyers, preached the war's end, and congregants prayed for it to be so.

By night in New York, a crowd engulfed St. Patrick's Cathedral. Candles flickered in the night. Thousands sang "America the Beautiful." In

New York mayor John Lindsay speaks at an antiwar rally at Columbia University in New York City, on Moratorium Day, October 15, 1969. Lindsay gave a half-dozen speeches that day advocating an immediate end to the Vietnam War.

Washington, after nightfall, Coretta Scott King led twenty to fifty thousand in a somber march to the White House. They walked slowly downhill, beneath a sliver of moon, the floodlit Washington Monument at their back. "How are you doin' tonight, officer?" asked one plump redheaded marcher. He greeted every cop this way.

"They sure are polite," one black cop told another.

"They sure are," the other replied.

"Do you think they're coming round this block more than once?"

"There's just a lot of them."

They passed the White House and sang John Lennon's new anthem to "give peace a chance," one immense slow wave of quivering candlelight. Inside, Nixon sat alone and scribbled at the top of his yellow pad, "Don't get rattled, don't waver, don't react."[1]

◆

That same day, John Lindsay had City Hall draped in mournful black and purple bunting. There he spoke of peace, of why he ordered flags lowered. It was supposed to be just another speech. But this crowd had short hair, bouffants, chore coats, pressed shirts. They booed him. Someone shouted, "Put that flag up, Lindsay, you creep!"

An hour later, Matthew Troy, a powerful Queens councilman, navigated the catwalk atop City Hall and hoisted the flag to the pole's summit.

"Huzzah!" the crowd yelled.

In the west section of City Hall Park, staff were oddly absent when it was time to lower the flag. At police headquarters in Little Italy, the flag remained high, as it did at all five borough halls. The city flag was lowered at the Municipal Building; the American flag was not. At Nelson Rockefeller's Manhattan office, the flag was not lowered. An American Legion leader telegrammed Lindsay that lowering flags represented "a capitulation to the enemy." The head of the firefighters' union called the moratorium a "national disgrace." The cops' labor chief said it was "wholly inimical to the national interest." The blue-collar *Daily News*, the nation's most-read newspaper, deemed M-Day, as it was called, "National Disgrace Day" and "National Aid-to-the-Enemy Day." The Veterans of Foreign Wars called for a "silent counter-action."

Colleges were especially quiet in old Dixie. The University of Texas at Austin had the largest outpouring in the Southwest. Four thousand demonstrated. It was not even a tenth of the student body. At Texas Tech, where some twenty thousand matriculated, only three hundred turned out. Fifteen thousand students attended Oregon State; only one thousand demonstrated. A thousand came out at Philadelphia's Temple University; the school's enrollment, thirty-four thousand. Politicians exhibited the same. It was notable that about a fifth of senators endorsed a moratorium in wartime, but that also meant four-fifths did not.

The governor of Oklahoma proclaimed it "patriotism day." In Atlanta, the mayor ordered flags lowered. But at state buildings, where Georgia governor Lester Maddox reigned, flags remained at full staff. The mayor of New Britain, Connecticut, ordered flags flown from utility poles. At the veterans hospital in Cleveland, NBC reported that the veterans there generally opposed the moratorium. The far-right John Birch Society termed the moratorium an "act of treason," rhetoric echoed by the mayor of Savannah, Georgia, where at doorstep after doorstep flags flew at full staff. Barry Goldwater said that the North Vietnamese could only interpret M-Day as a sign that "the United States is beginning to weaken." "I have to put myself in the enemy's position," he added, "and if my enemy looked like he was weakening, I certainly wouldn't be willing to go to the peace table." On the eve of the moratorium, at a tribute dinner for Dwight Eisenhower (it was his birthday), the dais included Ike's widow, President Nixon, and California governor Ronald Reagan. Earlier in the day, if only to becalm activists, Nixon expressed respect for protestors' right to dissent. Reagan scorned activists who carried the flag of those killing American boys and gave "comfort and aid to the enemy." As Pat Buchanan once observed of the onetime Democrat, "Reagan had the zeal of the convert."

It didn't help the antiwar cause that, with M-Day bearing down, North Vietnam's premier called the moratorium a "worthy and timely rebuff" of President Nixon. In Philadelphia, the suburban transportation chief draped his buses and trolleys with flags. While M-Day was observed in Boston's prosperous suburbs and on Boston Common, it was quiet in blue-collar South Boston and the black community of Roxbury, like the black areas of DC and other cities. Nationwide, throughout the day, numerous motorists drove with their headlights on as a statement of support for the war effort. At the space program in Cape Kennedy, Florida, thousands of cars ran their lights, as did New York City police cars, fire trucks, buses, and taxis. At Brooklyn College, while hundreds of students demonstrated, twenty squad cars encircled the campus with their headlights on. Downtown, at the demonstration at Wall Street's plaza, fifty tradesmen gathered at the outskirts, mostly steamfitters and sheet metal workers. The hardhats chanted, "No surrender!"[2]

In Queens, it was Game Four of the World Series. New York's *other* baseball team had been a laughingstock for years. Now the Mets were chasing their miracle. Before the game, baseball commissioner Bowie Kuhn agreed to place the flag at half staff. But the Marine band and the military color guard refused to perform the national anthem if the flag was lowered. Meanwhile, New York baseball legend Gil Hodges, a former Marine, lobbied insiders to raise the flag. The Mets had invited more than two hundred injured veterans from a local naval hospital. Some came in uniform, others wore blue hospital pajamas. Chrome wheelchairs glinted in the sunlight. The vets demanded the flag be flown "two-blocked," to its full height, or officials would have to "fight us," said one twice-injured sergeant. The specter of handicapped vets storming the field proved too much. The commissioner relented and notified Lindsay. But it was too late for the band to show. So Gordon MacRae, of Broadway fame, told Shea Stadium he'd have to perform a capella. He encouraged Mets fans to "show the country" how they sing the anthem. Elder baseball greats watched from their seats—Casey Stengel (enlisted for World War One) and Joe DiMaggio (enlisted for World War Two). The network camera panned the stadium—little boys in blazers sang the anthem, a cop saluted, players had their hats over their hearts—as the stadium's flag rose high above center field.[3]

There remained deference to the presidency. The counterculture, Vietnam, had not changed that. Only Watergate would. Richard Nixon had an emerging credibility problem on the war, but it had not convinced most Americans to turn against his command of the war. This was an era of polarizing culture warriors. But most Americans viewed the actual war with nuance. Since August '68, the majority deemed Vietnam a "mistake." Six in ten said so on the eve of M-Day, a new high. Most Americans, however, wanted a "phased" pullout over an immediate withdrawal, and many doves still trusted the president to administer it. The moratorium had shown what was possible. It was of historic scope. Yet, as one poll found afterward, more Americans also concluded M-Day was a "bad idea," rather than a "good" one. Senator Ed Muskie hinted why. The Democratic leader called the moratorium a "unique and somewhat awkward experiment" to change policy in "public view" of our enemy while at war. He supported the moratorium but also echoed why many questioned it. By the end of the day, the antiwar movement had turned toward the mainstream. But it had far to go. There was reason to believe it could get there, if it did not reverse itself radically.[4]

The day after M-Day, the blowback was buried by the big story: a historic mass protest for peace (that was peaceful). *Time* devoted two issues to the moratorium. "With scattered exceptions, the moratorium was a dignified, responsible protest," CBS's Walter Cronkite assured Middle America. "It was a display without historical parallel, the largest expression of public dissent ever seen in this country," read *Life*. "We made our point without tearing things down," said one moratorium organizer. As one Columbia student remarked, it was "nice to go to a demonstration and not have to swear allegiance to Chairman Mao." And the Mets won too.[5]

| "Law and Order" and the Decline of Cities

Nixon's inner circle worried that Moratorium Day signified a new Middle American peace movement. Chief of Staff H. R. Haldeman felt a "great" sense of "relief" after he learned only two million demonstrated. But for the president, the outpouring was still too vast, too respectful, to sleep easy. With M-Day, Nixon realized that "American public opinion would be seriously divided by any military escalation of the war." The president sweated how to buy time and urge resolve.

At his convention speech in 1968, Richard Nixon spoke of "sirens at night" and "Americans dying on distant battlefields" and "hating each other, fighting each other, killing each other at home." He asked, "Did we come all this way for this? Did American boys die in Normandy, and Korea, and in Valley Forge for this?" As he had throughout the campaign, he pledged to be the "voice of the great majority of Americans, the forgotten Americans, the non-shouters, the non-demonstrators," to enforce "law and order" amid historic upheaval and ensure "an honorable end" to Vietnam.[1]

Nixon won despite his abundant personal flaws, despite rifts with his party's establishment, despite a third-party candidate siphoning GOP votes, despite being written off by the commentariat years earlier. A 1962 ABC special was titled *The Political Obituary of Richard M. Nixon*. *Time* magazine's headline: CAREER'S END. "Barring a miracle," read *Time*'s 1962 epitaph, "Richard Nixon can never hope to be elected to any political office again." As Nixon's demographics guru Kevin Phillips later put it, "For the first time since the founding of the Republican Party in 1854, a Republican president had been elected over the opposition of the principal residential citadels of Megapolitan money, media, and fashion."[2]

It also helped to be the candidate challenging the divided party of an unpopular president. Chicago '68 had made that much clear. A few days after Chicago, Pat Buchanan counseled that Americans want "a man with some steel in him." Nixon should "use the demonstrators, the worst of them," as a "foil," a means to attract "the Silent Majority, the quiet Americans whose cause is just." Nixon underlined the Silent Majority sentence. More than a year later, Moratorium Day threatened that foil and Nixon's ability to retain his electorate. So it was, only a few weeks after M-Day, that Nixon gave his first address summoning the "great Silent Majority."[3]

◆

Richard Nixon's reach for the Silent Majority exceeded the war and put words to the coalition he had long sought. He wanted Americans to see him as a man able to steady the ship, steward the storm, a man who accepted responsibility, who could still bring order to the nation's tumult.

The issue of "law and order" crashed over American politics and shaped elections large and local. It was an issue that predated Nixon's 1968 campaign and agreed with him, and one he amplified when it suited him. During the general election, a Nixon television ad flashed images of menace and violence and spoke of soaring crime rates. It showed whites. But liberals worried the public saw blacks. "You can't vote your hates, you have to vote your hopes," Hubert Humphrey implored. But Americans sought stability by 1968, as the balance between freedom and order seemed excessively tipped to the former. "I know they'll call me an old fogey for it, and they're probably justified, I think freedom has reached a point where it is creating disorder and forgetting that order was its mother. It is destroying its mother," said historian Will Durant in this era. "Freedom has to be moderate or it destroys itself." The issue, though, reverberated because it was not abstract. It was a matter of experience, of a place. "Law and order" was born out of the decline of America's cities.[4]

In January 1969, Daniel Patrick Moynihan warned the incoming president that there was a national "urban crisis." Moynihan was a Democrat from JFK and LBJ's Labor Department, best-and-brightest erudite, affable yet pugnacious. Nixon hired him to run urban affairs. Fresh from a Manhattan conclave on city decline, Moynihan was shaken. America's great metropolis was "coming to pieces," the conference's rapporteur concluded, and it betrayed a national plight. If the "crisis of the cities" should continue, Moynihan warned, "democracy would break down."[5]

In 1965, John Lindsay originally campaigned as Gotham's elixir. He said he did *not* agree that the "city is too big to be governed by one man." A Lindsay flyer told of murder, rape, assault, theft, stressing the frequency of offenses, that the city's crime rate had "jumped" by a third in a decade. In one television ad, Lindsay stared into the camera and said that "loud voices from City Hall" told New Yorkers that the city was "getting better and better." The camera shifted to images of Lindsay standing amid ramshackle buildings and rubbish. "Yet, before this very day is over, someone will be murdered. Children will be bitten by rats. Negros will be denied jobs because of their race. Fifty thousand drug addicts will need another fix." The ad showed a vagrant. "Fifty jobs will leave the city." The ad showed a storefront FOR LEASE sign, an impoverished mother and child, smokestacks. "Something can be done."

A pillar of the old Republican establishment, the *Herald Tribune*, ran a series that year on the "City in Crisis" (the lead author, Barry Gottehrer, later joined Lindsay's staff). *Time* magazine described the city circa 1965 as a "cruel parody of its legend," a "shiftless slattern, mired in problems that had been allowed to proliferate for decades." One Lindsay slogan, which was lifted from a columnist: "He is fresh and everyone else is tired."

Lindsay was slim and square-jawed and stood six foot four, with bright blue eyes. He was the son of an investment banker who earned his way onto the Social Register. Lindsay attended Buckley, prepped at St. Paul's, matriculated at Yale, where he rowed crew and was selected for Scroll and Key (his twin brother joined Skull and Bones). In 1949, he married Mary Anne Harrison. Lindsay met Mary Anne at the wedding of Nancy Bush, the daughter of Connecticut senator Prescott Bush and the sister of another Yalie, a Skull and Bones man too, George H. W. Bush. In Congress, Lindsay represented the "Silk Stocking" district on Manhattan's East Side, among the wealthiest wards in the United States. It included homes of the Northeast GOP old guard—Nelson Rockefeller, Jacob Javits, and Thomas Dewey. When he was a congressional freshman, fifty reporters ranked Lindsay among the top ten most influential in Congress. By the time he ran for mayor, at age 43, his campaign announcement won the covers of *Newsweek, Life,* and *Look* magazines. With success, the covers of *Time, Newsweek,* and *Life.* At the victory party, the *Voice's* Jack Newfield reported the gleeful crowd had "Princeton and Radcliffe etched in their Scott Fitzgerald faces." Read one Manhattan billboard, JOHN LINDSAY IS SUPERCALIFRAGILISTICEXPIALIDOC IOUS. Reporters from Peru to Denmark to Italy covered him. He was the dashing man of central casting and the press fell hard. Indeed, John Lindsay was said to have Kennedy magic.[6]

But the fairy tale eluded him. In November 1965, *Time* pictured him before the Manhattan skyline, his eyes as blue as the sky and level with it, superlative personified, a man equal to towers. Three years later, on the eve of the 1968 election, *Time*'s cover exhibited Lindsay surrounded by a New Wave nightmare, a red collage of scared children, cops, tipping skyscrapers. The headline: NEW YORK, THE BREAKDOWN OF THE CITY.[7]

Still, even as the city's decline earned coverage, this superhero was framed as just another casualty of Gotham. Lindsay had inherited a mess. If viewed continentally, the urban crisis exceeded any city or man. Washington played its usual role. In the nineteenth century, the government helped spur the transportation revolution of canals and railroads, which boosted cities such as New York and enabled the western expansion (the travel time from New York to Chicago decreased from three weeks to two days). After World War Two, federal policy helped underwrite flight from cities, with programs from the Servicemen's Readjustment Act (generous GI home loans) to the Interstate Highway System.

These policies were accompanied by the Great Migration. Until 1910, about nine in ten blacks lived in the South. Over the next three decades, about two million impoverished blacks fled the racial caste system of the South for the urban North. It was a "one-way ticket," as Langston Hughes wrote. The mechanization of cotton picking helped accelerate the migration, and the black exodus doubled in two generations. Between 1940 and 1970, at least four million more blacks trekked northward. They came from the southern seaboard, from Virginia tobacco farms and the rice fields of South Carolina, up along the coast to settle in great cities from Philadelphia to New York. They came from the remotest depths of the Mississippi Delta and plantations across the Cotton Belt, up to the industrial shorelines of the Great Lakes, to Chicago, to Milwaukee, to Detroit. "From the early years of the twentieth century to well past its middle age, nearly every black family in the American South, which meant nearly every black family in America, had a decision to make," wrote historian Isabel Wilkerson. That decision changed America's cities. In 1910, blacks constituted 2 percent of the nation's two largest cities (New York and Chicago). Between 1940 and 1970, amid flourishing wartime industry, the black population skyrocketed—Chicago, from 8 to 33 percent; New York City, 6 to 21 percent; Los Angeles, 4 to 18 percent. Detroit's black population rocketed from 9 to 44 percent. For nearly a century since the Civil War, "only the South had to contend with the contradiction between the national creed of democracy and the local reality of a caste system," wrote historian Nicholas Lemann. "The great black migration made race a national issue in the second half of the century." At the same time, Puerto Ricans also migrated northward and mostly settled in Gotham. New York City's Latino population soared from 2 to 16 percent between 1940 and 1970, while the city's white population decreased from 92 to 63 percent.[8]

This massive migration of blacks and Puerto Ricans northward coincided with the loss of good blue-collar work, as factories abandoned northeastern cities, later the North, and finally America. In New York City, officials noted by 1969 that "most of the poor are white" but "hardest hit are the younger low-skilled blacks and Puerto Ricans" because the "growth sector of the city's economy is in white-collar and skilled blue-collar work," but the "growth in the labor force cannot qualify for either." It was tragic timing for recent migrants, within a larger tragedy. As factories disappeared, the quality of life in cities also deteriorated. And what happened, what would happen, happened so fast, so completely, that later generations would hardly recognize the blue-collar New York that once was.[9]

◆

A postwar bestseller named New York City the "greatest manufacturing town on earth." Manufacturing and wholesale trade remained the city's largest employers into the fifties. As historian Joshua Freeman noted, midcentury New York had more manufacturing workers than Los Angeles, Philadelphia, Detroit, and Boston combined. But between 1959 and 1964 alone, the city lost a hundred thousand manufacturing jobs. Other blue-collar industries faded as well. Between the early fifties and the mid-seventies, Gotham lost about forty thousand longshoremen jobs. Ports rotted. Industrial neighborhoods wasted into slums. "The consequences are ominous," said one regional planner at the time. There were some seven or eight million jobs in the New York region. Only two million remained in the city proper by 1970.[10]

The deindustrialization of America had begun. The nation's trade surplus fell 60 percent in the sixties. There would be no trade surplus at all by 1971, for the first time in the twentieth century.

Gotham was a leading indicator. Everything seemed to go bad, even the air. New York City's mortality rate from pulmonary emphysema increased 500 percent in the 1960s. A medical examiner spoke of rural residents' "nice pink lungs," while New Yorkers' "are black as coal." Over a Thanksgiving weekend in 1966, a haze of sulfur dioxide and carbon monoxide clouded the cityscape and—not for the first time—killed several hundred. On a daily basis, the pollution left a dark film on windowsills, seeped inside homes, and seemed to remain on children even after their bath, as one mother complained. At the same time, hundreds of millions of gallons of raw sewage discharged daily into New York's greasy Hudson and East Rivers.[11]

By 1968, *U.S. News & World Report* wrote of the city's "chronic chaos" and quoted an "important business leader" comparing New York to a "disaster area." The report was not considered alarmist. The city felt increasingly dysfunctional. In Lindsay's first term, city worker strikes paralyzed the subway system (on his first day) and stopped garbage collection, and a walkout by teachers shuttered public schools for more than a month. In the winter, snow seemed to be cleared too slowly. New Yorkers depended on a crammed subway system that, in the sweltering summer of 1970, had air-conditioning in less than a tenth of cars. In turn, the decade began with a 50 percent subway fare increase, while on subway trains, a streetwise man no longer kept his wallet in his rear pocket. Women dreaded night-shift commutes.[12]

In the sixties, nothing challenged cities like crime. By the time Nixon campaigned in 1968, eight in ten Americans agreed that "law and order" had "broken down" in the country. More than six in ten Americans believed local courts dealt with criminals "not harshly enough." Or as Gallup reported after one poll that year, "Crime and lawlessness are mentioned nearly twice as often as any other local problem." When Democrats gathered in Chicago, half of all women in America said they were "afraid to walk at night" within one mile of their home.[13]

The 1968 Democratic Party platform, however, spent fifteen thousand words before it considered the issue of "justice and law." The platform read: "We pledge a vigorous and sustained campaign against lawlessness in all its forms—organized crime, white collar crime, rioting, and other violations of the rights and liberties of others. We will further this campaign by attack on the root causes of crime and disorder." The deemphasis of street criminality was deliberate. LBJ's attorney general, liberal icon Ramsey Clark, betrayed the mindset with his summary of crime in the sixties: "The white middle class city dweller by contrast is likely to be the victim of violent crime at the rate of once every 2,000 years, while upper middle income and rich suburbanites have one chance in 10,000 years." The mental gymnastics required to suggest that concern over crime was a figment of paranoia and white racism continued in certain intellectual circles for a half-century thereafter. For example, the 2017 Pulitzer Prize winning *Blood in the Water,* on the 1971 Attica prison riot in upstate New York, used scare quotes around the issue—"crime problem." The book detailed that in 1964 "the nation's crime rate was historically unremarkable," noting homicide's infrequency per hundred thousand people (always true) and citing the higher murder rate early in the Great Depression (while ignoring the plummeting murder rate in the quarter-century after or that since, concern was tied to a rising homicide rate that by 1973, broke the record last seen in 1933).[14]

In the sixties, America's violent crime rate (murder, rape, robbery) increased 125 percent and the property crime rate (burglary, larceny, car theft) increased 110 percent. Anxiety over crime permeated to such an extent that America developed a means to quickly call for help, 911.[15]

"In New York City, in the heart of town—not only in the slum areas—people are afraid to go out at night," said one Manhattan assemblywoman. "What you really have, or almost have, is battle conditions in New York." As early as 1964, the New York police commissioner confessed that city law enforcement was engaged in "a war that seemingly has no end." Between 1965 and 1966 alone, Lindsay's first year in office, city robberies increased 264 percent.[16]

Worse still, the number of murders tripled in New York City in the sixties, even as the population remained steady and the rate of solved homicides declined. As crime increased nationwide, in fact, the likelihood a crime would lead to imprisonment declined fivefold between 1962 and 1979. Locally, the surge in crime preceded John Lindsay but also worsened on his watch. During his mayoralty, murders in New York increased at the second-highest rate among big cities. Movies conveyed the mood: *Midnight Cowboy* 1969, *Little Murders* 1971, *Death Wish* 1974, *Taxi Driver* 1976.[17]

Public schools were among the saddest casualties. The city's High School Principals Association published a report in 1969: "Disorders and fears of new and frightening dimensions stalk the corridors of many of our schools. Yet in the face of these obviously clear and present dangers, our Board of Education has virtually abdicated its responsibilities." By May 1970, the school superintendent said, "Efforts to stop pushing drugs in school areas are fruitless."

Urban nihilism had become conventional. Harvard law professor James Vorenberg, former director of LBJ's Crime Commission, reported in 1969, "To a considerable degree, law enforcement cannot deal with criminal behavior." He advised more antipoverty initiatives instead. Come 1970 in New York, there was a new blight. In subway tunnels, "graffiti addicts equipped with felt tipped pens or even spray cans" plagued stations. Three years later, six in ten subway cars and half of all city public housing would be "heavily graffitied." Worse was ahead.[18]

"Overshadowing all other grievances in New York is the issue of 'law and order,'" the *Washington Post* reported in 1969. "Millions of New Yorkers live in daily fear for their lives and their property. Huge sections of the city become ghost towns at night." In 1971, remarkably, *Life* centered an issue around home security. The cover pictured a woman timidly peering through her gated window. "In every large American city and in the suburbs as well, burglars and robbers wage their guerilla warfare against homes," it read. The magazine offered advice on alarms. It concluded, "If a burglar *really* wants to get into your home, he'll get in."[19]

As *Life* alluded, crime's impact went beyond cities. In 1968, when Gallup asked Americans if they were "afraid to walk at night" near their home, half of residents in central cities said they were. So did one in three suburbanites. Still, the closer people lived to America's troubled downtowns, the more they feared becoming a victim.[20]

◆

In the late 1960s, one of New York's elder intellectuals, literary critic Irving Howe, recalled being harassed by a student radical at Stanford University. The student hassled Howe for not being fullhearted about "the revolution." Howe turned to him and said, "You know what you're going to be? You're going to be a dentist."[21]

Because, while all of that counterculture, urban tumult, and flagging opportunity for the working class took place, something else did too. Gotham augured yuppiedom—the young and cerebral workforce of the embryonic information economy. Between 1950 and 1970, the share of single New Yorkers earning high middle-class wages increased eightfold. One former industrial neighborhood south of Houston Street—known as Hell's Hundred Acres or the Factory District—was rechristened Soho by the nouveau chic, as the *New Yorker* reported in 1970. One early denizen ranted about "the forces of Greenwich Village encroachment." Galleries opened. There were "incredibly cheap" sculptures, priced at a half-year's salary for a blue-collar worker. One gallerygoer was wowed that executives had moved into SoHo.[22]

The proto-yuppies were not nearly enough to stave off urban decline. Most strivers still crowded into well-heeled greenbelts in this era, replete with strict zoning laws. At the same time, Greenwich Village had changed by the late sixties. The "once-blithe spirit" was darkening, reported *Newsweek*. A *Times* headline in August '68: DERELICTS AND HIPPIES ARE MAKING WASHINGTON SQUARE A NIGHTMARE AREA. (Washington Square Park was in the heart of the Village.) Crime challenged liberal sensibilities. As one editor who lived in the area put it, "It's simply a matter of survival." By the early seventies, the nation's most famous "radiclib newspaper"—*Newsweek*'s descriptor for the *Village Voice*—ran a "crusading series of articles attacking antipolice sentiment." "It's a heavy scene here," said Villager Camille Billops, a young black artist who later became widely known in the art world. "I used to think I was safe because I'm black. Well, that just isn't true. Black people are getting ripped off right and left. I even have fantasies of doing junkies in." She added, "I've had it. I'm so tired of being scared."[23]

The Village's youthful avant-garde also included Edmund White, who became an admired writer. White offered this stroll down memory lane:

A woman I knew bought a brownstone in the Village for thirty thousand dollars and said to me, "I know I'll never get my money out, but I'm sentimental about the city." Uncollected garbage piled up along the curb. The sidewalks were cracked and tilted by tree roots. Streetlights burned out and weren't replaced. The crime rate was high. My little apartment was broken into, despite the metal gates on the windows. . . . Burglaries were so common that no one paid much attention to them except the victims. . . . When I moved to Rome in 1970, I suggested to an Italian friend that we switch sides of the street to avoid confronting three teenagers coming toward us. "Why?" she asked, astonished. In New York we paid the cabdriver to wait at the curb till we were safely inside past the locked front door. We were always aware of everyone within our immediate vicinity. . . . We made sure we had at least twenty dollars with us every time we left home so that a robber wouldn't shoot us in frustration, but were also careful not to carry more—nor to be too well-dressed. . . . As we approached our apartment building we prepared our key in our pocketed hand so that we wouldn't fumble at the door a second longer than necessary. We walked in straight lines down the sidewalk and only at the last moment did we veer off toward our door, not wanting to signal our intentions or our vulnerability to a watching mischief-maker. On the subway we didn't look at other passengers.[24]

The crime problem in the city, like the nation, was complicated by politics. In Lindsay's first term at least, wrote biographer Vincent Cannato, "the police were under orders not to arrest disorderly young people on the streets of Greenwich Village." Locals chafed. The West Village—or more accurately the South Village, as it was called—was still an Italian neighborhood. Bleecker Street staples in the late sixties: coffee from Porto Rico Importing Co. (No. 194), Vegetable Garden (No. 233), Ruggiero's Fish Market (No. 235), A. Zito & Sons bakery (No. 259), Faicco's Meats (No. 260), Onofrio Ottomanelli (No. 281). Nearby, Frank's Pork Store on Carmine Street, two more Genovese butcher shops and Joe's Dairy for fresh mozzarella on Sullivan Street, not far from Raffetto's for fresh pasta. These merchants and their customers were concerned about increased crime. Lindsay focused elsewhere.

It would take several years for Lindsay to treat crime with an alarm commensurate with the public mood. By contrast, he took graffiti seriously early on. Lindsay would favor the rhetoric of antiwar activists on the Vietnam War by 1970, and sometimes cataclysmic rhetoric about the state of America. But he was more reticent on the issue that most plagued cities, even as Lindsay became a spokesman for cities nationwide by earning a leadership post on the Kerner Commission on civil disorder.

Meanwhile, America's largest city center became a red-light district. Pimps and prostitutes and pickpockets overtook Times Square. Storied theaters were replaced by marquees that read, XXX LIVE SHOW. In neon, PEEP. Signs everywhere, ADULT MOVIES, 25¢. Electric red, SEE LIVE ACTION SCENE. More peep shows. Fetishes, including bestiality, were advertised on storefronts. Accordingly, in 1968, bestiality was onstage. *Futz!* was a play about a farm boy lusting after his pig. A *Times* critic described it as a "parable of nonconformity" and the playwright as a "baroque artist" who "embroiders wildly on fevered fantasies." Said one cop on Forty-Second Street, "If a little old lady wants to buy the *Times*, she has to climb over three rows of *Screw* [magazine] to get it." Said the mayor, "I don't think that it's gotten worse."[25]

Cops bristled when Lindsay understated the difficulty of their job or "meddled" in their affairs. Policemen also believed that the pressure to let delinquency slide benefited Lindsay's base—hippies and minorities. As a candidate, Lindsay had proposed reforming the police force. He vocally supported the Civilian Complaint Review Board, a longtime effort to establish a permanent agency to monitor police abuse. When the board was on the ballot, Lindsay's staff sought to make New Yorkers "ashamed" to oppose it. One Lindsay billboard ad: DON'T BE A "YES" MAN FOR BIGOTRY, VOTE "NO." At one point, the cops affirmed the inference. Their union boss said, "I am sick and tired of giving into minority groups with their whims and their gripes and shouting." Lindsay's push to retain the civilian complaint board was overwhelmingly voted down. That failure cowed Lindsay with the cops for a period, leading him to help bury one corruption scandal. The civilian complaint board's opposition came from outer borough whites (in Queens, more than two to one against). The politics of the issue had shifted from a referendum on police abuse and bigotry to a referendum on crime. It also turned out that suggesting people are racists for not supporting your position turned off the very people you needed to turn on.[26]

Likewise, the average cop loathed Lindsay when he downplayed the worst that came with their work. The 1967 Spanish Harlem riot conveyed why. The Justice Department's definition of a major riot included more than three hundred participants, disorder exceeding twelve hours, gunfire, violence, looting, and arson. The Spanish Harlem trouble began after a midnight knife fight. A Puerto Rican man allegedly threatened a white policeman with a blade. The cops killed him. Mayhem followed. On the *second* night, *Newsday* reported, there were six more hours of "wild disorder in the seething East Harlem ghetto." Some twenty-five stores were looted. Bottles and rocks showered down on cops. There was gunfire. A thousand cops were deployed. Mayor Lindsay rushed to the scene in the predawn light. He was told the violence would return again with nightfall. Lindsay, however, said East Harlem was "virtually normal." Nightfall came, and the third wave with it. Two thousand rioters "rampaged through Spanish Harlem, smashing, burning, and looting." Fifteen hundred cops were now deployed. There was rooftop sniper fire. Cops, in bulletproof vests and steel helmets, ducked gunfire for twenty minutes. Cops returned fire. A mother was shot through the head. Her daughter was injured. The disorder crossed the East River into the Bronx. It spread downtown. Stores were looted on Fifth Avenue. Elsewhere, cops were injured and a 16-year-old boy was killed. Meanwhile, between the second and third nights of havoc, Lindsay assured New Yorkers the mass violence was actually a protest. "There was no riot," the mayor insisted to reporters. "This was a demonstration."[27]

CHAPTER 6

The Political Fallout of "Law and Order"

A FEW MONTHS before the 1968 election, when people were asked which candidate was best at handling "law and order," Richard Nixon and George Wallace ranked ahead of the onetime Minneapolis mayor who had lessened crime and reformed police, Hubert Humphrey.[1]

"With half of women in America uptight about law and order what was the liberal response? 'Law and order,' they said, 'is a code word for racism.' In other words, 'Lady, you're not really afraid of being mugged; you're a bigot,'" read *The Real Majority* (1970). "Instead of saying, 'We are *for* civil rights and *against* crime,' many seemed to feel that anyone against crime must also be against civil rights."[2]

By deemphasizing crime, the left effectively tolerated it in the name of toleration (e.g., Ramsey Clark's mental gymnastics, Humphrey suggesting that voting on crime was voting for "hate," or the Democratic platform in '68). With overemphasis, the right demagogued the issue (see: Wallace, George). "Nixon took pains not to inflame," wrote biographer John Farrell. "He was offering calm and accord—not further division—to fretful Americans. The intentional polarization came later—during his presidency." Still, the Nixon campaign knew that stressing "law and order" carried racial overtones. The Catholic minorities—"Irish, Ital, Pole, Mex"—were "afraid of Negroes," H. R. Haldeman noted following a meeting with Nixon in July 1968. Haldeman added that Nixon "has emotional access to lower middle-class" whites—It was "not fair" to call them "racist," he wrote, because they were "concerned" about "crime & violence." Simultaneously, liberal leaders feared that spotlighting crime cemented stereotypes of blacks. Still, as cities grew more dangerous and residents became desperate to curb criminality, it felt like a luxury to talk of causes. Some liberals' suggestion that criminality was largely society's fault, thereby transferring the agency of the criminal onto the victim (because the victim is part of society), rubbed many the wrong way, especially considering it came from the same side that roused against "blaming the victim" in other circumstances. It seemed like more armchair bloviating by people who didn't fear walking home at night or hadn't had their shop looted. The public demanded that—however tricky the task might be—Democrats show firmness and demonstrate concern equal to their distress, or someone else must. Some politicians came closer to finding the balance. Bobby Kennedy campaigned in the 1968 primary by stressing his tough-on-crime record as attorney general. He still retained his civil rights bona fides. By 1968, enough people seemed to believe Bobby Kennedy was fair enough to be firm.[3]

The issue was delicate, however. Like poverty, crime concerned racial disparities, no small matter in the civil rights era. As *Time* reported in 1970: "The rising level of crime frightens the Middle American, and when he speaks of crime, though he does not like to admit it, he means blacks." But those frightened by crime were not only Middle Americans or whites. Most crime was then, as now, committed within racial groups (whites hurt whites or blacks hurt blacks). By the sixties, blacks were more likely to be victimized by crimes and more likely to commit crimes. In 1969, for example, a black woman was 3.7 times more likely to be raped than a white woman; a black person had at least a 3.5-fold higher probability of being robbed than a white person. On the other side of the issue, one study looked at the 543 murders solved in New York City in 1966: blacks committed about 60 percent of the murders, whites 20 percent, Puerto Ricans 12 percent. A study of Chicago homicides from the mid-sixties to the dusk of the seventies reflected a similar pattern. Between 1980 and 2008, when reliable national data became available, blacks were victimized by murder at 6.2 times the rate of whites and they committed murder at 7.6 times the rate of whites. At the same time, anger over crime transcended race. In autumn 1968, 35 percent of all whites were scared to walk at night within a mile of their home, but so were four in ten blacks. New York's leading black newspaper, the *Amsterdam News*, wrote in a 1967 editorial: "We can't get rid of crime by ignoring or compromising with it. And we can't use slingshots or statistics to fight animals bent on killing."[4]

There were occasions when Lindsay's soft touch helped. On the night of April 4, 1968, Lindsay was enjoying a Broadway musical with his wife. A member of his protective detail handed him a note. Martin Luther King had been assassinated. Lindsay returned to his residence. He spoke with aide Sid Davidoff. Lindsay said he wanted to go to Harlem. "Let me at least get up there and see what it's like," Davidoff replied. Davidoff and Barry Gottehrer jumped into their city-issued black Mercury, switched on the siren, and raced up FDR Drive. In north Harlem, a thirtysomething assemblyman, Charles Rangel, thought that "the country was coming apart." He too hurried to Harlem's main thoroughfare, 125th Street. Davidoff arrived and spoke with a black Muslim leader, who went by Allah. Davidoff phoned the mayor, said it was a scene of "sorrow and grief," and it could turn ugly fast. Lindsay said he was coming. "There's no guarantee of your safety here, you cannot come up here," Davidoff recalled telling him, and Lindsay responding, "It's where I belong." Lindsay arrived with a detective and an aide at about half past ten. Allah indeed provided—protection, that is. Harlem's organized crime boss, Bumpy Johnson, sent his daughter to walk with Lindsay as well, a signal that this white man was to be left alone. Rangel joined Lindsay too. He thought Lindsay was a "pretty courageous guy." Thousands were in the streets. Anger was palpable. Leaders feared chaos. This was America's largest black neighborhood. Lindsay stood before a crowd and "looked straight at the people on the streets and he told them he was sick and he was sorry about Martin Luther King," wrote columnist Jimmy Breslin. About two hundred youths chanted, "Martin Luther King! Martin Luther King!" Lindsay approached them and asked, "What are you doing?"

"We're marching for King," said one youth angrily.

"Then I'll lead you and we'll march together," Lindsay said, wisely pivoting.

He led them for a block or so. The march broke up. He attended a meeting with Harlem leaders. Around eleven, Lindsay was streetward once more. Near him, there was pushing. Angry shouts. The crowd became "hostile." Black leaders pressed for calm. Lindsay tried to speak and was shouted down. Cops tussled with a few people. Missiles were thrown (perhaps bottles, and it's unclear if they targeted the mayor). A limousine pulled up. Lindsay was pushed in by his bodyguards and the limo sped off.

In the days after, the rough edges of the story got sanded down, to the extent they were reported at all. The *Christian Science Monitor* quoted a Lindsay aide who said that the crowd surrounding Lindsay was actually "quiet and *not* unfriendly." The narrative veered into the white savior fairy tale. Lindsay was credited for New York City avoiding a riot, for being a "key factor in preventing disturbances," reported the *Boston Globe*. Alistair Cooke, a prominent British correspondent, reported that Lindsay was "highly praised" across America for his city's "remarkable placidity" in the wake of King's killing.[5]

Placid, Gotham was not. About a week later, the NYPD released the statistics. "Property damage and arrests" in the previous week had been "almost on par" with Harlem's weeklong riot in 1964 but more widespread in several black sections of the city, the *Times* reported (on page 35). One immense improvement: there were few complaints of police brutality this time. Because, as Alistair Cooke also reported, the police were under the "strictest orders" to keep cool, and the cops did, at times exhibiting "superhuman" restraint. The NYPD reported 534 incidents of riot arrests (arson, burglary, disorderly conduct), compared to 600 in the 1964 riot. Arsonists burned at least sixty properties. A *Times* editorial still headlined NONVIOLENT CITY. The newspaper made its case by comparison. That Gotham was "extremely fortunate" to avoid the blanket turmoil of many cities (which it was and did). The *Times* extolled Lindsay's "élan," credited him with the city's "nonviolence," and wrote that Lindsay's visits to black areas were as "crucial as they were courageous."[6]

In subsequent weeks, to drive home the valor, Lindsay was commonly compared to Mayor Daley of Chicago. After King's death, Daley ordered cops to "shoot to kill any arsonist or anyone with a Molotov cocktail in his hand in Chicago." Lindsay invited the contrast and chided, "We don't shoot kids in New York City."[7]

◆

The day Martin Luther King was killed, New York senator Robert Kennedy was campaigning for president in Indianapolis. He trashed his speech, climbed atop a flatbed truck, and broke the news to a black crowd. There were gasps and people cried out. He continued speaking and the crowd seemed to calm. "For those of you who are black and are tempted to be filled with hatred and distrust at the injustice of such an act, against all white people, I can only say that I feel in my own heart the same kind of feeling. I had a member of my family killed, but he was killed by a white man." Bobby quoted Aeschylus. He spoke of the wisdom born of despair and the "awful grace of God." He said America must surpass its divisions and muster "compassion toward one another." He urged the crowd to return home and pray. "We can do well in this country," he continued. "The vast majority of white people and the vast majority of black people in this country want to live together, want to improve the quality of our life, and want justice for all human beings that abide in our land." And still he reached back to the Greeks, as some politicians could back then. So he spoke on, of a need to "tame the savageness of man and make gentle the life of this world."

It was a glimpse into why so many Americans, after King's death, invested so much hope in Kennedy. Though his remarks were "almost unnoticed" in the national media at the time, as the *Daily News* reported, Bobby had somehow bridged the races on this night, of all nights. And to America, he was Bobby by now, the first name of the third son to inherit his father's expectations after Joe's death, after Jack's death—and now, with King's death, America's expectations too. Historian Doris Kearns Goodwin recalled a "frenzy" that year, a sense that "revolution was really around the corner." "On the other hand," she added, "there was a group of Americans who felt that only Bobby could heal the divisions, that because he was tough and because he was straightforward and because he was passionate, he could bring the blue-collar workers and the blacks together."

We'll never know if he could have done that much. RFK's feats were later embroidered. "It was during the Indiana primary that we saw Kennedy's astonishing chemistry with white ethnic workers from the steel mills of Gary," reporter Jack Newfield wrote in his RFK biography. It was not, however, RFK's "chemistry" that was "astonishing." After the 1968 Indiana primary, polling showed Vice President Hubert Humphrey had the most support from blue-collar whites. Bobby Kennedy was competitive among blue collars, however, and twice as popular as Humphrey with blacks. (The New Left's favorite, Gene McCarthy, had almost zero black backing, a problem that plagued the favored candidates of upscale white liberals until, and again after, Barack Obama united them with blacks.) "What made Kennedy so unique," Newfield wrote, "was that he felt the same empathy for white workingmen and women that he felt for blacks, Latinos, and Native Americans." That empathy, in this era, had become rare. In the end, Bobby never had the chance to prove what was possible. For he too was killed that year.[8]

The RFK coalition was feasible. Even on issues as toxic as crime and race, alliances wasted away, unrealized. There was a consensus among blacks and whites that crime was a serious problem and the courts had become too lenient on criminals in this era. The majority of blacks *and* whites also felt that societal inequities contributed to crime (such as poverty). But they didn't thusly conclude inequities pulled a trigger. Both whites and blacks seemed to want a firm hand but also recognized the need for a leg up. This potential black-white consensus got lost as the era's liberalism tended to dodge the issue and Nixon seized it. (Notably, liberal politicians' relative inattention to crime early on, allowing the issue to fester, reduced public sympathy for societal factors and for criminals by the eighties. That inattention bolstered severe overcompensation, such as mandatory minimum sentences. In 1980, a majority still thought prisons should "rehabilitate"; by 1993, only a quarter of Americans said "rehabilitate," and six in ten thought prisons should "punish." Meanwhile, racial inequities worsened. By the end of the eighties, despite drug use declining, blacks were at least five times more likely than whites to be arrested for drugs.) But back at the dawn of the seventies, as the nation endured its first crime wave since becoming *the* "affluent society," blacks and whites implored politicians to strengthen policing.

The more money people had to shield themselves from crime, however, the less likely they were to worry about it. When whites are divided into five income brackets, the poorer the household, the more likely they were to think "law and order" had "broken down." Blue-collar white women and white men were more likely to worry about crime than their upscale counterparts. The majority of whites also thought a "lack of support for local police" was a "major" cause of disorder, and even near the height of the Black Panthers' influence, a plurality of blacks agreed that a "major" cause of lawlessness was inadequate support for law enforcement.[9]

"Where once our cities were urban meccas, they are now miserable slums," read one 1969 *Times* article. "Our cities, once melting pots, are now powder kegs."[10]

If America's largest city was a microcosm of urban decline nationwide, Newark was the powder keg—or the "nightmare," as another *Times* article reported. Joined with Gotham in the blue-collar coastal megalopolis, Newark was disproportionately dependent on the fading factories and port economy. In fact, the nation's first large container docks were constructed in Port Newark (an innovation that decimated the jobs of longshoremen). At the outset of World War Two, one in ten residents of Newark was black. By 1970 the majority were black. The city's troubles predated much of that migration and harmed migrants. In the 1930s, federal appraisers recorded Newark's high tax rate, high debt, high rate of residents receiving relief, and the "strong tendency for years for people of larger incomes to move their homes outside the city." Unlike Detroit, which had a sizable black middle class, Newark's descent was so precipitous that few were surprised the city exploded during the 1967 riots. Neither city ever fully recovered from the riots. But Newark began low and sank lowest. By 1971, Newark had the nation's highest crime rate, the largest share of slum housing, and the highest rates of infant mortality and venereal disease, as well as the highest share on welfare rolls. For all that, the remaining homeowners faced the second-highest property taxes in America. If you could get out, you cut your losses and did, though urban blight polluted local suburbs too. The waterways across north Jersey were so contaminated, fish were now commonly seen without fins or tails.[11]

"The cities of America are where the crisis of American civilization is happening," Theodore White wrote. "If the decade of the 1960's can appropriately be called the Decade That Gave Goodwill A Bad Name, it is not because of the Vietnam war—it is because of what distant goodwill has done to life in the big cities. All the programs had been advanced by Democratic thinkers practicing the best doctrine of the day; but theologians put doctrine above experience. The Movement insisted on more of the same for the seventies."[12]

◆

Even the New York Stock Exchange and the New York Yankees pondered moving to the suburbs. Corporations forsook Gotham, from PepsiCo to the American Can Company to Shell Oil. Between 1967 and 1974, the number of Fortune 500 headquarters in the city fell from 139 to 98. Companies were following their employees. In the fifties, more than 850,000 New Yorkers left Gotham. In the sixties, almost one million whites left, and like in other cities, most took with them an impression—of high crime, poor schools, riots, racial strife, dysfunctional and aloof governance, burdensome and wasted taxes, central city rot. Between 1950 and 1970, New York's nonwhite population increased from 13 to 37 percent, even as the city's overall population remained constant. Between the fifties and the mid-seventies, nearly two million middle-income New Yorkers abandoned the city, while almost an equal number of poor residents moved in. By 1970, New York City's welfare rolls (north of one million) exceeded the population of every American city save six. Almost three in ten New Yorkers were on some form of public assistance, while the city's collapsing middle class decimated its ability to raise the tax revenue to fund social services.

Mayor Lindsay still championed a vast expansion of municipal programs. As the seventies dawned, the city expanded the nation's largest metropolitan health care system and offered free open enrollment in the city's university system to all high school graduates. Open enrollment turned the "poor man's Harvard" into an educative boondoggle. City College had produced four Nobel Prize winners in the years after the Great War; by the early seventies, over half of its incoming students required remedial courses. Meanwhile, social service and welfare payments doubled to become the budget's largest expenditure.[13]

At first, Mayor Lindsay and other leaders could delay balancing the city's checkbook. The mid- to late sixties had a strong national economy and a Wall Street bubble, which gassed the city's burgeoning financial services industry. The dusk of the sixties forced the fiscal reckoning. Since midcentury, Americans had taken for granted steady prices and rising wages. But high inflation hit. Then, come 1969, a recession too. A blue-collar worker with three dependents in New York City had the same purchasing power in 1970 that he had in the late fifties. At the same time, the city's income taxes were 50 percent higher than the next twenty largest cities. Business taxes were hiked as well. Higher taxes pushed more employers to leave the city, research found. And still Gotham's balance book tinted redder. Between 1961 and 1975, city debt nearly tripled.[14]

"Since 1898, New York had become America's largest and most important metropolis," journalist Ken Auletta wrote. "Then, in the 1960s, New York stopped growing. Each year, the budget would come up short; each year, officials would devise a temporary solution by taxing a little here, borrowing a little there, fudging everywhere they could." Some sounded the alarm. "We're going broke," the city's budget director said in 1969. That same year, the Citizens Budget Commission called New York's finances "a picture of gloom." It warned that the city faced "choices between what is wanted and what can be afforded."[15]

Yet even as New York City slouched into the seventies, it remained the economic and cultural engine of the world. Its population still exceeded forty-two states. The growth of suburbia, while immense, was also sometimes overstated in this period. In 1950—before new superhighways were built, the crime wave developed, many GI families nested in greenbelts, and millions of black migrants came north—27 percent of Americans lived in suburbia. By 1970, 37 percent of the public lived in suburbia. It was the balance that changed. In 1950, more Americans lived in cities than suburbia. By 1970, suburbanites slightly outnumbered residents of central cities.[16]

And as whites left cities, liberal activists often reduced all of their motives—soaring crime, sinking public schools, pollution, congestion, the high cost of living—to whites' worst motive: racism, or its popular euphemism, "white flight." Yet whites fled cities with lots of blacks (New York) and cities with few blacks (Minneapolis). And not only whites sought greener pastures. Between 1964 and 1969, 600,000 blacks nationwide abandoned central cities. Overall, the suburban black population increased from about 750,000 in 1960 to about 3.5 million in 1970 and to north of 6 million by 1980. Meanwhile, while one in seven white New Yorkers left the city in the sixties—which was the equivalent of all Baltimore residents leaving Baltimore—the corollary held as well: most whites remained. White suburbanites, in this era, were wealthier and better educated than whites in more urban and more rural areas. As one of the period's labor historians,

Gus Tyler, put it, "The truth is that many whites cannot move, because they cannot afford to. Typically, they are white workers of more recent stock: economically unmonied and geographically immobile."

To city fathers, New York could withstand the hemorrhaging of blue-collar work because employment overall improved into the late sixties. It was how Washington later viewed America's deindustrialization. The new city jobs were concentrated upscale. Meanwhile, social programs focused downscale. Whites still constituted the largest number of the city's poor. But it was working- and middle-class residents who represented most New Yorkers in 1970. That middle grumbled amid a new liberal outlook and strategy— government programs focused down and cultural politics focused up, even as the economy was beginning to shift against the middle class, eventually concentrating wealth within the penthouse crowd. However incongruent it would be to later generations, as the sixties became the seventies New York City was the picture of the Middle American squeeze. Said one dress manufacturer, "This is becoming a city with white-collar jobs and blue-collar people."[17]

CHAPTER 7 | Blue-Collar Whites Are "Rediscovered" (in Middle American Gotham)

A MONTH AFTER King's death, it was peak Lindsay. *Life* pictured him on the cover as the wise man—his chin resting on his palm, a contemplative stare, those blue eyes. Cover line: THE LINDSAY STYLE, COOL MAYOR IN A PRESSURE COOKER. In turn, New Yorkers adjusted to those pressures. They were now getting "police locks" that barricaded the front door with a steel bar. Even in casual settings, such as during a movie, women guarded their handbags. New Yorkers began walking more briskly to bypass beggars, buskers, and men urinating on the sidewalk. The *New York Post* had a daily update: "Today's Air: Samples taken by the Air Resources Dept. during the last 24 hours at 10 points across the city showed that the air was unsatisfactory." On a good day, the air was deemed "acceptable." For the most part still, within the prestige press, Lindsay remained unsullied. His recent accolades, for how he mayored King's death, bestowed a glow. So *Life* gave him the Full Kennedy. There was the image of him with the masses. The image of him in command. The image of his beautiful family. It explained the "Lindsay style—a compound of energy that keeps him going through eighteen-hour days, courage that takes him into threatening riots, and a flair." They were suckers for his flair. His face was now careworn. His brow creased. His blond hair grayed. And to most of the media, Lindsay was better for wear. The first picture inside *Life* portrayed his noblesse oblige—virtuous blue blood photographed beside cheerful blacks. It went on like that. Three days later,

Lindsay was on the cover of *New York* magazine. The handsome face was centered on a campaign button. It read, LINDSAY FOR PRESIDENT.[1]

Lindsay's star was now bright enough for veepstakes. The period's partisan tectonic shifts remained unsettled. There was a drive for the GOP to turn leftward. LBJ's historic landslide had been less than four years earlier. One night, as Nixon's aides escaped the city for the sea air of Montauk, they squared off on who should be vice president. Conservative Pat Buchanan supported Reagan. Moderate Ray Price supported Lindsay. Nixon seriously considered Lindsay, according to speechwriter William Safire. Nixon was no Goldwater. He was a moderate on issues from the environment to civil rights. (Nixon helped pass the 1957 Civil Rights Act and supported LBJ's Civil Rights, Voting Rights, and Fair Housing Acts.) Nixon had long needled the right wing as well. He disavowed Joe McCarthy in 1954. He labeled John Birch Society members "nuts and kooks." By 1968, Nixon concluded: his embarrassing failure to win the California governorship proved a Republican could not win *without* the right wing, even as Goldwater's walloping proved a GOP nominee could not win with *only* the right wing. "Nixon was a

Richard Nixon and John Lindsay at the Commodore Hotel in New York, September of 1968. (AP Photo)

pragmatist," Buchanan reflected. "He would have been open to it, if John Lindsay could win the thing for him."

At the 1968 GOP convention in Miami, over bourbon and Scotch inside Nixon's penthouse suite, Lindsay had his advocates. Ohio governor Jim Rhodes was among them. But southern power Strom Thurmond said no. Mr. Conservative, Barry Goldwater, said no. Lindsay and the "new Nixon" also both came from New York (which could trigger an arcane Electoral College issue in a close race). The GOP was also moving south and west. Lindsay recognized his improbability before the first clap of the gavel. At the convention, Lindsay passed a note to campaign chronicler Teddy White. Lindsay wrote that he must be "free to speak out on issues," if selected. It was purportedly meant for Nixon. But Lindsay surely was minding a larger audience. He hoped the note would be leaked. White obliged. He reported that Lindsay "probably already eliminated himself" with a note of "awesome sternness." In the end, Nixon solicited emerging liberal hero (Lindsay) to introduce his choice, the future Silent Majority pugilist (Spiro Agnew), at the convention.[2]

◆

By January 1969, in cold and rainy Washington, the new president experienced an unfamiliar warmth. Reporters would fake it, even if they did not feel it. They had been humbled. Even Dick Nixon would get a media honeymoon.

Nixon's unexpected presidency had led the prestige press to reassess many of its assumptions, including whether America's intelligentsia understood Americans. "The liberal Eastern Establishment found it was not needed on election day—which made its leaders take a second look at the Forgotten American, at an angry baffled middle class that, paying the bill for progress, found its values mocked by spokesmen for that progress," wrote Garry Wills in *Nixon Agonistes* (1970). "These voters felt cheated, disregarded, robbed of respect; and unless their support could be reenlisted, the Establishment's brand of liberalism would perish as a political force."[3]

That second look began with Chicago's aftermath. "Mayor Daley and his supporters have a point," wrote Joseph Kraft, a left-leaning and influential columnist. "The most important organs of the press and the television are, beyond much doubt, dominated by the outlook of upper-income whites" and "are not rooted in the great mass of ordinary Americans."[4]

Media executives agreed. "The blue- and white-collar people who are in revolt now do have a cause for complaint about us," a media boss told *TV*

Guide. "We've ignored their point of view." Clarified another, "We didn't know it was there!"[5]

"A working-class father who may have sacrificed for years in order to send his son to college cannot remotely comprehend why middle-class youths cry that 'the system' is rotten," read *Time* soon after. "To him, they are all spoiled brats . . . to whom everything has been offered and from whom nothing has been demanded."[6]

America had overlooked its middling white masses somewhere between this new "passionate clash" from the "alienated left" and "the alienated right," wrote Richard Goodwin in the *New Yorker* several weeks before Nixon's inauguration. The "lower-income urban white," Goodwin continued, is "in a no-man's-land between black poverty and what he sees or imagines of middle-class affluence." He reminded readers that these whites felt beset by their cities—the poisoned air, the receding parkland, the congestion, and that "his own streets are unsafe and, increasingly, streaked with terror." And yet, he added, they had "no sense that there is anything he can do to arrest the tide."[7]

◆

Weather forced John Lindsay to recognize that tide. In February 1969, New York City experienced its worst snowfall in eight years. It was a Sunday. The official in charge of managing snow plowing was upstate. The city lost a day. Nearly four in ten pieces of snow removal equipment were inoperable. Three days later, the city remained snowed in. Forty-two people died in the blizzard; half hailed from the blue-collar and middle-class borough of Queens. The United Nations undersecretary general, Ralph Bunche, a Queens resident, telegrammed Lindsay on Wednesday. In his seventeen years in his neighborhood, the telegram read, he had "never experienced such neglect in snow removal as now." The undersecretary added, "This is a shameful performance by the great City of New York, which should certainly condone no second-class borough."

Lindsay felt unfairly blamed for the weather. During one visit to Queens afterward, he was heckled by blue-collar whites. He presumed some were Jewish. One woman approached and offered reassurance. He was still a "wonderful man," she said.

"And you're a wonderful woman," Lindsay replied. "Not like those fat Jewish broads up there," he added, pointing to the female hecklers. Near him, reporters from the AP to the *Times*. One in three New Yorkers was Jewish. Lindsay needed them to win reelection. The comment would have potentially sunk his Jewish support and hardly endeared him to liberal women. It was never reported contemporaneously. A *Times* reporter later explained the editor's reasoning: "You don't kick a man when he's down." Conservatives could be forgiven for wondering if they would have enjoyed similar generosity.[8]

Later, in a private letter to Lindsay, Jimmy Breslin comforted the powerful and assured Lindsay that his afflicters were the bigots. By snowstorm, Breslin wrote, blue-collar whites didn't "really mean snow." He explained, "Snow is white and you're really thinking about black." These New Yorkers didn't *really* share the UN leader's view that their neighborhood was treated as "second class." They weren't *really* exasperated by years of metropolitan dysfunction. Even rising crime Breslin waved away as fear of the "black face." It was a view Breslin also tendered publicly, though less explicitly. This was why on one Sunday in the summer of '69, when visiting a crowd of thousands at an Irish hurling game inside Gaelic Park in the Bronx, Breslin was greeted with shouts of "scum" and "fat bum." The gifted columnist was celebrated as the chronicler of the little guy. With that honor, he sometimes felt empowered to stress the worst in them to explain all of them. Thusly, Breslin continued, the snowstorm backlash—nay, crime; nay, the entire "political campaign"—had "come down to just one word: black." This "fear" derived from truth irrefutable: "All white people seem to have an unconscious reflex against black people." The letter resonated with one aide, Jeff Greenfield. Greenfield forwarded copies to the entire senior staff, urging "every word of it" to be "read slowly."[9]

Yet it was a mayoral election year. And in 1969, the city was too blue-collar to write off *all* of them. Lindsay's greatest hurdle to reelection was not the old guard, those *Herald Tribune* Republicans. It was *Daily News* blue collars. Lindsay's braintrust decided they needed to fathom why they had a problem, however belatedly.

A month after the blizzard, March 1969, came the first effort. The memo reported that blue-collar whites faced new "financial insecurity," rising crime, rising taxes, shoddier city services, and a menacing uncertainty ("the possibility of riot or disturbance over anything, at any time"). They felt a new culture had "undermined" their values. The internal memo also noted, "They are treated like second-class citizens—taken for granted, short-changed, in terms of visible public attention."[10]

By April, Pete Hamill wrote of a "revolt" in "the white lower middle class." "Say that magic phrase at a cocktail party" and "monstrous images arise." They were seen as "the murderous rabble: fat, well-fed, bigoted, ignorant, an army of beer-soaked Irishmen, violence-loving Italians, hate-filled

Poles." First the *New Yorker*. Now *New York* magazine. These were sincere and searching looks from urbane high ground. *New York* concluded its story by assuring readers of Hamill's blue-collar credentials. Its readers shared their city and race with blue collars, but little else. This issue of *New York* included a full-page ad marketing Pan Am's "holiday tour" in the Soviet Union. One could feign Trotskyite but savor like a czar—see "subways like art galleries, grand ballet," and "vodka and caviar that never ends." Other full-page ads sold "icy-toning mist" and jets to Britain.

Hamill wrote that the white workingman was often a veteran who resented "double standards," that his "neighborhood is a dumping ground," that he works "very hard" at "dangerous" and "joyless work" but still "prices are too high." Hamill raised race barside and found men who thought blacks had "been given too much" and others who thought blacks "got the shaft." A typical guy returned from the Korean war to "discover that the GI Bill only gave him $110 a month out of which he had to pay his own tuition" and so he could not afford college. Now he lived with "desperate" public schools, polluted streets, dangerous parks. "For him, life in New York is not much of a life" and he "feels trapped and, even worse, in a society that purports to be democratic, ignored."

"Very disturbing," Nixon scribbled on the article after reading it. He asked, "What can be done about it?"

The Labor Department was already researching blue-collar discontent for the president. In the months ahead, Nixon launched a "Middle America Committee." Middle Americans were still not his voters. They were also no longer firmly Democratic voters. Politics was in flux. And it was especially soft in the middle. In 1968, Democrats saw their steepest decline in support from whites in the middle third of earners. But they were not yet with Nixon. Plenty still voted Democratic. In New York, in 1968, Nixon lost the Bronx and Brooklyn by two to one. Meanwhile, a faction registered their discontent with a third alternative.[11]

George Wallace was a southern Democratic segregationist with a pancake face and prominent eyebrows and pomade-slick hair. He was a child of the evangelical South, a bantamweight who had won his state's Golden Gloves title twice and he politicked like one. He had made his name as a schoolhouse-door racist. In Alabama, only five years earlier, he had shouted, "Segregation now, segregation tomorrow, segregation forever!" Yet since he challenged rich frat boys as a class president in college, Wallace also punched up. On the national stage by 1968, he was running "because the steelworker, the paper worker, the rubber worker, the small businessman, the cab drivers are getting tired of the intellectual morons in Washington and in the liberal newspaper offices and the federal judiciary telling them" what to do. He campaigned against those "pseudo intellectuals," "beatnik professors," "left-wingers," and a media that "looked down their nose" at blue collars and "called us rednecks" and "think you don't understand." He campaigned as a little man for the "little man" (he was also little, five feet six inches, which tickled Freudians). He asked voters, "Can a former truck driver married to a dime store clerk and a son of a dirt farmer be elected President?" Yes, said a third of the electorate in Wisconsin and Indiana, and more than four in ten Maryland voters, during the '68 Democratic primary. Afterward, the left tended to write off Wallace's 1968 Democratic supporters as northerners with hearts below the Mason-Dixon line.[12]

Ted Kennedy sought to convey what else moved them. He channeled Bobby. "Most of these people are not motivated by racial hostility or prejudice," Kennedy argued. "They feel that their needs and their problems have been passed over by the tide of recent events. They bear the burden of the unfair system of Selective Service. They lose out because higher education costs so much. They are the ones who feel most threatened at the security of their jobs, the safety of their families, the value of their property and the burden of their taxes. They feel the established system has not been sympathetic to them in their problems of everyday life and in a large measure they are right."[13]

◆

By August 1969, *Harper's* featured an essay on "'the forgotten man,' perhaps the most alienated person in America." It talked of paycheck-to-paycheck whites in the "gray area fringes" of cities or cheaper suburbs, of an emerging "malaise that lacks a language."[14]

John Lindsay received a large internal study on blue-collar whites a month later. It underscored how they were "alienated from government," "forgotten," and, for the first time since World War Two, financially stuck. The confidential Lindsay study also concluded that because "poor is synonymous with black, frustration has increasingly taken on racial overtones, but the basic cause of the frustration is the economic squeeze."[15]

Working Americans Are Rediscovered, headlined the *Washington Post*. Blue-collar whites had been overlooked for so long, the surge in attention was front-page news. "Preoccupied with upper-class discontent on the campuses and with black rumblings in the ghetto, the alienation of the working class has been largely ignored by both the media and politicians," the *Post* reported. "We're trying to find out what is bothering them," explained

Lindsay's media guru, David Garth. "Our problem is that we never had contact with those neighborhoods until last year." It was almost as if the pale masses were right about that Yalie after all.[16]

By October, *Newsweek* delved into this emerging discipline of plain people anthropology. Out in "square America," the magazine discovered, "they want everyone to just quiet down and just quit threatening to destroy what they have worked so hard to build and preserve. They are hostile toward poor and rich alike—toward the poor for being on welfare, toward the rich for not paying taxes." Blue-collar whites thought the "economic pie is dwindling." The magazine reported a "new populism" was emerging from the "yawning gap between the intellectual and the common man, between the governors and the governed." A cop who became mayor of Minneapolis summarized his supporters this way: "Lookit, we're sick of you politicians."[17]

By January 1970, as the Ford Foundation decided it needed to sponsor a "Conference on Blue-Collar Alienation," *Time* magazine named "Middle Americans" its person of the year. Several years earlier, *Time* had set a new standard in media jaw-jawing over youth, handing its annual honor to the baby boomers, who "loom larger than all the exponential promises of science and technology." They shall "cure cancer and the common cold . . . lay out blight-proof, smog-free cities, enrich the underdeveloped world and, no doubt, write finis to poverty and war." Baby boomers had been told they were special so often, for so long, others could almost—almost—not blame them for believing the hype. In 1967, *Time* had a psychedelic cover—THE YOUTH, THE HIPPIE. The hippie, *Time* expounded, used drugs for "kicks," sure, but sometimes also as a "kind of sacrament." A UCLA study, it noted, discovered a "subspecies" of LSD users were cosmic pilgrims. Their drug use was "primarily eucharistic in nature." "Blowing your mind" was reframed as Christian mysticism. The magazine carried on: "It could be argued that in their independence of material possessions and their emphasis on peacefulness and honesty, hippies lead considerably more virtuous lives than the great majority of their fellow citizens." Wrote *Time* in August '69, after a certain music festival in upstate New York, "The real significance of Woodstock can hardly be overestimated." But *Time* would try. Woodstock conveyed "the unique sense of community that seems to exist among the young, their mystical feeling for themselves as a special group, an 'us' in contrast to a 'them.'" Even the commission that investigated the Columbia occupation—before unspooling the unpleasantness—chose to begin its report with this bromide: "The present generation of young people in our universities is the best informed, the most intelligent, and the most idealistic this country has ever known." The blue-ribbon sycophancy of America's new cultural filiarchs continued until the highbrows' bête noire (Dick Nixon) won, and as these things go, over-compensation followed. America's most influential magazine noticed its own readers and stamped its imprimatur on the trend. *Time* magazine wrote of Americans who lived around the center of mores and income and country, as well as coastal blue-collar clusters. Those people were worried that America was "no longer the dream as advertised." They wondered if "they were beginning to lose their grip on the country." They "felt ignored" or "treated with condescension." "No one celebrated them. Intellectuals dismissed their lore as banality." In turn, *Time* reported, the mainstream media had obsessed for years over the counterculture, college kids, hippies, and "angry minorities." And before the media saw it, Nixon sensed it. "Nixon was pursuing not so much a 'Southern strategy' as a Middle American strategy." With Nixon, Middle Americans thought they found a voice. They increasingly "flew the colors of assertive patriots." They were beginning to "assert themselves."[18]

◆

By the seventies, the New Left seemed to diminish the value of a good day's work, notions of duty and honor, and what we owed our country and those who defended it. Blue-collar whites knew what the other side of civility was like. They bought into the system because, like most Americans by the 1950s, they had lived the hardscrabble life. Tens of millions recalled the Great Depression, the roving multitudes searching for work, the fathers who disappeared, the mothers forced to give up one child to feed the rest—mustard sandwiches on stale bread. The wars too, the Second World War and Korea, the boys who came home but seemed to have left something of themselves back there. Whatever their gripes, they knew the sight of better days. So they embraced a stability absent from America for decades, even cherished it. That's what the counterculture neglected. Baby boomers' "square" parents and countrymen had endured terrible economic hardship and war. Even radicals might desire peace and quiet after that.

The counterculture was also not as radical as advertised. There were utopian movements in the nineteenth century, some forty communes in upstate New York alone, including the "plural marriage" of Joseph Smith's first Mormon community. At the Oneida Community, which lasted decades, property and spouses were communal. During the Roaring Twenties, a new class of youthful urbanites had disposable income, began their own sexual revolution, flaunted conventional mores (women especially), and reveled. Births to unwed mothers doubled between 1940 and 1960.[19]

Antiwar activism was also precedented. New England leaders proposed seccession from the United States over the War of 1812. The Draft Riots were an antiwar insurrection. World War One sparked an immense antiwar movement. In 1918, socialist leader Eugene Debs declared: "The working class who fight all the battles . . . have never yet had a voice in either declaring war or making peace." And Debs was jailed for the speech. The federal government arrested some two thousand Americans during the Great War for merely advocating draft resistance.[20]

Yet people are creatures of recent context. In the fifties and early sixties, most American children had been raised in an environment of comparative stability, prosperity, conformity, and prudery reinforced by the broadcast age. Hollywood censors had imposed strictures: lovers were not to be filmed horizontal, and at least one partner must keep a foot on the floor at all times. By 1969, the Academy Award–winning film Midnight Cowboy featured Joe Buck (played by Jon Voight) as a gigolo having varieties of sex in myriad positions: with a cake-faced older lady uptown, with a boyish young man in a dark theater, with a fur-coated socialite after a psychedelic party. Says a fat prospective pimp, lamplit in a bathrobe, "I'm gonna run you ragged!" "Wooooha!" hollers Joe Buck.

By the late 1960s, as activists became more aggressive, whites were often portrayed as consumed by social resentments, none more than race. Even Jimmy Breslin, a columnist considered sympathetic to the average Joe after all, had interpreted backlash over lax snow removal as backlash against blacks. During the 1968 race, Nixon aide Kevin Phillips told Garry Wills that the "secret of politics" was "knowing who hates who." Writers later applied Phillips's comment to Republican race-baiting. But to a degree Phillips didn't grasp, the public held a deeper contempt for white college activists. In 1970, a fifth of whites said Hispanic or indigenous activists "who agitate for more equal treatment" were "harmful," and 42 percent said the same about "blacks who demonstrate for civil rights." By comparison, 53 percent of whites thought "people who picket against the Vietnam war" were "harmful," and a slightly larger majority said the same about "student demonstrators who engage in protest activities" (a plurality of nonwhites also disapproved of student demonstrators). Blue-collar whites consistently disfavored activism more than their upscale counterparts. But here too, the campus protestors bothered them most. Half of whites with no more than a high school education saw civil rights activists in a negative light, but two-thirds of them said the same about student protestors. In comparison, less than a fourth of blue-collar or poor whites disapproved of Latino or indigenous activists. There was little societal tension, little competition for jobs, between downscale whites and Latino or indigenous activists in this era (similar to the dynamic between upscale whites and blacks—who rarely competed for jobs, societal status, schooling, or housing).[21]

At times, blue-collar whites were more supportive of black civil rights than wealthier Americans. As Richard F. Hamilton noted in comparing whites outside the South in 1963, seven in ten whites with white-collar work said "Negroes should have as good a chance as white people to get any kind of job," and nearly nine in ten blue-collar whites agreed.[22]

Backlash over the era's sexual revolution was also misunderstood. Years in, not only Middle Americans—or working-class whites—preferred modesty. Two-thirds of all whites, as well as a majority of better-educated whites and young adults, believed that "when sex is out in the open, such as in motion pictures," it is "less attractive." Women desired more public modesty than men, but men sought it as well.

Meanwhile, Joe and Jane America were not especially vexed by the hippies. Most Americans spurned certain attributes associated with them: disrespect, condescension, provocation. But only about a fifth of all Americans, and an equal share of whites, thought hippies were a "danger to society." The generation gap, a fixation of the era, was exaggerated. Sure, older Americans did not commend hippies' actions and lifestyle. But most grayhairs did not fret the longhairs. Barely a third of Americans middle-aged or older saw hippies as a "danger." It was the same with Vietnam. As one poll captured in 1969, nearly six in ten adults in their twenties were now doves, the same share as adults age 50 or older.[23]

The blowback over hippie style was likewise overstated. Their fashion was often mistaken for the issue, but outward traits were mostly a shorthand for expressing deeper disputes. Indeed, less than a fifth of the public was bothered "a lot" by young people's hair, talk, and clothing. The richer white people were, the less annoyed they were by hippies. In any case, no significant slice of America revered the flower children. When asked if they "approved" of counterculture style, scarcely more than a tenth of Americans said yes. In other words, most Americans were not uptight over hippies. They simply didn't dig them. And they had their reasons.[24]

The counterculture had inverted common values. Serving your country was now bad. The flag was denigrated. "Suckers" worked for "the Man." Marriage was compared to "colonization." Housewives were compared to servants. Being a workingman, once a badge of honor, was the image of the piggish and plodding yeomanry, a genus of man presumed too dumb to even recognize its ennui. And the condemnation often came from "rich kids" able to "turn on, tune in, drop out"—those who could afford to be a hippie.

John Lindsay came to personify what bothered them. He seemed to celebrate the people who looked down on them, and court everybody but them. Lindsay was regularly in the media politicking in black and Puerto Rican areas, or with the white opera crowd. But in Italian or Polish or Irish sections of the city, as his aide admitted in 1969, Lindsay and his staff "never had contact with those neighborhoods until last year." "There was a whole world out there that nobody at City Hall knew anything about," said another aide, Nancy Seifer, who tried for a year to connect Lindsay with white ethnic groups. "These were the people who were paying the bills, and who felt they were getting nothing. But there didn't seem to be any real interest. . . . If you didn't live on Central Park West, you were some kind of lesser being."[25]

Lindsay had "the best accents of an enlightened Tory," the *Economist* wrote. A few reporters began to suggest by 1969 that their Tory might not understand commoners. Lindsay was a banker's son who had gone to all the best schools. He was applauded at all the best schools. He was publicized with all the best people. He was celebrated in all the best media. He even seemed to strut like he was goodness itself, and if you were not with him, then you must be . . . bad. All the while, blue collars pushed ahead—many feeling unappreciated, tolerating absent opportunity, as their city fell apart, as they got the sense that their grievance was not only ignored, but invalidated by their betters. And then came Vietnam.[26]

The torrent of articles on blue-collar whites, like the research on Lindsay's desk, overlooked the centrality of the war within the culture war, and what was uniquely polarizing about this war. Still, as pundits pondered blue-collar angst, that angst seeped into popular culture, and the war came with it. Late in 1969, Creedence Clearwater Revival released their hit "Fortunate Son," giving rare voice to the class conflict over the war. Soon after, Merle Haggard's "Okie from Muskogee" topped the country music chart. "We don't burn our draft cards down on Main Street. We like livin' right, and bein' free," Haggard sang. "We still wave Old Glory down at the courthouse." He quickly followed with another hit, "The Fightin' Side of Me." In it, Haggard sang: "I don't mind 'em . . . standin' up for things they believe in, [but] when they're runnin' down our country, man, they're walkin' on the fightin' side of me." In 1970, Haggard was named country music's Entertainer of the Year.

"Here were these [servicemen] going over there and dying for a cause—we don't even know what it was really all about—and here are these young kids, that were free, bitching about it," Haggard once said. "There's something wrong with that and with [disparaging] those poor guys."[27]

CHAPTER 8

Those Who Did the Fighting
and Dying

IN WORLD WAR Two, Hollywood's Jimmy Stewart, Clark Gable, and Douglas Fairbanks Jr. served. Iconic athletes served, from Joe Louis to Hank Greenberg to Joe DiMaggio. The sons of power who also served and sometimes died in combat included Franklin Roosevelt Jr. and Elliott Roosevelt, Teddy Roosevelt Jr. (World War One veteran too), Stephen Hopkins (son of FDR's closest advisor), Henry Cabot Lodge Jr. (a Brahmin and progeny of senators), Peter Lehman (son of New York governor and banker Herbert Lehman), Peter Saltonstall (son of the Brahmin politician Leverett Saltonstall), John Eisenhower (Ike's son, served in Korea as well), George H. W. Bush (son of senator and banker Prescott Bush), as well as John F. Kennedy and Joseph Kennedy Jr. Reportedly, after hearing of his little brother's heroics, Joe Kennedy Jr. volunteered for a dangerous mission. Elliott Roosevelt witnessed Joe Kennedy's plane explode. The Roosevelts, the Kennedys, and the Bushes were not in Vietnam.[1]

John Lindsay also served in World War Two. "Twenty percent of my class at St. Paul's was wiped out," he recalled. Lindsay's prep school, St. Paul's, lost 104 boys during the Second World War. In Vietnam, St. Paul's lost three.

In 1969, when the white working class was being "rediscovered," Harvard and MIT began a study of "what makes" the blue-collar workingman "tick." They needed only to explore their backyard. Harvard College lost about 450 alumni in World War Two. It lost 22 alumni in Vietnam between the classes of 1945 and 1968. Viewed another way: Harvard and MIT graduated 21,593 students from 1962 to 1972; of them, 14 students, or 1 in 1,542, died in Vietnam. Over the same period, in nearby blue-collar South Boston, 1 in

80 draft-age boys died in Vietnam. As one *Harvard Crimson* writer argued in 1966, "The present draft code [is] one of the clearest examples of class-privilege legislation in American history." Or, as war reporter and Harvard alum David Halberstam told James Fallows, "Almost as many people from Harvard won Pulitzer Prizes in Vietnam as died there."[2]

Unlike any time since the Civil War, Vietnam revealed what sort of boys did the fighting and dying in war. Still, a half-century after the war, some academics argued this class divide was a "myth." Yet perhaps even more than the Civil War, the Vietnam War asked rich boys to risk little compared to most American boys. White college graduates were 7 percent of all soldiers who fought in Vietnam, though, for example, in 1969, 38 percent of all college-age whites were enrolled in college. When young servicemen are compared to civilians of the same generation with a similar education, college graduates were roughly 6.5 times *less* likely to serve in Vietnam—high school dropouts were about twofold more likely to serve.[3]

In all, most soldiers who fought in Vietnam were whites with a blue-collar or poorer background. They typically were high school graduates, raised somewhere between poverty and the middle class. Hundreds of thousands of poor boys did fight in Vietnam. A fifth of soldiers in Vietnam were white high school dropouts, above their share of the US population. Poor boys did more than their fair share. But they were not as likely to serve as blue-collar Americans. The least privileged were the least likely to pass the military's educational standards and other requirements. The war was most aptly a division between blue and white collars, and, like counterculture politics, it was also a divide between those likely to come from the industrial economy and those increasingly concentrated in the new information economy.[4]

The Korean War's class divide was more modest than Vietnam's, but it existed then too. High school graduates were significantly more likely to serve in Korea than those with college degrees. Overall, from 1964 to 1973, among some twenty-seven million draft-age men, about a tenth served in Vietnam and another 30 percent served elsewhere. One generation earlier, during Korea, two-thirds of eligible whites and half of eligible blacks served in the military. Another study placed the Korea-era rate as high as 70 percent. Service was near universal throughout World War Two. Blacks served in Vietnam in numbers proportional to their share of the population, though they did more than their part in the war's early years as well as on the battlefield. But because black civilians were inordinately impoverished, class divided whites more than blacks. As one large Veterans' Administration study found, "White veterans are actually more likely than black veterans to be drawn disproportionately from the working class." Like downscale whites, blacks and Hispanics were also more likely to experience serious combat. Indeed, it was not only that affluent whites were less likely to serve, they were also less likely to experience the worst of the war, and thus less likely to die.[5]

Three in four Vietnam veterans saw Americans killed or wounded. But here too, a soldier's risk related to his class. Nearly half of all veterans of Vietnam (white and minorities) were frequently engaged in combat, compared to about a third of soldiers with an upscale background.[6]

For decades, James Fallows did yeoman's work refuting those who denied Vietnam's class inequality. In 1969, Fallows was completing his last year at Harvard. To avoid service, the six-foot-one-inch Fallows arrived at Boston's Navy Yard on draft day weighing 120 pounds. He later wrote of the experience:

> Virtually everyone who showed up on Cambridge day at the Navy Yard was a student from Harvard or MIT. There was no mistaking the political temperament of our group. Many of my friends wore red arm bands and stop-the-war buttons. Most chanted the familiar words, "Ho, Ho, Ho Chi Minh, NLF is Gonna Win." One of the things we had learned from the draft counselors was that disruptive behavior . . . might impress the examiners with our undesirable character. . . . Later in the day, even as the last of the Cambridge contingent was throwing its urine and deliberately failing its color-blindness tests, buses from the next board began to arrive. These bore the boys from [working-class] Chelsea, thick, dark-haired young men, the white proles of Boston. Most of them were younger than us, since they had just left high school. . . . I tried to avoid noticing, but the results were inescapable. While perhaps four out of five of my friends from Harvard were being deferred, just the opposite was happening to the Chelsea boys. . . . We returned to Cambridge that afternoon, not in government buses but as free individuals, liberated and victorious. The talk was high-spirited, but there was something close to the surface that none of us wanted to mention. We knew now who would be killed.

Fallows wrote of a friend, a fellow Rhodes scholar and corporate lawyer, who told him, "There are certain people who can do more good in a lifetime in politics or academics or medicine than by getting killed in a trench"—a perspective about as undemocratic, as narrow a definition of human worth, as it was prevalent in cosmopolitan circles. Fallows spoke of the "bright people of my generation who made a cult of their high-mindedness," even as they "so willingly took advantage of this most brutal form of class discrimination."

He asked, "Why, especially in the atmosphere of the late sixties, people with any presumptions to character could have let it go on?"[7]

The hypocrisy was rife. Gallup found that a majority of male collegians in 1967, and half of all students, said they considered themselves a "hawk" concerning Vietnam. Yet two-thirds of those same students objected to the idea that "the same proportion of college students should be drafted as youth who do not go to college." As John Helmer wrote, "The Vietnam War was planned by college educated and relatively affluent Americans in Washington, and fought in the field by the less educated, the economically disadvantaged, and the poor."[8]

Not all "fortunate sons" let others go in their place. LBJ's son-in-law, Marine Chuck Robb, served in Vietnam.

John McCain, a handsome flyboy and admiral's son, was shot down over Vietnam on his twenty-third sortie and imprisoned for years—enduring torture, attempting suicide. McCain's father commanded American forces in the Pacific. McCain was offered early release. "I knew that they wouldn't have offered it to me if I hadn't been the son of an admiral," McCain once said. "I just didn't think it was the honorable thing to do."[9]

Al Gore, the Harvard educated son of a senator, chose not to serve as an officer but enlist, like his father's Tennessean constituents—though he would face less jeopardy than combatants as a military reporter. In 1969, Gore walked through Harvard Yard, short-haired and in his Army uniform, and students jeered him.[10]

"A large part of the American public really did look at the warriors and war in the same way," said Larry Berman, a Vietnam War historian. "It was a terrible thing to have done." It was not, for the most part, overtly done. The rare shouts of "baby killer" resonated because they captured a widespread psychic wound. Soldiering had traditionally offered commoners a pathway to societal respect. Vietnam changed that too. "Those of us who came back," veteran Ron Milam said, "we tried to hide that we were in Vietnam." The grievance often regarded lost honor rather than being spit on (though there was some spitting). Polling showed Vietnam veterans felt they were treated worse by the public than veterans of earlier wars. In fact, soldiers' outlook divided more by class than by race, be it on their cold view of draft dodgers or on whether their homecoming was "worse" than expected. The poorer (or the less educated) a white veteran was before entering the military, the more likely he was to hold a grudge about his homecoming, which hinted at the sense of lost status. Vietnam veterans experienced greater feelings of societal alienation than their civilian peers. That alienation was also twice as prevalent among blue-collar boys than among better-off veterans.[11]

"The critics are picking on us, just 'cause we had to fight this war. Where were their sons? In fancy colleges? Where were the sons of all the big shots who supported the war? Not in my platoon. Our guys' people were workers," said one Ohio veteran interviewed by Murray Polner for his book *No Victory Parades* (1971). The veteran, Steve Harper, spoke of witnessing a "resist the draft" rally in Chicago. "What about us poor people? For every guy who resists the draft one of us gotta go and he gets sent out into the boonies to get his backside shot at. One of their signs read WE'VE ALREADY GIVEN ENOUGH. And I thought, 'What *have* they given?'"[12]

"What he says, is something we all know, but prefer not to think about," wrote a young *Washington Post* columnist, David Broder, in 1973 of Polner's book. "This war, the longest war in our history, was also the least democratic war of our century. There was no equality of sacrifice. The children of the affluent—those in college or with subsidized early marriages—were, for most of the war, exempt from military service. Those who fought were, as Polner says rather cruelly, 'our new expendables.'"[13]

Veterans were not left proud. After Vietnam, a majority agreed that they "were made suckers, having to risk their lives in the wrong war in the wrong place at the wrong time." Back in 1970, America was only a quarter-century from World War Two, the epic and just war. The Korean War had not undermined countless boys' sense of duty, their sense of manhood, their fight. It was not only the grayed hawks who told those boys it was "their turn." There was also the barside vainglorious who projected Normandy onto the DMZ. Leaders said it. Parents said it. And good sons did their duty to country, after all. Good boys minded their parents, after all. Many fathers, and perhaps fewer mothers, took that filial piety—to them, their fellow, their leaders, and their country—and told the boys it was "their turn." Yet "good wars" also require parents to trust their children's fate to politicians. They also require young people to trust elders, march forward, and face the abyss. The criticism that weighs down history falls upon every leader who knew enough and yet was too timid to risk his political fortune, too afraid of taking responsibility for a lost war, or too willing to use abstract worst outcomes—a fear of Asia going red, or even California, it was said—to send other people's sons to war.[14]

Antiwar demonstrators said they were trying to bring those boys home. But their leaders marched beside the flag of soldiers who killed American boys in Vietnam, and some waved that flag or worse. In 1972, Hollywood star and activist Jane Fonda visited North Vietnam. She denounced American policy for a wartime enemy's authoritarian propaganda. She was photographed sitting atop a North Vietnamese anti-aircraft gun that targeted US pilots, a pose she regretted later in life. But the extremes were only part of it. As Teddy White put it, "The movement's theologians considered draft-dodgers and draft-bound alike equally innocent victims." But only one side risked everything. The majority of veterans did not think the movement personally blamed them for the war, but it seemed to diminish what they risked, as well as their service and sacrifice—to suggest some died in vain, or lost a limb in vain, or suffered it all in vain. It seemed to deem what was supposed to instill honor as dishonorable, or at least not honorable, and that charge usually came from those who had not seen what led them there, or how they served over there. It was again a matter of preaching. The comic self-importance was not funny if you were on the receiving end and had less status. It grated on you, then, the indignity of that moral certitude without sacrifice. They had the social position and time to both question society and escape the most demanding obligation to it. Few of those white college kids would have dared lecture a black man on fairness. But they had the gall to lecture whites with less status about social justice, though their sanctuary meant lowlier boys might die in their place.

In the end, most of the boys who went to war disliked the movement that said it wanted them home. When asked to rate the antiwar movement on a scale of hot to cold, Vietnam veterans' cold view of antiwar demonstrators was equaled only by their view of oil executives and surpassed in coldness only by their resentment of those who left the country to avoid the draft. They were far more likely to view antiwar demonstrators coldly than to see members of Congress and military leaders that way. And despite a vocal and notable few, such as John Kerry and Ron Kovic, only 3 percent of Vietnam veterans attended an antiwar demonstration where arrests were made. The disdain for draft dodgers was not unique to veterans either. Overall, only three in twenty Americans thought that "many young people" trying to "avoid the draft" was a "healthy thing" for society. Young people were less likely to disapprove, blue-collar whites were especially likely, but a majority of all segments of society opposed or did not respect draft dodging, in part because here too, those most able to evade conscription—and most likely to try—were the "fortunate sons."[15]

The draft boards were themselves a class screen. One 1966 study of the 16,638 draft board members nationwide found that seven in ten were white collar, and nearly all members were white. For those who were reluctantly drafted, resistance usually paid off, especially for those who could pay. Draft law became its own industry. By one calculation, of 210,000 accused draft evaders, more than 200,000 escaped conviction and fewer than 3,200 served any jail time.[16]

"To the devastating psychological effect of getting maimed, paralyzed, or in some way unable to reenter American life as you left it," said Max Cleland in 1970 Senate testimony, "is added the psychological weight that it may not have been worth it, that the war . . . left a small minority of American males holding the bag." Cleland, of small town Georgia, was the son of a secretary and an auto-parts salesman who was also a World War Two vet. He lost three limbs to soldiering and later became a senator.[17]

Six in ten Vietnam veterans also thought others were getting ahead while they served. But the grievance lingered deeper. Many veterans believed protestors' ferocity toward the war and soldiering masked other motives, perhaps none more than self-preservation, which research later affirmed. "That's certainly how a lot of veterans perceive it," historian Mark Moyar said. "That they were being slandered, accused of fighting a bad war, accused of doing bad things, so those who did not serve could rationalize their decision." "I don't blame anyone for not wanting to go," ironworker Charles Salli told a reporter in Manhattan. "Everybody gets afraid. But they're just like us. We had to serve and *our* sons had to serve. Why can't they?" Or as Vietnam veteran and novelist Larry Heinemann once put it, "I know there were many people who opposed the war for moral and political reasons, but I also know there were many people against it because they were chicken and because their mommy and daddy had money to keep them in the streets."[18]

In 1969, of the soldiers killed in combat who were from Long Island— which includes a section of New York City and dense suburbs—only one in eight had ever taken a college course. *Newsday* wrote: "Long Island's war dead have been overwhelmingly white, working-class men. Their parents were typically blue collar or clerical workers, mailmen, factory workers, building tradesmen."[19]

Even as the antiwar movement permeated New York City by the early 1970s, there were also three hundred thousand veterans in the city, more than the population of Wichita, Akron, or Tampa at the time. After Vietnam, one study found that a slim majority of the era's blue-collar white veterans were craftsmen. George Daly's father served in the Great War. Daly himself left high school early to fight in World War Two. Now the steamfitters' chief commended tradesmen who did their "duty." "Our guys," Daly said, "they didn't wait to be drafted."[20]

Most Americans who went to Vietnam were volunteers—they chose to go, to the extent a sense of duty or limited prospects amounts to a choice. Most World War Two veterans were drafted. Yet it was the Vietnam draft that tore America apart. That concerned many things. But one thing it concerned, which went underdiscussed during the war, was who went, and who died. Seven in ten Americans who died in Vietnam had enlisted. Some sought the fight, the chance to prove themselves. "I wanted to be a hero," former marine Roger Tuttrup told writer Studs Terkel. "I saw a little action. But I was no hero." The Hagel brothers, from small-town Nebraska, volunteered. A draft board member suggested Chuck Hagel reenroll in college to avoid the draft. His brother, Tom, requested to be deployed in Vietnam rather than accept orders to serve safely in Germany. Their father and uncles had served in World War Two. They had grown up around war stories. Chuck thought it was his time. Both brothers were injured multiple times. Chuck Hagel became a senator and led the Defense Department. "The Vietnam War changed every institution," Hagel once wrote. "America survived, but many Americans paid a terrible price for it all."

Numerous boys enlisted in the military to retain some choice over their fate. In his junior year of high school, Nebraskan William Abood watched recruiters knock on neighborhood doors. "Vietnam was always in the back of my mind," he said. When it was clear he was going to be drafted, he enlisted. He looked at a list of available occupations in the service. "Well, a mechanic, he wouldn't get shot at too often," Abood thought. Like Abood, many hoped to at least use the military to better themselves. Yet even these reasons—whether to accept their conscription or to enlist—were often not independent of other motives, such as a sense of male honor, or the weight of obligation to their country or fellow or their fathers' path. "I was not convinced that monolithic communism was going to take us down, but my country called," said Ron Milam, a Vietnam veteran and historian.[21]

"We're against the [Vietnam] War for what it does to families and human lives," said New York trade union chief Peter Brennan, a World War Two veteran, in 1970. "Who likes to look at a boy with his arms or legs shot off? But you've got to fight for your country." To him, one could disapprove of the war but feel duty-bound, because citizenship was not only about what it gave you, but also about what you gave it. And that meant in wartime, to the old-fashioned, a willingness to give everything.[22]

"I believed in a limited war, but my uncle fought in Pearl Harbor. My relatives all served," James Lapham recalled. "No question, I would serve." By 1970, Lapham worked as an electrician in New York City and attended graduate school part-time. "The majority of those guys working at the World Trade Center then, the majority of the guys I worked with, they were World War Two vets or Korean vets. I gotta stress this point: the construction worker was a different worker then. It was a hard trade. These were hard guys. They would go to the bar and drink a shot of brandy and a beer and then they'd be on the steel. This was a crew who fought the wars. They were hardened by their experience . . . these guys weren't going to take anybody insulting the flag or our country." Lapham continued, "People were getting tired of these demonstrations that were anti, anti, anti. I also didn't like [activists] closing down the campuses when I'm working, trying to maintain a family, trying to make my wife happy and find some time with my wife and kids. It was hard. Any chance I had, I had to do research to keep up with the kids who were going to school fulltime." He paused, then added, "Class is an important part of this."[23]

Students who couldn't afford to take enough classes to at least qualify for part time, but worked toward a degree after work, were also *not* eligible for student deferments. Some class-based deferments did end with the sixties, such as for graduate students. The draft moved to a lottery in 1969 for the first time since World War Two. Blue plastic capsules containing birth dates were drawn by hand before cameras. The draft didn't equalize service, but it helped. Only a tenth of Vietnam's veterans were whites with white-collar jobs before enlisting in the service, but they constituted a fifth of draftees. By 1970, about a quarter of American troops had some college education, though that was still only about half the share of their generation stateside. In late April 1970, shortly before Nixon announced the Cambodia invasion, the president ended the draft deferment for occupations and fatherhood. About 425,000 men were classified with occupations considered to be in America's national interest (effectively, young men deemed *not* expendable). It privileged white-collar careers—scientists, mathematicians, teachers. In New York City alone, between 15,000 and 60,000 teachers were young men with occupational deferments. Nixon also pledged to end the undergraduate exemption as well, if Congress gave him authority. But politicians were in no rush to break down that sanctuary. By then, 1.8 million young men had student deferments.[24]

"It was the poor farmer, the poor white and black in the city, who were fighting in Vietnam," electrician James Lapham said. "You just couldn't conceive it. A father took a kid down to the military and said, 'This is your future.'"

On May 4, 1970, in Cambodia, as 105-mm howitzers boomed shells into the jungle, four soldiers dug a bunker while listening to the Animals' "We Gotta Get Out of This Place." Elsewhere, written across a helmet was "better to kill than be killed." It was found in the dirt. About ten US soldiers, of the nearly 50,000 dead so far, were recently killed in a local operation. Some 335,000 US troops were currently deployed in the war zone. The Movement was a world away. The young soldiers shared a generation. But they did not need Kent State to weigh the war on its most mortal terms.[25]

"The whole notion of the generation gap during Vietnam was overplayed and the real story is the cleavage within the generation," former marine Jim Webb said in 1980. That was the "most veiled issue out of Vietnam," a "polarization" of cultures. It contributed to veterans' "alienation," which he also spoke of as an "isolation" compounded by having "nowhere to vent it" and "so the rage sort of erodes from the inside out." Webb was the son of a Second World War bomber pilot with Appalachian roots, the first in his family to graduate from high school. Webb's mother had a grade-school education and lost three siblings to illness in the poverty-stricken flatlands of Arkansas. Webb went on to lead the Navy and serve in the Senate. He long felt, as he put it as a young veteran, that servicemen's side was "maligned" for "its beliefs about societal duty." He also recalled that at Georgetown Law School, "in a student body of eighteen hundred people, I met three people who'd been in combat."[26]

Some fifteen million men avoided combat by working the system or taking advantage of legal havens. The future political leaders who evaded the war include Dick Cheney (student deferments and deferments for family hardship, as a new father), Bill Clinton (student and for enrolling in but never joining the ROTC), Newt Gingrich (student), Joe Biden (student), Donald Trump (student and medical, for bone spurs in his heels), Pat Buchanan (for arthritis), Mitt Romney (student and as a missionary), Michael Bloomberg (student and medical, for flat feet), Bernie Sanders (applied for conscientious objector status), Rudy Giuliani (student, occupational for being a law clerk, and medical for punctured eardrums). Other sons of power attained a coveted slot in the National Guard, virtually ensuring they'd never see combat, such as George W. Bush, Chris Dodd, and Dan Quayle.[27]

Fewer than one-fifth of young men with a student deferment came from modest circumstances. By comparison, seven of every eight protestors in this era had at least one year of higher education. There were also boys who had a way out but still went in. Robert McClure was the oldest of nine children on a Kentucky farm. His father obtained a deferment for him. McClure still served. "I was afraid that people would think that I was afraid to go," McClure said. Some young men who could have avoided the war but still went, such as John Kerry, came to resent politicians who dodged their duty but later seemed, in Kerry's view, carelessly willing to send other boys to other wars. But the class resentment permeated more. Once veterans came home and had the luxury to think about more than combat, they reflected the grievances of their societal station. Like most blue-collar whites, they saw antiwar activists as privileged peers who demeaned not only the value of their service but also their aspirations—stability, a college degree, suburban affluence. Abbie Hoffman once wrote his father, a businessman, "[I'm] trying to break away from the world you and Ma brought me up in." As wars can, the unpopular war intensified and revealed this class division because it concerned not only how one lives but also how one might die.[28]

America's small places proportionally gave the most. Military service is "the best thing a kid can do coming out of high school," said one Vietnam veteran from Beallsville, Ohio, in the Allegheny foothills. The town's 450 residents lost six sons to Vietnam, among the most per capita. Historian Christian Appy compared two sections of Alabama. Talladega's 17,500 residents included small-time farmers and textile workers. It was a quarter black and only a third of the townsmen completed high school. Talladega lost fifteen sons to Vietnam. About fifty miles west, in Mountain Brook, an upscale Birmingham suburb with a larger population, most residents were white and nearly every man graduated from high school. No one from Mountain Brook died in Vietnam. One study found that Americans who lived in towns with fewer than a thousand people died in Vietnam at rates four times greater than their share of the population. On the day of the Hardhat Riot, a boy from one of those tiny places, Johnsburg, Minnesota, joined the ranks of the Vietnam dead. Richard Matheis was born May 7, 1950. The day after his birthday, May 8, 1970, he was shot by friendly fire in Cambodia and died in the arms of his best friend.[29]

CHAPTER 9

The New Left and the "Great Test for Liberals"

THERE WAS A reasonable indictment to be filed against the status quo. At the cusp of the seventies, nearly one in three blacks lived in poverty. In 1971, the typical black 17-year-old still read at the same level as the typical white 11-year-old. Laws forbidding blacks and whites from marrying had only recently been deemed unconstitutional, in 1967. Meanwhile, the American Psychiatric Association still classified homosexuality as a mental disorder. The Stonewall revolt in the Village occurred in the summer of 1969, the same year Yale first opened its doors to female undergraduates. It remained constitutional to discriminate against women. Women were fired for getting pregnant. Banks commonly refused to issue credit cards to wives without their husbands' permission. Then there was Vietnam.

At the height of the 1964 presidential election, not too far from Kent State in Ohio, Lyndon Johnson pledged: "We are not about to send American boys nine or ten thousand miles away from home to do what Asian boys ought to be doing for themselves." His vice president had privately urged retreat. "People can't understand why we would run grave risks to support a country which is totally unable to put its own house in order," Hubert Humphrey wrote in a memo in February 1965. "It is always hard to cut losses. But the Johnson administration is in a stronger position to do so now than any administration in this century." Humphrey didn't espouse that view when he was his party's standard-bearer. Between 1965 and 1968—roughly Johnson's command of the war—36,540 American boys died in the fight.

During the 1966 midterm election, as Richard Nixon barnstormed America, he said that if the war continued into 1968 it would be a "great tragedy for the United States." As a new president in 1969, Nixon pledged

Vietnamization, the gradual handing over of the reins of the war to South Vietnam. Unless there was a "threat" from a "major power involving nuclear weapons," Nixon told reporters in July 1969, "the United States is going to encourage, and has a right to expect, that this problem will be increasingly handled by—and the responsibility for it taken by—the Asian nations themselves." In 1969, another 11,780 Americans died in that Asian war.[1]

Decent people hated this war. Years in, presidential promises unkept, millions of Americans supported the troops but rightly questioned why they were there. Coffins were returning from the jungles and mountains and mosquito infested deltas of a remote country on the other side of the world, and all for an undeclared war. The antiwar movement's moral gravity heightened in 1967, when Martin Luther King severed his alliance with LBJ and spoke against "fighting an immoral war." That same year, Robert Kennedy questioned "domino theory" logic, as he talked of "killing innocent people" because the Communists are "12,000 miles away and they might get 11,000 miles away." Meanwhile, Arlo Guthrie's "Alice's Restaurant" became a hit song. Woody Guthrie's son sang, upbeat and folksy, of dodging a New York draft board. Still America committed more boys, more billions. The troop levels exceeded Korea. The war outlasted World War Two. A veteran of both those wars, William Westmoreland, the commanding general who looked the part, told reporters in late 1967 that the war's "end" had begun to "come into view." But there was no landing in Sicily to show for it. No surge up Italy. By early '68, half of America questioned if there ever could be a turning point, a D-Day, beachheads to win on the way to winning.

In late January 1968, during the Vietnamese lunar new year (Tet), the North Vietnamese and Vietcong commenced a shocking offensive that struck thirty-six of the South's forty-four provincial capitals, including breaching the US embassy in Saigon. Tet proved a military loss for the Communists but a psychological victory. American wounded on color screens, in America's living rooms, amid reports of forces overrun. Walter Cronkite famously told viewers "the bloody experience of Vietnam is to end in a stalemate," that "optimists" have been "wrong in the past," and America must "negotiate, not as victors, but as an honorable people who . . . did the best they could." Westmoreland, *Time*'s onetime Man of the Year, had lost credibility. LBJ too. After Tet, for the first time and from then on, the lion's share of Americans thought the war was a "mistake." By March, antiwar candidate Eugene McCarthy mounted a stunning challenge to President Johnson in the New Hampshire primary. RFK entered the race. LBJ astonishingly bowed out. As Henry Kissinger later admitted, Tet was the war's "watershed" because "no matter how effective our actions, the prevalent strategy could no longer achieve its objectives within a period, or with force levels, politically acceptable to the American people."

Still the war went on. America's bloodiest years were '68 and '69. But the solemn and dignified antiwar movement seen on M-Day would radicalize with events. The gulf between a public who wanted the war done, and those who strived to end it, would only widen. The antiwar movement was becoming more hawkish in its dovishness. They exhibited the same zealous desperation as those generals who talked of taking the war to China. It was peace by any means necessary. Peace now! But unlike the generals, events on the ground were affirming the movement. The war was a quagmire. Thousands of Americans with bright futures to risk, risked their wellbeing and their chance at the "good life" to do good—and stop a calamitous war. Time would prove the numerous activists wrong who valorized Ho Chi Minh or understated the repression that would come if the Communists did win. But before the war ended, the Pentagon Papers would show the movement was right about central failings of the war effort and that "masters of war" had lied about it for years—on the effectiveness of bombing the North, on the standing and rectitude of our governmental allies in the South, on America's ability to win this war, on what all the dying was for. It made the antiwar movement more certain in its righteousness. The larger Movement came to define American power by how it had gone so wrong. And for numerous adherents, the anthem or the flag did not symbolize what was still good or right, but Middle America's refusal to recognize all of America's wrongs.

Yet the New Left also seemed to ignore all that had been recently accomplished. LBJ's achievements included the '64 Civil Rights Act, the Voting Rights Act, Medicaid, Medicare, Head Start, food stamps for millions, the National Endowment for the Arts. In 1970, 17.5 million whites and 7.7 million blacks remained impoverished. But between 1966 and 1969, the black poverty rate fell from 42 to 32 percent, the white poverty rate from 15 to 10 percent. "Looking back now, I'd say that because we were Americans emerging from the stultifying 1950s, we were extraordinarily naïve about both politics and esthetics—humorless, unseasoned, dogmatic because untested," wrote Edmund White in his memoir. "What was shared by these two doctrines—the continuing (and endless) avant-garde and radical politics—was an opposition to the society around us, which we judged to be both philistine and selfish. America had changed in seismic ways in the decades that preceded us, but we knew little or nothing about these forgotten changes."[2]

Vietnam had a way of eclipsing progress on the left, even as the wider public began to question why they must foot the bill for a federal largesse that increasingly left them out.

For liberals, by the 1970s, the radical rode herd over the era's activism, from Vietnam (yippies) to civil rights (Black Panthers). Reasonable people thought they could ride the wave and channel the din. After all, John Lindsay was the picture of the reasonable man. He was an heir to the northeastern Republican establishment, a political celebrity, a blue blood wooing hippies, a star giving way to a larger force.

◆

By Moratorium Day 1969, John Lindsay spoke like a man of the New Left. The moratorium arrived weeks before the mayoral election. Lindsay was a Manhattanite who became Hollywood, dreamed of leading Washington, but first he had to get past Queens. Or more accurately, he sought to win enough outer-borough New Yorkers and rouse his base. By M-Day, it was unclear he could. The right saw a chance to take down a nemesis before he got too large. After the moratorium, the conservative *Chicago Tribune* editorial board tellingly did not criticize Eugene McCarthy, Ed Muskie, George McGovern, or Ted Kennedy. It wrote of the "fitting response" to "Lindsay's contemptible attempt to exploit antiwar sentiment."

Barry Goldwater urged Richard Nixon to ignore the mayoral race and let John Lindsay sink with his city. Pat Moynihan continued trying to bridge a middle way. He wrote the president that while Lindsay was not "a special friend of yours in a political sense," he was "in awful trouble" and needed help. Nixon hung back. Lindsay lost the Republican primary, though he would still be able to run for reelection on the Liberal Party ticket. Lindsay had won nearly three in four Republicans in Manhattan, but the same share voted against Lindsay in Staten Island (where eight in ten residents were Irish or Italian). Lindsay won thirteen black or Puerto Rican districts in the outer boroughs. He won only one district that was predominantly white outside Manhattan—prosperous Brooklyn Heights, which was then heavily Wasp.

The night of the mayoral primary, Nixon told H. R. Haldeman to congratulate Lindsay. Haldeman informed Nixon, Lindsay had lost. Nixon "was amazed" and "pleased." Nixon told domestic affairs counsel John Ehrlichman to "be sure we are hands off in this race." Pat Buchanan could hardly contain his schadenfreude. He told Nixon that Lindsay's loss was a "permanent blow" to the "eastern liberal establishment." Barry Goldwater said to Bill Buckley that Lindsay's defeat "could well be the turning point," allowing conservatives to "shuffle off" the last liberal luminaries from the party.[3]

Lindsay had lost the GOP primary to State Senator John Marchi. Marchi was an Italian from Staten Island, but in all the wrong ways for the general election. Marchi was northern rather than southern Italian. He lived in a lovely hamlet on Staten Island. His mien was formal and learned. He would not siphon ethnic support from Democrats. Especially not from Mario Procaccino. Procaccino was born in a town near Naples, the son of a shoemaker. He arrived in America young, struggled with poverty, eventually graduated from City College and Fordham Law, and worked his way up the Bronx Democratic machine. He was short, stocky, waddling, with a pencil-thin mustache, the "little guy for the little guy," as Procaccino told voters during the mayoral campaign. In flashes, his campaigning was smart like that. Procaccino attacked Lindsay as a "limousine liberal," coining the term, arguing uptowners who supported Lindsay didn't care about the "small shop-keeper, the homeowner." That they "preach the politics of confrontation and condone violent upheaval," which created a disorder that "limousine liberals" escaped, with their doormen, their kids in private school. If handled delicately, perhaps an effective populism. Surely Procaccino would tread carefully on race in liberal New York. For the general election, GOP voters should split between the Republican nominee and the former Republican, Lindsay, now on the Liberal ticket. This was a Democratic town. The incumbent, Lindsay, stood atop a fallen city. Procaccino and Democrats couldn't lose.[4]

From his first day as mayor, Lindsay's troubles had seemed biblical. The transit strike forced tides of commuters to stream across bridges, to hitch-hike, only to be stuck in endless gridlock. City business was paralyzing. Lindsay tried to be stern. Days dragged on. He eventually recognized that even blue bloods must backroom. After thirteen days, with losses to the city and workers likely exceeding $100 million, Lindsay gave in to the union leader, a chinny old man who had once fought in the Irish civil war. Experts said Lindsay gave too much, however (twice the White House inflation guidelines). And his weakness with one union invited aggressors from others.

During that first strike, Lindsay tried to show solidarity. He walked miles daily, flashing his talk-show grin, sometimes strolling with stars such as Sugar Ray Robinson. Lindsay reminded New Yorkers that this was still "fun city." The fun continued from the transit strike to a hundred thousand tons of garbage stinking up the streets during the sanitation strike (where he did not capitulate), to impotence during a teachers' strike, to blizzard misman-agement, to finding himself atop a more fractured city beset by all manner of decay. It was not only blue collars who were frustrated. "I voted for him, and so did my wife, but I have a lot of regrets now," a Reform Democrat confided in 1966. "He comes on as if he's bearing the white man's burden," he added. "What bothers me about Lindsay is his lack of humility in trying to conquer that monster. He doesn't seem to know what he doesn't know."[5]

But, to save his job, Lindsay ate his humble pie. He pressed the flesh with the ethnics, sat with black-hatted Lubavitcher rabbis, endured the middle-class community centers, held the kiddies, reassured the elderly, and rallied his base—from Harlem blacks to gala whites. "Super Wasp," as *Newsweek* called him, was reportedly tireless.

See Super Wasp atop a dais, overlooking a black-tie Waldorf affair, speaking of "the splendid society of which we are capable," assuring the thriving they are as good as they think they are, this "galaxy of wonderful, committed New Yorkers here tonight." See Super Wasp speeding up the highway in his Caddy to the Bronx, removing the bow tie and donning his handy skullcap. See Super Wasp schmooze middle-class Jews. He speaks against Vietnam and wasteful budgets and of admirable social welfare policy. He downplays his activism and accentuates securing the city, as he regularly does (these days). See Super Wasp soothe the elderly in Manhattan, a crowd of three thousand wearing SENIOR POWER buttons. He notes that "crime can most affect old people." See Super Wasp regale on, new night, new gala, same charmer. There he is with boldfaced Lindsayites—entertainer Ethel Merman, actress Kitty Carlisle, fellow heartthrob Troy Donahue. No one would say John Lindsay went down without a fight.[6]

His core strategy was captured by an apology ad (where he never actually apologized). It pictured him open-collared, *Gentlemen's Quarterly* as ever, staring into the camera. He said, "I guessed wrong" on the blizzard and "that was a mistake, but I put six thousand more cops on the streets and that was no mistake." The candidate who once led with police reform now led with policing. It went on that way, until the camera zoomed in and he said that this was the "second-toughest job in America" but he wanted it.

Lindsay would outspend his opponents, combined, four to one. The *Times* editorial board allowed that, yes, "crime is rampant, race relations tense; transportation is archaic, housing inadequate; education is faulty, welfare burdensome; the streets are dirty, the air polluted; prices are high, and so are taxes," but it still endorsed Lindsay (in *two* editorials). In the campaign's homestretch, there were tickertape parades for the Apollo 11 astronauts and the "miracle Mets." It gave the city buoyancy. After the Mets' World Series victory, images were plastered across front pages (in the papers workingmen read) of Lindsay in the Mets clubhouse, being doused with champagne by players, like one of the boys. But perhaps Lindsay's greatest blessing came from Procaccino's errors. As DC influencers Evans and Novak wrote, Procaccino ran "the most inept Democratic mayoralty campaign in modern history." In the end, Lindsay cobbled together a new kind of liberal coalition—minorities, Jews, the otherwise liberal, white, and well educated, plus smatterings elsewhere. He won with 42 percent. "Why did Lindsay run so poorly?" analysts Richard Scammon and Ben Wattenberg wrote. It was because the mayor "allowed the election to be phrased as a referendum on law and order/race/crime." They noted that Hubert Humphrey in 1968, despite his failings on social issues, won 61 percent of liberal New York City, though Humphrey also faced two more conservative opponents. In the end, Lindsay earned only one in four white workingmen's votes. His minority investment paid dividends, however. As a third-party candidate, Lindsay impressively won more than eight in ten blacks, more than six in ten Puerto Ricans, and two thirds of Manhattanites. Read one *Times* headline: POOR AND RICH, NOT MIDDLE CLASS, THE KEY TO LINDSAY REELECTION.[7]

Mario Procaccino emerged from the race a damaged man. His campaign was branded racist (long after, the *Times* obituary adjudicated it a "thinly disguised attack on black and Hispanic people"). He had campaigned in liberal and tense Gotham on "law and order"—it was "crime city," not "fun city," he said. He had told a black audience, "My heart is as black as yours." It was an ugly assertion, a man trying to say he too had grown up the hard way. With that failure, and with his emphasis on crime (though Lindsay too had highlighted crime when he initially ran for mayor), Procaccino was stalked by charges of being "anti-black." It reduced him to tears on the campaign trail.

But there was a certain way that elites talked about Mario Procaccino. During the campaign, Woody Allen told a gala that Procaccino was probably "in his undershirt, drinking beer and watching Lawrence Welk on television." *Time* magazine noted Procaccino's "electric blue suits and watermelon pink shirts." The *New Yorker* wrote that Procaccino and Marchi "owe their victories largely" to racist whites, that it "did not hurt" their candidacy that both men were Italian, a "condition" they shared with 1.3 million New Yorkers. It conceded that to "many" Lindsay supporters the "New York redneck is probably an Italian" and that the "Lindsay men" speak of Procaccino as the "Little Napoleon of Backlash." The *New Yorker* soon spoke for itself, reporting that a "great many" city residents find it "impossible to believe that in this time of crisis in American cities someone like Procaccino could actually be elected mayor" because he is a "round pouter pigeon of a man, a graduate of"—ahem—"C.C.N.Y. and Fordham Law School," with "interests" limited to the "Little Italys of the Bronx." The *Economist* reported that the American "press has created" an impression of Procaccino as "emotional and not terribly bright." The city's most liberal daily, the *New York Post*, wrote that he looked like a "ward heeler, so much so" it was "hard to take him seriously." Correction, contended another writer—Procaccino's disposition was more like a "Bronx grocer." Another observer conjured old mafia flicks, writing of Procaccino's "George Raft suits" and comparing his supporters to "an old Edward G. Robinson movie." The National Urban League's Whitney Young characterized Procaccino's circle as new money—his words were "affluent peasants"—suggesting that the *paesani* funding him had cash but not civility. Read another newspaper, "If you put Mario Procaccino in a white apron he could be hawking mackerel at the Fulton Fish Market."[8]

"Especially must Italians wonder where contempt for a class leaves off and prejudice against Italians begins," Milton Himmelfarb wrote in 1973. "People who would not dream of telling Negro jokes regale each other with Italian jokes."[9]

"Not so long before this, these same white, lower class borough dwellers," historian Steve Fraser later wrote, "had been regarded as cultural heroes standing up to the fat cats, applauded for their everyman insouciance. Now they had become culturally disreputable, reactionary outlaws, decidedly unstylish in what they wore and drank and in how they played; they were looked on as lesser beings."

This condescension from the uptown left, increasingly echoing the New Left, was no aberration, which the era's liberal aberrations ably conveyed, much like the exception that proves the rule. There were dissident liberal thinkers who, similar to some reporters, heeded Chicago '68 and the Nixon shock that followed. "The left, preoccupied with its own oppression, could not see [white workers] as human beings with real grievances," wrote feminist Ellen Willis in 1969, a view considered "counterrevolutionary" within her New Left circle (she was the daughter of a city cop). "Liberal politicians (with the concurrence of radicals) dismissed the workingman's fear of crime as racist paranoia and his resentment at having to support people who did not work as social backwardness." Pete Hamill wagered that "a century of intellectual sneering at bourgeois values" had led "many intellectuals" to overlook or sneer at the "plight" of the blue-collar white. Hamill added that the era's cultural patricians "don't understand his virtues (loyalty, endurance, courage, among others) and see him only through his faults (narrowness, bigotry, the worship of machismo, among others). The result is the stereotype." "The social critics of the 1960s and early '70s are relatively affluent compared to the marginality and even joblessness they had experienced during the Depression," Michael Harrington wrote a few years later. "This change in their own class position may have made them less sensitive to the daily struggles of less favored people." "Liberals did not sympathize with the suffering of people like those who live in Canarsie," explained Jonathan Rieder, a Yale sociologist who in the seventies, as David Frum

quipped later, "spent two years living not in New Guinea or up the Amazon but in a place that his academic colleagues probably found even more exotic: the lower-middle-class neighborhood adjacent to New York's Kennedy Airport." "An extraordinary amount of bigotry on the part of elite, liberal students goes unexamined at Yale and elsewhere," wrote a Yale graduate student in 1969, Michael Lerner. "Directed at the lower middle class, it feeds on the unexamined biases of class perspective." He recalled hearing Polish jokes from Ivy Leaguers who would be aghast at black jokes. Lerner added, "Radicals gloat over the faulty syntax of the lower middle class with the same predictability that they patronize the ghetto language as 'authentic.'"
"It was clear enough to working-class kids like me that we were moving into a different class world when we became active on the left," wrote John Welch, a typical '60s activist save his working-class background. "Ordinary students who were against the war thought that workers were all crypto-Nazis. Many students and active leftists really did believe that 'working people are the enemy.' Of course, leftist leaders knew better . . . still, I can't remember how many times you heard people call common soldiers 'pigs,'" he wrote. "Working people often were talked about as if they were fat and satisfied, pigs wallowing in warm mud. The working class has 'sold out,' it's been 'bought off.'"[10]

Not so long ago—when elites needed hard men to defend the nation, to construct a superpower—the everyman was esteemed. Even within the churches of capitalism, such as Rockefeller Center, the laborer was drawn as if he was a Greek demigod. They were the grunts celebrated for winning the Second World War. They built the nation's cities, farmed its food, and spanned the continent with superhighways. And since FDR, most had backed Democrats because Democrats backed them and respected them.

Now New Left leading lights seemed to thrive in the nation blue-collar men helped build and protect, but portrayed them as bygone, square, simpletons, pigs, racists, sexists, warmongers. But it was the relative silence on who really went off to war that seemed to offer a window into what they most abhorred. As poorer boys forever had, many joined up, thinking they needed to go somewhere bad to get somewhere better. In other words, if at one time the masses had been seen rosily for their best, the new culture had swung radically. Ordinary men were framed as patriarchal oppressors. After all, the "American male is sufficiently vicious, virile and violent," explained Kate Millett in her influential book *Sexual Politics* (1970). The book earned her the cover of *Time*. It discussed the "privileged white man's general sway of empire" and his "dominant wrath," conveniently ignoring all the luxe white ladies atop the food chain, as well as the lowly workmen maltreated by "the

Man" daily. In fact, the "little guy" was told he was now a "big man" because he was male, doubly so because he was white. Thus, the disempowered were told they really had power. Even their feelings of alienation were invalidated. Struggling whites felt blamed for an elite corps of powerful men, though few had any relation to them. The new liberal culture seemed to disparage earned status—a workingman's respect, motherhood's respect, parental respect, elder respect ("Don't trust anyone over 30!" it was said), but most explosively of late a soldier's respect, and with that, the flag's respect, and with that, the dead's respect. And as this disunion took on the weight of war, divides seemed to devolve more readily into battle lines, and each side clung to the greatest offenses—the My Lai massacre or the "good soldiers" shamed for the "bad war." And while it was only a minority who shamed them, the criticism came from the sort long featured in the media for occupying halls and mistaking it for "war," for throwing rocks at cops and calling it "war," for taking refuge within campus sanctuaries while lecturing about "just war," even as others went off to the real war.

Protesters burn a US flag during an antiwar demonstration in Washington, DC, in 1969. (Hulton Archive/Getty)

And as the New Left outlook seeped into the center-left mainstream by 1970, its censorious side did as well. The nascent stereotype of the judgmental "limousine liberal" came to exceed the man it was first weaponized against (John Lindsay) and stick to the new liberal establishment he embodied. Lindsay, like others, could also be his worst enemy. The day after losing the GOP mayoral primary, Lindsay blamed his failure on "the forces of reaction and fear," on his opponents appeal to "built-in bigotry" and the "most base instincts." Lindsay later regretted the words. It rarely aided a politician to assume the worst in voters.

It was not entirely un-Lindsaylike, however. Lindsay was once asked a softball question: did he see any commonality between turn-of-the-century European immigrants and the city's blacks today? He could have affirmed the unique trauma of the black American experience, which was well known to America by the 1960s, while noting the millions of Europeans who fled poverty only to find poverty. He could have acknowledged that it was Wasp Brahmins (like Lindsay) who stood atop systemic discrimination against Italians, Irish, Jews. He could have said the earlier era's child labor was not slave labor, but neither was it kids' play. Instead, Lindsay replied curtly, "There is really no comparison."

Yet on one occasion, Lindsay deviated and noted "common afflictions." In August 1969, Lindsay spoke to civil rights leaders in Charleston. He jumped off his staff's research and the media's new interest in the overlooked masses. Lindsay said lower-middle class whites are also "deprived, of security, a sense of progress," and "shadowed by the threat of chaos" in cities. "Millions of working men and women, once thought of as part of an affluent society, are," he said, "finding, just as the blacks said a decade ago and the college students five years ago, that the system is not working for them." The speech was hardly noticed back in New York. Lindsay returned to the city, faced the unpromising odds he would be reelected, and doubled down on his base.

Bobby, Lindsay was not. But few were. After all, Hubert Humphrey had said "law and order" was about "hate," not about the rise in lawlessness and dearth of order. And Gene McCarthy could tip his nose with the best of them. A McCarthy aide once said the labor movement wasn't worth "the powder it would take to blow it to hell." During the 1968 Oregon primary, as Bobby Kennedy worked to cobble together a coalition of blacks and blue-collar whites, McCarthy told college students that RFK appealed not to the erudite like them, but to "the less intelligent and less educated people in America. And I don't mean to fault them for voting for him, but I think that you ought to bear that in mind as you go to the polls." In Arthur Schlesinger's words, McCarthy was declaring "a revolution against the proletariat."[11]

◆

By spring 1970, few mainstream politicians sought the New Left's favor more than the handsome Republican gentleman John Lindsay. About a half-year after the moratorium, Lindsay made a pilgrimage to Berkeley, the birth-place of student activism. He was the featured speaker at the University of California's Charter Day. The honor conventionally came with an honorary degree. But the university regents and the state's governor, Ronald Reagan, voted to deny Lindsay the commendation, which only bolstered Lindsay's appeal to counterculture students, long Reagan's adversaries. Lindsay's top aides, including Dick Aurelio and Jeff Greenfield, labored over the address for weeks. This was the epicenter of student activism. It was Lindsay's chance to become the candidate with the fire.[12]

In Berkeley's open-air Greek Theatre, atop the podium, stood Lindsay. He was tan. The gold-tasseled cap gave his eyes a cobalt hue. He seemed to personify, as ever, the establishment. Then he spoke of "disaffection and be-trayal" and how "we cling to our faith in our own efficiency, but we begin to see breakdowns everywhere." He railed against the powerful who "draft you to fight needless wars." (Of course, Berkeley's matriculants didn't fight in Vietnam, but it played well.) He spoke of powerful men who "pollute the air and water" and "perpetuate poverty" and "set the conditions which either ensure or deny a decent society." Still, he cautioned that turning to violence was "cowardly and immoral." He went on to express solidarity with the Movement all the same. He affirmed their belief that "institutions do not work." He continued, "Men, now in power . . . believe that the people of America are ready to support repression as long as it is done with a quiet voice and a business suit." Lindsay pushed on: "If you believe that the risks of freedom are preferable to the certainties of tyranny—if you believe that you do not cure an illness by silencing the outcries of a patient—then you must speak out loudly and clearly against this threat of a new repression." And the students acclaimed him. Of course, not all. This was Berkeley. Hecklers yelled, "Out of Vietnam! . . . Free the Panthers!" But the outbursts were rare. Repeatedly, students stood and cheered. Lindsay gazed at the Berkeley crowd and saw his future.[13]

And Lindsay flew away—well, not until later that day. He traveled to Stanford, where he repeated his cri de coeur. "It was a strange speech for a politician," noted a *Times* reporter, "self-doubting, pessimistic, deeply critical of established institutions." But the *Times* editorial board wrote that Lindsay "underscored his national stature as one of the few governmental leaders able to communicate with American youth." ("Youth" and "New Left" were often used interchangeably in the "paper of record," like most outlets.) The *Times* further commended Lindsay for standing before cheering students and "courageously" challenging the establishment.[14]

Serious minds now saw Lindsay as presidential timber. In the past three hundred years, only 2 of the 102 men who had preceded Lindsay in the mayoralty had attained higher political office afterward—DeWitt Clinton (governor, 1817) and John T. Hoffman (governor, 1869). But Lindsay was not the first New York mayor to look in the mirror and see a president, nor would he be the last. He was a favorite cover boy of magazines. The "strappingly handsome product of St. Paul's and Yale," read *Newsweek*'s latest Lindsay cover. He was gentlemanly good TV too. The star of *Bedtime for Bonzo* was the governor of California. People even talked about that B-lister becoming president one day. Ronald Reagan president, imagine that. The era's upheaval made anything seem possible. Why not Lindsay?

New York senator Charles Goodell said Lindsay had "a good shot" at the '72 Democratic nomination if he switched parties. "He will be a contender for leadership of the eastern liberal establishment and a major factor in the 1972 presidential campaign," the *Chicago Tribune* reported. "Astute politicians in New York infer from his campaign remarks that he aspires to succeed" Senator Edward Kennedy, whose was marred by Chappaquiddick, as the "heir apparent to the Democrat presidential nomination in 1972." Jack Newfield wrote in *Life* about how "tough" Lindsay was and that his inner circle and "army of college canvassers" believed he had "invented, in cynical, fragmented New York, the scale model for a national New Politics campaign in 1972." "Perhaps we are so familiar with him that we can't see the mystery anymore, that we know his blunders too well," Newfield wrote in another article, after witnessing Berkeley. "We forget the fierce fascination Lindsay holds for the young and black." *Newsweek* acknowledged the uphill climb but added, "After Eugene McCarthy's extraordinary 1968 insurgency, nobody with Lindsay's special potential can be lightly dismissed. His glamorous good looks are accompanied by a dynamic style, a 'Here's Johnny' celebrity on the TV talk shows and predictable appeal to minorities, the urban poor, and twenty-five million newly enfranchised young voters." (The voting age would change from 21 to 18 before the 1972 election, and there was much buzz that young people might make a president.) Subtly, Lindsay cut loose some of his Republican aides. One young journalist, Gloria Steinem, wrote after seeing the pilgrimage to Berkeley, "Lindsay just might be putting it together for '72." Steinem imagined him as RFK and Gene McCarthy rolled into one. That he could unite blue-collar whites and "disillusioned suburbanites" with youth, minorities, and cosmopolitans. The *Times* reported that Lindsay's campaign manager and now deputy mayor, Dick Aurelio, was being called a "president maker." Aurelio characterized Lindsay as a "great test for liberals."[15]

◆

In the land of unmagical thinking, where Dick Aurelio actually subsisted, Lindsay would beta-test a Democratic future—a high-low coalition, upscale whites and downscale nonwhites. And since the country was still very white, the strategy depended on youthful verve. So it was in Berkeley that gentleman John Lindsay secretly met with an occupier of Columbia, an organizer of Chicago '68, a leading sixties radical—Tom Hayden. To paraphrase the Grateful Dead, what a long strange trip it had been.

After Chicago '68, Hayden speculated that if the Democratic Convention had been in New York, Lindsay would have given the demonstrators Central Park and some 750,000 protestors would have come. As a congressman, Lindsay had voted for the Gulf of Tonkin Resolution. But by 1968, the New Left read signals. That February, Lindsay told University of Oregon students, "There is obviously much in our capacity to dissent from, to rebel against." In March, around the time of the Grand Central yip-in, Lindsay told three thousand students at Queens College that they should "join resistance movements." He encouraged students to become politically active but not use "harassment tactics," such as burning draft cards. He was asked about dodging the draft. The mayor said he would never counsel such. He also noted, as Richard Reeves summarized in the *Times,* that a "draftee had the option of declaring himself a conscientious objector." Reeves noted that Lindsay received "one of the most enthusiastic receptions of his political career." The next day, front page of the *Times,* MAYOR URGES YOUTHS TO AID WAR RESISTANCE. The headline was overstated, even unfair, but also impactful. In April, Lindsay stayed out of the Columbia occupation. Still, Lindsay assured New Yorkers afterward, he was a "disciple of change."[16]

Meanwhile, Lindsay's administration was secretly funding Abbie Hoffman (and continued to do so after the Grand Central yip-in). Lindsay aide Barry Gottehrer thought Hoffman had "credibility with young people that we needed" and hired him as a community liaison in the Village. Hoffman was also tasked with writing a pamphlet on navigating the city safely. The funding helped subsidize Hoffman's lifestyle and his first book, *Fuck the System*. A counterculture favorite, *Fuck the System* was effectively a travel guide for hippies in the city—how to obtain free food, free booze, welfare, free lawyers, and free phone calls: "A number 14 brass washer with a small piece of scotch tape over one side of the hole will work in old style phones (also parking meters, laundromat dryers, soda and other vending machines)."[17]

But with the Berkeley speech, Lindsay's embrace of the New Left was no longer peripheral. There Lindsay was, privately chatting with Tom Hayden in a hotel room. Hayden urged Lindsay to run for president on an antiwar platform. He hoped that Lindsay could rally youth, nonwhites, and the conscientious, and maybe, just maybe, save white-bread America.

Three years earlier, when America's cities exploded with riots in that "long hot summer" of 1967, Hayden had lauded the havoc: "A riot represents people making history" and "fundamental change." Hayden continued, "To the people involved, the riot is far less lawless and far more representative than the system of arbitrary rules." The riots had killed scores and decimated cities from Newark to Detroit. But Hayden explained, "Violence can contribute to shattering the status quo." The estimable *New York Review of Books* published the essay. The issue's cover featured an instructional diagram for a homemade Molotov cocktail.[18]

The article was published about a month after Lindsay described the Spanish Harlem riot as a "demonstration." There was an Orwellian quality to these New Lefties. Rampant graffiti was not a problem but high art. Norman Mailer clarified, if you sentence convicted graffitists to clean vandalized subway stations, it's like "condemning Cezanne to wipe out the works of Van Gogh."[19]

So graffitists were "Van Gogh." Theft and occupation could be "liberation." Riots were sometimes "demonstrations." The "highest patriotism" was exhibited by antiwar activists, rather than the boys fighting for their country. A Molotov cocktail could be a "protest." Even rape could be justified as "insurrectionary."

"Rape was an insurrectionary act," wrote Eldridge Cleaver in his 1968 memoir *Soul on Ice*. "It delighted me that I was defying and trampling upon the white man's law, upon his system of values, and that I was defiling his women." The *Times* called the book "brilliant," and christened it one of the ten best books of the year. The *Nation*: "Remarkable." The *Atlantic*: "Passionate and eloquent." The *Washington Post* was not as gaga. Still, it closed by extolling Cleaver's "brave and necessary adventure."

This was the cultural class Lindsay also occupied. That left became fashionable in the sixties, firstly among the heartfelt college set, then the intelligentsia, finally among celebrities and the professionally posh. Yet the outlook's appeal to the mainstream wore thin by 1970. Perhaps that shift was seen best inside a thirteen-room penthouse duplex on Park Avenue in that first month of the decade. Rich and famous whites fundraised and discussed underclass oppression with Black Panthers over silver trays of canapés. Some of the Panthers were to face charges for plotting to bomb retail stores, a police station, a botanical garden. In attendance were two journalists. Reporter one: the *Times* chronicler of patricians and parvenus, Charlotte Curtis, slim and elegant in black, studiously observing. Reporter two: Tom Wolfe, already well known, already perennially resplendent in vanilla suits, scribbling about, ballpoint to pad. (Barbara Walters was also present, though merely in her private capacity as a concerned socialite.) Curtis, in the *Times* society and style section, offered the first account. She reported it straight. She led with the Q and A between "the conductor laureate of the New York Philharmonic" and a "tall and handsome" Panther field marshal. The *Times* editorial board soon rebuked: "[The] emergence of the Black Panthers as the romanticized darlings of the politico-cultural jet set . . . represents the sort of elegant slumming that degrades patrons and patronized alike." In time, it would be Wolfe who memorialized the gathering. His twenty-thousand-word essay pierced the "delicious little agonies of the Radical Chic," this confederacy of afros and women with their hair just so, and all the "marvelous contradictions" of all sides, to borrow Wolfe's way with words. The essay infuriated black radicals and the white and woke, to borrow a term of a later day. "That bloodsucking Tom Wolfe," said the "tall and handsome" Panther field marshal. But Wolfe's prose mostly aimed upward and whiteward, if not also leftward. He was out to defrock America's cultural priesthood. The *New York Review of Books*—which Wolfe described as "the chief theoretical organ of Radical Chic"—saw fit to answer Wolfe's "frivolous account" with a gusty defense of America's well-meaning betters. Yet as historian Vincent Cannato noted decades after, this high-minded sympathy for the discontented rabble, that "radical chic, did not extend to the city's [white] blue-collar workers."[20]

CHAPTER 10

Building the Twin Towers,
Ethnic New York, and Race

IRONWORKERS SOMETIMES LOST sight of the land. They climbed atop the manmade world and the fog occasionally grew thick and the city vanished into vapor. "It was ghostly," one worker recounted. Atop the tower, there were giant cranes and their cables seemed invisible. As the steel floated out of the mist, a tag-line man used a rope and hook to steer it to the two connectors. These men stood highest, alone atop a column, waiting to bond the beam, often working without harnesses. The beam could jump with the wind and they needed to pivot fast and a harness could trap them. Once the new steel was in hand, it was hung and, in time, another deck was done. And upward they built, breaking for a brief lunch, which was often a sandwich while straddling some steel. On clear days, they could see all of Brooklyn, over Manhattan's cityscape, past Yankee Stadium, and far westward, to where New Jersey was green.[1]

The Twin Towers were Everest, the "big job" for the thousands of tradesmen and laborers who built a city of steel in the sky. By spring 1970, Lower Manhattan was "in a state of explosion," wrote architecture critic Ada Louise Huxtable. "The 110-story Trade Center will only be the tip of the iceberg. What is going on from the Battery to Brooklyn Bridge is the remaking of a city." Acres of Civil War–era row houses and colonial roads were demolished. The new southern face of Manhattan would be sheer skyscrapers of steel and glass. Huxtable coined it "New York's Second Skyscraper Age."

At the center of it all, the Twin Towers. In total, downtown would gain fifty million square feet of working and living space. The World Trade Center provided a fifth of it. To build the towers themselves, almost four times the total structural steel at the Empire State Building—more than two hundred thousand tons—would be lifted into the sky, ultimately more than a dozen stories higher than mankind had ever gone before. Originally, the Trade Center was not intended to push new heights. But Manhattan had the world's tallest building since 1908. It was the American century. In the sixties, Americans designed the first jumbo jet, completed the first domed super-stadium, built the world's longest suspension bridge, and launched the moonshot. The Twin Towers would "truly be the product of our time," said the principal architect, Minoru Yamasaki, in 1964.[2]

But first, the world's tallest towers needed to rise atop waterlogged soil. They excavated enough soil and debris—1.2 million cubic yards—to fill three-quarters of the Houston Astrodome. The quarried earth was used to expand the width of Manhattan by nearly twenty-four acres, the foundation of Battery Park City. In part to keep the Hudson River at bay, they built a reverse bathtub, two blocks wide and four blocks long, and anchored seven stories deep to bedrock.[3]

The most remarkable engineering feats were the towers. To maximize space, they created express and local elevators, creatively mimicking

The view of one of the towers under construction at the World Trade Center, New York City, on October 20, 1970. The Empire State Building is pictured in the background. (AP Photo/Jim Wells)

the subway. Most extraordinary, skyscrapers' skeletons would change. Skyscrapers typically relied on an inner spine of vertical columns. Instead, the Twin Towers vertical loads were mainly supported by an exoskeleton of crosscut-steel mesh. Disadvantages were examined, including one worst-case scenario: could compromising the shell lead to collapse?[4]

In 1964, one of the Trade Center's lead architects defended the Twin Towers' structural integrity. An example given: "The buildings have been investigated and found to be safe in an assumed collision with a large jet airliner traveling at 600 miles per hour. Analysis indicates that such collision would result in only local damage which could not cause collapse." The scenario was no hypothetical. In the last weeks of World War Two, a bomber got lost in the fog and crashed into the Empire State Building. In spring 1968, one group published a large ad in the *Times*. It argued that the towers' height was a "hazard" and featured a drawing of a passenger airliner about to collide with the Twin Towers.[5]

The World Trade Center's engineers and architects did not adequately consider how jet fuel, once ignited, could burn hot enough to collapse the towers. The scenario also seemed farfetched to them. By comparison, the benefits were certain. The open floor plans were a leaseholder's goldmine. Each floor contained an acre of usable office space. The magnetism of the towers' summit proved more fleeting. Before the Trade Center was finished, Sears announced that its new headquarters in Chicago would surpass the Twin Towers. So Gotham would lose this honor too. Developers still hoped to catalyze the area's rebirth. The Trade Center featured downtown's first new luxury hotel in 150 years.[6]

But the Twin Towers were ugly, as one envisions colossal rectangles of steel mesh. A "fearful instrument of urbicide," wrote critic Wolf von Eckardt. "Pure technology," Huxtable wrote. "It is General Motors Gothic." Previous peaks in the city skyline—the Empire State, Woolworth, and Singer buildings—valued immensity and aesthetics. But as journalist William Geist later wrote, the Twin Towers looked like "the box the Empire State Building came in." The exoskeleton also necessitated narrow windows. That denied the sense of grandiosity one expects inside towers. Critics also saw indulgence. Why have two? Why now? As the towers ascended, the city descended. The Twin Towers captured the space between the grandees' priorities and street blight. And though few realized it then, they marked a bygone era as well—the great city ceaselessly climbing skyward, an America forever reaching upward. And to the workers who had built so much and had come so far, by the time they realized all that could be lost, it already was.[7]

◆

In 1850s New York City, nine in ten laborers and seven in ten domestic servants were Irish-born. The majority of the city's poorhouse, as in Philadelphia and Boston, were Irish as well. Over the previous decade, 1.7 million Irish had fled poverty and famine for America, including Patrick Kennedy, the dynasty's progenitor, who listed his trade as "labourer." Within the Irish male workforce in New York, more than half of the laborers had a trade, from carpentry to coopers to gas fitters. But the Irish had also endured decades as a hated minority. In 1844 Philadelphia, a Protestant mob killed fourteen. In 1855 Louisville, an anti-Catholic riot murdered at least twenty. Still they came. By 1860, New York City's Irish population exceeded Dublin's. At least one in four New Yorkers and Bostonians was Irish-born.[8]

Meanwhile, the Germans arrived in larger numbers. Many were "forty-eighters" fleeing the failed revolution that swept Europe in 1848. The Germans were less destitute than the Irish. More settled in the country-side and went west. Irish and German insularity helped spur the "common schools" movement to encourage assimilation. One beneficiary was girls, who by 1850, unlike in any other nation, attended elementary school in about the same proportion as boys. Come 1900, Germans were the largest ethnic group in the nation. Their New York City population was only surpassed by Berlin and Vienna. Still, by 1910, a quarter only spoke *Deutsche.* World War One sparked anti-German hysteria, including at least thirty murders. German literature was burned. Beethoven and Brahms were deemed "the music of conquest" by the *Los Angeles Times.* The war, like its sequel, spurred mass assimilation.[9]

Assimilation came slower for others. Between 1845 and 1855, as America emerged from a depression, three million immigrants arrived in the United States. It was the largest proportional shift of foreign-born in American history, as historian James McPherson noted. Before 1840, most immigrants were Protestant and less than a third were low-skilled laborers. In the two decades after 1840, immigration rose sixfold. These newcomers were mainly poor Irish and German Catholics. This shift inspired the Know-Nothing Party to form in 1854, which elected more than fifty representatives that year. Some Know-Nothings blamed immigrants for all societal ills, "the destruction of a fancied golden age," wrote historian Sean Wilentz. But nativists also received disproportionate support from downscale Protestants who competed with immigrants for jobs and housing. "The poorer the city neighborhood, the higher the Know-Nothing vote," concluded historian John Mulkern in his study of Massachusetts, where nativist candidates won the governorship, state legislature, and all eleven House races. Secret societies formed to elect native-born Protestants. If an outsider asked about one New York society, with a million members, the member responded, "I know nothing."

The sectarianism of Christendom lurked beneath all of it. The American Catholic church had supported slavery but defended downtrodden immigrants. Evangelical Protestants opposed slavery but supported oppression of the poorest whites, including thwarting their vote. Some Republicans argued that their party seemed united by a "base alloy of hypocrisy," to quote an aspiring politician, Abraham Lincoln. As Lincoln put it, "How can anyone who abhors the oppression of Negroes, be in favor of degrading classes of white people?"[10]

The Civil War suspended all other disputes. It ultimately killed more Americans than all other American wars combined. During the war, in 1863, Congress introduced America's first draft. In the Confederacy, highborn boys and slave "overseers" could legally escape conscription. Similarly, $300 (roughly a laborer's average annual earnings) bought rich boys out of the Union draft. Meanwhile, many of the Irish were ill-disposed to go south to fight to free blacks, only to compete against them for work up north. "Those in the North, where the bulk of the Irish lived, would fight to preserve the Union, but their ardor cooled considerably once President Lincoln emancipated the slaves," historian Jay Dolan wrote. Most immigrants never saw slavery's horrors firsthand, which inhibited sympathy. Seven in eight immigrants settled in free states. In northern cities, industrialists also used free blacks and newly arrived Europeans to push pay down and break strikes. In June 1863, Irish longshoremen protesting poor wages were undercut by black strikebreakers. One month later, years of division culminated. The conscription law sparked the Draft Riot, the worst civil unrest in American history, when a mob of mostly lowborn Irish American boys rioted over the "rich man's war, poor man's fight." For four days, they attacked the homes of prominent Republicans and institutions supporting the Union, and they scapegoated blacks, burning the Colored Orphan Asylum and murdering at least eleven blacks, including some by lynching.[11]

Anti-Catholic bigotry persisted after the war. "If we are to have another contest in the near future of our national existence," President Ulysses Grant commented in 1875, the next civil war would be "between [Protestant] patriotism and intelligence on the one side, and [Catholic] superstition, ambition, and ignorance."[12]

By 1880, Irish Americans attained some stability. William Grace became New York City's first Irish Catholic mayor. The Knights of Labor formed, and at its peak about half of all members were Irish. The Knights of Labor fought for the eight-hour workday, equal pay for the sexes, a ban on child labor.[13]

Still by 1890, about half of New York City was German and Irish, slightly more than a fifth were native-born (often of English ancestry), while Russians and Poles were 5 percent, Italians 4 percent, and blacks, Hungarians, and French constituted somewhere between 1 and 2 percent each. By the turn of the century, Italian and Russian Jewish immigrants arriving in New York outnumbered Irish and German immigrants four to one. The city's Italian population tripled in the 1890s alone. Most Italian newcomers were male farm workers from the poor south. According to lore, said one Italian immigrant, when they got here they found "the streets weren't paved with gold, they weren't paved at all, and I was expected to pave them."[14]

Italians provided most New York construction and shoreline labor at the close of the nineteenth century. "We can't get along without the Italians," a city police officer said. "We want somebody to do the dirty work. The Irish are not doing it any longer." But Italians often didn't receive an equal wage. In 1895 New York, during work on the Croton Reservoir—once the city's primary source of drinking water—common labor's daily pay was $1.30 to $1.50 for whites, $1.25 to $1.40 for coloreds, and $1.15 to $1.25 for Italians. Italian Catholics experienced violent bigotry as well. In New Orleans in 1891, in the worst single incident of mass lynching in American history, eleven Italian immigrants were strung up. The *Times* editorial board had advocated greater Italian immigration, writing in 1874 that they "have nothing to do with trades-unions," are "accustomed to low wages," and would be protected from "Irish malcontents." Come 1891, the *Times* justified the lynching by deeming the victims "sneaking and cowardly Sicilians," a people with "lawless passions," a "pest without mitigations." The *Washington Post* reported that the New Orleans killers were not a mob but "cool-headed men" of "social standing."[15]

At the same time, millions of immigrants settled in New York City, which had the most crowded slums worldwide by 1900 and a death rate almost double London's, even as America's GDP surpassed those of Germany, Great Britain, and France combined. In the Lower East Side, workers lived in shabby and foul tenements that bred epidemics. In the 1850s, *half* of all children born in the city were not expected to live to the age of six. Surviving children commonly worked in grim factories. Garment workers, half of whom were women, worked in sweatshops so debilitating that as tuberculosis spread, it came to be known as the "tailors' disease" or the "Jewish disease." Ironworker deaths were common. Fathers' workplace injuries left countless families destitute. These miserable conditions led more than a third of new immigrants to *return* to Europe.[16]

Still more came. The industrial economy was fueled by laborers. As historian Richard Krickus chronicled, in the early 1890s, an Austro-Hungarian unskilled laborer earned 24¢ a day compared to the "astounding" daily wage of $1 in America.[17]

Senator Henry Cabot Lodge, an influential Boston Brahmin, welcomed fair-skinned "Teutonic Italians" from the North, but not the "dark-skinned Southerners." In 1911, the Federal Immigration Commission reported that southern and eastern Europeans were "far less intelligent than the old" immigrants; "racially," they were "unlike the British, German, and other peoples" who "came to be part of the country," while the new wave "come with the intention of profiting in a pecuniary way." Several years later, Madison Grant, a Manhattan topsider, authored a widely read book that popularized the notion of a Nordic "master race." It asserted that recent Mediterranean and eastern European immigrants were "of the weak, the broken, and the mentally crippled," and yet these "servile" races were "rising against the master race." The newcomers had less "mental ability," explained the *Saturday Evening Post*, and Americans should not "forfeit their high estate" by joining the "mongrel races."[18]

Woodrow Wilson personified America's tension with immigration. He vetoed a law that both excluded Asiatic laborers and required a literacy test for immigrants. He stewarded momentous laws for the underclass—eliminating child labor, securing an eight-hour workday, extending antitrust powers. But Wilson's administration also characterized recent immigrants as "low-browed, big-faced persons of obviously low mentality."

In Wilson's book *A History of the American People*, the onetime president of Princeton University wrote that "sturdy stocks of the north of Europe" were being replaced by "the lowest class" who had "neither skill nor energy nor any initiative of quick intelligence . . . as if the countries of the south of Europe were disburdening themselves of the more sordid and hapless." A Virginian, Wilson also wrote of "ignorant negroes" and touted the KKK as an institution to "protect the southern country from some of the ugliest hazards." Wilson's outlook later would be oversimplified as white supremacy, but it was more nuanced. Much as Italian laborers sometimes experienced the worst wages in the North, Wilson placed the Chinese above southern Europeans in his racial hierarchy. He explained, "The Chinese were more to be desired, as workmen if not as citizens, than most of the coarse crew that came crowding in every year at the eastern ports" from southern and eastern Europe.[19]

Nativist-Protestant angst and related social issues, in fact, shaped the first substantive Republican headway in the Democratic South, which was a matter of culture, not race. In 1928, Democrat Al Smith—aspiring to be the first Catholic president—was branded as a papist who was against prohibition, as a corrupted big city pol, as the candidate of "rum, Romanism and rebellion." Irish and Italians did overwhelmingly back Smith. (Identity politics was so formative that by 1932, even amid the Great Depression, Irish and Italians in Boston and New York provided *less* support for FDR than they had for Al Smith.) Ultimately, Republican Herbert Hoover trounced Smith. The party of Lincoln won five southern states—all in the socially conservative peripheral South, from Florida to Texas to Tennessee, revealing an oft-overlooked southern fissure that influenced American politics long after. It was the Deep South that generally followed the racist and racialist candidates after Democrats began championing black equality in 1948—Strom Thurmond's Dixiecrats that year, Barry Goldwater in 1964 (for opposing the Civil Rights Act and related dynamics), and George Wallace in 1968 (Wallace won two-thirds of the vote in Alabama and Mississippi but only a third of the Tennessee vote). New Deal politics, particularly FDR's abortive court-packing plan, helped unite Southern Democrats and conservative Republicans, at least according to one freshman congressman of the time, Lyndon Johnson. JFK observed the same trend later as president. "Some Democrats have voted with Republicans for twenty-five years, really since 1938," Kennedy said. "So that we have a very difficult time, on a controversial piece of legislation, securing a working majority."[20]

Into the 1920s, as the Great Migration of blacks began, most Irish and Italian workers remained manual laborers. Jews had moved up the economic ladder more rapidly, but like in the Old World, ancient bigotry resurfaced. The Jewish characters of popular dime novels around the turn of the century, wrote historian Michael Dobkowski, were "money-centered personalities" with "grotesque physiognomies," and were "always the exploiter, never the exploited." The era's populist movement was threaded with references to Shylock, the Rothschilds, a mingling of conspiratorial Jewish bankers with Christ's crucifixion. Later, Henry Ford subsidized years of antisemitic propaganda. At the same time, since the late nineteenth century, the Wasp ruling class shut affluent Jews out of elite circles, from social clubs to universities. In 1923, Franklin Roosevelt helped enact a cap on the number of Jews admitted to Harvard. Yale didn't end its informal admissions policy, which restricted Jewish enrollment to about 10 percent, until the 1960s.[21]

Yet in the Jazz Age, optimism pervaded. More Americans lived in cities than on farms. There was a stock market craze. Americans bought cars, electric refrigerators, and radios, and with that, they bought into consumer culture and entered a new age of broadcast mass culture. A hit song was "Blue Skies." The heavens seemed boundless. "We in America today are nearer to the final triumph over poverty than ever before," Herbert Hoover said in 1928. "The poorhouse is vanishing."

The United States became so poor during the Great Depression that some Americans sought a better life in Russia. One in four men was jobless. Industrial production declined by half. Nearly half of all banks failed. Went one motto: "Use it up, wear it out, make do, or do without." Millions became hobos. They learned tricks. Hot water and ketchup made tomato soup. Divorce declined, crime would decline, but child abandonment increased. FDR's New Deal would save millions from privation and the Second World War doubled wages and salaries, as the war effort amounted to one last jobs program. For blue-collar families who did not lose a breadwinner, the war opened the road to prosperity. Yet not for southern blacks or interned Japanese Americans. Less recalled, six hundred thousand Italian Americans were branded "enemy aliens." More than ten thousand Italian Americans were forced to relocate from the West Coast.[22]

It was a different America after the war. The nation accounted for half the world's GDP. The boom, as well as programs such as the GI Bill, helped families finally reach the middle class. Still, by 1970, three-quarters of Polish Catholics, two-thirds of Italian Catholics, half of Irish Catholics, half of Protestants, and a quarter of Jews remained blue-collar. The Wasp elite endured. But by 1970, the average white Protestant no longer embodied the American Dream. A quarter of Irish Catholics now earned at least a high middle-class wage, compared to only a fifth of white Protestants. In fact, American affluence had never reached white Protestant Appalachia. They were mostly descendants of Scots-Irish Presbyterians who since the colonial era traveled down the Appalachian spine. In the 1950s, the region lost half of its coal and agriculture workforce—more than 640,000 jobs. Still by 1965, a third of Appalachians lived in poverty. Indoor plumbing remained rare in remote counties. Even by 1970, after the "war on poverty" ameliorated some hardship, the region's per capita income lingered well below the national average and up to a million poor whites remained isolated in decaying mining towns and smaller communities, especially along the ridge lands of West Virginia and Kentucky, including what one government-backed agency called "a rural slum reaching over 1,450 square miles." Even among whites, the postwar years were not uniformly prosperous.[23]

In 1969, for a family of four in a city, the nation's median family income was not enough to provide a "modest but adequate" standard of living—and about half of New York City's whites fell below that threshold. Nationally, at the time, fewer than one in three blue-collar whites thought they were "better off" than five years ago. An equal few said they would be "better off" in five years. Even among those doing well, there was a sense that the good land was shifting against them, so soon after arriving on it. Between 1946 and 1970, the share of New Yorkers working as craftsmen, laborers, and foremen fell from 41 to 29 percent. Trade unionists were long considered the "princes of labor." Yet many of those blue-collar "princes," wrote Michael Harrington in 1972, were "neither poor nor affluent but in-between and distinctly deprived."[24]

◆

The steamfitters' chief in the seventies, George Daly, grew up during the Depression. He lived on an Irish block of the Village, near Italians, Poles, Ukrainians. The "Daly dozen"—six girls, six boys—attended Catholic school and worked young. Daly was a shoeshine boy—a nickel a shine, a penny tip. His mother, who descended from eastern European Jews, converted to Catholicism as an adult. She attended church daily and raised the family. His father was a steamfitter, like his Irish father before him, who joined the Knights of Labor.

Like millions of others after the Second World War, George Daly returned from the military and made a life. He was a handsome round-faced Irish boy, with strong shoulders and a soft voice. He became a steamfitter's helper, hanging pipe, working weekends, roadwork for a period, moonlighting as a prizefighter under Rocky Graziano's trainer. An uncle, also named George Daly, had been a likely contender for the championship but died of a burst appendix. The younger George Daly was a welterweight, fighting just under 150 pounds. He fought out of the crouch and his fellow steamfitters cheered him on in Coney Island. In time, Daly led them, supporting his family along the way. A veteran union tradesman now secured a middle-class life. All five of Daly's brothers and the spouses of his six sisters became steamfitters.[25]

These typical familial bonds led labor unions to resemble ethnic clans. By midcentury, different trade unions were known as mostly Italian or Irish or Jewish or Polish, or some mix of a few ethnicities but not others. The unions had followed the folkways of medieval guilds. They not only favored legacy families but also created obstacles for outsiders. Some trade union apprenticeship exams gave candidates an extra ten points if a blood relative belonged. It took a half-decade to train a pipefitter. As the *Times* noted, the Air Force trained a jet pilot in eighteen months; unwritten was that a *Times* reporter could be trained in less time. America's unusually steep vocational barriers also and inordinately pervaded white collar fields, from law to medicine. But with the civil rights era, the building trades felt pressure from activists, liberal politicians, and media coverage. Construction unions were forced to answer first, and for those who had not made vocational inroads— foremost among them blacks.[26]

Progress came slow, especially for a population that felt it had waited long enough for its slice of the American dream. In 1969, under the Nixon administration, the first federal push for implementing affirmative action focused on construction unions. Consequently, Washington's first program assigning racial quotas fell on blue-collar whites. The Philadelphia Plan mandated that federal contractors choose targets for minority employment within suggested guidelines. At the same time—perhaps heightened by a sense of scarcity from the recession and depreciating construction jobs—opposition to workmen quotas became more visible. In Chicago, white hardhats stormed a federal hearing on union discrimination. In Pittsburgh, thousands of white workers demonstrated against the mayor for stopping local construction while the city negotiated with black protestors. In April 1970, John Lindsay joined others and pledged to require at least one nonwhite trainee for every four journeymen working on city construction projects. Though like Nixon, Lindsay did not seek to publicize the policy.[27]

Many blue-collar whites came to question why affirmative action began with them. Why were they put on the line first for nepotism hardly unique to them? It seemed to capture how the era's liberal betters treated them. They felt like pawns of social policy that higher classes drafted yet escaped, not unlike the war, as if the wages of slavery and Jim Crow were northern workingmen's debt. They had seen blacks arriving in northern cities in large numbers within recent decades. Most northern whites recognized the unique injustice of the American black experience. But they noted that many of their people had arrived after slavery ended, and most had made their way in northern states. Many German and Irish had fought for Dixie, but vastly more fought for the Union and, by default, emancipation. The common white American rarely considered how the national economy had benefited from slavery, including early Gotham. Between 1700 and 1774 about seven thousand slaves of African origin were brought into the New York colony—roughly the city's entire white population in 1737, most of whom were Dutch and English. Decades after slavery's abolition in the city, northern longshoremen worked docks that serviced ships stuffed with cotton picked by southern slaves. Yet that linkage felt remote to northern white workers by 1970. And it didn't sit especially well for families living paycheck to paycheck in a failing city, with good blue-collar work on the wane. To most tradesmen, their primary estate was their union membership. That estate had required discrimination against other European ethnicities and now, by the 1950s—with large black urban populations and postwar growth—against blacks, and thus was shaped by racism and inseparable from America's history of it. Even those who acknowledged all that often didn't see why affluent advocates shouldn't go first. It felt like school busing would feel to them in the years ahead, or affirmative action as it spread. Colleges would enact policies to help racial minorities (disproportionately downscale) while protecting the estate of upscale whites through legacy admissions. After all, blue-collar whites' legacy was more likely building universities than studying within them. They saw hypocrites telling them to bear burdens that others benefited from more and had yet not answered for, or would not or could afford to never face, and yet still stood on soapboxes and morally judged them.[28]

In 1968, of the 1.1-million-member construction unions filing reports with the Equal Employment Opportunity Commission—a group deemed "generally representative" of the nation's 3.5 million unionized construction workers—blacks were 7.4 percent (about 4 percentage points below their share of the population) and Hispanics were 4.4 percent of members (about equivalent to their share of the population). Hence construction unions were about 88 percent white. By comparison, for the school year 1968–69, faculty members in higher education were 94 percent white. "While unions slow-walked integration, they were hardly repositories of segregation either," wrote Brendan Sexton in *Dissent* in 1972. He noted that trade unions were more diverse than the staff of the *Times* magazine, where " 'unions' (all unions, not just some of them) were recently described as the 'principal barriers' standing in the way of black progress."[29]

For his part, Nixon second-guessed the Philadelphia Plan. In January 1970, he read of AFL-CIO boss George Meany's criticism of the plan. Nixon worried it "hurts us," because "with our constituency we gained little." Still, Nixon expanded the policy from government contracts exceeding $500,000 to contracts exceeding $50,000, and added quotas for women. By midyear 1970, there were 407 minority apprentices in Washington, four times the number in 1964. Pat Buchanan, no fan of affirmative action himself, later defended his boss's positive impact. Buchanan noted that between 1969 and 1973, black employment on federal contracts rose from 4 to 26 percent.[30]

In 1970, plumber Patrick O'Connell didn't seem proud that his union had few blacks. But he didn't want to give his union card to a stranger over his son. O'Connell was 34, already three years older than his father, a cop, had been when he died. A Korean War vet, O'Connell had joined the Navy at age

17. It "was the best way that most of us got off relief," a Depression welfare program that the O'Connell family took with "terrible shame," he said. His hair was now streaking gray. He commuted daily from Long Island, where he lived with his wife and two children in a single-story frame home, with a well-cut lawn and a barking dog, on a block with three firemen and a few cops. "We can't give our kids college degrees," the plumber said. "All we can give them is the union card."[31]

"Some men leave their sons money, some large investments, some business connections, and some a profession. I have only one worthwhile thing to give: my trade. I hope to follow a centuries-old tradition and sponsor my sons for an apprenticeship," a union craftsman wrote in a letter to the *Times* (an institution that, like many, was privately controlled by one family and passed down between generations). The craftsman continued, "For this simple father's wish it is said that I discriminate against Negroes. Don't all of us discriminate? Which of us, when it comes to a choice, will not choose a son over all others? I believe that an apprenticeship in my trade is no more of a public trust, to be shared by all, than a millionaire's money is a public trust. Why should the government . . . decide how I dispose of my heritage?"[32]

Both Lindsay and Nixon similarly supported union integration. Nixon had more impact in Washington than Lindsay did in New York. Nixon overcame dismay over integration, nevertheless. As his speechwriter William Safire wrote, "The irony was that of all people, the construction workers had been given the hardest time by the Nixon administration." Nixon pushed integration in 1969, and at the same time, to fight inflation, he ordered a 75 percent cutback in new federal construction contracts.[33]

Construction was especially hard hit by the recession. Nixon's cutback made it worse. In May 1970, construction's unemployment rate had increased 112 percent from the year before to 9.1 percent, twice the national average. Some factors were not unique to the era. Automation continued threatening livelihoods and taught the working class to be skeptical of progress. Unionization peaked midcentury but it was not until about 1970 that membership began its permanent and soon, precipitous decline. For a period, the skyscraper renaissance helped insulate Manhattan. In 1968, New York accounted for a quarter of the nation's commercial development, as midtown experienced its own construction blitz. Downtown, the Twin Towers site alone employed about five thousand construction workers at its peak. But by 1970, even fortunate tradesmen knew they were on the back end of

A construction worker building the World Trade Center in New York City in 1970.
(Eddie Adams/AP)

their feast. They became more defensive about their jobs, however dangerous. About one worker died for every hundred who built the Twin Towers.

Elevator constructor Joe Kelly saw a close friend, a father of five, plummet twenty-five floors to his death at the Trade Center. But the pay was worth the risk. Kelly was a family man who hung on for years, "when every Friday the ax was falling." By 1970, the Twin Towers job paid him upper-middle-class wages. Kelly knew, like all, that proverbial famine would follow. He didn't use his vacation time. He caught a movie with his wife about every six weeks, sometimes getting a drink after at a "respectable place." He favored Johnny Cash and Jackie Gleason, attended Sunday midday mass, and was yet another military veteran on the steel. His yellow hard hat had flag decals and read FOR GOD AND COUNTRY. Patriotism was increasingly visible on construction sites. As the Trade Center hardhats would, when a skyscraper was completed, workmen often staked a large flag to the final column. They watched the crane lift the last steel, as it steadily ascended countless floors and the wind picked up and the flag waved and whipped in the thin air, at times violently.[34]

CHAPTER 11 | **Cambodia and Kent State**
May 1970

T HE WORST OF the war seemed over, and the division Vietnam had wrought seemed sure to subside with it. It was mere weeks after John Lindsay had summoned his inner Berkeley, in Berkeley. And for the briefest instant, Richard Nixon seemed to be listening.

On April 20, 1970, Nixon pledged the withdrawal of 150,000 troops. "Nixon talked like a man who believes the war in Vietnam is all but over," the *Chicago Tribune* reported. The Vietnam Moratorium Committee, which had organized the historic demonstration only a half-year before, was now being disbanded. The *Times* concluded the antiwar movement was "drained of vigor." Then, ten days after the pledged withdrawal, Nixon announced the expansion of the war into Cambodia.[1]

Activism exploded. From the University of Maryland to Oregon State, ROTC property was ransacked, vandalized, firebombed.

At the Pentagon, the morning after the Cambodia speech, the wife of a soldier in Vietnam thanked Nixon. It moved him. "You see these bums, you know, blowing up the campuses. Listen, the boys that are on the college campuses today are the luckiest people in the world," Nixon said. "Then out there, we have kids who are just doing their duty. . . . I am sure they are scared. I was when I was there. But when it really comes down to it, they stand up." The media spread the soundbite: the president called protestors "bums." It was fuel to the fire.

Police confronted demonstrators and militants coast to coast, including at a campus in Ohio—Kent State. In the small hours of Saturday, May 2, students rampaged through town, chanting, smashing dozens of storefront

A GI, with his M16 rifle over his shoulder, in the fish hook region of Cambodia on May 5, 1970, the day after the Kent State shooting and less than a week after President Nixon announced the expansion of the war into Cambodia. Student protests erupted nationwide, which led to the Hardhat Riot. (Dang Van Phouc/AP)

windows. By night, students set fire to the school's ROTC building, burned a flag, and cheered the flames. Firefighters arrived. Students pulled the hoses away. Some hacked at hoses with ice picks and a machete. Other students pelted firemen with rocks. The firefighters retreated. The blaze reached the ammunition stockpile. Outside, Kent State students could hear the ammo rapidly pop in the flames, *rat-a-tat-tat . . . rat-a-tat-tat.*

By Monday, May 4, Kent State was tense. The National Guard had arrived. Clashes persisted. Because of duty rotation, the guardsmen deployed Monday had slept just three hours the night before. Meanwhile, after days of college conflict, some parents worried. That morning, a skinny 20-year-old Kent State student from Long Island, Jeffrey Miller, put on his bell-bottoms and a maroon shirt. He phoned his mother, assuring her, "Don't worry, I'm not going to get hurt."

The campus bell tolled, summoning demonstrators to the grassy slopes of Kent's commons. It was sunny and students were cheerful. Some waved the usual revolutionary flags. Many shouted the usual antiwar chants. It was all so usual. The police bullhorned: "Leave this area immediately, leave this area immediately." Troops assembled with fixed bayonets. Protestors tossed stones, sticks, brickbats, rubble. Guardsmen formed a skirmish line. They held M1 rifles with an eight-round magazine and pointed them toward students. Most protestors didn't realize the rifles were loaded with real bullets. The troops fired teargas. Protestors, including Jeffrey Miller, hurled some canisters back. A teargas canister landed near the soldiers. Students cheered. Some chanted, "Pigs off campus!" The troops moved toward the students. Several students tossed more stones and rubble. The guardsmen ascended a hill and formed another skirmish line at the crest. More than two dozen guardsmen fired. Some guardsmen, intending to miss, shot into the air or into the ground. Others did not. The gunfire lasted thirteen seconds, wounding nine and killing four. Jeffrey Miller was among the dead.[2]

Word first spread over chattering teletype machines and radio broadcasts. The Dow Jones suffered its worst daily loss since JFK's assassination. Activists attacked ROTC facilities from Rhode Island to Kentucky to Missouri. At the state university in Stony Brook, Long Island, two campus buildings were set afire. Arsonists struck the gym at the University of Alabama. Two firebombs hit the ROTC at Ohio University. Students burned multiple buildings at the University of Wisconsin and the "cops threw tear gas at almost anything that moved." *Time* magazine reached for Yeats: "All changed, changed utterly."

In Massachusetts, twenty thousand students forced the governor to lower the statehouse flag. But at San Diego State College, a football center single-handedly held off 150 students trying to lower the flag, and became a hero in the conservative city. Up the coast, at Berkeley, students set an Army vehicle afire and hoisted a burning American flag.[3]

Most DC colleges shut down, but the city avoided the worst. Rennie Davis, of Chicago '68, urged one college crowd to form "national liberation brigades." American University students pelted cops with rocks. Cops fired teargas. A young woman "spit at" one cop, screaming, "Fucking pig! . . . filthy swine!" Later, she handed a flower to another cop and said, "It's not your fault, but what do you expect us to do?"[4]

In the New York City metropolitan area, more than a dozen colleges and universities closed. Uptown at Columbia, a contingent of students— Ivy Leaguers calling themselves the "Third-World Coalition"—occupied a floor of the administration building. Thousands of Columbia students rallied into the night. Students blocked the West Side Highway during rush hour. Near the United Nations, young people hurled stones at police. Downtown at NYU, activists occupied several campus buildings. In the mathematics department, radicals held a $3 million government computer ransom for $100,000 (capitalists, these were not). Proceeds were to be used to free Black

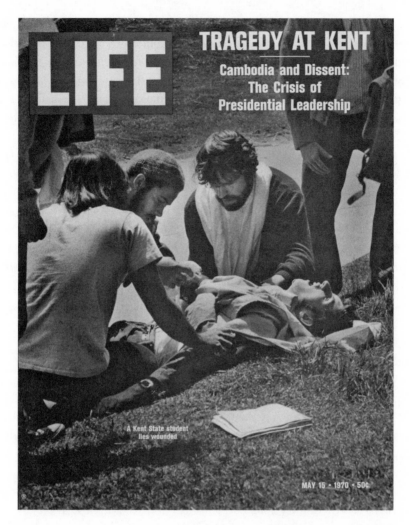

TRAGEDY AT KENT

Cambodia and Dissent:
The Crisis of
Presidential Leadership

A Kent State student
lies wounded

MAY 15 • 1970 • 50¢

The cover of *Life* magazine after members of the National Guard opened fire on protestors at Kent State University in Ohio, May 15, 1970. (Howard Ruffner/Life Picture Collection/ Getty)

Panthers. When the police charged in, a cop saw a lit fuse burning toward gasoline bombs. He stomped it out. On the street, in front of the modernist student center, the pavement was gooey with animal blood. A "guerrilla theatre troupe" had reenacted Kent State. At City College, which was officially now closed, like NYU, students raided the ROTC office and used the contents to fuel a bonfire.[5]

Peaceful activism also intensified. Between the Cambodia speech and Kent State, about twenty new student strikes were declared daily. After Kent

State, daily student strikes increased fivefold. Even then, the protests felt provocative to viewers watching the activism unfold in the news. They saw signage—HEIL NIⱧON, read one—or students holding inverted American flags or waving the Vietcong flag. In all, more than five hundred colleges and universities temporarily closed—about one in three nationwide. Ivy League colleges shuttered, from Brown to Princeton to Columbia. When Princeton put the prospect of closing to a vote, yeas were 2,066 and nays 181. In Georgia, all public colleges shut down. Even Governor Ronald Reagan sent about one million collegians home, closing California's entire university system.[6]

"Surely, the most critical week this nation has endured in more than a century," the *New Yorker* wrote afterward. "The war has made us warlike." Yet with that eloquence, the *New Yorker* also hinted at how the liberal mainstream tolerated, sometimes affirmed, the radicalization of its progeny. The influential magazine wrote that the extreme response to Kent State, which included campus bombings nationwide, was "necessary to awaken" Americans.[7]

◆

Inside the White House, aides felt besieged. It was an "absolutely poisonous" period, recalled William Smyser, a member of Nixon's national security staff. "We were not only fighting the North Vietnamese, we were fighting the Americans." "The city was an armed camp. The mobs were smashing windows, slashing tires, dragging parked cars into intersections," Nixon speechwriter Ray Price recalled. "That's not student protest. That's civil war."[8]

It was civil conflict unseen since the Civil War. From January 1969 to April 1970, the country suffered more than 4,300 bombings. In New York City alone, between August and November 1969, bombs exploded at the Marine Midland Building, the federal office building, the Armed Forces Induction Center, Macy's Herald Square, Chase Manhattan Bank's headquarters, and the General Motors Building. In March 1970, in the basement of a townhouse in Manhattan's Greenwich Village, two detonator wires accidentally crossed; dynamite blasted upward through the floors and the house tumbled into a cloud of rubble. Investigators discovered it was a Weathermen bomb factory. The ex-wife of actor Henry Fonda (Jane Fonda's father) aided some survivors. Actor Dustin Hoffman, another neighbor, raced to save his artwork. There was enough dynamite to explode every home on the block, if detonated. The cadre's leader, Terry Robbins, had told Mark Rudd a few nights earlier, "We're going to kill the pigs at a dance at Fort Dix." Rudd "assented." After leading the Columbia occupation, Rudd and other radicals had eventually formed the Weathermen, a leftist terrorist group that fancied itself freedom fighters. "At that point, we had determined that there were no innocent Americans, at least no white ones," Rudd wrote. In the house, if doubt was expressed, a honkey countered, "You're just accepting your white-skin privilege." Rudd heard of the explosion that night. "A red gash split open in time," he wrote of his grief. He did not consider all those servicemen and their sweethearts saved because that shrapnel bomb—dynamite wrapped with nails—never exploded the dance. Three Weathermen died. One was Ted Gold, one of the leaders of the Columbia occupation. Another was Diana Oughton, a great-granddaughter of the Boy Scouts founder. She had grown up on a Tudor-style estate and gone to the best schools. She volunteered after college, but in time became melancholy and dated SDSer Bill Ayers—another "rich kid radical," a business executive's son who later became a Weatherman. Ayers was reportedly her greatest "influence," and after Chicago '68, the two of them, like Rudd, aligned with the radical faction. The nation's leading liberal student group, SDS, had a schism. And Oughton's extremism did not abate. Their cadre's leader, Terry Robbins, also perished. He was a "fierce" little terrorist for "liberation" (who "regularly hit his girlfriend," noted Rudd's memoir). Robbins had once recruited militants at what was then an obscure Ohio college, Kent State.[9]

Like the war, the turmoil was televised—nightly. As a New Jersey autoworker said of the antiwar activists, after Kent State, "You can't turn on the television without seeing them do something else." Longshoreman John Cooke, who unloaded cargo from a pier near the rundown far West Village, started to feel like the television provided "a one-sided point of view from demonstrators," night after night.

"War, and the efforts to end war, looked alike on TV. They all just looked like more war," as Rick Perlstein wrote in his history of the era. This is how most Americans experienced the tumult. Collegians protesting on TV lived different lives. In this era, only about one in ten whites had a college degree. Among Americans in their late twenties, the share with a four-year degree increased from 6 to 16 percent between 1940 and 1970. But more were in school—36 percent of college-age youth were attending college in 1969. A university degree was a ticket to the Establishment. From elite schools, that degree provided the pedigree to lead it. The best schools offered an aura similar to nobility of earlier ages, without a corresponding ethos of obligation—whether to parents, estate, or country. The average college student body was also disproportionally upscale. In 1969, among affluent families with college-age dependents, two-thirds had a child attending college full-time, compared to less than a fifth of poor families. Yet the majority of children in colleges were also the first in their family to receive a degree. Campus culture was personal to those blue-collar families. They looked upon the schools, accurately, as roads to affluence that were unavailable to them. Seven in ten whites without a college degree (most of whom had a high school education or less) thought in 1970 that "a college education almost automatically guarantees a higher standard" of living. To blue-collar America, college represented their hope for their children. Yet what they saw, on television or elsewhere, seemed to dismiss them and that.

The most elite schools were the most liberal. When colleges were divided into three tiers of selectivity based on SAT and ACT scores, 67 percent of students at the best schools identified as liberal or far-left in June 1970; by comparison, the equivalent share in the middle stratum was 53 percent and in the lower stratum 44 percent. The polling also indicated that, in contrast with less-prestigious schools, the best schools made students more liberal, compared to their views when entering college. And since the best schools meant liberal schools, the counterculture revolution infused highbrow culture. Faculties drifted still more leftward, but universities remained a bastion of privilege and exclusivity, especially within the Ivy League. At the same time, students at lower-status schools were not only more likely to be blue-collar. They were also most indicative of the broader American mindset. Students at the lowest tier of schools were *more* likely than collegians with greater status to say they would "accept the draft call and serve," and they were also the *least* likely to think their fellow students endorsed antiwar demonstrators. One *Fortune* poll found that a slim majority of students at "forerunner" schools—the more distinguished colleges—thought America was a "sick society," but only a third of all college students agreed. When "forerunner" students were asked to name someone they admired, Che Guevara ranked ahead of all presidential candidates. The finance magazine noted that few of these students had ever experienced scarcity.[10]

This fact had not escaped baby boomer parents and grandparents. In 1970, most of blue-collar America could recall the threadbare years of World War Two, when soldiers were heroes. A third of Americans were at least teenagers during the Great Depression. They had seen poverty unimaginable to suburban baby boomers. They were also raised before the concept of a "teenager"—and the leisurely self-exploration associated with it—was mainstream. By the seventies, Nixon aide Pat Buchanan's comment that student activism represented "the revolt of the overprivileged" was a rather conventional view.

There were exceptions. Jerry Rubin was the son of a truck driver. Yet New Left luminaries, like the typical college-educated activist, were disproportionately the children of affluence. It was not only the "rich kid radicals," such as Weathermen Bill Ayers and Diana Oughton. Abbie Hoffman's dad owned a medical supply company. Tom Hayden's father was an accountant at Chrysler. Jane Fonda was the daughter of a famous actor and a socialite. Rennie Davis's father was the chief of staff of the Council of Economic Advisers under Truman. David Dellinger grew up wealthy and attended Yale like his father, whose friends included Calvin Coolidge.

"From the point of view of the Polish television watcher on Milwaukee Avenue in the northwest side of Chicago, the longhaired militants and their faculty patrons are every bit as much part of the Establishment as are the presidents of corporations," wrote Andrew Greeley, a Catholic priest and a public opinion researcher of the era. "The peace movement is seen as very much of an Establishment movement, working against the values, the stability, and the patriotism of the American masses, which incidentally are seen as footing the bill for Establishment games and amusements."[11]

◆

As news broke of Kent State, Nixon aides clustered around the teletype machine in the press office. White House counsel Chuck Colson watched the "grim-faced" staff. He thought of the violence after King's death. Later, he went to the oak-paneled White House mess. He stared at the color television in the corner. "Dinner plates were untouched, red-jacketed stewards stood frozen in place, White House staffers sat in stunned silence, their eyes fixed on the grisly tragedy being replayed before them," Colson wrote in his memoir. "Then, on the screen, appeared a sobbing grief-stricken face, the father of Allison Krause, who was dead. [The father said] 'The president is to blame!'" Colson felt defensive, guilty, finally "unclean." He couldn't eat.[12]

Privately, Nixon was in shock. "I could not get the photographs out of my mind," he recalled. "I could not help thinking about the families, suddenly receiving the news that their children were dead because they had been shot in a campus demonstration," Nixon continued. "I thought of my own daughters," of them "learning to talk and to walk, and their first birthdays, and the trips we took together . . . getting them through college and then—whoosh—all gone."[13]

It was a shock of his making. Calling militants "bums" was, as the *Economist* put it, a "foolish rhetorical self-indulgence." Nixon's driest tinder was the president's unfulfilled "assurances that peace was on the way," the magazine continued. The president had enabled the "outburst of rage."[14]

The film *Patton* came out that year. Nixon became obsessed with it. It was an immense film and sentimental about war. Nixon had a biography of Patton bedside. The film showcased the man Nixon wanted to see in the mirror. And after Kent State, he tried. Nixon had an outstanding memory and was among the most well-read presidents of the century. Yet he admired men of action. In schooldays football, Nixon hurled his 140 pounds at players and was, almost invariably, the boy flat on the grass after. He was no athlete. But he quickly got up and returned to the line. He persisted. He tried to be a tough boy. He wanted to be a hard man. The first White House comment after Kent State began conventionally. The pro forma expression of grief: "The president shares the sadness of the parents involved." Then Nixon Pattoned: "This should remind us all once again that when dissent turns to violence it invites tragedy." "We have to stand hard as a rock," Nixon told Henry Kissinger. "If countries begin to be run by children, God help us."

So Nixon played unfazed for the cameras. But the upheaval ate away at him. It was Cambodia, campus unrest, the media fixation on protests against the war. Everything felt against him. Three National Security Council staff resigned. So did his director of student outreach. Second-guessing was rampant—of his crumbling promise of peace, of his ineptitude at waging war, of his presidency. Nixon wallowed with "deep resentment," H. R. Haldeman recalled. The man who embodied all the power felt alone in the storm, without the visibility needed to find a way out. Nixon tried to be a "firm rock" but he was "deeply wounded by the hatred of the protestors," Kissinger wrote. He came "close to cracking" and lost "the confidence to have any confidence," Pat Buchanan remembered. Advisor Jack Brennan "had never seen him appear so physically exhausted." For the second time in a week, Nixon retreated to Camp David.[15]

"Those few days after Kent State were among the darkest of my presidency," Nixon later wrote. "I felt utterly dejected."[16]

CHAPTER 12

Kent State Shakes New York

JOHN LINDSAY FELT compelled to do something. "Activist groups began to put pressure on City Hall," recalled Deputy Mayor Dick Aurelio. Young aides urged Mayor Lindsay to lower flags citywide to mourn the Kent State Four, as the dead were now called. But lowering the flag for Moratorium Day caught blowback. Staff debated. They could at least create an elegiac atmosphere at City Hall. Aurelio chimed in, "Who could possibly object to honoring four dead students by lowering the flag at City Hall?"[1]

Meanwhile, city activists became electrified. Student protestors began to gather at the epicenter of global capitalism. They rallied against the draft, against the masters of finance, against the "masters of war." Chants ricocheted in the cavernous downtown. Demonstrators held antiwar placards and waved Vietcong flags and swamped Federal Hall's steps. The students were, at first, scarcely aware of the construction workers watching from their steel perches above.

Two days after Kent State, two thousand future doctors and nurses marched from City Hall to Manhattan's southern tip. Many came from the city's prestigious medical schools—Columbia, Cornell, NYU. It was a solemn wave of white along Broadway—students in white medical coats, white tunics, white dresses, and black armbands.

At one point, several construction workers walked to the head of the march, carrying an American flag. "A minor conflict developed," read a police report. "Personnel stepped in."

At Wall Street, some of the graduate students trailed off. Outside Federal Hall, near the Stock Exchange, three thousand students rallied against the war.

In the Village, a throng of students marched uptown. They fattened their ranks at Union Square and persisted northward.

Chants echoed off skyscrapers: "One-two-three-four. We don't want your fuckin' war! Two-four-six-eight. We don't want your fascist state!"

At times, bands of youths charged into the streets, kicking over trashcans, snarling traffic, shouting, "Avenge Kent State!"

Some students chanted up Broadway and neared the site where, three years earlier, the elegant Singer skyscraper had been demolished. (Briefly the world's tallest skyscraper in 1908, it was the highest tower ever intentionally demolished.) Its replacement, the US Steel building, was still only a skeletal twenty-eight floors. The Twin Towers were rising directly westward.

Scattered ironworkers gazed down at hundreds of students along Broadway and pelted them with aluminum cans, milk containers, small pieces of rubble.

Students fled for cover. One skinny girl, college age, was cut on the head. Other protestors taunted the workmen: "Jump! Jump! Jump!"

Inspector Harold Schryver, the commanding officer, bullhorned the workmen to stop. Columnist Pete Hamill saw this much. Hamill asked Schryver if he was "going to make arrests."

"Don't worry about it," Inspector Schryver replied.

"You expect these kids to respond to law and order and you won't go up and make arrests?"

"Law and order," Inspector Schryver replied. "These bums don't respect anything."

Schryver ordered a sergeant and four patrolmen inside the construction site. But when the cops reached the open steel up high, they turned back. "The building superintendent was told to get word to the steelworkers," a cop reported.

Meanwhile, at the southern tip of the island, at the base of another unfinished skyscraper near Battery Park, medical students scrapped with about five hardhats. Workmen said the students desecrated the flag. The students said the workmen heckled them.

Students persuaded Trinity Church leaders to create a permanent first-aid center. Both sides seemed to expect worse violence.[2]

◆

A tribal tension had infused downtown. "Most afternoons, my friends and I took our brown bag lunches down to Battery Park to watch the hawks and the doves argue over what course in Southeast Asia the Nixon administration should take," said Joe Guzzardi, a young Merrill Lynch investment banker.

"It was good theater. We didn't have a stake in it, one way or another. We were conflicted about the war," he added. "We were opposed to the war but equally opposed to spitting on the flag and the burning of the flag."[3]

Lindsay aide Sid Davidoff recalled that one day, around the time of Kent State, "we had to pull [mayoral advisor] Jay Kriegel out of actually being beaten up" by some workmen. "Jay was slight, wasn't like me. He was an intellectual, Harvard. He looked it. He was physically being assaulted."[4]

At City Hall, Mayor John Lindsay met with two Kent State students. Afterward, Lindsay proclaimed Friday, May 8, 1970, a "day of reflection" over Kent State. He ordered public schools closed.

Lindsay felt that he was ahead of the fervor. The day before Nixon's Cambodia speech, when campuses were calm, Lindsay spoke at the University of Pennsylvania. "For the first time in one hundred years, sane men worry about the violent end of America," he told students. Lindsay denounced violence. He also expressed "unending admiration" for protestors "willing to take the consequences." He added, "These are the guys who are heroic."

The Ivy Leaguers cheered.

This mayor of a riven city was picking fights, even as he spoke of peace. The *Times* headlined: MAYOR SUPPORTS DRAFT RESISTERS.

In the days after, Lindsay's staff sought to tamp down that storyline. They told reporters he had only conveyed his respect for lawful civil disobedience. But for those on the other side, it was the Lindsay they had come to dislike. The headline felt right even if the specifics were wrong. The New York leader of the Veterans of Foreign Wars declared Lindsay persona non grata. On Moratorium Day, McGovern had called demonstrating the "highest patriotism." Now Lindsay deemed demonstrators truly "heroic."

Lindsay and McGovern were courting the antiwar movement, and it was unmooring them from the public. At times they'd realize it and offer some penance—affirm servicemen's sacrifice or talk of the common people—but soon enough the New Left rhetoric would resurface. And since people tend to recall what offends them, the benefit of the doubt faded. Only about a tenth of Americans thought the "real heroes of the Vietnam War are those who refused induction and faced the consequences, and not those who served in the Armed Forces." The same survey data hinted how the unmooring happened. The loudest voices of the era were youthful activists. They dazzled and intimidated liberal politicians. The prestige press obsessed over them. They also spoke for few. Most young adults didn't even side with movement zealots. Only a fifth of young people agreed that the "real heroes of the Vietnam War are those who refused induction." This same few disagreed with the notion that "veterans should feel proud to have served their country."[5]

But with Kent State, Lindsay believed a "major shifting of opinion" was afoot. He wanted to represent that future. He felt like the future. On Wednesday, May 6, Lindsay was the headliner for a media banquet. It was his chance. He was ready to confront a president.

Inside the Plaza Hotel's Baroque Room, Lindsay stood above the magazine industry elite and summoned a new "not-so-silent majority." He eloquently spoke against descending into "violence in opposition to violence." He also spoke of "revived antiwar legions" below crystal chandeliers.

"There is a whole new generation that comprehends with far greater clarity than their scared and weary elders," he said. He did mention the "brave young men sent to the bloody war," only to quickly return baseside. He spoke of the city's forty-two colleges and universities, of the student strike, of silent classrooms, of a broken nation. "Our hold on the future is very frail," he said. "For the first time in a century, we are not sure there is a future for America."

Soon again, he lurched moderate. He emphasized the "need for civility" and "binding America."

Lindsay was eyeing the presidency. He was trying to straddle the incongruent, to be both cool breeze and brimstone. As the *Times* reported, it was "a major speech obviously keyed to a national audience."

"When you tell the disaffected that riot and bloodshed are not the way, they reply that this nation is following a similar way in Southeast Asia," Lindsay continued. "When you counsel restraint, and peaceful action, their reply is, 'It doesn't work. So if the system spreads violence in the name of peace, we'll do the same.'" And there he was, defending the "disaffected that riot" and saying, "We'll do the same." Lindsay had not imagined that his language could, soon enough, justify his antagonists as well.[6]

◆

The next morning's *Daily News* carried a dispatch from Ohio: IN KENT, A WIDE TOWN-GOWN GAP. The same could be said for the national media's backyard. All three TV networks were based in New York, as were radio, book publishing, the magazine industry, three of the six most-read daily newspapers in America (and that's excluding the *Wall Street Journal*). Yet as much as 1968 had awakened the prestige press to backlash, few of these national reporters, living in the city, realized that the troubles of flyover country were their own.

At City College, a construction worker grabbed a student protestor by the lapel and yelled of fighting in Vietnam, of killing, and under his vicious rant was an outcry, that he was not ashamed. Other workmen roughed the boy up.

The college kid reached into his backpack, palmed a large conch shell, and slashed one of the men across the face.

The societal fissure did not entirely escape the *Times*. The newspaper dispatched one of its reporters to the borderlands of the New York metropolitan region—Mahwah, New Jersey—to familiarize readers with foreign views. Mahwah was located where the New York State Thruway cut into the foothills of the Ramapo Mountains. The township had a Ford factory, a walled city of sorts, that extended more than 170 acres and assembled eight hundred cars daily.

It would be a decade until the last car came off this assembly line. That closure inspired one more Bruce Springsteen dirge for the workingman, "Johnny 99." In 1980 alone, at least two hundred thousand auto workers were laid off nationwide. A study two years after Mahwah's closure found that a majority of those workers remained jobless.

This was 1970, though. America still had a trade surplus. The Northeast actually had major auto factories. And Mahwah employed 4,700 breadwinners, some of whom rose before dawn and commuted from Harlem or Brooklyn for the good work.

Some of those men were angry at the guardsmen. Kent "makes me want to vomit," said a portly man with a beard who worked electrical maintenance. "To think, they fired into American citizens. Bullets are no match for rocks." The cluster of men nearby grumbled. The reporter discovered that, as polling would soon demonstrate nationwide, most of the workers blamed student activists for Kent State.

"They go to college to raise hell, especially the rich kids," one autoworker said.

"These guys are supposed to be going to college to learn something," another workman said. "What are they doing? Burning down buildings. Locking up teachers."

"They're supposed to be our future leaders," said another. "If I had a chance to get an education, I wouldn't be wasting my time on the streets."[7]

Tomorrow, the students' reaction to Kent State would make the *Times*'s front page. And this small article—which offered hints of the class divide on the day hints would no longer be needed—was buried inside, beneath the extended coverage of collegian unrest.

◆

The hippies' and hardhats' outlooks were, by now, almost inconceivable to each other. Yet circumstance had compressed that cultural and class divide into the narrow landmass of Lower Manhattan, only about a kilometer wide near Wall Street, back then. It was a maze of slim streets and colonial byways that cut at odd angles beneath the rising skyline, where thousands of blue-collar men worked on beams and steel decks, in the open air, staring down at the students, who were, again, protesting.

It was May 7, 1970. The last president not to attend college, Harry Truman, celebrated his eighty-sixth birthday in Missouri. In Washington, President Nixon said there would be no more talk of "bums." He vowed he also wanted peace. Tomorrow, after the Knicks-Lakers championship game, Nixon was to face reporters and speak to the tumult. The day after, in DC, a national rally for Kent State. Collegians were already converging on the capital. In New York alone, several trains and more than fifty buses were booked to shuttle students to Washington. Another ten thousand New York students planned to carpool.

Campus unrest escalated still more. Most protests were peaceful. But enough were not for the upheaval to seem everywhere—leading the television news, the radio updates, the front pages of newspapers tossed to doorsteps nationwide. Students at the University of Missouri and Syracuse University burned effigies of the president. Firebombs exploded in ROTC buildings from Nevada to Ohio. At the University of Wisconsin, firefighters doused more than forty blazes on one day alone, as guardsmen patrolled the campus for the fourth day and the school's president decided to resign. Campus buildings were burning across the land, in California, in Illinois, in Alabama, in New York City—at Fordham and the Brooklyn campus of Long Island University, after activists followed through on threats and set the humanities building ablaze. Student radicals had threatened to blockade Manhattan's bridges, tunnels, and highways. After intense negotiation, activists balked. Midday, some students still caused gridlock along the Long Island Expressway.[8]

At the same time, at 76th Street and Amsterdam Avenue, Manhattan's Upper West Side, three to five thousand students gathered outside a chapel and were eerily quiet. They were here for the Long Island boy killed at Kent State, Jeffrey Miller.

He was from Plainview, Long Island. His father was a typesetter for the *Times*. Miller's image had led newspapers—the dead boy facedown on the pavement, a girl kneeling over him, her arms spread, screaming anguish. Yesterday, at a hometown memorial, he was eulogized by JFK's wordsmith Ted Sorensen.

In the city, at the formal service today, Dr. Benjamin Spock stood at the fore of the pale blue chapel. Spock's child-rearing guide was outsold only by the Bible, with sales north of twenty million copies by the late sixties. He had, indeéd, written the gospel of postwar parenting. Spock instructed parents to trust their instincts, favor love over authority, and relax boundaries (though not entirely). Critics said he incubated a new era of mass permissiveness and youthful entitlement. "Is Dr. Spock to blame?" asked one *Newsweek* cover. The answer: "If Dr. Spock didn't exist, it would have been necessary to invent him." Spock "had become a bogeyman." In one review, *Time* was more critical of Spock and the likeminded. "Whatever their merits, the books produce a good many faddishly permissive parents," read *Time*. "Often a father is more involved in living up to his child's expectations than the child is in living up to his." For those looking, the young radicals reflected the trend. Mark Rudd's mom reacted affectionately to hearing that he led the Columbia occupation ("My son, the revolutionary," she said). It was an "absolutely typical" reaction of Columbia militants' parents, who were "more loving than judging," the *Times* reported after interviewing the college's radical leadership. This permissiveness was new to America back then. *Newsweek* granted, "There was principled anger over the nation's family doctor counseling, or at least sanctioning, draft dodging." "Your book was almost a bible to me in raising my children," wrote one upstate New York mother. "But now what you have done turns my stomach. We teach our boys to be men, and now you're tearing that down." The same letter bags, however, also included plaudits. Wrote another mother, "If you ever begin to lose courage in your present struggle, think of the thousands of mothers and sons you are speaking for."[9]

These were indeed the parents he spoke for. Spock said Jeffrey Miller's death "may do more to end the war than all the rest of us have been able to do during the past five years of escalation." Miller's family sat in the front row, beside Mayor Lindsay and his wife, listening silently. Hundreds sat in pews behind. Spock continued, "Very few people are privileged to make this kind of contribution to humanity."

Outside, it was cool and bright and breezy. The crowd's size was "reminiscent" of "movie stars' funerals," reported the *New York Post*. Thousands pressed nearer and cupped their hands behind their ears, to hear the weak loudspeaker. Police politely requested students leave room for traffic on the avenue. A girl handed a cop a daisy. One sign evoked Nixon's remark: WE ARE ALL BUMS. Another placard displayed the enlarged image of Miller's dead body; written across the image in blood red was the word AVENGE.

Inside, Senator Charles Goodell spoke of "meaningful death." A rabbi intoned in Hebrew—psalms, the mourner's prayer. Another rabbi quoted John Lennon, asking America to "give peace a chance."

The redwood coffin was wheeled down the aisle. Hundreds wept. Miller's roommate Steve Druckner, his skullcap atop his long hair, embraced a girl holding a daisy.

After the funeral, as the hearse was loaded, Druckner filed out with the mourners and saw the crowd—thousands of youths, silent. They held their arms outstretched in a tide of peace signs. With tears in his blue eyes, he turned to the crowd and said, "You're beautiful."

Students followed the cortege up the avenue. Sunlight glinted off the hearse's polished rooftop. The march concluded at Eighty-Sixth Street. Some youth continued north to Columbia. Others entered Central Park. Hundreds more took the subway to a Wall Street rally, where protestors were angrier than observers had known them before.[10]

◆

Manhattan's original city hall was a center of colonial history, from the Stamp Act Congress of 1765 to the Confederation Congress two decades later. After it was remodeled, the building was renamed Federal Hall. The first United States Congress wrote the Bill of Rights there. And in 1789, it was where George Washington took his oath of office.

Thousands of young people crowd the cortege bearing the body of Jeffrey Glenn Miller afer funeral services in New York City, May 7, 1970. Miller was from a New York suburb on Long Island. He was one of four students killed by national guardsmen at Kent State three days earlier. (Paul DeMaria/AP)

Even then, the day revealed America's veneration of the everyman. George Washington had an inauguration, not a coronation, in a world of kings. His title did not take on the airs of royalty. He did not wear the finery of London or Paris, as the colonial gentry was wont, but donned brown Connecticut broadcloth. The ceremony would not be hidden from the people inside a palace. Washington walked outside onto the second-floor balcony and took the oath before the sovereign multitude.

Back then, Wall Street's plaza was the city's largest intersection. In the streets, one witness said, the "throng was so dense that it seemed as if one might literally walk on the heads of the people." Few were close enough to see that, in one congressman's words, "time has made havoc" of Washington's face. Instead, they saw a balcony of dignitaries. At the center, the enigmatic man, unusually tall, clad in a double-breasted suit, a sword at the hip. His hand was on a Bible. It was a shout from the judge that told them the oath was completed—"Long live George Washington, President of the United States!" Washington bowed.[11]

By 1970, the current Federal Hall (called the Subtreasury Building for years) was itself 135 years old. It was closed for renovations. The interior had degraded. The façade remained familiarly grand, Greek Revival, a frontage of Doric order, eight columns and eighteen steps of marble. It was a favorite hub of demonstrators by now, at the center of the world's unrivaled economic power. It was also a pleasant place to gather. The plaza was an airy exception to the cramped caverns of downtown Manhattan.[12]

Thousands of activists were already there by the time the funeral attendees arrived. Before the afternoon, they would demonstrate at City Hall and police headquarters, stage sit-ins, and rally more at Wall Street's plaza. For now, student leaders stood atop the marble stairs and bullhorned chants.

Placards: I'M A BUM FOR PEACE. KENT: NIXON'S THE ONE. IS MY LAI IN OHIO? In the crowd, a blonde's blue chiffon blouse was tied above her navel. "Peace now" was written across her bare midriff.

"We're not asking anymore, we're demanding," said an NYU law student with collar-length hair, the mic periodically squealing as he spoke. "Wall Street, the stock market, gonna be closed tomorrow," he spoke on, jabbing his right index finger. "Let me just say one thing about violence. I'm not sure where I stand on violence, whether I'm for or against it," but violence against cops is "suicide." The police were inexpressive, some with their arms folded, a row of blue caps and helmets on the high stairs, between the activists and Federal Hall's sun-drenched columns. "We're gonna stop Wall Street tomorrow," the speaker continued. "We're gonna stop New York City on Monday. And we're going to bring the whole country down with us next week."

Cheers. Fists raised into the air.

"There were students from all over the city," said NYU freshman Nancy Brachfeld. "The demonstration was peaceful."

The NYPD found the kids "particularly troublesome" and "disruptive."

"The flag of the communist Cuban government; the Black Panther banner; and the Vietcong flag were flown from the [Federal Hall's] steps, the latter flag from the hand of the statue of George Washington," stockbroker Robert Parker said. "There were also the placards of 'Kill the Pigs.'" He added, "The police kept their calm." Not everyone else did.

At noontime, as Jeffrey Miller's funeral procession continued uptown, twenty to forty hardhats marched east along Wall Street. The plaza was crammed with seated protestors. Students gradually stood and turned to the commotion.

"It's the patriots, it's the patriots," said an activist on the steps.

"It's the patriots, is right," confirmed another.

"Keep cool," a speaker said into the mic.

The hardhats arrived two abreast, some with small flags fastened to their helmets. Two large flags flapped at the helm.

"Keep cool." Both sides shouted and cursed the other. "No violence, no violence," another speaker yelled into the mic. A dozen scuffled. The crowd jumped back. "No violence," the speaker shouted. "Don't you fuckin people understand?"

Cops split it up a half-minute later.

The crowd chanted against the war.

A bushy-haired activist took the mic. He told the crowd to "wait a second" and "shut up" and "dig on this." The crowd stilled. "Dig these mother fuckin [construction workers], right here, [a] hand full of people controlling you. Kick their mother fuckin ass."

Speakers tussled with him to regain the mic.

"Kick their mother fuckin ass!"

Organizers grabbed the mic. One asked, "What do you want to do, start a riot?"

◆

Patrolmen escorted the construction workers out of the plaza. After the Wall Street rally, a pack of youth neared the US Steel site.

From the upper girders—beer cans, fruit, gravel rained down. An Associated Press photographer was slashed across the face, as was a young attorney purchasing cigars during lunch.

Construction workers and antiwar protesters scuffle near Broad and Wall Streets, May 7, 1970. The fight broke out midday after twenty to forty construction workers holding American flags confronted student demonstrators. (John Rooney/AP)

Near Battery Park, ironworker Eugene Schafer stood atop a girder. He was in his early thirties, big-shouldered, with a doughy double chin and black horn-rimmed glasses, a veteran like most tradesmen. He watched marchers brandish Vietcong and Cuban flags. "Anybody who raises an enemy flag in our country is a traitor," he believed. Schafer found an American flag and waved it at the steel's edge. Activists yelled up. Others offered him their middle finger. He sprinted down to the street, where he said he was "mauled, kicked in the groin, and the flag was torn away from me and ripped up in pieces."

These were not the flower children of midtown's *Hair*. To be sure, thousands of the students downtown—like the majority of American collegians—didn't want to use violence in order to end violence. Many were in the streets to honor the Kent State Four. But the mood was less Moratorium Day than Chicago '68. The fringe felt vindicated. The crowd seemed more yippielike—more militant and more outrageous. Radicals hoped to draw out the repressive authorities before the cameras, to show the pigs' true nature.

By about four in the afternoon, most of the students gathered at Union Square. NYU's Nancy Brachfeld, who marched with five hundred from Wall Street, arrived with the rally well under way. Students sat down in the road. They blocked traffic along Fourteenth Street, a major thoroughfare. Thousands thrust fists and waved placards and shouted for peace.

"After the first hour, police tried unsuccessfully to persuade the demonstrators to leave," ABC News reported. "After the second hour, police moved in."

A phalanx of helmeted police marched forward and hit the mass at once, scattering the youth, jabbing students with their clubs. Some students hurled rocks and bottles at the cops, and the cops escalated in kind, clubbing the college kids, the wood sticks cracking off heads and welting backs, even as cops dragged other protestors along the cement like squealing animals. "Total confusion prevailed," Brachfeld said. "We did not know where to run. The policemen started beating up everyone."

As the afternoon lengthened, the NYPD started to receive peculiar phone calls. At 4:20 p.m., a brokerage house employee said he had heard, from a guard, that construction workers would "start trouble" tomorrow at the peace rally outside Federal Hall. Between 5:45 and 6:10, police logs recorded three separate entries of another warning: "Rabble rousers will break up the rally at the Stock Exchange and then proceed to City Hall."

Meanwhile, in midtown, Nixon's communications director, Herb Klein, taped his appearance on tonight's *Dick Cavett Show*. Klein was calm and insistent. Nixon was trying to do "the right thing." Trying to negotiate peace. Trying to ensure South Vietnam remained free.

Cavett asked if the president had ever considered abandoning the war.

Klein replied that if the United States did, it would be "the greatest bloodbath."

The opposing view came from a Vietnam veteran against the war. John Kerry was still nearly a year from his speech before the Senate, from wondering, "How do you ask a man to be the last man to die in Vietnam?"

Kerry wore a starched collared shirt and maroon tie, his jacket buttoned, his long slender frame resting back confidently in the plush red chair. He was the picture of the uptight suit that many hippies were uptight about, until he spoke, his cadence languid and definite all at once.

"When I was in Vietnam, I have to say to you, I just could never feel I was fighting to save that country." He spoke, instead, of feeling "like the German," of "occupying," of "imperialism." Young Kerry was channeling the New Left, staring down Nixon's man.

At 10:25 p.m., about an hour before *Cavett* aired, the NYPD received another warning. A student organizer told the cops ten thousand protestors would demonstrate tomorrow at the Stock Exchange. "We anticipate violence from the construction workers," he added.

Many workers had decided as much. The clash earlier in the day was "the straw that broke the camel's back," one workman later said. Some of those men worked in the Bowery, a wasteland about two miles uptown. At lunch, they had marched past modest Chinatown markets and a Little Italy still brimming with fluent Italian, past slum-chic Soho, down past City Hall, to the Financial District. There they "attacked" demonstrators, the worker said. "Then they came back and said that everyone had to go out Friday—all the workers from the World Trade Center, the US Steel building and Manhattan Plaza—and break some heads."[13]

PART 2 | "Bloody Friday"

CHAPTER 13 | "U—S—A. All the Way!"
May 8, 1970

A SLATE-GRAY MIST lingered above the bay and the wind kicked up and came over the rotting docks and blew the thin rain sideward against the half-built skyscrapers rising at the city's southern edge. At the base of one tower, as ironworkers smoked beneath scaffolding and talked, a police car drew up curbside. "Fellows," a cop said, "there's another demonstration at the Subtreasury Building," which was also called Federal Hall. Ironworker Eugene Schafer, still smarting from confronting peaceniks and getting "mauled," grabbed one of the American flags on site, and the ironworkers spoke of comeuppance.

At City Hall, a caller reported that workmen planned to "knock heads" with the kids protesting the "Nixon-Kent thing." Soon after, at a quarter past nine, the NYPD was told that a "disorderly group" would burn down 40 Wall Street. A minute later, someone phoned the police and said that construction workers "might cause trouble" for the demonstrators downtown. Another caller pegged the attack at noontime and warned, "Construction workers at the Twin Towers are going to take care of the protestors on Wall Street."

The NYPD relocated a crowd control squad from Queens to the Financial District.

On Wall Street, as the rain dissipated, a thousand students shouted beneath the smoky sky, "One-two-three-four. We don't want your fuckin' war!"

The chanting was loud enough to be heard inside stockbroker Robert Parker's office on the fifty-third floor of 40 Wall Street. A half-block away, on the seventh floor, executive Walter Hendrickson found the repeated profanity "disgusting." A woman from the same building phoned the police about the vulgarity.

The demonstration was relatively civil, however, compared with the chaos since Kent State. Speakers firebranded the familiar: "Get out of Cambodia!" "You brought down one president and you'll bring down another!" "Close down the movies and the plays." One speaker railed, "Off the pigs!"

About twenty cops manned Federal Hall's marble stairs. They were mostly twentysomethings. Baby-blue helmets with chin straps, gloves, narrow ties, long buttoned coats. In the streets below, scattered knots of policemen looked on as well.

Deputy Chief Inspector Valentine Pfaffmann stood at the periphery. "Prevent assaults on demonstrators," Pfaffmann told a sergeant, and keep the sidewalk "fluid." Yesterday, he warned, hardhats and hippies had scuffled at lunchtime.

The crowd fattened on Wall Street. The NYPD detoured traffic. A white boy held up a red sign for the Black Panthers: FREE ALL THE POLITICAL PRISONERS. FREE HUEY + BOBBY. Beside him, a placard read: STOP THE KILLING IN CAMBODIA AND KENT. Another handwritten sign: KENT-BODIA.

Students awaited yippie leader Abbie Hoffman. The NYPD radioed an alert, warning Hoffman was coming. But the organizers were unsure he would show. The morning's cold rain had tapered expectations, if not also relaxed student ire citywide for the first time since Kent State, four days earlier. Only a thousand, of the ten thousand expected, had arrived so far. Activists still intended to shut down Wall Street. As one protestor put it, "We have to close down the financial centers of this country because they help carry on the war."

With Abbie Hoffman's arrival uncertain, the headliner was Paul O'Dwyer, a man of the Old Left with rare reach in the New. The son of struggling Irish schoolteachers, and one of eleven children, O'Dwyer arrived in America as a young man. He worked docks. Packed garments. Eventually, he made his name as a champion of the underclass. His elder brother became the mayor of New York City. But the activist wanted inside too. Paul O'Dwyer was one more pol chasing Bobby Kennedy's Senate seat.

O'Dwyer put on his best political bonhomie and glad-handed bystanders and hopped a puddle. He was a small man with a disheveled white mane and wild gray eyebrows and wore a baggy suit reminiscent of old sack-suited professors. At the outskirts, watching, businessmen with brokerage jackets, tightly knotted neckties, narrow-shouldered blazers, putty raincoats, snap-brim caps and fedoras, holding boxy briefcases, leaning on furled umbrellas.

The inner crowd sat and stood along Wall Street. The students wore bandanas, tartan slacks, frayed bell-bottom jeans, mackinaws, serapes, corduroy blazers, suede buckskin with fringe, thick knitted sweaters, the usual small buttons on big lapels, the usual faded Army field jackets. A half-dozen students made origami hats from newspaper and wore them for the rain. A young woman read the *Times* with a stack of broadsheets on her head. A cigarette stub burned between her fingers. Beside her sat a bearded boy in a green military coat. With the public schools closed to honor Kent State, some teenagers and teachers came too. Among them, seven staff members from an alternative progressive school uptown, including a future Democratic city leader, young administrative assistant Ruth Messinger. There were black kids here and there. Some with big afros. A few Puerto Ricans too. But it was mostly the usual pale college kids. A lot of glasses and good listeners. Girls with center-parted long locks and tawny lips. Boys with adolescent beards and severe stares.

Paul O'Dwyer, his voice still hinting Irish, brushed his bangs off his creased forehead and spoke of the "children of the working class," of families "loaded-down with taxes." He talked of a "message we can give them, which I think will bring that group over to our side." This was how to "end the war," he said. "We can end it now. We can end it immediately. And we can end it before these demonstrations cease—"

"End the war on the Panthers!" someone yelled from the crowd. "Power to the Panthers!"

O'Dwyer persisted. "This is the thing—"

"End the racist war in South Vietnam!" The protestor stepped forward. He was chubby, college age, a white boy with an afro of curls. He thrust his left fist into the air. "End the racist war in South Vietnam!"

"We will talk to everybody that listens to us," O'Dwyer said. "The whole world is in shock." O'Dwyer tolerated these interruptions now. This was no longer his left.

Few activists still believed they could jawbone peace. But the New Left was invested in the Free Speech Movement. Even critics were invited to have their say. One student, bespectacled and bearded, held the silver "fat Elvis mic." He prepped the audience for outrage. "No matter what he says, no matter how bad it is," the speaker warned haltingly, "please be quiet and listen to his point of view."

The new speaker exuded Establishment. The jacket and tie. A Wasp face with a Roman nose. The side-swept hair, straight and trim with delicate bangs, a tidy mustache, pinkish skin. A cigarette cindered in his left hand as he mellowly said, "It's fine to demonstrate and everything but when you start burning down buildings—"

The crowd hollered and brayed. Heads shook dismissively.

The organizer raised his palm to mollify them.

The speaker waved his left hand inward, gesturing as if to say, Bring it on. "It's okay for you to yell but I can't, right?"

The crowd's mau-mauing loudened.

It only riled him. "I'm for America! I love America!"

Once more, the organizer lifted his palm. More students hollered and booed.

"I love America!" The mic was soon passed.

"We all love America," said a boy in a floppy woolen hat. "It's the people who run it that we can't stand."

Scattered applause. A girl yelled, "That's what I'm sayin'."

Someone sang "Hey Jude" over the PA system. Hundreds joined in. The Beatles's final album was officially released today.

At five minutes to eleven, the thin rain returned. Scores opened their newspapers and held them over their heads like pitched rooftops. Few protestors left. Most remained unaware of the warnings.

Just in case, Chief Pfaffmann radioed: "Construction workers would appear from [the] Twin Towers site." The chief also dispatched two patrolmen to the World Trade Center site to "interview foremen, ascertain facts, and dissuade." He insisted, "Prevail upon the workers." The chief presumed the workers, and his own men, would heed him.

In a dorm room lounge uptown, beside the dingy East River, one student organizer nervously twirled a coiled phone cord. The lounge was chock full of first-aid kits and bulky ink-based duplicating machines and fliers and crinkled soda cans. Bruce Biller, a small, 23-year-old med student, was coordinating a new corps of volunteer paramedics from Hunter College and NYU's medical and dental schools. Biller was on the phone with a medic deployed near Wall Street. A workman had warned a nurse that hardhats would "beat up the demonstrators" at noon. The source "apparently" was a construction worker from the Bronx, who worked at the Twin Towers site. Biller hung up and called 911. Fifteen minutes later, he dialed 911 again.

At 11:26, a sergeant sent out an alert over NYPD dispatch: "Two hundred construction workers expected to enter crowd at Wall and Broad to create havoc. Also, rumors of a few thousand students coming to Wall and Broad from Queens."

Rumors spread within the crowd. A speaker announced that if hardhats "come" at them, "don't try to fight them." After all, the speaker added, "The police are here to protect us."

At the top of the steps, in front of the helmeted police line, a girl with a white motorcycle helmet stood beside another activist. They waved a Vietcong flag.

Some protestors began to trail off. They were asked to stay, to reinforce the ranks, to make a stand. "Nobody's going to move us," a speaker yelled into the microphone. "Let them come! We'll show them! We won't be chased away."

From afar, the cross-cut steel shell looked like a rusty car radiator grille, and while the South Tower remained small and skeletal, the North Tower approached the height of the Chrysler Building. Its red bones were only exposed near its peak, which seemed to fade into the sky on days such as this, when the haze hung low on the city.

Two patrolmen circulated around the muddy gravel below. They spoke with foremen about the rally and radioed back that the Twin Towers "workers are not involved."

Forty-two floors above, Joe Kelly heard talk of getting involved. The steel was slick and the wind harsh, but the smog abated at these heights. The workmen spoke of yesterday's clash, of another demonstration today.

Kelly was six foot four, fit, blue-eyed, with a pudgy nose and receding red hair that was cut close. After discharge from the Army, he slogged a few years as a seaman on oil tankers. He returned stateside, enrolled in night school, and put in seven years as an apprentice. Now 31, Kelly worked the largest elevator constructor job in the world.

Workday mornings—like his neighbors: a bus driver, a policeman, a steamfitter, a TV color processor—Kelly left his wife, Karen, his baby, and two small strawberry-blonde daughters at his modest brick-and-shingle house on Staten Island. He mounted his turquoise Triumph 500 cc motorcycle, parked it in the steel belly of the ferry, climbed the metal stairs, and sat on a wood bench and skimmed the *Daily News*. When the ferry screeched against the wood pier and docked, he drove a mile to the Twin Towers. He parked near the rusty elevated West Side Highway and, with thousands of workmen, walked in the shadow of the partially built Twin Towers, entered the gray wooden shanty, and donned his plastic helmet, which was yellow and had flag decals and the phrase FOR GOD AND COUNTRY.

Kelly's half-hour lunch break approached. He had never marched over anything before. But he'd reached his "boiling point." Kelly descended and joined about fifty tradesmen, to "see what this peace demonstration was all about."

Along Wall Street, scores of new demonstrators arrived from the east. One leader bullhorned: "Watta we want?"

"Peace!" the marchers responded.

"When do we want it?"

"Now!"

In front of Federal Hall, a thousand protestors rose up and turned to the new arrivals and roared, tossing fists high beneath the cool gray sky.

The leaders of the march were clad in more faded military coats, more armbands. But the two hundred followers were boys with cherubic faces and oversized jackets, girls with headbands and ribbons in their hair—the big collars, the big glasses, the big hair of the era. Near the front, one boy with mop-top hair held a red placard that read, STOP NIXON'S WAR. The chanting became frenzied.

"Watta we want? When?"

"Peace now! Peace now! Peace now!"

Twenty minutes to noon. Bruce Biller, the coordinator of the medics, dialed 911 for a third time. He was connected to the temporary police headquarters on Wall Street. Inspector Harold Schryver assured Biller that they "had a sufficient number of patrolmen on the scene." Besides, they "had learned that the construction workers were not coming."

The hardhats had not showed. The protest concluded gradually. Some students strolled uptown for another rally. A thousand demonstrators remained. Some witnesses estimated twice that. The students chatted casually. One *Times* man noted that the crowd was in "good humor."

At first, few noticed the dozen workmen wading into the mass. At the fore, a man grimacing, his yellow helmet backward, his hands in the pockets of his chore coat. Another man with a wide fleshy nose and sideburns and a helmet adorned with flags. A fair-haired older man in brownish coveralls. Behind him, a little man pinched a newly lit cigarette. Near him, a tall hardhat with a lineman's build. They entered slowly, single file. A senior NYPD officer glanced at the hardhats and turned away.

Another group of hardhats neared Wall Street's plaza.

"Give 'em hell, boys," a patrolman shouted. "Give 'em one for me!"

The lunchtime crowd thickened to thousands and construction workers continued filtering into the plaza, until hundreds of workmen were seen parading up Broad Street's slim corridor. They were several men abreast, moving in a loose phalanx with heavy footfalls, wearing colored helmets, flannel, tattered trousers over steel-toe boots, shouldering big American flags, bellowing, "U—S—A. All the way! U—S—A. All the way!"

NYPD chiefs counted four hundred hardhats now.

Cops formed a line. They contained the hardhats where Broad Street fed Wall Street. The workmen moved four American flags to the fore of their ranks. A few hardhats held up a lean workman. The workman lifted a flag high above the fray.

The streets were now brimming over. A businessman stood on a lamppost, holding a file folder. The police created a demilitarized zone of sorts, separating the hardhats and the students by twenty to forty feet, each faction volleying chants.

Students swung their arms overhead and hollered louder.

Hardhats responded with their middle fingers and shouted out: "We're number one! We're number one!"

More workmen wandered into the mass and assembled at the rear, including about thirty ironworkers from the west. "I carried the flag up Broadway and Wall Street and I could see three or four blocks of faces—a complete sea of faces of chanting people against the war in Vietnam," said ironworker Eugene Schafer.

Another contingent of hardhats cheered: "Hey, hey, whaddya say? We support the U.S.A.!"

Patrolmen Michael Stokes, a 26-year-old who lived near the withering industry of Queens's western shoreline, saw a separate contingent of workmen, about two dozen, walking northward on Broad Street. They shouted, "Love it or leave it! Love it or leave it!"

As midday neared, the sun burned through the clouds and the day warmed and the air became heavy with humidity. Thousands heard the clamor in their offices. Typewriters stopped and phone receivers were set on cradles and chairs swiveled. Legions of office workers descended to the streets. It was now tough to enter the plaza. Spectators stood up on their toes and craned their necks. Strangers asked the person ahead of them, What's going on? Inside adjacent office buildings, plenty of clerks and bankers and secretaries and lawyers worked on. Still, on floor after floor, tower by tower, thousands collected at large windows, cranked them open or lifted wooden frames, and stared downward. The throng consumed the cavernous streetscape, leaving it difficult to discern where the sidewalk ended and the road began.

"Peace now! Peace now!"

"Love it or leave it!"

Hardhats gestured with their hands, challenging the peaceniks to come at them.

Some workmen now held white leaflets with American flags and the words RALLY FOR AMERICA.

Deep within the pack, a group of workmen pushed "anyone who happened to get in their way," said Arlene Gross, a computer programmer in her early twenties, who watched from the sixth floor of 20 Broad Street, which was located beside the Stock Exchange. On the floor above her, elderly executive Walter Hendrickson watched hardhats assemble as "spectators in the street and the employees in the various buildings cheered them on."

For a few minutes, it was no more than that, each tribe shouting anthems and insults, seemingly delimited. Some cops now stood at ease and chatted with the hardhats.

There were workmen well north of six feet and intimidating from browridge to boot. Yet plenty of the hardhats were no taller than the students. But the shorter guys were often broad-backed. The skinny workmen had veiny forearms, hands thick and cracked and callused from day after day after . . . years of manhandling steel or brick or blasting a riveting gun. At the vanguard, a few dozen men, including a big man, black Irish with a spotted yellow helmet, his checkered-flannel sleeves rolled up, as he hollered at the students, his hands cupped around his mouth, trying to be heard. Beside him, a young man, nostalgically cool, like a handsome Buddy Holly, with a modest pompadour and black horn-rimmed glasses and a pencil behind his ear. To his left, a squirrely little man with a blue helmet and a sinewy face and protruding ears. Over his shoulder, another big man with pale skin and black hair and a fixed stare. His mustard-yellow hard hat was adorned with an iron cross. Many were tanned from working the high open steel. They had boots and white cotton socks and baggy slacks and some wore shirts with their name on their breast. These were clean-shaven men, ranging from their twenties to their fifties. Some of the older guys were fleshy, shirts protruding at the paunch. Most of the men, though, were trim enough to give chase.

Students abruptly pressed forward, juiced by these gritty men who were now proxies for the warmongers. The youthful ranks were, in this instant, emboldened. It was mere days after the breakdown of civil order at Kent State. Yet these revolutionaries remained confident enough in the system to believe that the police would maintain order, that there were rules of engagement, that the hardhats would be held behind enemy lines, that the means of combat were words.

"Fuck you and Nixon too!"

"Take a bath!"

"Commies!"

Hardhats tossed aluminum cans. Men nudged frontward. More shouted. More swollen hands cupped mouths.

The cops linked arms and formed a human chain that spanned the width of Broad Street. It was difficult to hear the person beside you. Police loosely assembled a second line parallel with the first.

Curbside, a group of Wall Street men—slim twentysomethings, side-parted hair, ties, shirtsleeves—smiled and waved their arms and joined the hardhat anthems. At least a thousand local workers now cheered the hardhats.

The students sensed a tidal shift. Hundreds of them retreated into a solid mass at the base of the steps and the Washington statue. The statue was massive and bronze and someone had scratched FREE BOBBY into its stone pedestal.

The crowd tightened around the students. The building was at their back. The students were surrounded.

About twenty thousand people crammed several blocks now, Assistant Chief Inspector Arthur Morgan estimated. Morgan was a veteran of tumult, including the '67 Harlem riot. Although by 1970, every NYPD leader had experience with upheaval.

Bystanders stepped on toes. A man in a blazer climbed a stop sign. A hardhat scrambled up a lamppost. Police radioed for assistance. More squads were deployed. In the street, hardhats pushed against the police line.

"Take it easy," cops yelled. "Keep back."

The police pulled some workmen aside. The hardhats said that Federal Hall belonged to all the people but was missing its American flag. The flag had not been hoisted due to the rain, but none there knew this. The hardhats blamed Mayor Lindsay's order to lower flags for Kent State.

"All we want to do is put our flag up on those steps," one workman said.

"If you try, there'll be blood to pay," Inspector Schryver reportedly replied.

Chief Morgan, also in the parley, told the workmen that they must apply for a permit to protest here, like everyone else.

"The construction workers at this time gave every indication that they were unorganized and had no specific plan of action, and that the sudden interest and support shown by local Wall Street workers appeared to surprise them," Chief Pfaffmann later reported to Internal Affairs.

The hardhats returned to their ranks. Workmen chanted on and the crowd with them. Each side had instigators hurling insults across the police line. The cacophony drowned out sirens.

"There was yelling, pushing, and shoving going on between the construction workers and the peace groups," said one young patrolman in the plaza, Wilton Sekzer. "The construction workers wanted one-half of the Treasury Building." Their pushing got "stronger."

More flag-waving hardhats arrived.

"Love it or leave it!"

"Peace now!"

Inspector Schryver saw the police line "waver and bend." It now "appeared to be a matter of minutes before the police would be overrun."

Bottles sailed through the air. Chief Morgan was nearly hit. Chief Pfaffmann reported that the "missiles were thrown from the ranks of the demonstrators." A camera captured one hurled from those ranks.

At the fore of the students, kids angrily flashed peace signs and cursed the war, the president, the workmen.

"Fuck you and Nixon too!" students chanted on, fists and middle fingers aloft. Some screamed, "Fascist pigs!"

Hardhats replied with their middle fingers and fuck-yous and a barrage of slurs—"Bums! . . . Faggot! . . . Commie!"

Electrical supply salesman Bob Barber was on his way to worship at old Trinity Church. But he saw the flags, heard the chants. It felt patriotic to him. He impulsively joined in.

A few rabble-rousing businessmen filed into the front of the hardhats. More white collars collected at the rear and boomed along. NYPD commanders estimated that eight hundred office workers now bolstered the hardhats' ranks. Chief Pfaffmann reported more "pressure" on police.

Still more construction workers arrived. Men with red helmets and check-ered shirts came from the west, cutting through the crowd along Wall Street.

Inspector Schryver encouraged students to leave the area.

Hardhats unfurled a massive flag. Bystanders cheered.

Peaceniks continued to aggressively chant.

The students had the loudspeaker. They tried to outcheer the hardhats as though it was an all-American pep rally. It only aggravated the workmen more. More hardhats pushed against cops. More fuck-yous. More middle fin-gers. Other men had their hands at their sides, curling their fingers into fists.

The workmen blasted forward. The first police line broke. "You can't go!" shouted one police supervisor. The second cordon stopped the men. Some patrolmen shoved hardhats back. The hardhats heaved forward. In the hardhat ranks, a few men had lead pipes wrapped with burlap and held them low. Cops backstepped.

A student waved a Vietcong flag from the steps.

The hardhats hollered and booed and the girl with the white motorcycle helmet did not relent.

The last police line broke.

CHAPTER 14 | Melee

HARDHATS BLITZED FORWARD and the crowd panicked—screaming, shoving, thousands running and tripping and pleading for a way out. Antiwar signs were dropped. One girl fell and hit the ground "with a sickening thud." She was trampled. "All these construction workers seemed intent on reaching [the] Vietcong flag," said attorney Leon Ciferni, looking on. Some hardhats charged headlong, elbows splayed, plowing through the crowd, cutting it in two. Hardhats attacked any boy who looked like a hippie. One student keeled over, retching, as the tide of men crushed over him. The big black Irish hardhat with the spotted helmet struck one student, soon another. At Federal Hall's colonnade, a hardhat grabbed a peacenik's collar and punched him. A student shoved the hardhat in the back. Another workman charged in and the scrum fell. One workman tackled a peacenik against a column. More hardhats swarmed.

Drew Lynch, a slight 19-year-old protestor, was hit in the left eye. "As I was spinning around, another construction worker hit me across the nose and in my right eye," Lynch said. He collapsed. Amid the blur of rushing legs and boots and splashing filth, "I was hit in the ribs and across the eye with a metal pipe." Lynch took more blows, kicks to the face, to the groin. A cop dragged him out of the melee as he bled. "Get the fuck out of here!" the cop yelled. The construction workers "beat any persons who did not clear out quickly enough," another demonstrator said. A small high school senior, Barry Cohen from Brooklyn, was cold-cocked in the face and lost consciousness.

More hardhats arrived, some from the east along Wall Street, others up Broad Street. They saw the brawl and men waved their fellow to help and a

Construction workers storm Federal Hall's steps to raise a US flag and scatter student protestors at the outset of the Hardhat Riot, May 8, 1970. (Carl T. Gossett/The New York Times/Redux)

pack charged ahead, one man holding his flag like a torch as he ran. The vanguard wedged into the masses. More hardhats followed, plunging into the breach, swimmers to the sea, arms whirling. The crowd gasped.

The sidewalks were packed at both ends. Strangers stood with their backs pressed to buildings, hoping the rampage would pass them by. Others dashed for safety inside doorways. Some escaped, including a law student who marshaled an NYU flock. Countless more were trapped. Friends were separated. Many students tried to outrun the men. But there were too many people to move quickly. Wild-eyed strangers pressed and jostled and screamed for help. Scores fell on the crooked, dank cobblestones. The "press of people" knocked a 17-year-old demonstrator, Nina Jaffee, to the sidewalk. "I became hysterical and was lying on the ground screaming," she said. Someone pulled her free of the panic and helped her behind the colonnade.

"I was petrified," said Pace College freshman Martin Dolgow. A policeman pushed him into some girls and hollered: "Come on, you kids. Get out of here. Get out of here!" Dolgow fled along Wall Street, where he saw a cheering businessman and a grinning cop.

More workmen cut into the center of the plaza. At the fore, a gloved man carried a huge flag. Another hardhat supported the pole. Electrical salesman Bob Barber and other men strained to touch the flag's fringes as if they were touching honor. Nineteen-year-old Michael Doctor ran up the steps to help hold a peace banner aloft. The banner was jerked from his hands. He turned to see who it was. "Some guy belted me in the face," said Doctor, a slim six-foot-four Pace College student with long dirty-blond hair. "I reached up and pulled him down the steps, threw him on the ground, and jumped on him," he said. "As I sat on him, holding him down, he continued punching me in the face." Other hardhats surrounded Doctor. He was soon battered from "all sides." A patrolman pulled him from the brawl by his hair.

The shouting and shrieking and screaming became one frenetic din as the melee consumed the plaza. Hardhats threw rabbit punches and jabs. They pulled students' jackets over their heads before spinning their fists up. Some workmen waved their arms downward, urging the men to calm. Others clasped their rabid kindred from behind, pulling them off bloody hippies before it was too late.

"Jesus Christ," one observer mumbled, likely a reporter. A handful of journos had nested atop Federal Hall's stairs.

"You better get some more cops here, man," another onlooker said. He turned to a cameraman and told him, "If they come up here, you're going to get killed."

More hardhats bounded up the stairs, scattering hippies and reporters alike. Later, a local network cameraman was seen with an "obvious scalp wound," but it's unclear when he was injured or how.

Michael Doctor was prostrated and disoriented at the bottom of the steps. Another hardhat punched him in the face, threw him onto the pavement, and leapt onto his back. More workmen kicked him. He blacked out.

Atop the stairs, workmen tossed their arms up and lifted their helmets. Below, men carried a massive flag over them like a tent. The flag flowed up the steps, as though it were rising with a wave.

From above, where George Washington was inaugurated, at the white marble center of the financial world, it was bedlam, an electric multitude of brawling and bullying and fear. Said one accountant, it was "animalistic."

"A melee of fistfighting that entrapped thousands of employees," the *Times* reported. "There was blood on many faces," the *Post* reported. "Limp bodies were being carried off." It was a "battle," narrated a CBS newsman in real time, a "wild, swinging melee."

Stock Exchange worker Reid Menting witnessed a hardhat kick a girl on the ground. "I saw two patrolmen rush over to the location and take the construction worker away," he said.

Pace freshman Stephen Rich held a girl up on his shoulders. She yelled down to him what she saw. "She could not see the end of the stream of yellow," he recounted. "There was a huge crowd of peace demonstrators." Hardhats were "piling in and beating the kids."

The crowd pushed a half-dozen students against the steps and toppled them. Strangers and friends tangled. People yelled and there was a smell, a reeking, some blend of exertion and fear. Students jostled to get sweaty strangers off them. A hardhat looked down at NYU student Stephen Yaffe. The hardhat clenched his fist and lunged at Yaffe, who rolled to his left. The fist grazed Yaffe's ear. The hardhat disappeared.

"Get on your fucking feet!" a cop yelled down at Yaffe.

"Help me," he replied. "I can't get up."

The cop yanked Yaffe up by his arm. Yaffe's female friend was distracted and still on the ground. The policeman lifted her up by her hair.

The rank-and-file cops were often the same generation as the students. Patrolman Eugene Greenlaw was 21. He lived in the first mass-produced suburb, Levittown, a postwar magnet for young GIs and blue-collar whites (a covenant forbade black residents for the first few years). The 750-square-foot homes were tract-housing clones—four rooms, no basements, no logical place for a washing machine. But it was *yours*. Most Levittown men commuted into the city on workdays—police officers, bus drivers, firemen, tradesmen. Greenlaw was insistent, though, that he "tried to stop [the hardhats'] charge." He reported to superiors, "I held my night stick out in front of me with both hands and started to push back against the crowd."

Patrolman Greenlaw was hit. A flagstaff likely speared him. It was too crazy to be sure. His upper lip was busted open and a tooth was chipped. He fell and stood himself up. "I pushed my way back up to the top of the steps," he said.

Patrolman Wilton Sekzer, age 25, said the hardhats first "broke through on the east side" of Broad Street. In that instant, he was on the west end of the plaza. "We kept sidestepping, trying to keep the crowd back." Another patrolman, John Burns from Queens, said that after the "main body" of the hardhats "hit our line," the cordon broke. "We were unable to hold them back." He added, "As they broke through our lines, they rushed toward the students and I followed, still trying to hold them back." Many onlookers, like the Stock Exchange's Reid Menting, said the cops had made "a determined effort to prevent the construction workers from getting through their control."

Yet to "reporters at the scene," according to the *New York Post,* it seemed like the police only offered "token resistance." ABC News reported that "police did little to stop" the initial onrush. Numerous witnesses avowed the same. Pace student Martin Dolgow said after the first hardhats broke the line, the police "let the others through." NYU medical student Jack Shonkoff saw the original charge and said, "It appeared to me that the police made no effort to stop the construction workers." Brooklyn College student Rifka Keilson said in her sworn affidavit that police "made little attempt to restrain" the hardhats. She added, "Police stepped to the sidelines or up the steps of the Treasury Building and stood watching with folded arms."

Howard Bushman, a young Wall Street lawyer, saw the melee commence. He was standing catty-corner from the steps, across the street. "If the police had taken firm, decisive action at the inception," he thought, violence would have been "prevented." Soon, the violence closed in on him too. Abruptly, near him, Bushman saw a hardhat attack a skinny longhair. Two cops broke up the fight.

Bushman pulled one policeman aside. "I think you ought to make an arrest," he said.

"What for?" the cop responded.

"I'm sure you saw this incident."

"Do you want to make a complaint?"

"I guess, I better make a complaint." Bushman gave his information. Said he was an attorney.

"Were you injured?" the cop asked.

"No, but I don't believe you have to be injured to make a complaint."

Bushman convinced these cops to ask the identity of the attacker. The hardhat was in his early twenties and lived with family—his sister, his mother, his grandmother—in a single-story brick and shingle bungalow in Staten Island. He handed over his green journeyman card to the cops. Bushman noted the name. But the cops refused to cuff him.[1]

More workmen bulled into the masses. The crowd roared. New throngs pushed for escape. Some slipped in street puddles. Thousands remained trapped.

Patrolman Burns was forced against the steps. "All the while," he said, he was "trying to keep the two groups apart and break up fights." He reached the pedestal beneath the Washington statue. He was shoved to the ground and twisted his ankle.

At the southeast base of the stairs, as a half-dozen police officers tried to steer the masses eastward, Patrolman Sekzer got kicked in the leg and fell, spraining an ankle as well. He shambled forward, pushing his way to the statue base. Another cop lifted him out.

Construction workers attack students at an antiwar rally in New York's financial district on May 8, 1970, in what came to be known as the Hardhat Riot. (Bettmann/Getty)

Above them, a man with a duckbill helmet and a tool belt pushed a hippie over a platform edge. The hippie fell, his arms reeling with panic. Students below reached up to catch him. The workman grabbed another hippie by his belt and hurled him into the crowd below.

The trampled girl, who had fallen during the hardhats' first charge, was now "bleeding profusely" from her head. Rifka Keilson watched paramedics carry away the girl and saw "construction workers beating other demonstrators with flagpoles."

After the "side of the police line just melted away, and those yellow hats charged up the steps and began to beat up students, I ducked around through a nearby underpass to get on the other side of the crowd," recounted a workman, one of the few who spoke in detail with reporters afterward, anonymously. "And as I was hurrying through," he continued, "a policeman stopped me."

"Did Twin Towers get here yet?" the cop asked him.

"No," the worker said, "they haven't come yet."

"Gee," the cop replied, "I wish they'd hurry up and get here."

Atop the steps, a sergeant tried to separate the factions. He ordered about six cops to form a vertical line up the stairs. East side, hardhats. West side, hippies.

A construction worker hurls someone into the crowd during the Hardhat Riot, May 8, 1970.

On the steps, police corralled some hardhats and tried to drive the youth back. A few teenage girls got trapped in the melee. They saw cops club students. Strangers stumbled into each other and screams rang in ears. One hardhat yelled, "Let the kids out!" Some men listened. At least one of the girls escaped.

A hefty man climbed the pedestal of the Washington statue. He looked like any other suit, tie and blazer and middle-aged. Then he debased a flag—tearing at it with his hands, or ripping it with his teeth (witness accounts varied).[2]

"He spit on the flag! He spit on the flag!" Joe Kelly, the Twin Towers elevator constructor, heard.

A fair-haired young attorney, Michael Belknap, saw the hefty man bite it twice. "As soon as I saw what he was doing, I knew there would be trouble," Belknap later told the cops.

The hefty man stuck his thumb to his nose and waved his fingers, razzing the hardhats.

Hardhats began swinging away at the man's feet. Two men climbed the pedestal. One was a construction worker, the other wore a business suit. The men tussled like children quarreling at Washington's feet. The construction worker hit the hefty man in the face. He fell hard.

"Kill him!" someone yelled.

Workers punished the man with blows. Patrolman Burns, grounded on the steps with his twisted ankle, saw a man who "pulled down" a flag get "socked."

"There just seemed to be a rush, a mob scene," Joe Kelly said. "The chant then was, 'Get the flags up on the steps where they belong.'"

Hardhats charged across the steps. "There was fighting going on all over," Patrolman Stokes said.

A businessman lifted Patrolman Burns up, retrieved his helmet, and guided him out. Finally, police pushed forward and shielded the hefty man.

Michael Belknap told the cops he was a lawyer. He asked to see the injured man. Another young lawyer, Richard Fleischmann, spoke with Assistant Chief Inspector James M. Taylor (Taylor had been one of the commanding officers involved in the Columbia occupation). Fleischmann, wearing a business suit and tortoiseshell glasses, was nose to nose with Chief Taylor, who was tall, silver-haired, his shoulders adorned with stars. Fleischmann identified the lead attacker. It was an electrical foreman from Long Island who went by Richie. Fleischmann asked the chief to arrest him. But Chief Taylor said they couldn't arrest "anybody under the circumstances."[3]

In the crowd, "people were in a panic," said Gerry Oliffe, a twentysomething copy editor. His girlfriend, 22-year-old Lucile Mendelovitz, said she was "really scared."

Patrolman Stokes tried to return to the high ground. The stairs remained slippery from the rain. He was knocked by someone and "fell backwards." His head snapped back and his helmet hit the sidewalk hard enough to chip. He was "momentarily dazed." Two guys helped him to his feet. He "collapsed to the sidewalk once again."

Chief Taylor saw that his men were "overrun." Standing on the west side of the steps, he ordered cops to regroup on the lower stairs. Some did. He saw fights bursting out seemingly at random. "Police tried to get through the crowd to break them up, the fight would stop, and other fights would break out," Chief Taylor wrote later in his internal report.

Deep in the crowd, Ruth Messinger said it was "constant turmoil." She heard some demonstrators shouting at officers: "Why aren't you arresting them? Why are you pushing us?"

At the crest of the steps, in front of Federal Hall's colonnade, hardhats lifted their helmets and waved their flags and the masses cheered them. Police were scattered between the men, and even those with helmets, with visors down and nightsticks by their side, did nothing as the hardhats celebrated atop the stairs. "We just stood there," Patrolman Eugene Greenlaw later told police investigators in a rare admission, though—like all the internal records—the comments were never made public. The cop added, "The construction workers had completely taken over."

No reinforcements yet. The Special Events Squads, platoons of thirty to forty-five cops trained in crowd control, were spread from Columbia University to Union Square. Police expected more Kent State aftermath. So far, only a crowd-control squad from Queens had been redeployed downtown.

Hardhats planted flags on the Washington statue. Workmen saluted.

"We took the steps! We took the steps!" hardhats chanted. One of them was Milton from Queens. An electrician, he was big and balding, with glasses and green work clothes. He held his arms high in victory, king of the mountain. In the crowd below, laborers and office workers joined in, including two young men in ties and shirtsleeves. One of them waved both fists overhead elatedly. The other man, bespectacled and bony, shouted along. Beside them, a thickset man with a concave nose and a round chin. He wore a quilted chore coat and a flag-decaled hard hat and waved a small flag with his right hand, yelling with his kindred, "We took the steps!"

"Broad Street and Wall Street were filled with people as far as the eye could see from building line to building line," Chief Pfaffmann reported. He estimated the crowd now at twenty-five thousand. "Many cheering the construction workers."

In the buildings overhead, workers tossed tickertape and computer punch cards out of their windows. Confetti glittered in the air.

Hardhats continued amassing atop the steps, clapping their hands, bellowing "Hoo-ah," chanting on, waving American colors still.

"Wow," said Jack Friedman, an underwriter in his early thirties. "It was just like John Wayne taking Iwo Jima."

CHAPTER 15 | "About Time the Silent Majority
Made Some Noise"

A FATHER'S GRAND feats can underline a son's failure. The "good war"
lorded over Vietnam this way. V-E Day had been twenty-five years
earlier, to the day, May 8, 1945. The anniversary marked the Nazis' defeat, the end to the worst theater of the war. Pacific combat continued. But
Americans still rejoiced. Boys were coming home.

The news arrived on May 7, a day earlier than Allied leaders intended.
The AP violated the embargo. Teletype machines worldwide printed the bul-
letin. It was about half-past nine in the morning in New York City. Word
spread over the radio. There was yelling in the streets. Horns honked citywide. So many New Yorkers reached for telephones at once, city phone lines
jammed. The news caused Manhattan's natural traffic patterns to reverse.
As if water flowed upstream, cars and people amassed in midtown into the
afternoon. Countless didn't want to commute home. A half-million people
celebrated in Times Square. Tickertape showered streets from midtown to
downtown. In the Financial District, the mass smothered Wall Street's plaza.
Nearby, Trinity Church was at capacity. New Yorkers stuffed the street outside to pray. Americans were filling houses of worship nationwide. A dozen
blocks north of Trinity Church, inside City Hall, Mayor La Guardia gave an
afternoon radio address. He alerted the public that the city would officially
mark the occasion the following day, May 8, 1945, after President Truman's
speech. Most offices and factories continued business as usual. The nation's
manufacturing hub, New York City, was not easily shut down. Countless
workers couldn't celebrate until their shift ended. As evening arrived, the
wartime brownout ceased. The lights turned on in Times Square. Broadway

was again the Great White Way. As New Yorkers reveled into the small hours, the cityscape glowed in full for the first time in years.

On the morning of May 8, President Truman's address earned the largest broadcast audience since the advent of radio. Many wartime factories gave employees the day off. After Truman's speech, a quarter-million more packed Times Square. The Stock Exchange observed two minutes of silence for the dead. The entire police force went on duty. More than seven thousand civilians also volunteered to assist the NYPD. This was World War Two. People joined up. Wartime factories were filled with women and men too old to serve. "Victory begins at home," went the slogan. The nation was united in wartime. The bulk of the servicemen had known only one president. He had shepherded the United States through the Great Depression and World War Two, until about a month earlier. As victory over the Nazis was celebrated, flags remained at half-staff to mourn Franklin Roosevelt.

A quarter-century later, V-E Day was scarcely remembered in the city. Vietnam veterans couldn't conceive of the hero's welcome that had greeted many of their fathers and uncles on these selfsame streets. The *Times* passingly mentioned V-E Day inside the paper, buried within a story about Ike's papers. The news was instead dominated by the unpopular war.

In the streets now, most of the police and hardhats were veterans of earlier wars, or had kin there, or knew someone well enough, over there. Patrolman Wilton Sekzer, the son of a World War Two vet, had volunteered for Vietnam and returned stateside emaciated, just 110 pounds. Many hardhats could recount some version of that, from elevator constructor Joe Kelly to ironworker Eugene Schafer. Schafer had fought more than two years in Korea and it was never a memory he fully discarded, all those months in foxholes. More of the elder tradesmen—whether Peter Brennan or George Daly—had served in the military, like the police commanders. Long before he became an NYPD chief, Valentine Pfaffmann was just another GI wounded in action during World War Two.

Cops and construction workers were not only closer to the military by experience, kin, and kind. Big-city police departments also had a hierarchy similar to the military. Their work, like many skyscraper trades, came with peril. Both jobs shared a martial quality as well, as Gay Talese noticed in his 1964 book on the building of the world's longest suspension bridge, the Verrazzano, which connected Staten Island to Brooklyn. "Building a bridge is like combat," he wrote, "the language is of the barracks, and the men are organized along the lines of the noncommissioned officers' caste." And as in war, sometimes the young bridgemen "like to grandstand a bit, like to show the old men how it is done," and they will swing on cables or straddle beams, "and sometimes they get so daring they die."

The hardhats and the cops were of a similar mind. Inspector Schryver later reported his men were overrun and that he instructed subordinates "to protect the people." Yet Schryver's account overlooked what he undoubtedly knew. "These bums don't respect anything," Schryver had said of the peaceniks, after all, the day before. Tradesmen and cops hailed from the same neighborhoods. They had similar upbringings. They often attended the same churches and frequented the same bars. They looked the same, disproportionately ethnic whites and short-haired. One nickname for the cops was "fuzz," possibly because many police enlisted straight from the military and thus had buzz cuts. "A lot of police, on their vacation, we used them to work in the construction industry," steamfitters leader George Daly explained. Both police and tradesmen tended to also be "sportsmen," as Daly put it. Some of them, like Daly, had professional prospects. More commonly, they were schooldays athletes. Elevator constructor Joe Kelly had been a forward on his varsity high school team. He'd played ball four nights a week until he was married. Now he coached children for a Staten Island parish. These were the same men now in the streets, atop the steps, cheering and policing (or not policing).

Antiwar activists regrouped near the base of the stairs and chanted. They still sought to make a stand. Joe Kelly thought they looked "un-American." A group of protestors linked arms. They assumed safety in numbers. An NYU law student and "legal observer," Frank Fioramonti, asked patrolmen for their commanding officer. They waved him off. The entire scene was "turmoil," he said. "There was a breakdown in command control."[1]

Violence rippled outward. A young man was kicked on the ground beside a telephone booth. The boy cowered into a ball. A hot-dog vendor bent over his pushcart to see the boy. The boy remained curled in a fetal position, too terrified to move, even after his attacker ran off. Inside the telephone booth, a man continued his conversation. Elsewhere, a guy called a hardhat a "motherfucking fascist." That too came to blows, as packs of students ran off, trying to flee through the horde. One young couple, Gerry Oliffe and Lucile Mendelovitz, were knocked over by the crowd. They disentangled themselves from the pile, saw an elderly man with a bloody face, and crawled inside a building lobby.

Elsewhere, a gray-haired workman called a pack of students "communists." "We're not communists!" a girl screamed back. The workman swung at one young man and missed but the follow-through of his haymaker hit a girl.

A construction worker and businessman attack a young man at the periphery of the Hardhat Riot, May 8, 1970. (Neal Boenzi/The New York Times/Redux)

A boy picked her up and "felt a rain of blows" to the back of his head as he carried her away in his arms.

An elderly husband and wife got separated in the panic. An ambulance was stuck in the massive crowd. Nearby, NYU film student Harry Bolles shouldered his bulky Arriflex 16 mm motion picture camera. To record audio, his friend carried a large tape recorder. Bolles, a little stocky, a little tall, with frizzy hair and long sideburns, lived in a tenement in the low-rent West Village. He had filmed some Wall Street clashes but decided to go a block south, where it seemed safer. At Exchange Place, a man said he was "bothering" workers. "I'm not," Bolles replied. "I'm here filming, man." Bolles was politely asked to leave. Bolles politely replied, "No, I'm sorry." Someone yelled, "They're gonna kill him now!" Shouts from the pack, "Oh God . . . Jesus . . . shit." Another man shouted at Bolles: "You stop taking pictures. Right now!" Bolles stopped. A worker still struck him. Five or six hardhats rushed in. Bolles was pushed to the pavement. Kicks and punches—to his back, to his neck, to his legs. Then they were gone. He gathered his broken camera and crawled inside a liquor store.

Frank Fioramonti, the legal observer, approached a middle-aged police captain and asked his name.

The captain hesitated, stared at him, and then replied, "Jones."

"Do you have a first name?"

". . . Jeffrey."

There was no Captain Jeffrey Jones in the NYPD.

Two blocks south of Federal Hall, on the twenty-eighth floor of one office building, workers gathered at the window. They gazed at the colored helmets, the flags flapping above tens of thousands, the mass covering the streetscape.

Jean Sookne, a petite middle-aged secretary, saw about two hundred workmen parade north toward the plaza. The crowd parted before them. Suddenly, a cop car moved out of the intersection, out of their way. The hardhats "dashed forward like mad dogs."

"I broke down and cried," Sookne continued. "I turned away from the window. I couldn't look anymore. I went into the ladies' room and I cried. I knew it would be horrible." She later heard "other employees laughing" by a window. "Tickertape was raining down on the construction workers, spurring them on." Some of her coworkers were awed. One shouted, "Look at that!"

At the Banker's Trust tower, a dozen workers gathered on a narrow stone ledge. In the street, one shoe was atop a white sedan. Bloody hippies were being pulled out of the multitude.

A block west of Broadway and Wall Street, an office worker saw two contingents of hardhats merge and "strike the students," some with "iron tools." She watched as the cops "stood passively by."

Elderly executive Walter Hendrickson, watching still from his office window, thought police were doing an "admirable job under the circumstances." "The construction workers were jeered and insulted by vile language," Hendrickson said. "Somebody had to shut them up."

Ironworker Eugene Schafer saw an American flag get "torn up" by a peacenik. A workman told a reporter that some students had "spit on the flag." A 28-year-old clerk on his lunch break, Alfredo Fernandez, saw an antiwar activist try to "rip" an American Flag. The young investment banker who often watched hawks and doves argue over lunch, Joe Guzzardi, was several layers back. "A lot of flags were getting stomped on," he said. "There were a lot of hippies out there." The hardhats were "pushing, shoving," swinging "blows," Guzzardi said. Though he was impressed, as some hippies "held their own."

A middle-aged man ascended the stairs and tore down an American flag and got punched in the nose.

A kid flailed at Joe Kelly. Kelly had not hit anyone for at least a decade. "I gave him a whack and back he went. He went down, I know that. And I just figured he wouldn't be back for more."

Police repelled one pack of workmen, escorted them a few blocks, and "dispersed" them. More hardhats walked up Broad Street. At Federal Hall, more workmen funneled off the steps and into the masses crowding the plaza and the streets. Students felt safer in packs. Some goaded workmen and refused to retreat. Hardhats got hold of several. More beatings. More passive cops. More fleeing droves. An ambulance siren wailed over the din.

Nearby, a hippie was knocked flat. Workers kicked him and lashed him with their helmets.

After fifteen minutes of chaos, backup arrived. Officers cleared the stairs, though many hardhats had already run off, chasing students in the streets.

On Federal Hall's stairs, a senior officer bullhorned, "Let's all go home. Give us a break."

"It appeared that the situation had returned to normal," went one NYPD report.

It didn't feel normal to thousands in the plaza. By now, stock market activity had "slowed to a crawl" as "brokers, analysts, investors, and office help poured out of the buildings or clustered at windows," the *Wall Street Journal* reported. On Broadway, a recent Yale Law grad, Frank Nestor, gave a thumbs-down to parading hardhats and was blitzed. One hardhat punched Nestor in the mouth. His front teeth caved in. Nestor fell to the sidewalk. His colleague "ran frantically, looking for policemen." Nestor was kicked and stomped on. "Don't kill him!" someone shouted. "Please, don't kill him."

It was "savage violence," according to lawyer Bill Hubbard. He found a senior officer.

"I'm a lawyer," Hubbard said on the steps. "Why aren't any arrests being made?"

"Get him off here," the officer snapped at another cop.

"What's the problem?" a cop asked Hubbard.

"Why aren't any arrests being made?"

"On what grounds?"

"Assault and battery."

"Nothing like that. This is only harassment."

At one intersection, another lawyer witnessed police stopping hippies but not hardhats. The antiwar protestors wanted to get into the main square with a TV cameraman.

One of those cops, big and clean-shaven and about 30, left his police line and requested a bandage from a medic. Someone asked the cop, "How come you let the construction workers through the line and stopped the students and the press?"

"We're with them," the cop replied.

At old Trinity Church, midday Mass was under way. The service was dedicated to Kent State and all the war dead. The priest stood at the side of the altar, before an ornately carved wood lectern. He talked of covenants and offerings and coming together. Injured students were carried down the nave's side aisle to vesting rooms. The priest, Vicar Donald Woodward, was clean-cut and wore thick black glasses and retained a boyish countenance, though he was middle-aged. Sometimes, from his office, he would gaze out the window at the unfinished Twin Towers.

The original Trinity Church burned down in the city's great fire during the Revolution. The second Trinity Church's regular worshippers included George Washington. New York City was then the nation's capital. James Monroe was married and eulogized at Trinity. John Jay was a churchwarden. Alexander Hamilton baptized his children at Trinity. Later, he was buried in the churchyard. Hamilton's gravestone was still visible from the street, on a small plot in the shadow of the modern city.

More injured arrived at Trinity. Parishioners' eyes wandered from the priest. Father Woodward curtailed the service. Protestor Drew Lynch waited for help. His mouth was cut and swollen and his eyes were flecked with blood and the skin beneath was inflamed with blots tinged violet. The wife of the separated elderly couple was helped but quickly left to find her husband. Two medics carried in Pace student Michael Doctor. He only now emerged from unconsciousness.

High school senior Barry Cohen had one eye bashed in. He also could not recall anything between being struck and being carried into Trinity. Young people were now, a reporter noted, stuffing aisle after aisle with "broken teeth, broken noses, and bloodied heads," sitting, waiting, "stunned, crying, and cursing."

In the streets, Yale Law grad Frank Nestor finally got to his feet. Still more strikes hit him—blows to the side, to the groin. He got loose and ran, spitting blood. His colleague could not find a cop to help and hurried back to Broadway. Nestor was gone and "the crowd was in a state of turmoil."

A *Newsday* reporter saw a girl spit in the eye of a hardhat. The hardhat pushed her down subway stairs. A girl screamed at cops, "Pigs, pigs, fascist pigs!" A workman yelled, "Communists!" The newsman later, it appears, spoke with one of the first hardhats at the plaza, the big man with the iron cross on his helmet. The hardhat said, "It's about time the Silent Majority made some noise."

On Exchange Place, about forty students were chased and attacked by hardhats. A girl tried to help her boyfriend and she was "knocked down and then trampled."

A block east, at around the same time, a young finance clerk had his peace button torn off and was flattened.

"Stop it!" someone yelled. "You will kill him."

Two blocks west of Wall Street's plaza, from the thirty-second floor, stockbroker Edward Shufro watched through binoculars. He told the *Times* that he saw two men in gray suits "directing the construction workers with hand motions."

The police, however, struggled to control the "hostile" hardhats because the workmen were "leaderless," Chief Morgan reported. His men were also "vastly outnumbered" by the "massive counter force." Chief Pfaffmann was shocked by the hardhat turnout and their rage. "Totally unexpected," he reported internally. He saw a "spontaneous" horde that came from all directions, riled up with "patriotic fervor." The counterprotestors would scatter, he said, only for word to crackle over the radio of trouble elsewhere.

Victims were being carried beneath the stone archway at 20 Exchange Place, a Depression-era skyscraper that once had the largest telephone exchange and the largest pneumatic tube system in the world. Suddenly, these elite buildings, their grand lobbies, were locking doors and becoming makeshift shelters.

A block uptown, on the southern side of Wall Street, a student with a long doughy face, filming hardhats with his small Super-8 camera, was mobbed and beaten. The workmen disappeared. A cop escorted the bloody boy from the horde.

Charles Thompson, who was born in the early 1890s, found refuge inside one Wall Street lobby. Cops asked if he wanted to go to the hospital. He said no. He wanted to find his wife. But his wife found him. "I was in shock" at first sight of him, she said. He was banged up but okay. She had only lost a shoe.

As anarchy seemed to spread still more, Collette McGovern watched out of an eighth-floor window on Wall Street, three blocks east of Federal Hall. "My stomach sickened at the sight of two-hundred-pound brawny helmeted construction workers beating up skinny under nourished hippies." It was "an appalling breakdown of law and order." She felt "officers used construction workers to do their dirty work and were glad to have it done."

"No sooner was one dispute quelled when another would arise," Inspector Schryver reported. "Many student demonstrators and their sympathetic bystanders would imprudently challenge the workers with obscene statements and gestures and the workers would respond."

Near Federal Hall, a businessman's head was gashed. A block west, still along Wall Street, John Koshel watched a hippie get beaten and said several cops saw but did nothing. Koshel, a blue-collar kid who became a lawyer, watched other cops step into a scuffle. One man, dressed like a security guard, told the police to get lost. The patrolman told him to move, or he'd be arrested.

Construction workers march carrying flags on May 8, 1970. At the margins, bystanders and businessmen joining the workmen. At the outset of the Hardhat Riot, eight hundred office workers stepped off the sidewalk and boosted the hardhats' ranks.

"It will take your club and gun to do that," the man responded.

The patrolman walked away.

For periods, the fights seemed everywhere, primal and pervasive, terrifying some, exhilarating others. Elsewhere downtown, at the same time, you heard only a faint roar, like the crowd at a baseball game heard from a stadium parking lot, and the distant sirens were the sole clue something had gone wrong. Hundreds of office workers now threaded the hardhats' lines and chanted along with them. More applauded from the sidewalk. Clerk Alfredo Fernandez thought it was "wonderful," as he cheered the hardhats for confronting the "spoiled brats who needed a long-deserved spanking."

On some roads, spectators could have mistaken the scene for the Fourth of July. Workmen paraded, belted out American ballads as flags flapped, and bystanders acclaimed them. On William Street, which was speckled with puddles from the morning rain, a group of ladies—wool coats, bouffant hair, headscarves tied over hair and under chins—applauded from the sidewalk. The men strode in their helmets and shabby canvas coats, smiling, chins protruding proudly, inhaling long drags from their cigarettes. On another block, a teenager followed hardhats. Outside a building entrance, several young men in military uniforms cheered. In another pack, a young man in a suit marched shoulder to shoulder with a pale man who had sunken eyes and welding goggles. Elsewhere, a Staten Island postal worker, who looked even younger than his 18 years, marched excitedly. Beside him, a man in an old steel helmet and dirty dungarees held a huge flag. Ahead of him, a workman with thick arms and a frayed white undershirt also marched with a big flag. Several rows back, another suit helped keep a flag aloft. It was a sudden new alliance, throughout downtown, workmen and businessmen, cheering, "U—S—A! U—S—A!"

CHAPTER 16

Violence Becomes "Contagious"

IN THE WIDER world, some one hundred thousand students protested in Sydney against Kent State and Australia's involvement in Vietnam. In West Berlin, five hundred students rallied. Many compared the Americans to the Nazis. In London, where Frank Sinatra prepped to give a charity performance, one fangirl being Princess Margaret, pig heads were dumped in front of the offices of US corporations. The front doors of the London offices of American Express, Pan American Airways, Dow Chemical, and Bank of America were painted with animal blood. Students protested in Paris over Kent State. In Tokyo, 3,500 leftist students and workers demonstrated against the United States. Thousands of students in Havana paraded in "homage" to the Kent State Four.

At Camp David, as the Hardhat Riot was under way, Richard Nixon went swimming. He tried to reach H. R. Haldeman after; no answer. He tried to reach Henry Kissinger; no answer. Nixon's family arrived at Camp David, hoping to calm him. Aides worried for him. "The very fabric of government was falling apart," Kissinger later wrote. "The Executive Branch was shell-shocked." Kissinger concluded that there was "no alternative" but to hold fast on Vietnam. Soon after, though, Kissinger confided to Arthur Schlesinger, "I have been thinking a lot about resignation." While the White House splintered after Cambodia, key figures agreed on the need for some conciliation with protestors. The Nixon administration permitted tomorrow's massive demonstration, commemorating Kent State, on the greensward south of the White House. Many presidential advisors feared tomorrow's demonstration might lead to more shooting. "A very strange feeling as the White House and DC batten down for another siege," Haldeman noted. Still, Nixon olive-branched on. The president appointed a prominent university president to advise him on campus distress. Nixon told reporters, "I recognize the profound concerns that are rending campuses today" and called for "mutual understanding." Vice President Spiro Agnew, long Nixon's pitbull, said the Kent State guardsmen might have been guilty of murder, stunning the press corps. Agnew also offered bromides, standard for anyone but Agnew, explaining that young people represented the "hope of the nation." Some 250 State Department and foreign-aid employees delivered a petition protesting the war's expansion into Cambodia.

In New York City, outside downtown, it was almost normal. NBA players were already arriving at Madison Square Garden. In midtown, a few thousand antiwar protestors peacefully paraded ten blocks from Senator Jacob Javits's office to Governor Nelson Rockefeller's office. On Fifth Avenue, a teenager with shopping bags, enjoying the day off from school, was approached by a reporter. She didn't want to give her full name. The reporter explained she "seemed embarrassed to be caught doing anything as frivolous as shopping." She assured the reporter that she was "very concerned" and had marched earlier in the week. Nearby, the midtown march had stalled traffic. Horns bleated. Protestors chanted. A red furniture truck clanged along the broken concrete and squealed to a stop before the crowd. The police ordered it forward. The young driver told a cop, "I won't start this truck up to run people down." A cop ticketed the driver. Demonstrators slapped peace stickers on the truck's metal trailer and passed around a white hat to cover his fine. He soon drove off to cheers and peace signs, waving goodbye with a fistful of dollar bills.

Nearby, at Fifty-Sixth Street and Sixth Avenue, teenagers carried a flag mounted upside down at half-staff. A construction worker "jumped" them and bruised at least one boy. At Fifty-Seventh Street and Seventh Avenue, some fifty female students marched. Signs read, END THE WAR; STOP THE KILLING. Feminist Bella Abzug stopped by. (A big personality, rarely without a big hat, she was running for Congress and would win. Her slogan, "This woman's place is in the House.")

The protestors picketed in front of the ornate Art Students League, which happened to be located across from a construction site. About forty floors above, hardhats hurled bolts, coffee, nuts, and bits of rubble at the protestors. One woman twisted her ankle dodging debris. Another student was cut on the arm. Abzug's campaign manager shuttled her to the hospital.

Meanwhile, Mayor Lindsay was not yet, it seems, aware of what was going on downtown. His administration separately reported that it would ramp up an investigation into police graft. At Gracie Mansion uptown, Lindsay carried on with meetings into midday. As the riot overwhelmed Wall Street, the police log noted that Lindsay came downtown, just north of City Hall. There, at Foley Square, a crowd of several hundred assembled for yet another antiwar rally. Speakers inveighed against the war. It was all very normal, until rumors reached the crowd of trouble near Wall Street.

At Pace College, near City Hall, students collected signatures for an antiwar petition. They had set up a table at the bottom of Pace's steps. Antiwar flyers were weighted down by bricks. Other collegians milled in the plaza as a handful of bloody students trickled back from the Financial District, limping "in pain," a professor said. There was "a lot of excited talk" about the Wall Street melee, said a Pace dean who happened by. Inside, on the third floor, a student interrupted a history class and shouted for help from anyone with first-aid experience.

Students gathered on Pace's rooftop and gazed toward Wall Street, trying to see if a riot was coming their way.

Across the roadway, inside City Hall, Deputy Mayor Dick Aurelio, Lindsay's "president maker," heard of disturbances, merely disturbances. Brass-tack and husky, with a thick mustache and thicker sideburns and big black glasses, Aurelio oversaw Lindsay's world—and in his absence, effectively the city as well. But the police did not report the worst to Aurelio. He soon would see that for himself.

◆

Hundreds of hardhats trundled uptown, chanting on, their objective unknown, even as roving packs went their own way. They swept through some side streets older than the United States, cobblestone byways so narrow the sun scarcely cracked the skyline, and there was frantic patter, crashing metal and thuds and screams, then something else behind you.

New Yorkers accustomed to staring coolly forward now minded their periphery. Onlookers stood back from clashes. Yet still they lingered, cutting in, casting prying glances, countless anxious but unable to turn away, anesthetized desk workers touching the animal.

It was not always clear who was the hunted and who was the hunter. Tribes blended. Office workers joined with hardhats. Hippies fled into the crowd. It was difficult to discern a peacenik from a shaggy civilian. And to be sure, the hardhats did not see peaceniks as innocent civilians this day, not the day they declared "enough" and "threw hands" for America.

"Quarreling and struggling became contagious," Inspector Schryver reported. "There were no well-defined lines." Chief Morgan also described the violence as "contagious." "Police personnel, regardless of rank, were involved in breaking up fights," Chief Pfaffmann reported. "Conditions were near chaotic."

Hardhats did not always meet words with violence. A local worker in his young twenties, Paul Petraro, said for "five minutes" he "heard two female students passing insulting and vile remarks" to about a dozen hardhats. "I could see the workers were angry but they never went after them."

Across from Federal Hall, a ginger-haired construction worker shimmied twenty-five feet up a lamppost, flag in hand. He glanced at the multitude and eyed the light, an orange fire globe beside an air raid siren. To mount the flag, he removed wing screws and detached the orange globe, which was about six by ten inches and made of a heavy industrial plastic. He dropped it. It hit a protestor, a boy with black-rimmed glasses and a flannel CPO jacket. The boy collapsed limp.

Patrolmen surrounded the boy. "There was a lot of screaming," 19-year-old bookkeeper Susan Huckvale said. "The kids were upset and scared." The hardhat unscrewed the large bulb from the lamppost and let it go. It struck Huckvale on the right side of her face and cut her scalp and she "bled profusely." A coworker was also cut. Several men offered their handkerchiefs to stop the bleeding. The young women ran off.

Atop the light pole, overlooking tens of thousands, the hardhat planted the flag. He might have been Joe Kelly's partner, Tommy. (Joe Kelly recalled seeing Tommy climb up a light pole on Wall Street and mount a flag "to a great round of applause" from the crowd.)

Susan Huckvale's head was still "bleeding badly." Another woman asked a cop to get her an ambulance. "I don't think we can get one. I'll find out," he said. The cop returned a minute later. "I'm sorry. We can't get one."

The girls found a taxi. But a herd of strangers surrounded the cars. The meter ticked. The driver slapped the horn. A boxy Checker cab was down the street, the "on radio call" sign half-lit. No cars moved. The driver pressed down the horn and the sound dragged on and then he let it go. The girls footed it to the hospital.

At Federal Hall, even as hardhats accumulated near the colonnade, some students refused to be scared off. Each side still cursed the other. One student chucked a metal can up at a hardhat. A workman caught the can and ripped it in half. A 15-year-old saw rocks and a cinder block thrown from the steps. Alan Waldman, a Xerox machine operator, saw a "very angry" hardhat hurl the cinder block. From the crowd, a rock struck the 15-year-old and cut his face. Police broke into the melee, swinging nightsticks. One cop hit a student in the rib cage and the kid collapsed.

Police drove a contingent of students northward along Nassau Street. The cops were now spread thin, lost in the crowd, interjected in some places, watching impassively elsewhere. One bystander said that even when cops tried to help, they were "just overwhelmed."

Nearby, a hardhat gripped a student's camera strap and began choking him with it. A high school senior, Andrew Phillips, got into an argument with a businessman and was soon jumped by hardhats. Other high schoolers darted for safety through a revolving door, only for the doorman to chase them out.

Finally, a crowd control unit arrived at Federal Hall. The bulk of the hardhats were driven southward, it seemed. The streets were still boiling over, tens of thousands, curious, scared, bloody. At 12:40, the NYPD log recorded: "No further help needed." Commanders would underreport the violence, the crowd, the prevailing sense of chaos in these minutes. It's possible some did it intentionally. It's also possible they were fed bad information. Most patrolmen were too deep in the horde to have perspective. Some cops might have also been unwilling to "rat on" the hardhats.

Five minutes later, another crowd control unit arrived from Queens. NYPD field commanders sighed relief. A thousand hardhats trooped to Water Street, at the island's southern edge. Cops trailed them. Two chiefs were told that the hardhats "broke up and returned to their work." But a third commander, Chief Morgan, noted in his internal report that after the thousand were "dispersed," they "reformed and marched up Broadway."

They were already pushing up Broadway. "U—S—A. All the way! U—S—A. All the way!" It boomed off the sheer towers, block after block of skyscrapers, as workmen filled the avenue. Spectators clustered curbside and New Yorkers flung open office windows and cheered. The first men to land on the moon had been lionized here eight months earlier. The "miracle Mets" soon after. Now these nobodies tramped up the great avenue, while tickertape drifted overhead. Someone shouted from an office window, "Good job, men." Another bystander yelled, "It's about time!" A worker later told reporters, "It was amazing, like a crowd cheering the gladiators coming into the colosseum."

Northward, more superpatriots, more hangers-on, and soon some of the same men cycling again through the plaza, which remained engulfed with colored helmets, a throng chanting nearly to the man, waving fists and flags, including ironworker Eugene Schafer, wearing his flag-adorned red helmet, gripping his big flagstaff, shouting along. Near him, a smiling cleanshaven businessman. More hardhats in flannel and overalls. A bearded angry man, tie loose off the neck. A workman, his helmet decorated with a lightning bolt, gazing bewilderedly at the crowd. At least one woman, wearing glasses, waving a small flag. A fathom back, a Scandinavian giant, blond flattop, high-rooted nose, attached earlobes, protruding chin, prominent browridge, finely dressed, beige raincoat, scowling, chanting too, as police watched from the steps above.

Ten thousand people were near Federal Hall. But at least twice that number now filled neighboring streets. Some hardhats were north of Wall Street, while the mass of men was still behind them, trekking uptown and spilling over into the plaza, though the NYPD was ignorant of most of it. The police had no bird's-eye view. No cops were deployed to building rooftops. No helicopters buzzed overhead.

It was in these minutes that the NYPD reported all-clear, even as violence broadened to more blocks. A young man made a sarcastic remark to workmen. He was punched in the stomach. A young woman was struck in the face while other men scrapped. A hardhat beat a kid for calling him a "fascist." A student demonstrator was yanked down from a building ledge and beaten. A "chunky" photographer wearing a gray suit took pictures from atop Federal Hall's steps. Stock Exchange worker Reid Menting saw a hardhat slug him. The photographer toppled backward into the crowd. Alan Waldman, the young Xerox operator, watched more than six hundred hardhats "marching briskly east." Waldman wore large mod glasses, brown slacks, a red flowered tie, a blue sport coat with a button that read: WAR IS NOT HEALTHY FOR CHILDREN AND OTHER LIVING THINGS. He stretched out his arm and gave the peace sign, and workmen surrounded him. A little guy snickered, "He's going to get it now." One workman gripped Waldman's tie and pulled it tight, steering Waldman's head like a wrestler. Waldman covered his face but strikes crushed through his guard and he was punched to the pavement, his nose bleeding, his mouth bleeding. Still more men attacked him.

"Everything happened real fast," Waldman recalled. "They were just a sea of faces."

He got free and scrambled over the hood of a gray car. The crowd parted. Workmen ran around the car. They cut him off and mobbed him again, and he took more strikes, but somehow freed himself. A small man leapt on his back and threw hooks to his face. Waldman shook him off. Waldman "took a shot in the eye and saw stars" and his legs gave out. He got kicked on the ground. He crawled for safety. He curled into a ball and waited out the blows until "somehow" the "horror" ceased, and the men melted into the masses.

The police controlled the stairs of Federal Hall, and little else. Cops engaged arbitrarily, often not at all. In the thick of the crowd, unless beside an attack, one could only know it by the shockwave—first uproar, then the flight for safety. Some brawls, however, were widely seen, as now. Five hardhats were chasing a hippie inside the plaza. At the fore of the workmen was an ironworker called "K.O. Joe."

K.O. Joe lived in East Flatbush, Brooklyn, among working-class Italians, Jews, and, more recently, blacks. Age 27, Joe had been busted in his late teens for using counterfeit bills. At the age some kids went to college, he got work as a hack driver, only to get in more trouble with the law. Since becoming a tradesman, though, he'd been clean. He spoke at a measured, ponderous pace. But now he was raging mad and, to the unknowing bystander, baleful. He had a muscular neck, a square jaw, thick black hair, and thick sideburns. Wire cutters, the big sort skyscraper workers used, were tucked in his rear pocket. His canvas coat had K.O. JOE lettered on the right chest panel. Stenciled on his metal helmet: K.O. JOE in large type across the front, his union insignia, and GOD BLESS AMERICA.

K.O. Joe jarred bystanders at first sight. Some attorneys stood on the south side of Federal Hall, fixated on him, as he chased the hippie, brushing the lawyers. The hardhats began "kicking and pushing" the hippie, attorney Kenneth Orce said. His colleague Eugene Scheiman saw the hardhats "severely beat" the kid with their fists, feet, and helmets. Another young lawyer, Lorin Weisenfeld, turned his head and saw the hippie cowering, trying to escape.

In the plaza, K.O. Joe caught the hippie and struck him within "full view" of the police on the steps, Orce said. It must have been "obvious" to police, Weisenfeld said.[1]

Community schoolteacher Andrew Lachman separately reported seeing K.O. Joe "kicking, pushing, and punching longhairs" in the middle of Wall Street. "Several police officers saw this and did nothing," Lachman added. A young law clerk, Max Chale, watched K.O. Joe repeatedly kick the youth but said cops facing the fight did nothing.

The hippie ran behind one of the lawyers, Weisenfeld. K.O. Joe shoved Weisenfeld five feet back and struck the hippie, until the boy escaped into the crowd.

Two of the lawyers found cops, to report what happened, and said that "after some hesitation, two policemen stepped forward." Weisenfeld watched patrolmen usher K.O. Joe away.

Five minutes later, the lawyer saw K.O. Joe again, on Broadway, walking freely.

The young lawyer was furious that K.O. Joe was free after all that. It wasn't even about Joe. The lawyer was mad at the anarchy, the cops' laxity.

He had witnessed an attack and identified the assailant. He had done what was right and felt compelled to see it through. So Weisenfeld approached a new patrolman. He urged the officer to arrest K.O. Joe. He said he'd file charges himself, if that's what it took. The cop escorted Weisenfeld and K.O. Joe away from the heavier crowd—a block north of Trinity, near Cedar Street and Broadway. Leonard Weil, an attorney who didn't know Weisenfeld, overheard the exchange.

"I want him arrested," Weisenfeld told the cop.

"What happened?" the officer asked.

"He struck me," Weisenfeld said. "I want him arrested."

The cop said he could not arrest K.O. Joe because he had not witnessed the assault. Weisenfeld could make a "citizen's arrest if he wanted to, but if it turned out to be a false arrest he might be liable in Civil Court," as Leonard Weil heard it. "In my opinion," Weil said, "the officer's actions were designed to discourage an arrest."

K.O. Joe and Weisenfeld were placed inside a squad car. One of the cops in the car was a 22-year-old patrolman who lived along Bay Ridge Avenue, in working-class southwest Brooklyn, near many tradesmen. Weisenfeld recounted what happened next in an affidavit. The Bay Ridge Avenue cop turned to K.O. Joe. "You should have kept going, Joe," he said.

The cop looked at Weisenfeld and asked, "You a lawyer, bud?"

"Yes," Weisenfeld said.

"What's the charges?" the cop asked.

"It is a case of assault."

"I see," the cop responded. He turned back to Joe and said, "Joe, I guess this guy's gonna complain that you hit him, right? And you're gonna file a cross-complaint, right, saying that he hit you, right?"

"Yeah, yeah," K.O. Joe replied, "that's what I'll do, right."

From the outside, the First Precinct was palazzolike. Its white stonework gleamed beside the murky East River. Inside the stationhouse, the fluorescence tinted sallow. The air was stale, unventilated, that smoky musk people were accustomed to indoors. Index fingers stabbed at typewriter keys and phones rang and cops asked questions, including the desk officer now, barking at Weisenfeld: Joe "has some rights too." The other lawyers listened but said nothing. The officer carried on. The desk officer told Weisenfeld he'd already gotten Joe detained. He said Joe could countersue. Weisenfeld let it go and left. Even this affluent white lawyer felt powerless with the police.

At Exchange Place, a Wall Street salesman noticed about one hundred bystanders "gathering" around a teenage demonstrator and a workman. The workman was the electrician who had cheered atop Federal Hall's steps a short while ago. The electrician "tore" a peace banner from the boy's hands and called him a "commie." The teenager tried to retrieve it. Someone grabbed the boy, shook him, and shouted, "You better get out of here, hippie!"

Banker Robert Bernhard happened by. He was the last Lehman descendant to serve as a firm partner. A Navy veteran in his early forties, with thin brown hair, Bernhard joined Lehman Brothers soon after graduating from Harvard Business School. On the street, well-barbered and business-suited, he tried to retrieve the banner. He elbowed the boy behind him and told the electrician, "Relax, he's only a kid. You're a grown-up. Take it easy."

Another man, wearing white overalls, grabbed the banker's collar and threw him against a telephone pole. The man clutched the banker's throat with his left hand and raised his right fist. The salesman pulled the man off the banker. The electrician, who started the fight, pulled pliers from his back pocket and gashed the salesman's head. Bystanders gasped. The salesman collapsed.

The banker, Robert Bernhard, asked a friend to call the police. He went back to help the salesman. The salesman was already rushing to the hospital. Bernhard saw hardhats "chasing the kids" on Broadway. It was, the banker said, "mass confusion."

Hundreds of hardhats chanted past the World Trade Center. Up in their aerie, ironworkers gathered at the steel's edge and drummed the naked beams with tools. The metallic clang resounded off buildings. Other men gazed down from scaffolding and derricks and rafters. A cop car crawled along at the rear of the men, its beacon revolving, blinking red. Behind, streams of tickertape lined the avenue.

Some police predicted the hardhats would return to work. Chief Taylor wagered not. He overheard men rail against Lindsay. He knew what this sort thought of the mayor. They were like Taylor's men. And the common cop was no fan of Lindsay.

Sixty feet above Chief Taylor, at Broadway and Liberty Street, Ed Hatrick gripped a beam of the rising US Steel building. Hatrick was an ironworker, midsize, mid-forties, with thinning salt-and-pepper hair below his flag-adorned helmet. He saw a "parade of construction workers" tramping up the avenue, waving flags, bellowing Americana. The image moved him. He descended and joined in.

At the same building, Robert Daub, an engineer in his late twenties with brown hair and brown eyes, decided to also follow the parading hardhats. "I knew nothing about the parade and was curious," he said. "I did not have permission to leave my job and felt I wouldn't be missed."

Some hardhats glimpsed the half-built Twin Towers. All marched on. Soon they were shouting, "Get Lindsay! . . . We want Lindsay! . . . Lindsay must go!"

Chief Taylor rushed to the fore of the pack, his aide trailing him. With a walkie-talkie, Taylor ordered a crowd control squad redirected from Wall Street to City Hall. They heard static and clicking on the radio.

At Trinity Church, the injured kept coming. At least forty now sat on the cold checkered ceramic tile, filling aisles, some collapsed against pews. Medics rushed between head wounds, scar-pink welts, bent and bloody noses. Xerox man Alan Waldman, the shaggy-haired twentysomething beaten for flashing a peace sign, had his lip stitched by an NYU med student. Waldman's eyes were bruising dark. His nose still bled. Film student Harry Bolles rested against the stone wall. His NYU film camera had been worth as much as a new car. He held its remnants in his lap.

Outside Trinity's ironwork fence, bystanders and students spilled off the sidewalk. Abruptly, workmen hopped over a car and jumped a man and tossed him to the ground. Several people fell. The men knocked a middle-aged woman down. She screamed. Men were on top of her. Still she screamed. She said she felt "hysterical." Someone got her out. Her right knee was cut. Her stockings were torn. Someone found her shoe. She sat down. She couldn't stop trembling.

Cops began to clear the portion of Broadway near Trinity. A redheaded patrolman with a potbelly swung his baton at students. A lieutenant, a tall and broad officer with a gold-braid-trimmed cap, grabbed the red-headed patrolman, spoke to him privately, and dismissed him.

Nearer to the World Trade Center, Chief Taylor still followed the throng of workmen. He told his aide to call for backup once more. Again, he heard only static, to the extent he could hear anything over the clamor. Hundreds chanted on, "Lindsay must go!" Some workmen pointed their flags toward City Hall, as if to show the way.

Nearby, a half-dozen blocks north of Trinity Church, hardhats attacked a teenage demonstrator and an elderly businessman. The businessman collapsed and was kicked where he lay.

At the same intersection, Broadway and Fulton Street, a reporter saw a workman pounding a young man. A patrol car pulled up. One cop opened the door and the peacenik bolted.

"Did you get one for me?" the cop asked the construction worker.

"Yea, pal, yea," the worker replied.

Beside City Hall Park, a Pace College student waved down a patrol car. Norman Kaish was only 125 pounds and five foot five. Still, he tried to break up a fight a few blocks south. Kaish straddled both tribes. He was a student and the son of a Queens electrical contractor. He had said as much to some workmen. That he was "on their side," even as he tried to save a hippie from being beaten, and took a punch for it.

Kaish stepped to the patrol car, pointed to a pack of hardhats nearing City Hall, and told the cops, "Better request more help."

"This is nothing," one policeman replied. "You should have seen what happened on Wall Street a little while ago." The cop smiled and drove off.

A few blocks south, Chief Taylor's radio calls still met static. He ran to get ahead of the horde. He worried that City Hall remained unprepared. The hardhats continued up Broadway. Bystanders hugged the sidewalk. The yellow sedans did not honk for the workmen to make way. Taylor was panting. He stopped, bent down, palmed his knees. The World Trade Center's North Tower loomed behind him. Atop it, a red and white crane lifted a steel beam. The beam floated upward and soon was lost to the sky. In the street, Taylor stared at the workmen. He understood them. The cops had battled hippies all week. The hardhats were hardly the only ones pissed off at the kids who wreaked havoc citywide. But this was out of hand. Hardhats were now near federal and local courthouses, municipal buildings, City Hall. The police hadn't put down the riot on Wall Street. The chief now worried it was too late.

| "We've Lost Control!"

THE ELMS HAD leafed early and were damp from the morning rain. Sunlight winked between branches. The first hardhats assembled beneath the tree canopy. It was a quarter to one. Some men still shouldered American flags. Some still boomed "U—S—A!" Some still waved their fists in the wind.

Other men milled about on cracked paving stones. One hardhat kicked up divots in the grass, staring at the dirt, agitated. Another rubbed his knuckles on his undershirt.

Across the park, nearly two blocks away, a cordon of cops guarded the entrance to City Hall. The regular detail at the mayor's office included ten patrolmen and one sergeant, though one record logged upward of nineteen cops on-site. The policemen had helmets and wood billy clubs and holstered pistols and formed a skirmish line across the width of the bone-white stairs.

Abruptly, ten to twenty hardhats charged toward the police. They ran through the park, scaled the fence, rushed up the stairs. Cops collected into a skirmish line. Yellow and blue helmets collided and the police held the line, such as it was. The workmen retreated. Officials were encouraged. "I was assured that the police had everything under control," recalled Deputy Mayor Dick Aurelio, who sat on the second floor inside, commanding City Hall in John Lindsay's absence. They did not know what was coming.

Men shouted, "Hey, hey, whattya say? We support the USA!" Hundreds arrived at City Hall Park. Chief Taylor neared them. He saw patrolmen arranging wooden barricades and exhaled. Backup must be en route—any minute now.

As the mass coalesced, men's eyes were trained on City Hall. Shouting persisted: "Where's Lindsay? . . . Lindsay's a rat! . . . We want Lindsay! We want Lindsay!"

At five minutes to one, the NYPD log recorded: "Large number of construction workers heading north on Bdway. Heading for City Hall." An NYPD operations officer warned City Hall.

In the park, Chief Taylor stepped onto a wooden bench and told the workmen that City Hall's grounds were forbidden.

"Listen to the lieutenant!" someone yelled.

Somebody else called the men a "disorderly mob."

"On to City Hall!" yelled one hardhat. Then another.

Taylor overtook the workmen at the north end of the park. He glanced around the periphery. Still no backup.

On the steps, police re-formed ranks. Six to ten mounted police arrived. They wore glossy blue helmets and shiny black boots and hailed from a NYPD stable on West Twelfth Street, just south of a "no-man's-land of grimy warehouses and butcher shops," as the *Times* described the Meatpacking District at this time. The mounted police were deployed along the north side of the fence, between the hardhats and City Hall's plaza. The broad horses whirled toward the surging men, their hooves clapping pavement, their tails swaying with an even calm, as cops gripped the reins tightly.

Chief Taylor ordered a captain to hold the line.

The hardhats were again five hundred strong. Still, they balked at the cops' resolve. They hadn't come to fight their own kind.

Electrical salesman Bob Barber remained with the men. He had helped hold a flag aloft for the past hour.

A construction worker pointed to City Hall's rooftop. They noticed the flags at half-staff. More men pointed their index fingers toward the cupola.

"Put the flag at full mast!" someone yelled.

"Raise our flag! Raise our flag!" the hardhats chanted.

The young engineer Robert Daub had intended to only "observe" what was going on. Now he too chanted for the flag to rise.

A 60-year-old city clerk, eating lunch on a park bench, saw about twenty hippies and "so-called students" near the workmen. Their antiwar slogans became "some of the most vulgar profanity you can imagine." They "insulted the mothers of the policemen and the counterprotestors." The patrolmen exhibited "great restraint." The hardhats nearby likely did not notice the taunts. They were fixated on City Hall. More workmen bisected the park. The chanting spread: "Raise our flag! Raise our flag!"

Construction workers demand Mayor Lindsay raise the flag atop City Hall. The flag was lowered to half-staff to commemorate Kent State. (Librado Romero/The New York Times/ Redux)

Up ahead in the plaza, hardhats shoved aside two rows of wooden barricades. City Hall's iron doors were slammed shut. Construction workers sprinted toward the patrolmen atop the steps.

There was an absence of sirens. An absence of backup. A new NYPD head-quarters was being built within eyeshot of City Hall. It was to be rectangular and brutalist, like so many new eyesores of the era. The NYPD's current headquarters remained in Little Italy. It was a sight, classical, with arched doorways flanked by stone lions and massive Corinthian columns, its original cornerstone laid in 1901 by Teddy Roosevelt, a former police commissioner.

That headquarters was less than a mile uptown. But still no reinforcements. The only visible force deployed remained on the steps. Roughly ten to twenty cops in close ranks, guessed Martin Boland, a Pace College security guard. Boland was middle-aged and average size. His station happened to overlook City Hall. The large roadway separating Pace from City Hall, Park Row, was split by a partial sidewalk and fencing. Park Row fed uptown and downtown traffic as well as the ramp to the Brooklyn Bridge, where traffic into the city was stalled beneath the web of steel cables.

The guard saw thousands gravitating around City Hall. At the center, he estimated as many as a thousand hardhats. He heard the shouting. As the horde heaved forward, he wondered if he should do something.

Near the guard, outside Pace's plate-glass doors, students stared across the roadway.

The security guard was stationed at the fore of Pace's new indoor complex, which consumed about two city blocks. It was steel-framed with big windows, an airy lobby, a courtyard. At the rear half, there was a tower of glass and concrete rectangles. Vice President Hubert Humphrey had attended its unveiling last year, which elicited an antiwar march. The complex had replaced one of the first skyscrapers, the New York Tribune Building. The *Tribune*'s original masonry headquarters had been overrun during the 1863 Draft Riots.

The Civil War still loomed in the American mind in 1970. That year, more than ten million tourists visited its five main battlefields, from Gettysburg to Shiloh. Tourism at the same battlefields would decrease by two-thirds nearly a half-century later, despite the nation's population increasing by about 125 million. It had been only in 1956, fourteen years earlier, that the last documented Civil War veteran died, a New York–born man named Albert Henry Woolson. And now another riot, another divisive draft, another "rich man's war, poor man's fight."

The security guard had seen plenty of students, the militant kids, rally wildly over this war. He had seen worse on the tube. Kent State was at the back of most people's thoughts. But this was the first time the mayhem felt viscerally ominous. This mob was near. They were not college kids. They were the roughneck sort. And they seemed about to invade City Hall. He was unaware that these men had already overrun the Financial District, and that they had bum-rushed students. But many Pace students were hippies. The security guard knew the sight of fire nearing gasoline. The guard, with the assistance of a few faculty, snaked a metal chain through the handles of five of the six sets of doors and locked them. He sought to protect the property and the students inside. He didn't imagine that students might need those doors to escape.

At Foley Square, only a few blocks north of the mayor's office, government workers continued rallying against the war. Later, to excuse their meek presence in the Financial District, the NYPD logged that the mayor requested "a heavy police detail, including plenty of high-ranking officers," at Foley Square at a quarter past one. Another record pegged the time at half past one. It was clearly after the mob had reached City Hall.

By one o'clock, not only did NYPD command know that "large numbers of construction workers" were "heading for City Hall," but word had reached Foley Square too. In the square, Lieutenant Jerome Simon overheard some demonstrators discussing trouble at the mayor's office nearby. Lieutenant Simon, a onetime machinist who had seen all kinds of unrest in his decades on the force, was alarmed enough to leave his post at the square and "check the situation."

At about the same time, a 26-year-old city worker, James Stiles, also heard "people talking about the construction workers fighting with the peace demonstrators." Stiles decided to see for himself too.

Manhattan borough president Percy Sutton, a trailblazing black politician in the city, and the deputy borough president, Leonard Cohen, left the rally prematurely as well.

In the square, speakers spoke of wasted lives, wasted billions. Suddenly, scores of students ran into the square. Someone shouted: "The construction workers are beating up the demonstrators in Wall Street and at City Hall!" From the podium, the official hushed the crowd.

At about the same time, John Lindsay came, spoke, and left. Chief Pfaffmann recorded that when he arrived at the square at 1:40, Lindsay had "already appeared, spoken, and departed for Gracie mansion."

After the riot, a newswire reported Lindsay's presence at Foley Square but wrote that he had been "unaware of the developments" at that time. The *Times* and other outlets reported that Lindsay had been at Gracie Mansion during the riot, and in constant contact with staff by telephone. In fact, the mayor spoke as the riot enveloped downtown, and instead of driving into the storm, only a few blocks south, Lindsay withdrew uptown to his residence.

The Manhattan political chiefs, Sutton and Cohen, could only get twenty feet from City Hall's steps. The crowd was too vast. Too impenetrable.

Deputy Borough President Leonard Cohen, a native New Yorker and a graduate of City College and Columbia Law School, was middle-aged, with a wide smile and large brow. He had worked to take down one of the last Tammany bosses, before rising through the city machine himself.

Now he stared, openmouthed, pushing up on his toes. He saw a "large mass of men," about five to six hundred, with yellow hard hats and American flags, pushing against the front of City Hall, "shouting slogans and chanting angrily." The men drove forward and reached the foot of the steps. Suddenly, they surged up the stairs "as if to storm City Hall itself."

The hardhats splashed over the steps and buffeted against the police like waves battering a hull. This was the oldest city hall in the nation. It had austere portraits of men long dead and Corinthian columns and a grand marble staircase. But the workspaces were mostly a dimly lit warren of alcoves and small rooms overstuffed with people. An exception was John Lindsay's office, at a corner of the second floor, which was palatial, sunlit through frosted glass, and empty today. On one wall hung a picture of Fiorello La Guardia. La Guardia had led the city through much of the Great Depression and World War Two. He had been a progressive Republican like Lindsay. But La Guardia had been more than a foot shorter and bullishly charismatic and a man who leapt into political trenches. Lindsay tended to appear aloof, often summoning a vacant smile. Sometimes he twirled a small sword-like letter opener as he listened to staff in meetings and his attention seemed elsewhere, until he'd interrupt an aide midsentence. The inner man was a mystery even to his staff and the newsmen who studied him daily. Lindsay was the sort of politician who needed the people to love him but didn't really *need* people. Many of his aides were true believers, however. They were blinded by his star, but they rightly, and deeply, admired his principles. Lindsay was a man of principle. And even if these blue collars felt that Lindsay, and the uptown left he embodied, ignored or condescended them—blacks and Puerto Ricans did not, and that was no mean feat of conscience. "Lindsay came into the office believing that the establishment had created walls," said aide Jay Kriegel, "and it was a closed system and minorities had been shut out of the system." That focus, unlike with RFK, often limited Lindsay's ability to consider a wider lens. Still, Lindsay's cosmopolitan crowd aside, at least he was especially attentive to blacks, who most needed and deserved it. Journalist Noel Parmentel perhaps put it best, in the context of the promiscuous comparisons between Jack Kennedy and John Lindsay.

"Jack Kennedy was not in John Lindsay's class," Parmentel said. "John Lindsay is not in Jack Kennedy's league." Both men attracted a common sort of political aide—young, serious, shrewd, striving, including a few whiz kids. "The City Hall of John V. Lindsay," wrote one *Times* man early in the mayor's tenure, "is a busy, often congested place, peopled by serious young men who hurry through the corridors, clutching papers in both hands and leggy girls who scurry about brushing back their long straight hair with ink-stained hands." Deputy Mayor Dick Aurelio dressed young, wide ties and pink and purple shirts, but he was older, a practical man, a onetime newsman. His office was near Lindsay's. Aurelio heard the noise and stood and gazed out the window and realized how bad it really was.

The police rushed to form "solid ranks," two rows deep. They shifted their weight frontward and some held their clubs across their chest. The workmen rammed them and cops absorbed it and gave only inches and tried to give no more. Below, cops dashed across the plaza. Some yanked iron barricades along the pavement. They hoped to barricade off the hindmost.

"Raise the flag! Raise the flag!" Other men shouted, "Raise our flag!"

Chief Taylor asked Aurelio to placate the hardhats and raise the flag, at least until reinforcements arrived. Aurelio refused, according to the police.

At Chief Taylor's request, Aurelio met with a four-man delegation of hardhats. The construction workers outside "became increasingly impatient and agitated." Still more "climbed the fence and spilled into City Hall plaza."

A mayoral aide tried to calm the workers through a bullhorn. On the steps, a policeman spoke with several hardhats and took notes. One was recorded as T. Owens, likely steamfitter Thomas Owens, who worked at the Twin Towers site. An unidentified hardhat told the cop, "We want the flag up."

"Our flag, all the way up, the American flag at full-mast," Owens said. "'Cause Lindsay came out with some pretty terrible anti-American statements claiming the boys in Canada are really the true heroes of the war." Owens continued, "This is the Silent Majority, but they are not silent anymore. They can't take these hippies anymore, because they don't speak our language. We built this city. The steamfitters. The elevator construction workers. All of us. We built every building that they want to burn down."

The workmen continued chanting for the mayor's downfall and for the flag to be raised. They consumed City Hall's steps and pushed frontward, inching closer to the doors. Other hardhats assembled at the rear, booming along. There, deep in the crowd, 18-year-old Joseph de Chaves noticed a cluster of hardhats giving him "dirty looks." He walked away. He heard, "Get him!" Fists struck him and felled him. The horde passed over him. The men disappeared. De Chaves was attacked, he wagered, because of his shoulder-length hair.

On the lower stairs, young mayoral staffer Donald Evans stood with a few reporters. "Stop acting juvenile!" he told some workmen. A hardhat swung at him. "I stepped back quickly and he missed," Evans said. Some newsmen thought Evans was hit in the face. "He never touched me," Evans later told the cops.

Several steps above Evans, cops glanced sidelong. No backup in sight. Central command knew that a "substantial sized unformed detail" remained deployed a few blocks north at Foley Square, where it was peaceful.

From within the crowd, Chief Taylor shouted into a walkie-talkie.

Over the police radio: Mobilize motorcycle units citywide. The order was logged at 1:20.

The deputy mayor watched the mob and gulped. Hundreds of furious men were nearly inside City Hall, seemingly still amassing momentum. The danger felt imminent to Dick Aurelio. And the cops' indifference baffled him. "I watched [hardhats] singing, yelling, calling Lindsay all kinds of names and their fury was intense and the police were sitting there, staring at them, doing nothing," Aurelio recalled. "We had protests all the time at City Hall," he continued. "They were always permitted to go to the edge of the area where the parking was and certainly not allowed to get to the steps."

Queens powerbroker Matthew Troy weaved into the crowd on the steps. Troy was the councilman who had defied Lindsay on Moratorium Day and raised the flag over City Hall. Blunt, quick-witted, and burly, Troy had led a march supporting the Vietnam War years earlier. By his account, he warned Aurelio to place the flag at full staff to settle the crowd. He too wanted it raised. He saw the student protestors as "snotnoses." He watched hardhats demand Lindsay "raise the flag" and was "thrilled to death."

The outlying crowd now included two leaders of a small right-wing weekly newspaper based near City Hall Park, the *New York Graphic*— publisher Ralph Clifford, a 42-year-old portly Korean War veteran, and a young assistant editor, Jeff Smith.

Assistant Chief Inspector Fred Kowsky, who led the Safety Emergency Division, had heard the calls for assistance on his walkie-talkie (Kowsky had led the police detail ordered to evict students from Low Library during the Columbia occupation). He arrived and saw Chief Taylor manning the front of City Hall's steps. Taylor was trying to calm the hardhats. Kowsky cut through the crowd to Taylor. The chiefs huddled. Kowsky soon entered City Hall.

"There was a tremendous amount of noise and the situation had all the earmarks of a very disorderly condition, which could escalate into much greater proportions," Kowsky later recorded. "I deemed [this] to be a very critical situation based on experience from the past and my own observation at the moment that this crowd offered every possibility of invading City Hall."

Inside City Hall, beneath the rotunda's soaring dome, the deputy mayor jabbed his finger at Chief Kowsky. "How the hell did this get out of control?" Dick Aurelio yelled. "Why aren't they protecting the door?"

"We've lost control!" the chief blurted out. "We've lost control!"

Kowsky's face was flushed red. Sweat traced his cheeks. He urged Aurelio to have the flag raised.

Aurelio didn't want the mob pacified this way. He believed the flag should be lowered for the Kent State Four. Still, he was no ideologue. He glanced at Kowsky. Thought about the "fury" outside. "Such a frenzy out there, right before my eyes." He worried about the "headlines of City Hall taken over by protestors." Aurelio recalled that it "unnerved me and it panicked Kowsky. He wasn't his usual self. He was sort of a calm guy who took everything in stride. But it was a very riotous scene."

Aurelio sighed, "Raise the flag."

From the street, the crowd gazed upward and stilled. A middle-aged postman was atop City Hall's copper-covered rooftop. He neared the white limestone tower. Beneath the cupola and its statue of Lady Justice, he hoisted the American flag.

The crowd cheered and whistled. Men tossed their helmets skyward and waved their flags like eager Boy Scouts. Soon the masses sang "The Star-Spangled Banner" and "God Bless America."

"It damn near put a lump in your throat," said Joe Kelly, the Twin Towers elevator mechanic. "It was really something. I could never say I was sorry I was there." In his gut, he had a "very proud feeling," and "if I live to be one hundred, I don't think I'll ever see anything quite like that again."

The Manhattan deputy borough president was not proud. "While the national anthem was being sung," Leonard Cohen said, hardhats "mingled with the police on the steps." City worker James Stiles stood atop a concrete divider at the Brooklyn Bridge ramp. He saw some cops "throw their hats into the air" with the workmen.

Construction workers spilled off the steps and celebrated in the plaza.

"Okay, the flag is raised," shouted a middle-aged man in a suit. "Let's go get our pay checks and get drunk."

The crowd was unresponsive. Countless continued singing.

Abruptly, there was rhythmic shouting. Leonard Cohen was close enough to hear it. A pack of students were now trying to drown out the American song with antiwar chants. Near Cohen, the crowd became "tense."

Lawyer Michael Belknap heard the uproar on his walk back from Beekman Hospital. He had looked in on the man who desecrated the flag at the Washington statue, trying to be charitable. Now he was nearing the masses around City Hall.

Elsewhere, students began arguing with construction workers, until someone swung a fist. Hardhats hit a young man and tried to pull him over the iron railing that encircled the park. Pace physics instructor Melvyn Oremland grabbed the boy's arm and tried to pull him back. A businessman helped. They pulled him free, only for the businessman to begin choking the boy. Oremland shoved the businessman back.

On the west side of the steps, a man in a "placid business suit" tried to film the scene and was attacked by some workmen, who quickly fled. The man with the camera was bleeding. With a companion, he found some cops. He asked to press charges.

"We can't do anything at the present time," a cop replied. "There are five thousand fights and we can't handle them."

In the plaza outside Pace, about fifty students chanted the familiar: "One-two-three-four. We don't want your fuckin' war!"

Back near City Hall, about ten students "ran into the construction workers and attempted to take one of the American flags," said James Martin, who worked for public broadcaster WNYC and was at the edge of the plaza. The students failed to grab a flag. Martin watched them flee across Park Row to Pace.

"Let's get the kids," one hardhat said.

From the flat rooftop of Pace's new building, students draped a "huge" banner constructed from white bedsheets. Black lettering read: VIETNAM? CAMBODIA? KENT STATE? WHAT NEXT?

"Get the hippies!"

Fifty to seventy-five workmen plowed through the crowd, entered the roadway, leapt over the iron divider, and blitzed Pace. A school dean, Walter Joyce, was pushed aside as a "maze of people" sprinted past him.

"The construction workers are coming!" a student shouted in front of Pace.

"Get inside!" cried another.

Students turned, stumbled, pushed frantically. They were "running in panic and screaming for everyone to get off the street," said Pace junior Michael Seltzer.

"They're coming!" yelled a student inside the lobby.

It was a "a mob scene," said lawyer Michael Belknap, who also shouted for students to get inside.

People were "screaming and running from City Hall," said Ed Tilson, a young civil engineer. Tilson looked up at Pace's front rooftop. He saw a banner that read, 30,000 IN VIET NAM, 4 AT KENT STATE. Another student waved a Vietcong flag.

Up high, in Pace's tower, a peace banner billowed in the wind. Below it, a small banner hung in a window read: WAR KILLS. Ahead of the tower was the four-story frontage, a modern steel-framed glass encasement. More students gathered there, on its rooftop, holding antiwar banners, at least one Vietcong flag. As the charging workmen neared the entrance below, students used their elevated position to hurl rocks, bottles, and brickbats at them (in other words, the collegians were tossing rocks from a glass house).

In the street, workmen dodged the rubble and debris. Some hardhats hurled it back.

"Kill those long-haired bastards!" a worker shouted near Pace's entrance.

Students yanked at the doors. But the 110-foot entrance was reduced to one set of doors. Students bottlenecked at the doorway. The *Daily News* described them as "terrified."

It was "chaos, a panic, like a cattle stampede," said Pace graduate student Tom Norton. Norton was safely inside but his friend Stew Litvin was trapped with the students at the doors.

Hardhats reached the students. Litvin was blindsided and punched in the face and pushed to the pavement. "I tried to curl up into a ball to protect myself," he said. He was stomped on. "I then got to my hands and knees and began to crawl away."

A foot struck the left side of Stephen Rich's cheek. Earlier, Rich had escaped okay from the Wall Street turmoil. He was now on the ground, his jaw displaced, taking kicks. A medic dragged him to safety.

One Pace assistant professor, Ivan Rohr, held the glass door open and tried to help students inside.

"Call the police!" Rohr shouted inside.

"It was like a panic breaking from a theater fire," Rohr recalled. "Girls tripped and fell in the doorway, screaming. The construction workers began to smash at the students."

"Leave them alone!" Rohr yelled at the workmen.

Another Pace faculty member tried to funnel youths to safety. He saw workers "beat students with fists, feet, pipes, wire cutters," in Pace's plaza. Rohr also saw a man clasping an iron pipe taped at both ends. He saw another hardhat wielding a foot-long wire cutter. The workmen "were provoked" by students and let loose, said John Arnold, a commuter student and a Goodyear salesman, only for hardhats to attack "anyone who got in their way."

Adman Jack Corwin—a small man with bushy eyebrows, a brown mustache, and dark tortoiseshell glasses—watched the Pace students on the rooftop and the hardhats rushing the kids at the entrance and "feared the construction workers would get to the roof and throw the students off."

Outside in the plaza, five construction workers knocked a student to the pavement. The security guard clasped one of the workmen by the neck. He tried to drag the hardhat away, only to be punched to the concrete. He was struck still more. He yelled that he was "not for any group." The men disappeared.

Grad student Tom Norton tried to pull students through the doorway. A fist struck the right side of his jaw. He grappled with the workman and both went to the ground. "I felt like I was fighting for my life," he said. Someone "kept kicking at me." Other students broke in and "rolled the construction worker off and stomped the hell out of him."

A student, wearing a peace armband, was semiconscious, and being carried to Pace by two peers. Two other students tried to help Stew Litvin to safety. Dozens of students rushed into the complex and up the stairs. But plenty of college kids remained stuck outside. Some seemed too scared to move.

A few floors above, inside Pace, "everyone started pulling chairs out of classrooms to barricade the elevators," junior Michael Seltzer said. "We pulled fire extinguishers from the wall and locked ourselves in a classroom."

City worker James Stiles—still perched near the Brooklyn Bridge onramp—saw some ten fights occur, uninterrupted, near police.

Lieutenant Simon was among the cops atop City Hall's steps. He had seen the hardhats "charge" at Pace. The lieutenant worried City Hall could be flanked by them. He told Chief Kowsky as much. Kowsky told him to get another captain to guard City Hall's rear.

At Pace, the melee continued unpoliced. Pace VP Stanley Mullin watched from across the street. He saw one student "thrown to the ground" and a hardhat jab him with his flagpole. Another workman swung a tool with a "hammerlike stroke" down at the boy.

Adman Jack Corwin ran toward a fortysomething Pace faculty member, who was ushering students inside. Corwin begged, "Get the students off the roof."

"They have a right to demonstrate too," the faculty member replied.

Corwin retreated into Park Row, the large roadway between Pace and City Hall. He watched students continue chucking rubble at the hardhats.

Fighting spread beyond the plaza and into the edges of the crowd, near City Hall.

"I saw one construction worker kicked in the balls," Corwin said. "He fell down and turned completely white. Three construction workers tried to help him, with stones flying all over the place." Nearby, one student fought with three other workmen. A cop intervened at "a critical moment," Corwin said.

"Break it up!" the cop yelled. "Cut it out!"

Corwin turned his head and "saw several students beating a construction worker as badly as the other construction workers had been beating students."

Ed Tilson, the young civil engineer, thought he saw one student knocked out and another student in trouble as hardhats mobbed him.

"You will kill him!" Tilson shouted.

Tilson grabbed one of the hardhats by the neck and was punched. Men ganged up on him and knocked him over. He yelled that he was on no one's side, and it worked here too. The pack stormed off. It was "hardhats and a motley crew of disgruntled office workers," reported a Pace finance professor. He saw students flashing their middle finger at hardhats. Soon, beside him, "fists were swinging and everybody was hitting everybody." The only cops he saw were near City Hall. "I couldn't believe what was happening." He "was engulfed" in the melee. It was "turmoil."

Workmen picked up two-by-fours that had been left by a contractor and hurled the wood at Pace's glass doors and windows. The security guard tried to shield himself. The lumber, the debris, battered his forehead and his left wrist.

A young man, in his mid-twenties with sideburns and a mustache, joined with the hardhats. He was a City College student. He too tossed rocks at Pace. Physics instructor Melvyn Oremland asked the rock-thrower to stop. The rock-thrower replied, "These damned kids have closed me out of my college! "

The finance professor cowered behind a parked car. Even so, he was hit in the head by debris. He ran to the hospital.

A lawyer watched, slack-jawed, as hardhats were "beating young men on the plaza in front of Pace College within clear view of a group of police officers and approximately thirty patrolmen." He howled at a captain to arrest attackers. The captain "refused."

On Pace's rooftop, students lost their grip on the large antiwar banner. It fell to the ground. Hardhats grabbed it, tore at it, set it afire. It burned below a copper sculpture titled "Brotherhood of Man."

"IT WAS CLEARLY a class thing," Susan Harmon said. "They didn't bother about me." Harmon, a city childcare worker in her late twenties, was thin and had brown hair and was tall and "gentle-looking." She had seen Mayor Lindsay speak in Foley Square and noticed cops leaving. She followed. She listened to the mass sing patriotic standards. She watched people run across the roadway toward Pace and also heard, "Get the hippies!"

Now she walked the fence line of the plaza. A young man was prostrated on the pavement. Five construction workers were beating him. A short workman raised a long metal bolt clipper above the kid's head. She grabbed the man by the arm. He shook her off. She grasped the back of his jacket collar and yelled, "Stop it!" She tried and tried, shouting still, scolding them like "a mother talking to unruly boys," as she put it.

"Let go of me, bitch," the man shouted.

"No!" she shouted.

Three men shoved her against a parked car. They struck her several times. Although, she reported to the police, "they were not really trying to hurt me."

Another hardhat gripped her arm. "Get out of here, lady."

"No! No! No! I don't want to."

She pushed him away. He manhandled her and pulled her to the edge of the crowd and let her go.

She walked along the margins of the horde. "I had no cuts. There was no blood. I was just upset, angry, and excited."

About five hardhats stalked her.

"So, you want to be treated equal, huh?" one man bullied.

She kept walking.

Several workmen kicked her in the backside.

She walked over to the fence on Park Row. A young man hung on the fence, yapping at the men like a small dog, "I'm not afraid of you guys!"

"Shut up," she told him, "or you are going to get other people hurt."

He shut up. She was left alone after that. She returned to her office. There she sat. "I began to ache and cry. I was afraid my ribs were broken. I was scared."

Cops, here and there, did move fast to break up fights. Some sought to preempt the worst. There were officers who minded hardhats as they paraded, scrutinizing workmen's eye drift. But it was clear, already, that too many did too little. The cops had clubbed antiwar radicals yesterday for blocking traffic. But they had not clubbed the workmen for besieging City Hall. Now, dozens of cops coldly watched hardhats pummel hippies near Pace. Few cops were seen leaping into battles to save students. No hardhats were being dragged into paddy wagons. No one had yet seen a hardhat cuffed.

Southward, along Broadway, more hardhats were still marching toward City Hall, some with beers in one hand and tools in the other, chanting along.

A gray-haired officer stepped into their ranks and confiscated a big wrench from a hardhat. Close by, John Koshel saw a hippie give a peace sign to workmen. A half-dozen swarmed the hippie—soon punching him, kicking him, battering him with tools.

"About four police ambled up from some fifty feet away" but "took no action," recounted Koshel, the blue-collar kid who'd become a lawyer. He watched the hardhats push on, undeterred. He soon saw a longhaired student flat on the ground. One "well-dressed woman standing on the curb" said something that "provoked" other hardhats, Koshel continued. Some men sprayed her with beer. A cop on a scooter revved up his engine, sped near, but did no more. "This is the frightening aspect," added Koshel, a onetime Army infantry veteran. "The construction workers were just running wild."

By Pace, Ray Randolph arrived at the fringes of the melee. "I heard all this noise," he recalled. He had seen Mayor Lindsay speak at Foley Square. He'd heard talk of "trouble at City Hall" and "worked my way through the crowd."

A fresh-faced graduate of the University of Pennsylvania's law school, Randolph was a few inches taller than average, thin, blue-eyed, with wavy light brown hair that highlighted red. He had grown up in New Jersey farm country, the son of a homemaker and a union machinist, a "lower-middle-class" world, he said. He was unaware, in his childhood, that he had an-cestral ties to Plymouth Colony via one Nathaniel FitzRandolph, a founder of Princeton University. His family's wealth had been washed out in the

Depression. Randolph now lived in an apartment in Brooklyn Heights, where he occasionally came across Norman Mailer. Sometimes, after work, he crowded into McSorley's in the Village with colleagues. McSorley's was a wood-doored taproom that lacked air-conditioning in the summer and was warmed by an antique iron potbellied stove in the winter. Its two rooms were cramped with the stink of men and stale beer and loud voices cured by cigarettes. Yet one could get two ales for fifty cents, nosh on liederkranz and onion, and revel in dim nostalgia. It was famously the city's oldest pub. And it still refused to serve women (but soon, in August 1970, the municipal government and a federal court would force McSorley's to liberate).

Ray Randolph's focus that summer was his chance at one of the strongholds of American law. He was clerking at the federal courthouse beside Foley Square, the prestigious US Second Circuit appellate court, where he worked under the particularly prestigious Judge Henry Friendly (future Supreme Court chief justice John Roberts also clerked for Judge Friendly as a young man). Randolph would go on to become known as A. Raymond Randolph, a judge on the US Court of Appeals in DC, the second-most-influential court in the country.

Now, though, young Randolph watched and wanted to help somehow. He saw a sergeant with the cops on Park Row. He asked the sergeant if he was going to "take any action to stop the commotion in front of Pace." The sergeant ignored him.

At about that time, nearer to Pace, a young employee at the city's human rights commission happened upon the melee. Samuel Sherman watched about five students get punched, kicked, knocked down, and beaten still. This was "Nazi stuff," Sherman yelled at a workman his age. The workman said he would "kick my ass," Sherman recalled, if he didn't back off. Sherman backed off.

Nearby, a student at Brandeis High School, Peter Giagni, walked into the fray and told one hardhat to leave the banner alone. Giagni was leveled. Workmen stomped him, breaking his nose, smashing his head. He squirmed to shield himself, until he moved no more.

To anyone who has been in a fight, especially when outnumbered, a minute is an eternity. Near Pace, by now, there had been some fifteen minutes of brutality with police looking on but no policing. And it was getting worse. In the buildings overlooking the street, office work nearly ceased. Rumors spread of the melee below. Workers bunched at windows. A young secretary, Ronnie Spinelli, worked on the top floor of an early skyscraper, a sixteen-story Romanesque building that had once headquartered the *Times* when the area was known as "Newspaper Row." Spinelli stared out an arched window.

She had seen the peace banner burn. She had seen students try to retrieve it and get set upon. She had seen one construction worker "stomping on" a hippie's "face and stomach."

"What upset me to the point of physical sickness was the fact that the police stood there and didn't even attempt to help the students," Spinelli wrote Pace's president several days later. "A few policemen tried to break up a fight, only after the students were already beaten up." In her view, the police were "indifferent." Most were merely "watching," standing there "like tin soldiers."

Physics instructor Melvyn Oremland walked to a boy "covered with blood" and helped him to safety. He looked around and felt a sense of "futility." He saw four or five workers with clenched fists pound a student to the ground. Oremland was taller than average, solidly built. But he stood back. He said, "I assumed I would also be beaten."

Thousands of spectators moved like erratic waves, pulled with each gasp in the crowd, or the sight of men running, or shrieks of fear. It was morbid curiosity and concern and the primitive thrill of raw violence. The center of the action often moved suddenly and mass brutality accumulated rapidly, as a leaking dam might swiftly flood, and the crowd soon followed, gawking at the violence until they feared it, sometimes fleeing one brawl to run headfirst into another. It was one thing to mind your surroundings on dark streets. This was Manhattan in 1970. But around City Hall, dayside, regular New Yorkers were caught off guard by the sheer ferocity and volume of the violence. Fear took hold of people. They fled wildly, knocking over strangers at times. Many seemed anxious about what to do, when no one does anything. It was as Hobbesian as that, in the worst pockets of the mass. Scores of onlookers kept expecting riot-ready cops to throttle the rampage. But none did. Plenty of folks missed the blood by happenstance. They were in a safe crook of the crowd, unable to see what all the yelling was about. Sometimes it crept. People heard shouting or sensed danger. Then bystanders described experiencing a sudden outburst, near them, around them, for mysterious reasons, like an electrical storm, as men's arms flailed and strangers spit red and hippies were hit in the jaw, the solar plexus, seen gasping, taking blows to the back as they ran off. Most bystanders, those beside fights or caught in them, could only see the brawl near them, unless they were in an elevated position, like the boy who climbed a lamppost or office workers crowding their windows or the cops on the steps or the students atop Pace's rooftop, tossing rubble down at the workmen, even as streetside, more hardhats still arrived and picked up rubble and hurled it back. At Pace's doorway, a group of students were still trapped outside, screaming for sanctuary. Workmen got hold of them and beat them with their fists, tools, debris, as students cried out and some fell headfirst onto the pavement, as if chopped down.

"I watched in amazement and then horror as patrolmen, and police cars and [police] scooters, stood idly by while workers severely beat two students, throwing them over the guard rail surrounding the park," said Norman Kaish, the college man and electrical contractor's son. "Other workers then kicked them while they lay helplessly on the ground. I could not believe that the police were doing nothing."

Most of the students who had been crammed together near the doorway, who had not gotten ensnared with the hardhats, were inside Pace by now. But scattered beatings and brawls persisted.

Nearby, a junior city planner, Ed Wolner, noticed about a dozen cops on the sidewalk, across Park Row from Pace. They were "in a military 'at ease' position and facing Pace" and "did absolutely nothing."

In Pace Plaza, a group of hardhats mobbed another longhair. Students gawked from inside the lobby. Spectators gathered closer. The kid was punched in the right eye and collapsed. Workmen stomped him, kicked him. He grunted pain and gasped.

Michael Belknap nudged sideways to the fore of the crowd and stepped forward. He was still several months from thirty, still idealistic, still surefooted. An associate at a prestigious law firm, Belknap looked like a scion of the Wasp establishment—six feet tall, solid, and with wispy blond hair. Workdays it was Brooks Brothers suits, a white or blue dress shirt (only white or blue), and a "regimental tie," as he put it. He no longer wanted to be a corporate lawyer. He was a Democratic candidate for the state senate. He hankered to write a novel, though he kept that much to himself.

Belknap was the son of a Chicago advertising executive. He had attended New Trier, one of the most acclaimed and prosperous public high schools in the Midwest. As student council president, he had met Martin Luther King Jr. He became a Harvard man, college and law school. Nearly a decade later, when Robert Kennedy was murdered, Belknap could not turn off the television. A few days after, on a work trip, he met with a business executive in Philadelphia. The executive said that he was "glad that little shit got killed" because "he deserved it."

"That was the point where I felt I had to do something else besides corporate law," Belknap recalled. He began to work for Hubert Humphrey and attended the '68 Democratic convention in Chicago. But Belknap did not fight in the streets. One day, as the chaos outside the convention worsened, he was in his hotel room and smelled fumes. He left to see the disorder for himself. As teargas dissipated, he happened upon a friend. Belknap asked his friend to dinner. His friend declined his invitation because "I'm going to be bailing kids out of jail." Belknap decided to become more active. He lived a few blocks north of Washington Square Park and regularly attended political meetings in the Village. He became acquainted with feminist activist Bella Abzug and friendly with a young pol representing John Lindsay's old district, Ed Koch. He served as a marshal for demonstrators on Wall Street and a reader at Trinity Church on Moratorium Day. Like Mayor Lindsay, he had traveled leftward from the moderate Republican Establishment. And it had taken him here—to ensure that a man who desecrated the flag had representation, because everyone deserves legal representation, to see an unfair fight and step forward.

The longhaired boy was still splayed on the ground, helpless. Workmen continued hammering him with kicks.

"Leave him alone!" Belknap yelled. "He's hurt!"

The hardhats backed away. Belknap stepped between them and the kid.

"Is he one of them or us?" a hardhat shouted.

"Commie kid," another replied.

"Commie bastard deserves to die!"

Belknap was hit in his right eye and floored. He was dazed, grounded, unsure who or what struck him. Kicks battered his body. He curled inward. He tried to cover his head with his hands. Boots barraged his back and face. "He's hurt!" someone yelled. His body writhed. He felt lightheaded. His vision blurred.

The men stopped battering him. They stared down. Belknap wasn't moving.

The workmen dashed off.

Beside Belknap's unconscious body, the longhair he had sought to help curled into a fetal position. Finally, someone pulled the boy along the gravelly cement, freeing him from the fray.

Belknap awoke in the street, flat on his back, confused, blinking. A white jacket was over him. There was yelling and screaming. Legs sprinted by. Young medics tended to him. Belknap could not focus clearly. He realized he had blacked out. The medics asked if he could move. He didn't feel he had a choice. They helped him inside Pace's lobby, along with the longhaired boy.

In rooms beside the lobby, students and faculty barricaded doors. Inside the registrar's office, furniture was pushed against the door. The blinds were lowered. Someone frantically, repeatedly, dialed 911.

Outside, hardhats continued bombarding Pace's entrance with debris.

Windows shattered. Plate glass crashed into the pavement.

Hardhats leapt inside the lobby.

From a distance, the deputy borough president saw hardhats attack students outside Pace. Leonard Cohen glanced back at the cops. "Police were laughing and smiling and others [were] amiably chatting together and with construction workers," Cohen swore in an affidavit. A middle-aged attorney in the crowd, Lothar Nachman, also saw police "just standing there laughing and enjoying themselves."

A young city housing administrator, Robert Smits, approached two cops nearby. "Students are getting beat up at Pace College," he said. "Why don't you go over and do something?"

"We don't have any orders to cross the street," one answered.

"If I was getting murdered, you wouldn't cross the street? What is this?!"

Fights broke out near Ray Randolph. He saw no cops close by. A pack of spectators, mostly in suits and ties, had gathered in a horseshoe formation. He walked over. Three hardhats were about to gang up on a student. "I thought I could help the kids," he said. Randolph had wrestled in college and high school. "I rushed in."

He took about three steps and was struck in the groin. A hardhat lifted a steel pipe overhead and swung it like a tomahawk. Randolph glanced up before realizing what it was. The pipe smashed his eye socket.

Randolph collapsed. He still got a good look at one attacker, who wore a white helmet and was a few years older, a few inches taller, six feet and solid, with sandy hair and a red-checkered shirt. But he was gone as fast as he'd come. Randolph stood himself up. The pipe had left a vertical indentation in his face across his right eye, which was already bloodshot, the skin around inflaming. The wound got "pretty ugly, pretty quickly," he recalled. His vision blurred and he felt dizzy. He steadied himself, before circulating through the crowd, searching for that red-checkered shirt with his good eye, hoping "to find that son of a bitch."

"They're coming after us!" some kid yelled from Pace's rooftop. A dozen more hardhats "stormed" Pace's lobby. Workmen rushed up the stairs inside. Other hardhats pulverized students. It seemed like workmen were "swarming in all directions" and "swinging at everybody," said William Collinson, a Pace administrator. One hardhat struck students with an iron pipe. Some bashed students with metal wastebaskets. They tossed tables and chairs. More windows shattered. Young people cried out.

A hippie crashed through an outer window. Nursing student Mary Webb saw the boy's body shatter the glass from the lobby. She ducked down as ten hardhats tore through Pace. She saw one well-dressed blond young man with a "severe injury" to one eye. She pressed a compress to his bad eye. But he needed a hospital.

Inside the barricaded registrar's office, students peeked through the blinds and saw hardhats "throwing furniture" as students fled in the halls. One girl mumbled, "My God, it sounds like war out there."

Upstairs, Room 300 was converted into a first-aid station. An NYU medic examined Michael Belknap. Someone said the "workers were coming." Belknap stood bolt upright and rushed to the stairwell and descended with others. He slipped out the rear, setting off for Beekman Hospital.

Outside, Ray Randolph saw about twenty cops hustle inside Pace. The cops "took no action against the construction workers who were standing on the steps," the future federal judge said. "However, I saw two students struck by a patrolman on the north end of the line of patrolmen." Randolph also saw a cop "push a photographer who was attempting to take pictures."

Police entered Pace. Assistant professor Ivan Rohr saw a cop reach for his revolver.

"Don't draw your gun!" Rohr shouted.

Another professor, Leonard Bart, also screamed at the cop not to use his gun.

The cop hesitated. "What the hell else am I supposed to do?" he asked. His gun remained holstered.

Helmeted cops arrived, at least eight. Soon more.

The hardhats filed out "unimpeded," said Melvyn Oremland, the physics instructor.

No cops were seen pursuing the workmen.

In the lobby, Professor Bart "begged the police to leave some men at the front door, but I was ignored and the police disappeared into the building."

Pace VP Stanley Mullin entered and went to the roof with a school engineer. On the rooftop, Mullin saw about twenty-five students gathered on the parapet. Two were carrying fire extinguishers. Mullin told the engineer to get the police.

Helmeted cops cleared Pace's rooftop. Patrolmen confiscated metal bars and one machete from the students.

More workers rushed "the building for the second time," Professor Bart said. They began "smashing windows with trash cans, two-by-fours, iron pipes." Jeff Smith, the *New York Graphic* assistant editor, later "acknowledged" to police that he had "invaded" Pace with the hardhats as well. An NYPD internal record termed Smith a "rabid right winger who has a particular hate for the hippie-type student."

Outside, from above, it looked like a massive "unruly mob," said a young secretary, Christine Prasse, who was now watching from high in the Municipal Building, about a block north of Pace. She saw two columns of cops, each about eight men deep, marching toward Pace. Cars were stuck in the roadway.

Community college student Michael McNamee ran into Pace to help. He saw workmen bombarding a student with their yellow and blue helmets. A cop stepped in. The pack fled.

All day witnesses noted helmet colors to identify assailants, but that did not help much. At the Twin Towers, elevator constructors such as Joe Kelly wore yellow helmets, but so did metal lathers, excavators, and masons. At other sites, sheet metal workers wore blue helmets. So did ironworkers. Local dock builders wore blue and yellow. Electrical installers wore blue at one site and orange at another. Insignias betrayed more. Several men were seen with "AB" on their brown helmets. They were probably from American Bridge, a division of the waning behemoth US Steel, whose bridgemen had helped construct the great Verrazzano in the early sixties.

Helmeted police formed a line blocking Pace's entrance. The hardhats and their allies walked off. Some jogged across the roadway toward City Hall. Again, no cops gave chase.

Inside, students and staff peeped between window blinds and realized the coast was clear. They removed barricades from doors and exited through the lobby. Glass shards cracked beneath their feet. A dean "noticed some policeman on the steps of Pace remove an empty wine bottle from under one student's coat and a knife from the hand of another student."

Reinforcements cordoned off Pace's new complex. At an old campus building nearby, students were told to remain in their classrooms because "construction workers were rampaging through the new building."

Around this time, human rights worker Samuel Sherman saw a thin man "wearing a gray business suit with a red, white and blue armband" run by him "shouting directions and gesturing." But it's unclear who this man was or whether the men were merely behind him or heeding him, though Sherman's impression was the latter. It's possible that man was the *New York Graphic's* Jeff Smith, or the weekly's publisher, Ralph Clifford, who was in a gray suit and in the area at the time.

Nearer to City Hall, Victor Ross, a black 18-year-old banking trainee, saw a businessman on the ground. He glimpsed hardhats fleeing Pace. Ross reached to pull the white businessman up. In a blur, Ross was hit in the right eye. He tried to fight back. Someone else grabbed him. Another man hit him. Ross went down. A stranger kicked one of the hardhats to the ground. Cops pushed in.

Ross saw the main attacker. So did another witness. The hardhat was stout, with dark hair beneath his helmet. He wore a green shirt, faded gray khakis. The cop chastised him. No cuffs came out.

Ross's head was "hurting." He approached a cop who was about six foot five and well built. Ross told him he'd been assaulted. The cop ignored him. Ross said he could identify the attackers. The cop ignored him. Ross approached another officer on City Hall's steps. "I am too busy now," the officer replied. A black lady told Ross that medics were at Pace, where it was now safe.

In the crowd, many still didn't feel safe. Joseph Chan had escaped unscathed from the Wall Street melee. Then a workman punched Chan in the cheek over, he guessed, his antiwar armband. He found a patrolman, a veteran of a crowd control squad who lived upstate. Chan asked him to arrest the aggressor, whose helmet read "AB." The cop turned away. Chan touched his arm. Asked again. The cop glared at him as if he was going to "assault" him. Chan felt "frightened" and fled.

Elsewhere, Mayor Lindsay's bullish aide Sid Davidoff strolled toward City Hall. He hadn't heard of Aurelio's order to raise the flag. "As I arrived, I saw a guy on the roof of City Hall raise the flag back to full mast. I was incensed," he said. "And the construction workers are singing. They're singing the national anthem!"

Davidoff acted on instinct. He was determined to lower the flag, to ensure that the mayor's decree was observed, to honor Kent State. "So I ran into the back of City Hall with a couple of the other guys."

The mayoral aide sprinted up two flights with coworkers in tow. He climbed the ladder to the rooftop and lifted the metal hatch and pushed it aside. He saw the postman who had raised the flag, stalked over, grabbed him, and forced him down the ladder. He told a coworker to close the hatch and sit on it. Davidoff walked to the cupola and grabbed the lanyard and lowered the flag to half-staff.

The crowd erupted with rage.

Davidoff walked to the edge of the rooftop. He gave the peace sign.

Workmen bellowed and swore and shouted.

"Lindsay's a Red! Lindsay's a Red!"

Police put their helmets back on.

| "I'm Not Having City Hall
Taken Over on My Watch"

S CORES OF HARDHATS hopped City Hall's fence, leapt over the hoods of
boxy police cars, and toppled iron barricades. Several hardhats ran with
flags pointed forward, like soldiers brandishing their colors. They sprinted
through the parking lot and past half a dozen mounted policemen. The
horses' ears perked and their tails rose, but reins were held steady. On the
steps, the police closed ranks and leaned into the charge. The men collided
and it was a mess of shoving and shouting. Police backpedaled to the barred
front doors.

Mayoral staffers pressed against the windows above as men shouted rage
and sunlight glimmered off the colored helmets and flags below.

On the stairs, Captain John Reilly yelled at his men to hold the line.
Reilly was middle-aged and Irish born and his men were far outnumbered.
"There was pushing and shoving by everyone," Reilly reported. Reilly bent
down and clutched his stomach. He "felt a severe pain." Reilly was unsure
what happened. He slumped behind his men.

Off the stairs, construction workers charged City Hall and bumped into
strangers and rushed students, and as with Wall Street, order burned away
in seconds. It was a free-for-all once again, amid thousands so frenzied and
so close that you feared falling into a fight, as sirens blended into shouts
and strangers jostled to clear out. Scores cut off the person in front of them,
glancing back, sometimes so distracted by the fear at eye level that they
slipped on storm drain runnels or tripped on curbs or each other. Some
students pushed hardhats back and tossed fists, until they were overrun.
They were "physically no match for the construction workers," said John

Chapman, a young insurance worker. The bulk of the crowd, students and bystanders alike, fled in a loose herd. Hardhats tackled hippies and got hold of other stragglers by the tails of their shirts or by scoop-kicking them from behind, tripping them, flooring them, and then pouncing, punching. Some students crawled for escape as they took kicks to the stomach, to the face. Students pulled themselves into a ball, covering their heads. From the ground, it was a terrifying barrage of heels, shins, steel toes. One boy, college age, was knocked cold and his legs went limp and his face hit the pavement and his body jerked. He went into convulsions.

More hardhats stormed City Hall's steps.

"Hundreds of construction workers were pressing, trying to get into City Hall," said Lindsay aide Sid Davidoff. "They were incensed."

"They had better get that flag back up to the top of the mast," thought Joe Kelly, the Twin Towers elevator constructor.

The NYPD reported that construction workers were within a "fraction of reaching the entrance" of City Hall.

Inside, Sid Davidoff hustled down the marble staircase and saw Chief Kowsky, who was now yelling at Deputy Mayor Aurelio. Kowsky wanted to arrest Davidoff, to drag him out front and show the workmen they had the man who had lowered the flag.

Davidoff was "perplexed." He thought he had done "the right thing."

Kowsky saw Davidoff and took out his handcuffs.

"Chief, what's the problem?" Davidoff asked.

"Don't 'chief' me!" Kowsky yelled. "I'm not having a riot at City Hall. I'm not having City Hall taken over on my watch!"

"Look, we don't need to arrest him," Aurelio said. "He'll go back to his office. We'll work this out."

Outside, helmeted police pushed back and held the line and brandished their clubs but did not use them. Other patrolmen fanned their palms down, trying to encourage calm. A city worker thought "it was a miracle" the cops were holding the hardhats back.

"Raise the flag! Raise the flag!" the crowd shouted.

A group of about eight schoolgirls in their late teens, lots of bobbed bangs, stood deep in the crowd, chanting with the men.

On the rooftop, the American flag whipped with the wind. Two plainclothesmen teetered over to it. They struggled with the lanyard until the flag inched upward.

In the plaza below, the massive crowd cheered and doffed their helmets and sang "The Star-Spangled Banner" once more. Other men saluted, including ironworker Ed Hatrick. Still others clapped a hand over their heart.

Men turned to each other and shook hands and "slapped each other on the back," adman Jack Corwin said. "Some of the police were also smiling."

"Get your helmet off!" a workman yelled at policemen gazing upward.

Some cops smiled "sheepishly" and at least five removed their helmets. Some cops saluted. Others sang along.

As cops removed their helmets and talked "amiably" with those who were besieging City Hall, the deputy borough president, Leonard Cohen, was again incredulous. Dick Aurelio watched "policemen just chatting with each other and looking at the scene like spectators."

"I saw ten or fifteen police, who intermingled with the construction workers, join with the workers in singing 'My Country 'Tis of Thee,'" said Karen Burkhardt, a student at Brooklyn's Pratt Institute. Burkhardt said she saw some cops reveling and tossing "their hats in the air."

"The flag went back up and everybody seemed nice and happy and again they started singing 'God Bless America' and the national anthem and again it made you feel good," elevator mechanic Joe Kelly said. "Not that I like seeing those four kids out in wherever it was, Kent, get killed. I don't like to see anybody get beat up, never mind lose their life." Though he added, "I don't think Mayor Lindsay has the right to put that flag at half-staff. That flag represents this country."

A hundred students amassed on the east side of the plaza in front of City Hall. As the crowd sang of the "land that I love, stand beside her," hippies began chanting against the "fuckin' war!"

Hardhats glanced their way.

At first, ten kids were "shouting peace slogans," said 26-year-old Alvin Matz, a law clerk. But soon, as the hardhats sang, "the kids started shouting obscenities."

It was "evident" to roughly two dozen cops on the steps that the "dissident students" were playing with fire, said 26-year-old attorney Leonard Spivak.

The crowd sang on. Students chanted on.

Nearby, Jack Corwin saw about seven black young men, "well built, neatly dressed in sportswear, bushy hair, well-trimmed," walking southward, stopping east of City Hall's steps.

"I distinctly heard one say, 'Get that fucking flag down,'" Corwin said.

A veteran plainclothesman, Herb Robles, also heard some young people "making derogatory and inflammatory remarks" from the sidelines.

In the plaza, workmen and students cursed each other. Attorney Leonard Spivak wondered why the commanders were not redeploying some cops into the crowd. Corwin saw some hardhats close in around one of the black hecklers.

Chief Taylor was deep in the hardhats' ranks. Lieutenant Simon saw Taylor standing on a railing dividing the park from the plaza, urging hardhats to cool down. "I thought that he was in danger and started towards him," Simon reported. "I had to push my way through" to Chief Taylor.

Sirens wailed and red lights flashed meekly in the sunlight as police cars inched into the horde and parked along Park Row. One patrolman worried his car would be "damaged by the crowd." He moved it onto a median across from Pace.

In the plaza, hardhats attacked, again. Students fled and fought and fell and bled, again.

"People were running in all directions," ironworker Ed Hatrick said. One student was dragged seventy-five feet along the pavement, only to be lost in the multitude.

Near the eastern end of the steps, six hardhats surrounded a thirtysomething and punched and "stomped him," said Jules E. Yarnell, a middle-aged lawyer, a former World War Two Army captain. Yarnell ran to a police captain. "They're killing someone over there!" he shouted. "Can't you get your men to arrest them? Why can't you stop them?!"

The police captain gave him a "blank look and turned away."

"Do you have orders not to arrest?" Yarnell asked. "You're not a representative of New York's Finest! You're nothing but a horse's ass."

Elsewhere, attorney Leonard Spivak watched as "about forty construction workers charged into the crowd" and began "pushing and swinging" while "some students threw glass bottles" at the workmen or flailed to defend themselves, even as far more dashed for escape.

The deputy borough president, Leonard Cohen, estimated that one hundred hardhats were attacking now, swinging away at anyone who looked like an ideological foe. Cohen "shouted and shrieked" at cops to help, including an officer with a walkie-talkie. But the cops "did nothing." Cohen glanced toward City Hall. He saw the police remaining "steadfastly on the steps," some cops "laughingly joining with the assailants" while students were "brutally beaten."

In the streets, a person was knocked out and not moving. Over him, one man in a blazer signaled for a medic. A boy, college age with trim mop-top hair and a scarf around his neck, held his arm outstretched, palm up, his mouth open, as if he was yelling, Stop!

The confrontation between hardhats and the black hecklers escalated fast. "At first the blacks fought shoulder to shoulder in a semicircle or V-formation," Jack Corwin said.

Plainclothesman Herb Robles saw a few hardhats team up on one of them, a tall guy in his twenties with an afro. The workmen flung kicks. The tall guy was "giving them a good battle," until he went down. Spectators were "surging" so densely that they pushed the brawl to the parked cars near the trees. Fighters tripped on the metal fenders and fell against car hoods.

Robles became "concerned" the black kid "would be seriously hurt." He rushed in and tried to keep the workmen back.

"I'm a police officer!" Robles yelled. "Cut this out!"

Hardhats jumped over car hoods. Some of the black youth hopped the fence. In this corner of the melee, perhaps a dozen brawled—headlocks, grappling, fists—as bystanders tried to flee into the tree line or squeeze between cars. Countless ogled, spellbound. For here it was, in the tide of this white riot, an exception, whites versus blacks, the era's neurosis, a race battle.

Jack Corwin saw one of the black kids fall over the waist-high iron fence that enclosed the park. "Sometimes several blacks attacked one construction worker," he said. "Other times, several construction workers attacked one black."

Hardhats stood atop cars and craned their necks to see the brawl, at least three of them still holding large flags. A young man in white shirtsleeves raised both his palms up and yelled, as if pleading for calm. The clash ran into the blooming trees, snapping branches. Flowers drifted downward as men fought.

Overhead, debris flew and bystanders covered their heads. Some stepped back. Ironworker Ed Hatrick, likely watching the same white-black brawl, was now distracted, trying to dodge the debris sailing past his head. He ducked behind a car. A concrete chunk struck his chin. He collapsed, pushed

Construction workers fight student protestors and others at the edge of City Hall Park. (Leonard Detrick/NY Daily News/Getty)

himself up, and set off for the hospital. A colleague saw Hatrick "holding his chin, which was full of blood."

The plainclothesman, Robles, was trapped between cars and brawlers. He tried to split fighters. He was "getting hit from all sides." Someone smashed a metal helmet into Robles and he went down.

Meanwhile, outside the melee, attorney Leonard Spivak saw a pair of twentysomething women "exhort" policemen to help. Nothing came of it. He cut through the crowd. Approached some cops. "There's a riot over there!" he said. "You can be of service!" The police were not of service.

At Pace's campus across the roadway, college president Edward Mortola returned from a luncheon and learned that his school had been ransacked. About ten patrolmen were now guarding the new building. He phoned the police and the deputy mayor and requested more cops.

A sergeant descended Pace's steps. Ash blond with a paunch, he was a 41-year-old married father—of eventually nine children—who had worked as a railroad brakeman before joining the NYPD in 1953. Some students chased after him.

Back at Pace's entrance, lawyer Richard Fleischmann was shocked all over again. After witnessing the attack at the Washington statue, he had migrated here with the crowd. Two boys carried a wounded student to Pace's entrance.

"For God's sake, why don't you let them in?" Fleischmann said to an NYPD captain.

"No," he replied. "Orders are, no one can go in."

The captain "finally" let the students in. Fleischmann saw more fights. He urged the captain to "go out and stop it."

"My orders are to stay here," the captain replied.

Down Park Row, as attacks persisted, students harangued the ash-blond sergeant.

"Why don't you do something about this?" NYU student Abe Zerykier heard kids ask.

"In another minute, we are going to slaughter you," the sergeant said.[1]

Thirty to forty cops now guarded City Hall's steps. Thousands swamped the area below. A mayoral qualitative analyst, John Kaiser, stood by the cops on the stairs. He saw at least two dozen people fighting below. Kaiser overheard a lieutenant order patrolmen to "remain in position on the steps." The brutality was "increasing in intensity," Kaiser added. The lieutenant reiterated his order to not "intervene in the fighting."

Attorney Leonard Spivak asked cops to help. A policeman responded, "We have direct orders not to leave this assignment."

Deep in the crowd, Lieutenant Simon neared Chief Taylor. Then he saw someone go down. Lieutenant Simon heard, "He is one of ours. He's a cop!"

At the same time, on the steps, another lieutenant stood with a platoon. He was tall and slim and had a single bar on his blue jacket and a gold-banded cap. Mayoral aide Kate Klein, affable with a large smile and work ethic of equal measure, was now on the steps, behind the police line. She usually directed a staff of volunteers from a snug basement office. Because of the idle police, Klein got the lieutenant's name.

In the crowd, Lieutenant Simon rushed to the plainclothesman, Herb Robles. A dozen officers followed.

"Break it up!" a policeman yelled.

The brawlers were parted.

In the horde, plainclothesman Herb Robles felt "very weak" and "dizzy."

"I may pass out," he said aloud.

Two hardhats walked over to him.

"We didn't know you were a cop," one hardhat said. The hardhats apologized and carried Robles to City Hall for help.

Construction workers carry an injured man near City Hall during the Hardhat Riot.
(Frank Castoral/NY Daily News/Getty)

Lieutenant Simon turned again toward Chief Taylor. Someone kicked Simon's left leg. He took another kick to his butt. He fell hard enough to bruise.

Attorney Jules Yarnell had seen several fights since he called the NYPD captain a "horse's ass." About now, he watched half a dozen construction workers gang up on a businessman. "He dropped to the ground faster than any of the others," Yarnell said. The hardhats kept at him with their kicks. Yarnell, the middle-aged war veteran, "turned away." He "could not look." He "felt helpless."

The group of black youths walked southward along the park's eastern edge. On the sidewalk near Spruce Street, a slender middle-aged man approached them.

"Get the fuck out of here!" yelled the middle-aged man, who was also black. "This is not your fight. We'll tell you when to fight." The man made sure the youth left the area.

An injured young man during the Hardhat Riot. The small number of reporters present at the outset of the riot were quickly scattered, which led to nearly all of the assaults never being captured on film. Some photographers were also attacked and their film and cameras destroyed.

A block north, Chief Taylor was back on the steps, calmly speaking into a walkie-talkie. Reinforcements arrived. Fifty policemen now manned City Hall's stairs. Taylor ordered other cops to clear the area.

Hippies staggered in the street, holding each other up. Some limped alone.

The hardhats regrouped and shook hands, jabbed each other's shoulders jovially, while others shrugged coolly. Scattered men massaged their wrists and stretched out their fingers and cracked their knuckles. "I saw one or two policemen shaking hands with a few of the construction workers," said Robert Smits, the city housing administrator. Some four to five hundred workmen lingered in the area in loose knots, even as hundreds of other men decided to return full circle to Wall Street. As the throng of hardhats turned downtown, one cop muttered, "If I had my way, I'd let [the hardhats] have an hour with these kids."

CHAPTER 20

Full Circle to Federal Hall

WORKMEN STILL ROAMED the canyons beneath skyscrapers. At least half of the hardhats returned to work or went elsewhere. Others sought more fights. Scores repaired to musky local bars, had a shot, a draft or three, brandy, and soon, beer-scented, streamed out into the light.

Hundreds of workmen marched southward on Broadway. Just south of the park, human rights worker Samuel Sherman saw a lieutenant approach some hardhats.

"What do you have there, buddy?" the lieutenant asked one.

The workman pulled out a two-foot-long wrench.

"Well, don't use it," the lieutenant said, without confiscating it.

Sherman sarcastically echoed the lieutenant's comment. A middle-aged hardhat gut-punched him and walked away.

A few blocks farther down Broadway, a group of hardhats argued with a longhair in his late teens and beat him.

Sporadic violence had persisted near Wall Street since midday, even as the worst of the riot enveloped City Hall. But it felt like it was now getting worse, again. University of Michigan junior David Friedman stood on the south sidewalk of Wall Street, watching some one to two hundred hardhats parade before him. Friedman and another student gave the peace sign. Abruptly, Friedman was struck in the face and his nose was fractured; he fell to the sidewalk, spitting blood. He tried to stand. Strangers held him down. Men kicked him. Several students tried to pull him from the rabble. Two cops cut in.

A block south of Wall Street's plaza, a businessman grappled with a student. A hardhat, at least six feet and fit, bulled between them and wrestled the student to the ground. A potbellied cop stepped in and clubbed the student repeatedly. A cop car rolled up. The student was "bleeding from the head" and "semi-conscious." A cop shoved him into his car's backseat.

The plaza outside Federal Hall was still "filled with a mass of humanity," as young stockbroker Bob Stone put it. He saw a pack of fifty hardhats approaching along Wall Street. Workers periodically shot out of the pack. A hippie was punched. A longhair was shoved. The police were trying to "clear the roadway," he said, amid violence. Stone heard a police announcement on a bullhorn. Stone couldn't make it out. It was too noisy. More hardhats paraded westward on Wall Street, past him. A few ganged up on a student. The stockbroker wondered why so many cops did so little.

Thousands of people still lingered in Wall Street's plaza. A platoon of cops remained posted on Federal Hall's steps. More reporters had arrived by now. Onlookers gathered around interviews. The radio had reported rumors of clashes. Scattered paroxysms on Wall Street? A mass rampage? A white riot? New Yorkers wanted to see for themselves.

In the plaza, strangers asked cops, or the stranger beside them, if they knew what had happened. There was litter, streams of tickertape, abandoned antiwar placards dirtied by footprints, blood on the street. Once in a while, the crowd gasped over there or elsewhere. Another fight flared and disappeared as fast. The horde was still thick. Many in the plaza saw no bloodshed. At one point, collegians from Queens approached the police on the steps. One student asked why they were ignoring the workmen's attacks.

"What do you want me to do?" a cop replied. "We have two groups here."

A 60-year-old man walked over to the students and shouted, "You call them pigs and want them to help you!"

There were outliers. Twenty-year-old Steve Starer was nearby, with about a hundred demonstrators. Abruptly, a pack of hardhats came after them. One construction worker tackled Starer at the waist and took him to the street and pummeled him. A cop broke it up fast. The cop lifted Starer to his feet.

"Are you all right?" the cop asked.

"Yes," Starer said.

"Do you want to go to the hospital?"

"No."

The cop strolled away. Starer tried to do the same. But his leg "hurt" and he suddenly couldn't walk.

Back near the steps, the *Wall Street Journal*'s Michael Drosnin conducted interviews. Drosnin would go on to author *The Bible Code*, among other books.

He was only 24 then. A New Yorker by birth, a Columbia grad, Drosnin was reedy with long brown hair. He spoke with, among many, hardhat John Halloran.

"These hippies are getting what they deserve," said Halloran, a heavyset man who wore a reddish-brown helmet.

You hit anyone? Drosnin asked.

"No!" Halloran snapped.

A 23-year-old insurance worker "broke in." Stan Warsoff wore a blue three-piece suit. He had already seen a college-age hippie lying on the sidewalk "bleeding profusely from the head" while three hardhats beat him. It had riled Warsoff. He began berating the hard-hatted men.

The reporter turned back to Halloran, the construction worker. Drosnin asked, Would you hit a demonstrator?

"Damn straight," said another husky hardhat beside him. The husky guy lunged past Halloran and struck the insurance broker, Warsoff, and did not relent.

Halloran and Drosnin stayed out of it.

Police separated the men. One cop pulled the hardhat aside. Other cops surrounded Warsoff.

"I want that man arrested!" Warsoff yelled. "He assaulted me and I want to press charges. He's getting away! Get him!"

Paul Fusco, a *Look* magazine photographer, watched Warsoff plead for action. Fusco was thin, with big blue eyes, a divot above his lip, a faintly cleft chin, a creased brow, and receding brown hair that curled at his neckline. On the cusp of 40, he had photographed the Korean War and most famously RFK's funeral train—nameless town by nameless town, state by state, as Americans stood along the tracks to honor Bobby Kennedy, less than two years ago. One photograph captured a muddy boy saluting the train beside an older man, perhaps his father, as a woman stood on a dirt road, her hand over her heart.

Five to six cops surrounded Stan Warsoff as he demanded someone arrest the guy who punched him. "Where is he?" one cop said to Warsoff. "Point him out," another mocked. Paul Fusco saw police ringing Warsoff "so that he couldn't pursue the man he accused of hitting him." Fusco swore it was his "decided and unwavering opinion" that the cops "were hemming [Warsoff] in so that he couldn't act."

A photographer captured Warsoff speaking with a sergeant and Inspector Schryver. Both police commanders later shrugged the exchange off to internal affairs, claiming they arrived "after the assault had taken place."

"It was quite obvious that no one wanted to, or dared to," arrest the hardhat who struck Warsoff, Paul Fusco said. The police had the hardhat, he added, but "let him go."

The reporter, Michael Drosnin, tried to get the hardhat's name. He held out his press card. He asked if anyone would be cuffed. Half a dozen cops surrounded Drosnin. Cops jabbed him in the crotch with their clubs. They pulled at his clothes. They ripped his watch off.

Drosnin got loose. He approached a police inspector a few feet away. The inspector said he had seen nothing. Still, he got Drosnin his watch back.

Warsoff stalked away, visibly "shaken."

A call went out over the police radio. A few blocks north, on Broadway, hundreds of people were fleeing something.

Cops were drained by the day's "radio runs." Over the past hour, Sergeant Andre DiMarco and a patrolman had kept their helmets on in their car. One call after another to assist an officer. Two blocks south of the plaza on Wall Street, they trailed a parade of hardhats that trekked west and then turned up Broadway. Seven or eight times, they stopped the car to break up "large disputes." They radioed four calls for help themselves. More mounted policemen were deployed downtown.

On Maiden Lane and Broadway, in the shadow of the Trade Center and US Steel worksites, cops arrived to see hundreds "running in several directions." One man walked out of the thicket, bleeding from the nose.

"Arrest that man!" shouted 30-year-old attorney Joel Reiss, wiping blood off his lips. "I want to place charges against that man!"

The cops stepped between them. A financial analyst saw the worker slug Reiss again. Police cuffed the worker, an elevator constructor in his mid-forties, who said he wanted to file countercharges. Reiss, his nose broken, was arrested.

The center of trouble, however, was still several blocks up Broadway. Eight hundred hardhats from City Hall, Chief Morgan estimated, now marched toward Wall Street. Workmen banged car hoods, waved flags, chanted on, bellowed more Americana, including the "Marines' Hymn." Electrical salesman Bob Barber still upheld a flag.

A police car drove ahead of the men. Its beacon blinked red. Ruth Messinger and two of her colleagues at the community school, Andrew Lachman and Carol Lapidus, saw a construction worker on the trunk of one squad car. The workman had a blue hard hat and swung a large American flag back and forth as if he was "urging on" the men, said Lachman.

On Broadway, just north of Trinity Church, 61-year-old attorney Carl Melchior also saw a workman sitting on the trunk of the lead police car.

Businessman Eliot Karasick, now watching from his office window, saw two police cars crawl down Broadway. Hardhats sat on the trunk of each patrol car "waving American flags."

Near Trinity, students first heard a distant baritone, something like "Rah. Rah. Rah. Sis-boom-bah."

The men neared and the words cleared. "U—S—A. All the way!"

Joe Fiocca caught sight of the mass of hardhats from down the street. A volunteer legal observer, he glanced at the church gate and back at the vanguard, where workmen were "carrying steel rods and other weapons."

At Trinity, the first-aid overflow was in the churchyard. Students collected at the ironwork fence. A Red Cross medical coat was mounted on its spikes, meant to identify the first-aid station. As the workmen neared, students chanted loud.

About twenty hardhats rushed them.

Scores of young people, at times beaten unconscious, were brought to a first aid station inside Trinity Church during the Hardhat Riot. Throughout the church, as one reporter noted, victims crammed aisles with "broken teeth, broken noses, and bloodied heads," sitting, waiting, "stunned, crying, and cursing." (V. Shibla/The New York Post/Getty)

"Get inside!" Fiocca shouted.

The gate door was yanked shut. Vicar Woodward hurried to help padlock it. One policeman got in the workmen's way. The hardhats shoved him aside and tugged the gate. The chain held. Frustrated, the workmen climbed the gateposts and tore down the makeshift Red Cross flag. One hardhat pointed to the church standard and said, "Let's get the flag!" A few reached for it. A workman yelled that it was a church flag. Spectators said the same. Embarrassed, the hardhats slumped back.

Vicar Woodward "never thought" he would "see the day when I would stand behind the door of my church and see it stormed."

Inside Trinity Church, one demonstrator lay in the low light, beneath the candle-adorned alter, eerily limp. A bearded medic knelt over him and held his hand. On the other side of him, a young woman sat turned away, openmouthed, her eyes wide and distraught.

Outside, one medic said he had offered first aid to a hardhat who twisted his ankle. The workman "contemptuously" rebuffed him and limped off.

A crowd control unit was redeployed to Federal Hall. Hundreds of hardhats descended upon the plaza once more. Two thousand others pushed close. Scores had followed the men since noontime, including electrical salesman Bob Barber. There were stragglers, peripheral packs of men who had gone off on their own. Some would not pacify. But at Federal Hall, as the men regrouped at the steps, many were cheerful. They felt victorious. Still they sang the "Marines' Hymn." Still more "God Bless America." Still more chanted for the "U—S—A."

Still trouble persisted. One young man in cast-off Army fatigues climbed atop a newsstand. He photographed the workers. Hardhats knocked him off the kiosk and gave him a thrashing. A local TV news assistant hurried to his aid and was "bloodied in the melee." Freelance photographer Howard Petrick likely observed the same incident and approached some policemen.

"Why don't you do something about that photographer that was pushed off the newsstand?" he asked.

"Go to hell," a cop replied. "Mind your own business."

A half-block south of Federal Hall, people ran to Patrolman James McKeon. They were shouting, panting, telling him of a fight thirty feet away. McKeon could not see it through the "huge street crowd." He said, "I immediately pushed my way through." He saw a 22-year-old laborer, bent over, punching down at another young man with a "bright colored sports jacket," who was "trying to defend himself" from his back. The laborer was screaming, "Peace! Peace!"

McKeon grabbed the laborer. He began to arrest him. The laborer elbowed McKeon in his midsection and broke away. The cop chased him fifteen feet. McKeon grabbed him again. The laborer broke free again. McKeon chased him a dozen more feet. The cop swung his baton and it cracked off the laborer's head and knocked him to the ground. Other cops ran over. The bloody laborer was cuffed.

On Broadway, Paul Petraro watched students "yelling at workers" and "a melee developed." A few cops pulled fighters apart.

Near Exchange Place and Broadway, in an alleyway, 17-year-old Jon Kasso walked with a friend. The two boys turned up Broadway and ran into at least a hundred hardhats. Kasso's friend raised his hand and made a peace sign. "There's a couple of them," one workman blurted. They were rushed and beaten.

A block south of Wall Street's plaza, as some hardhats paraded, a black construction worker passed two men with Black Panther literature. One said, "Hey brother, you don't belong with them, come over here."

Soon after, a fortysomething in a blue suit got into a fight with these two black men. A half-dozen cops "appeared quickly," lawyer Gilbert Sandler said. The police were "indiscriminately swinging their clubs" at anyone in the scrum, Sandler added. Sandler and his colleague, Howard Ende, saw one cop club a longhair and flatten him. As the hippie bled from the head, a big cop stood over him and "appeared excited."

About ten minutes later, attorney Howard Ende said he approached Chief Morgan.

"Excuse me, sir, do these gentlemen have a parade permit?" Ende asked.

"Don't bother me," Chief Morgan replied. He "gently shoved me aside," Ende said.

At Federal Hall, police allowed Ralph Clifford, the gray-suited publisher of the "ultra-right-wing" *Graphic*, to speak at the base of the George Washington statue. Some workmen had already left. Thousands still looked on. The NYPD was desperate to disband them. So cops handed Clifford a bullhorn, perhaps because he clearly sympathized with the men and, with his suit, looked influential.

"I'm glad to see all of us here," Clifford said. "And three cheers for the construction workers!" Two men walked up the steps and flanked Clifford with American flags. Clifford veered into talk of "socialists." He glanced around the crowd. "All right, now. We've proved our point. Let's go." He added, "We must go home."

By midafternoon, the mob petered out. They were mostly becalmed by events. There was nothing left to fight. Tickertape littered curbs and gutters. The subway's thrum could again be heard through the street's steel grates.

The tide of injured finally ebbed at Trinity. A church lady offered coffee, tea, hot chocolate. Another woman carried a tray of sandwiches. A folk singer played his guitar. Paul O'Dwyer visited with the injured.

Bob Barschow's day was over. He had worked a day like any other. He was a lather's apprentice, mid-thirties, wearing workman's clothes. At Wall Street, Barschow descended some subway steps. He slipped his dull brass token into the slot and waited for the train. His supervisor was with him. A half-dozen black youths stood near Barschow. One said, "There's one of them." A big guy with big hair and a fedora stepped to him. The big guy pushed Barschow to the concrete. He kneeled over him, pinning him, punching him in the face, while another boy kicked him in the ribs on his right side. A businessman stepped in and kept the rest of the group back. The youth ran off.

In the streets above, squad cars and motorcycle units rumbled through cobblestone byways. Cops now seemed to be everywhere, while protests brewed elsewhere. The NYPD tracked hundreds of students uptown, a throng that originated from Columbia University. Still more activists marched in midtown. One thousand students stepped into Madison Avenue to block traffic. The NYPD received a report that "construction workers are going to show up" nearby, around Forty-Second Street, "for a possible confrontation with the students."

On Forty-Second Street, a group of Black Panthers paraded. A cast member of the musical *Hair* called the NYPD, perhaps to secure police protection. He said that "people in show business" would be holding a vigil tonight for Kent State. Another rally was scheduled in a few hours at the United Nations. It was going to be a long night.

Police deemed downtown "normalized," for now. Chief Morgan estimated that, by this time, the NYPD had broken up "several hundred individual fights" downtown.

One hardhat had been arrested.

At Pace, students were permitted to leave their classrooms. They were directed to exit the building "in groups of about thirty" and "cautioned to leave the area immediately." As some left, the police had to hold back lingering hardhats.

Pace's president messengered a letter to City Hall. He wrote of the "horde of men" who "invaded" the campus. He requested Mayor Lindsay "do everything possible to bring the perpetrators of this dreadful act to justice." The deputy borough president, Leonard Cohen, later telegrammed Lindsay that police "laughingly watched students brutally beaten."

At his residence uptown, John Lindsay digested reports on the riot. He was scheduled to catch a helicopter to Yale, his alma mater, and stay with its president, Mayflower highborn Kingman Brewster, an old friend—even though tonight, in Manhattan, the Knicks hoped to win their first NBA championship.

Meanwhile, Lakers superstar Jerry West stood across the street from Madison Square Garden. New Yorkers jaywalked. Jerry West waited for the light to change.

That afternoon, Vice President Agnew cancelled his plans to visit the city early next week.

At City Hall, on the mayor's behalf, Deputy Mayor Aurelio drafted a response to Pace's president: "I am appalled by the unprovoked and brutal attack." Tomorrow, the letter assured, the mayor would get answers from NYPD leadership.

Lindsay insisted Aurelio join him for the meeting. It was fine by him. Aurelio thought the cops' behavior had been "pathetic, passive, weak." He was furious that so many police sided with the construction workers.

In total, about sixty student demonstrators sought help at Trinity Church that afternoon. They had punched-in noses, busted lips, black eyes, gashes that could be stitched on-site. Some were likely suffering from concussions— the headaches, the dizziness, the absence of memory. A handful had "bad scalp injuries." Some needed hospitalization. But, as a reporter noted, "many young people were afraid to leave the church." Hardhats still coursed through the streets. And these white kids no longer trusted the police to protect them.

Most casualties were brought to Beekman. East of City Hall, it was the only hospital south of Canal Street, river to river.

Inside Beekman, the injured rested on gurneys with polished chrome rails and threadbare cotton sheets. They sat in plastic chairs between bland walls under buzzing fluorescent lights. It was loud, with nurses tending to wounds and orderlies dashing around. In rooms, nurses and doctors tended to bloody hippies. Dozens of victims waited their turn in the lobby, brooding in their chairs, some venting rage to reporters.

Michael Belknap held a cloth to his right eye, which was swollen shut, bruised, and caked with dried blood. His back had boot marks and was bruising in at least five places. Peter Giagni, the Brandeis boy who also had been knocked out, emerged from unconsciousness after several hours, wearing a hospital gown. His nose was fractured and it was still difficult to breathe. Patrolman Burns, who twisted his ankle, was among the first seen and discharged. Patrolman Stokes was seen too. He signed himself out. Will

Dorfer, the mid-twenties clerk who couldn't stand after his beating, left Beekman to convalesce at his parents' home in Syracuse. The salesman who helped the Lehman heir had the gash in his head sutured. Pace student Stew Litvin received five stitches. Ironworker Ed Hatrick received ten stitches on his chin. Victor Ross, the banking trainee who tried to help, had a serious concussion. He would not be discharged for three days. Charles Thompson, the elderly husband of the couple separated during one stampede, was confined to a hospital bed for fifteen days. Susan Harmon, the childcare worker who called the riot "a class thing" and clashed with hardhats, saw a doctor, had X-rays. They found no injuries. But she was unnerved. "They believe passionately that the students are destroying the country," she said of the hardhats. "They are very sincere and it's very scary." A City College student in "hippie clothes" said the hardhats "came at them like animals," and "we ran for our lives."

The NYPD claimed it had quelled the riot. But there was little reason for hardhats to remain. They had "taught those kids a lesson." They had taken the high ground of Federal Hall, of City Hall. They had raised the flag.

At the Trade Center, workers returned late from lunch, including Joe Kelly. "I was going to dock one man who came back an hour and a half late," elevator foreman Frank Pike said. But a workman told him, "'I saw these kids spit on the flag. What could I do?' How could I dock the man?"

Reporters flocked downtown. "A lot of us are World War Two vets and fathers and Purple Hearts," electrician Morty Grutman told one. "We're from a generation that believes the flag over everything. They were throwing confetti out of windows like we were heroes. But we're not heroes. We're just trying to be Americans."

South of Wall Street, John Riley's callused hand pointed to a flag. "A lot of good men died for that flag," he said. "We're not going to let a lot of long-haired kids and fast-talking politicians who make big money take it away from us."

Near Manhattan's southernmost point, where the ferries to the Statue of Liberty and Staten Island docked, Larry Tallman held his aluminum lunchbox and helmet, as he commuted home with fellow workmen. "I don't mind people demonstrating. But when these brats rip, spit on, and chew up the flag, what are we supposed to do, stand around and kiss them?"

Workers gathered around Tallman. The breeze wafted off the bay. Battery Park's old sandstone fort was ahead of them. Its flag was at full staff.

The reporter asked Tallman, Would you hurt demonstrators again?

"You bet. If they come back here Monday, we'll give them the chase of their lives."

"We'll kill them," his friend added.

PART 3 | Afterward and Aftermath

CHAPTER 21

The Days After: Knicks Utopia,
a Fraught City, and Nixon
at the Brink

Hours after the riot, less than three miles uptown, Madison Square Garden staged another America. It was the NBA championship's final matchup. "If there was a common cause left in town, it was the Knicks," *Sports Illustrated* wrote.[1]

The telecaster named the "superstars." The Lakers: Wilt Chamberlain, Jerry West, Elgin Baylor. He did not name any Knicks. NBA teams were already built around superstars. Yet the Knicks had reached the finals because of actual teamwork. The team's motto was to find the "open man" on offense—rather than depend on one man—and utilize a "helping defense." "None of us would be as strong individually as all of us were together," Bill Bradley said, "which was a very powerful metaphor that I think a lot of people in New York saw."[2]

Yet the team needed its center Willis Reed to cover all seven feet two inches of Chamberlain, the NBA's record scorer. By Game Five, with the series split, Reed thwarted Chamberlain early in the game. Then Reed collapsed on the court. "There goes the championship," Knicks starter Walt Frazier thought. "Without him, I didn't see any way that we could contain Chamberlain."[3]

Game Five occurred hours after Kent State. Marv Albert, the Knicks' play-by-play radio man, had a brother who attended Kent and fled the campus following the killings. The torrid era was like a sandstorm. It had a way of reaching into everything. "There was a scary, surreal nature to the shootings and a palpable tension in midtown that evening as my friend and I stepped out of the subway at Penn Station," wrote Harvey Araton, who was a high school senior and attended the game (he later became a *Times* sports columnist). "Upstairs, in the blue seats, the shootings dominated the pregame chatter, especially among the younger fans. As usual, the smell of marijuana wafted through our section. There was a feeling of restlessness in the crowd, an air of pessimism and fear that came close to resignation." Yet sports had always been an escape. And even with Reed out with a torn hip muscle, the Knicks relentlessly pressured Chamberlain. Stunning even themselves, they won. But the Lakers easily took Game Six in Los Angeles, with Chamberlain scoring 45 points.[4]

On the eve of the final game, no one knew if Reed would play. Few thought the Knicks could win without him. As players began to arrive at the Garden in the afternoon, and hardhats still coursed violently through downtown, Lindsay aide Sid Davidoff brooded in his office. He had been there since lowering the flag and reigniting the riot. Lindsay was still at Gracie Mansion. Later in the day, Lindsay called Davidoff and asked, "What did you do?"

"What did I do?" Davidoff repeated. "You wanted the flag at half-mast. This postman put it up." Lindsay was quiet. "The mayor would never react in the moment," Davidoff recalled. Davidoff remained in his office until nightfall contemplating his career's end. Meanwhile, Lindsay and Dick Aurelio digested the forewarnings given, the cops' indifference, the bloody magnitude of it all. Police Commissioner Howard Leary minimized the mayhem. "The sporadic assaults," Leary told reporters, "occurred on a hit and run basis, out of the immediate view and control of the police." Police had been, Leary alleged, "engulfed by the enormous noonday crowds and apprehension of the attackers was rendered virtually impossible."

Meanwhile, at five o'clock, one thousand youths stormed Grand Central Station, chanting "Avenge Kent State," obstructing rush hour. An hour later, the police reported five hundred demonstrators entering the nearby Port Authority bus terminal.

The NYPD received a "confidential" tip soon after, "info that there will be an effort to fire-bomb recruitment stations throughout [the] city."

Outside the Garden and throughout the city, commuters paid a dime for the *New York Post* at newsstands. The *Daily News* was only a nickel. But the *Post* was America's most-read afternoon newspaper. The front-page headline: WORKERS SMASH INTO STUDENTS HERE.

Inside City Hall, Dick Aurelio summoned Sid Davidoff to his office. "I was furious" at Davidoff and "angry that we were bullied" by the hardhats, Aurelio recalled.

Davidoff entered his office and said, "I don't know what to say—"

"Do you understand what happened today?" Aurelio interrupted. "You know how close we came to a riot within City Hall and to your arrest?"

"I don't know what to say to you. I mean, I thought it was the right thing."

"You understand?" Aurelio persisted.

"Yes, I do understand it," Davidoff said.

Aurelio eased back. He admired Davidoff. "It broke my heart" to raise the flag, he recalled. Aurelio looked back at Davidoff and told him, "I wish I would have had the balls to do that."[5]

Meanwhile, a mayoral aide called the police and expressed concern about hardhats attacking the thousands of students gathering in the early morning at Penn Station, where at least four trains were now scheduled to shuttle youth to Washington for the mass demonstration on Saturday. Dozens of buses were also chartered citywide. The NYPD assigned details for sunrise duty, covering the loading areas, such as NYU's campus in the Village.

At the Garden, tipoff time was delayed. Reed remained in the locker room. Hot compresses had not relieved the pain. Knicks' starter Dave DeBusschere tapped Reed on the shoulder. "If you can give us 20 minutes, we'll win," DeBusschere told him, as Reed recalled. The big man was injected with cortisone and carbocaine.[6]

"There is tremendous doubt" Reed would play, said the ABC telecaster.

7:34 p.m.: "Here comes Willis!" Marv Albert proclaimed. That night, most Knicks fans associated Albert's voice with the game. The local telecast was on a time delay. Radio offered the only live broadcast across the city.

As Reed exited the tunnel, stiff-legged and shuffling onto the wood floor, witnesses swore 19,500 fans smiled in near unison. A ball was passed to Reed. He coolly warmed up.

The national anthem played. In the upper decks, some young fans refused to stand.[7]

Tipoff. Reed didn't try to beat Chamberlain to the ball.

On the Knicks' first possession, Reed reached the free-throw line and received a pass.

Reed hit a smooth jump shot, the first score of the game. The crowd cheered, whooped, shook hands (the high five didn't yet exist).[8]

Reed hobbled back to defense. When he stood still, he placed his weight on his good leg. He didn't contest Chamberlain for a rebound.

Second minute. The Knicks had the ball. Reed was already downcourt, well outside the basket. He received a long pass.

Reed scored another jumper! The Garden thundered and even the young and earnest shot upward and boomed joy.

Reed would not sink any more baskets. But he had invigorated his side, and when he departed the floor with only 3:05 left in the half, the team had held Chamberlain to two baskets. The halftime buzzer sounded. The Knicks led by 27 points. They never lost the lead. New York won its first championship since the NBA had been founded twenty-four years earlier.

The Knicks had won true to form, with old-fashioned teamwork, from Walt Frazier's 36 points to Dave DeBusschere's 17 rebounds. It was the capstone of a storybook season, a reprieve from the divisive era. As Richard Nixon prepared to speak to Americans about Vietnam, restive youth stormed through Times Square chanting "Peace now" beneath pulsating neon light. News flashed that the National Guard was amassing for tomorrow's Kent State demonstration and the youth booed.

Knicks fans piled into bars, rejoicing. In the locker room, Knicks' player Phil Jackson answered the phone. It was the White House. Minutes before his address, Nixon congratulated Reed. Lindsay was not at the game. The mayor telegrammed the team congratulations (a copy was also sent to Ronald Reagan). Reed was named MVP. In the locker room, ABC's Howard Cosell told Reed, "You've offered, I think, the best of what the human spirit can offer."[9]

It was a welcome sentiment after the day's riot, after a week of tumult, after years of madness. People craved good old days. The 1897 Sears Roebuck catalogue was reprinted for reference libraries. The publisher was stunned when, in a fit of wistfulness, it sold two hundred thousand copies. A six-record album, *Golden Memories of Radio*, sold one hundred thousand copies. There was a Nostalgia Book Club. The club's president explained to the *Times* that "even the grim days of the Depression sound very good now." The *Times* article concluded by envisioning the future: "Can you imagine a sentimental look back at the Beatles, the miniskirt, Barbra Streisand?"[10]

Even the Knicks' two pale starters exhibited nostalgic unity. Bill Bradley was elegant, a bank president's son, a Princeton man, a Rhodes scholar. Dave DeBusschere was a workhorse who attended the University of Detroit and whose father hauled beer for a living. The team's racial cohesion was no less manifest. It was the nation's dream for itself, true on television if not in life, for a few hours, at least. "We had five guys that came from different and varied backgrounds," Walt Frazier later said, "but when we came to play as a team, man, it was something beautiful."[11]

◆

President Nixon returned from almost two days of seclusion at Camp David, still stuck in the darkness, as he later put it, still feeling "dejected." Key advisors were not defending him. Cabinet member Walter Hickel wrote, in a letter leaked to the press, that Nixon did "lack appropriate concern" for "our young people." Henry Kissinger and Daniel Patrick Moynihan would conclude Nixon was "on the edge of a nervous breakdown." It was the beginning of a long night and the "weirdest day so far" of Nixon's presidency, Chief of Staff H. R. Haldeman wrote later in his diary.

The president landed on the South Lawn and immediately hunkered down, as the hardhats returned to their homes for supper. Activists circled the White House grounds, carrying candles and haunting Nixon, as they had LBJ. "Protesters would scream things and the press would eat it up," White House social secretary Lucy Winchester recalled. "We were at war and [Nixon] took it hard." By 10 p.m., with the NBA championship over, all three networks went live to Washington.[12]

The president stood before reporters, his hands clasped behind him, his shoulders tilted forward, sweat glistening off his nose and collecting above his chin. Of the twenty-six questions asked, twenty-four concerned the protests and the war. Newsmen pressed him on Cambodia, Kent State, protest "intensity," his "use of the word 'bums'" to describe demonstrators.

Young people streamed onto the vast green space between the floodlit US Capitol and the Lincoln Memorial. The White House taped its windows, to prevent them from shattering, and encircled its grounds with about sixty busses, bumper to bumper. Five thousand troops were stationed in government buildings. In the basement of the Executive Office Building, across the street from the White House, the Eighty-Second Airborne wore full combat gear—including field packs and camouflage helmets. Some slept on the cold marble floor, others played cards, read, stared off. "It was haughtily reminiscent of what I had seen twice before in Central American countries," Chuck Colson wrote in his memoir, "uniformed troops guarding the palace against its enemies. But here in the strongest democracy in the world?" Pat Buchanan entered the basement for the five-cent cigarettes. He looked at one guardsman, about age 18, and saw a "nervous apprehension" about him, which he noticed in many of the young men. Fellow aide Steve Bull, who served in Vietnam with the Marines, also ran into them. "If you didn't experience it back then," Bull said, "you would have no idea how close we were to revolution."[13]

In New York City, just shy of midnight, Mayor Lindsay's office warned the NYPD of a tip it had received: more construction workers would likely confront students in Union Square at 6 a.m., as they prepared to caravan to Washington.

After the news conference, Richard Nixon walked upstairs and entered the Victorian parlor known as the Lincoln Sitting Room, which abutted his bedroom. From 10:35 p.m. to 3:54 in the morning, Nixon had forty-nine conversations. He spoke on the phone with family, seminal ministers Norman Vincent Peale and Billy Graham, political graybeard Thomas Dewey, Nelson Rockefeller, confidants such as Bebe Rebozo, members of his cabinet, and chronically to close aides. At 1:13, Nixon phoned NBC's Nancy Dickerson. When she answered, Nixon said, "This is Dick." It took her a moment to realize it was Dick Nixon. He sounded confused and digressive, but he added, "I really love those kids." At 2:02, Nixon hung up with Henry Kissinger and tried to sleep.

Near the White House, park policemen and students quarreled. There was yelling and rock-throwing. To avoid worse, cops funneled youth to the sprawling grounds near the Washington Monument, including the Ellipse parkland.

Nixon hardly slept an hour. He consulted more advisors and talked to UPI's Helen Thomas at 3:50. As the clock ticked near four, Nixon placed a record, Rachmaninoff's First Piano Concerto, on the turntable and blasted the music. The president peered out a window toward the Washington Monument. Nixon's valet asked if he needed anything. Nixon said no but asked, "Have you ever been to the Lincoln Memorial at night?"

At 4:35 a.m., they exited the White House. It was still dark, the air muggy.

"Searchlight is on the lawn!" radioed a guard, using the president's Secret Service moniker.

"Oh, my God!" said advisor Egil "Bud" Krogh, from the Secret Service command.

"Searchlight has asked for a car," crackled the Secret Service radio.

Before the hour reached five, Nixon left for the Lincoln Memorial. "I've never seen the Secret Service quite so petrified with apprehension," Nixon recalled.

The president and his valet ascended the fifty-seven white marble steps. Nixon read limestone inscriptions of the Gettysburg Address and Lincoln's Second Inaugural Address and stared up at the colossus, this picture of presidential greatness, never more distant to him. Then the president, the bête noire of the Movement, stepped toward a pack of bleary-eyed young men. Nixon attempted disarming small talk. He asked their home, their age, their interests. Some of the boys, standing close to the president, kept their arms folded. They wore tattered jeans, cardigans, collared shirts, surplus Army fatigues, and had "outlandish hairdos," as Bud Krogh put it. The morning was hazy and no one had slept enough, which only made it seem more surreal to onlookers, longhairs and crewcuts alike, all except solemn Dick Nixon. "His manner was intense—trying to reach out into them, to communicate with them. I've never seen him do it like this before," Krogh said. "He was trying to empathize with them as best he could."

"I know you, that probably most of you think, I'm an SOB, but I want you to know that I understand just how you feel," Nixon said. He careened between topics. He was exhausted and his eyes were bulbous and weighed down by bags. The crowd enlarged. Aides fretted. Outside the memorial, beyond the long reflecting pool, the Washington Monument glowed pink with predawn light.[14]

A young woman told the president: "We are willing to die for what we believe in."

"I realize that," Nixon replied. "Do you realize that many of us, when we were your age, were also willing to die for what we believed in, and are willing to do so today? The point is that we are trying to build a world in which you will not have to die for what you believe in."

The day broke humid. As the sun rose over Washington, the president's motorcade sped off.

Nixon visited the Capitol and later ate corned beef hash and eggs with staff at the Mayflower Hotel. The president was "completely beat and just rambling on," Haldeman noted. After, Kissinger worried that the Lincoln Memorial visit "was only the tip of the psychological iceberg."

Student protestors told reporters Nixon "didn't look anyone in the eyes," was "completely uptight," was "mumbling" and "absurd."

"He broke out of the cocoon that separates the president from the rest of humanity for three hours," wrote William Safire, "enjoyed a taste of real life and the bitter aftertaste."[15]

By midmorning, students assembled at the massive green expanse near the White House. One hundred thousand came, a gathering of the tribes. It soon was a steamy 90 degrees in the shade. Scantily clad youth splashed in the fountain. Students queued to sign a massive antiwar petition. A hairy male nudist carried an American flag. Students slapped tambourines, blew kazoos, patted djembes. Many wore moccasins, sandals, milled barefoot in the grass.

Everywhere, the flowy dresses, the floppy hats, the acoustic guitars. There were the girls with armpit hair, politically unshaven, liberated. The girls with charcoal lashes, airy blouses, braless. Pretty boys with hair near their small shoulders. The psychedelic hirsute boys, incensey, a blend of Rasputin and Jesus, Dionysian with a cause. The disparate black kids, the natural hair, the tapered Panther cool. The fastidious suburban white kids imitating Hindu mystics. Sunbathing couples embracing on the lawn. Smoke wafting. Tens of thousands were languorous as that. But the zealous, while fewer, held sway. Kent State had ensured that much.

Young men shouldered crosses and coffins near riot cops with white helmets. Signs and speeches urged "power to the people," an end to the war, an end to the draft, an end to the "systematic manipulation of our laws and

Yippie leader Abbie Hoffman uses a stars and stripes handkerchief at the antiwar demonstration in Washington, DC, May 9, 1970, the national demonstration to protest the Kent State killings. It was one day after the Hardhat Riot where construction workers attacked antiwar demonstrators over, among other issues, disrespect of the US flag. Abbie Hoffman was scheduled to speak at the student demonstration the workmen broke up, but did not show. (AP)

our constitution to oppress those who are fighting for freedom," as actress and activist Jane Fonda said, her hands on her hips before the nest of mics, a summer scarf around her neck. Dr. Benjamin Spock wore a tie adorned with peace signs and sweat glistened off his bald scalp and he spoke of the need to "demand" the war's end. A man carried a sign that read, HEIL NIⱧON. The *Times* reported that "the symbol was the raised fist and the word 'strike.' The demonstrators were constantly admonished to return to their homes, shut down the universities, engage in politics and work for a 'new order.'" It added, "The scene created the impression of a society in turmoil."

There was more peripheral violence. Teargas disbanded militants at George Washington University, about a mile from the White House. In the city streets, spasms of rock fights, shattered windows, crashed barricades. A coffin was hurled at the White House gate. It beckoned more helmeted police, more guardsmen, more teargas, more television footage of a troubled nation.

In the small hours of Sunday, a bomb shattered the glass façade of Washington's National Guard Building. The Weathermen claimed credit.[16]

Polls heartened Nixon. His approval rating held steady at 57 percent, even amid the student blowback. Half the country approved of how Nixon was "handling the Cambodian situation," compared to a third who did not. The public was against the war but trusted the president to end it. And like Chicago '68, Americans backed law enforcement over the alternative. Only a tenth of the public blamed the National Guard for Kent State.[17]

Walter Cronkite said recent events had "polarized not only the opposition to the war but also the opposition to the antiwar movement. New York City yesterday offered a chilling illustration of that division." Footage showed hardhats battling hippies.

By Sunday, Haldeman noted the president was "more relaxed" and "thinks we're turning a corner" because Nixon believed "the college demonstrators have overplayed their hands—evidence is the blue-collar group rising up against them, and [the] president can mobilize them."[18]

| The Riot Reverberates

IN NEW YORK'S UPPER East Side, while students rallied in Washington, John Lindsay and Dick Aurelio met with NYPD leaders for five hours. Afterward, the mayor and the police commissioner sat down before the microphones. Reporters piled in. Police Commissioner Howard Leary was grim-faced. The mayor scowled.

The commissioner acknowledged the warning calls. He said the cops had been badly outnumbered. They'd never expected to confront "such a large force." Still, he conceded that "even under those circumstances, some policemen were derelict in their duties."

Mayor Lindsay said New Yorkers had witnessed a "breakdown of the police as the barrier between them and wanton violence." Police "had a duty" to protect even "highly provocative" protestors. The mayor who called the Harlem riot of '67 a "demonstration" now sounded Nixonian. He scorned the "appalling," "highly organized and rough," "marauding bands of construction workers." Hizzoner pledged a "full report."[1]

Meanwhile, Americans unfurled their newspapers and sat down at Formica tables and read of the rampage over eggs and white toast. *Los Angeles Times:* WORKERS IN N.Y. BATTLE PROTESTORS, STORM CITY HALL. *Chicago Tribune:* WORKERS AND WAR CRITICS CLASH. *Boston Globe:* HARDHATS MOB STUDENTS, RAISE FLAG AT CITY HALL IN N.Y. ANTIWAR RALLY. *New York Times:* WAR FOES HERE ATTACKED BY CONSTRUCTION WORKERS: CITY HALL IS STORMED. The *Times*'s front page featured a photo of workmen surging up the stairs of Federal Hall, waving flags, the statue of Washington at the rear, looking away.

By Sunday, the cover of the nation's most-read newspaper, the *Daily News,* showed Nixon conversing with hippies. Above it: LINDSAY RAPS COPS'

'FAILURE.' Liberals pressed the mayor to offer more than words. Congressman Ed Koch, a brash and bald fortysomething, represented Lindsay's old district. "The police commissioner ought to resign—or be made to resign," Koch said.

Meanwhile, in the Financial District, city workers unloaded barricades from vans. Officials girded for more.

Seven thousand more marched on Monday. Hardhats and longshoremen and the random kindred—men with brokerage coats and starched-shirt clerks and coiffed ladies with quilted handbags. More bystanders hip-hip-hoobrayed from the sidewalk. More applauded from high-rise windows. More clouds of tickertape twisted in the wind between skyscrapers.

The throng marched from Battery Park to City Hall under a hot May sun. Again, they sang "God Bless America" and "The Star-Spangled Banner." An old flatbed truck carried flag wavers. At one point, hardhats banged oil drums beneath a flutter of tickertape. Cabbies and truck drivers rolled down their windows and stretched out their arms to shake workmen's hands. Bystanders stepped into the streets by the hundreds. The workers continued uptown and formed a crescent around City Hall. Lindsay never left his office. But he heard it. "Lindsay's a bum! . . . Lindsay must go! . . . We're number one!" One sign was stenciled, STOP AIR POLLUTION: MUZZLE MAYOR LINDSAY. A large placard pictured a flag and read HONOR AMERICA.

From the sidelines, riot-ready police looked on, some spinning their clubs. Thirteen hundred cops were in the streets—on foot, on scooters, on horseback, plainclothesmen too. The NYPD did not want more bad PR by allowing another BLOODY FRIDAY, to quote the headline in that morning's *Wall Street Journal*. At one point, Commissioner Leary surveyed the hardhats through sunglasses and scoffed at being pressured to deploy such a large force. "It's a big day—for the budget," he said.

Periodic violence persisted. On Broadway, a student was thrown through a shop's plate glass window. Cops quelled one workman ranting that kids are "not going to overthrow this country!"

Pace College was shuttered, like a third of colleges nationwide. A few hundred Pace students, at most, still took to the streets. Workmen were assembled across the roadway. Students shouted the familiar chants. One workman yelled from City Hall Park, "Come on, punks."

About twenty-five hardhats leapt across the median of Park Row and collided into the students. More shouting, more shoving, more fights. City worker James Stiles saw a hardhat level a longhair and boot-kick him in the body. A workman struck Stiles in the face. He fell and pulled inward and tried to use his arms to screen the strikes. He said, "I kept shouting that I was not one of the peace demonstrators and finally they left."

Mounted policemen came in fast. Patrolmen sprinted. The scrum scattered. It was over in a minute. Some cops carried students inside Pace. Nearby, a bearded city worker got in an argument with a workman. The hardhat jabbed him with a flagstaff and hit him.

On Broad Street, an International Business Machines salesman gave the peace sign. A hardhat lurched across a gray barricade and punched him in the mouth.

"The new Nazis: they're here," muttered a woman, watching nearby.

Several hardhats also restrained hotheads who were about to "get out of hand," the AP reported. Longshoremen said that union bosses had ordered them to "keep our hands at our sides."

Back near City Hall, hardhats chanted on. At one point, at the helm of the throng, some blue-collar boys saw a young woman, in short shorts and a tight white blouse, don a flag-adorned hard hat. Boys lifted her onto their shoulders and she smiled. Yet the playful quickly swerved serious when the counterdemonstrators were engaged. "People are fed up," said Geraldine Lee, a 29-year-old insurance underwriter. "Nobody has been speaking to the average worker. Nobody cares about what we want or how we feel."

A Brooklyn mother said she was worried about her teenage son being drafted. But she added, "I wouldn't want him to run into college and hide. I don't want him to think he can live off this land and not have to give something back."

By day's end, four hardhats were arrested for minor charges such as harassment. Three more arrests than during Friday's riot. Twenty-year-old Lennie Lavoro, a Twin Towers elevator constructor, was among them. That night, he returned to southeastern Brooklyn, to his small brick home, attached housing, the garage below the living room. "I don't care if a person stands on a street corner and tells everybody 'I don't like the war,' I don't like it either," Lavoro said. "But when they try to ruin the country and desecrate the flag, I can't stand it."[2]

◆

The next day, a thousand business school students rallied against the war outside the Stock Exchange. They had come from Harvard, Dartmouth, Columbia, NYU, MIT, University of Pennsylvania. The NYPD blockaded the students with barricades. The blue helmets seemed everywhere. The police kept the tribes apart. In the center, grad students with pressed shirtsleeves and neckties and blazers, held antiwar placards. Beyond the police lines, bunching into the barricades, a few thousand men with hard hats, wearing coveralls, names printed on their shirts, protesting the activism of America's future elite.

Workmen now too had a cause. In midtown, James Lapham entered a dank bar frequented by hardhats. "We got to go out and demonstrate!" shouted Lapham, the full-time electrician who also attended school and believed "class is an important part of" hardhat discontent. He led his own modest rally. Looking back, Lapham stressed that most hardhats were veterans. "They fought. And to see the American flag burnt and being spat upon—that was a different society. No one could conceive of that generation accepting things like that. So there are two sides of the story. The construction guys were beating up the students. But on the other hand, these kids incited people who fought for this country." He added, "Someone had to say enough is enough."[3]

Like never before, workmen demonstrated daily, largely downtown—a thousand or two some days, far more on other days. Men began coming down from midtown construction sites. Some workmen took half-day pay cuts to attend rallies. The ongoing protests attracted more white collars, more conventional conservatives, right-wing activists too. Meanwhile, far more American flags were seen affixed to wooden scaffolding and derricks and rusty beams. *Business Week* reported the scene after the riot: "As the days passed, it seemed that the whole downtown area belonged to the strapping men in hard hats."[4]

Fallout accumulated. The *Times* editorialized the day after the riot: "The hardhats, long scornful of excesses by privileged longhairs on campus, were obviously delighted" to "pour out their hatred on the students" and offer "their venom against the mayor, the most articulate spokesman in public life" for "college youth" and "for the right to dissent." Once champions of "law and order," hardhats had joined "the revolutionaries and bomb-throwers on the left in demonstrating that anarchy is fast becoming a mode of political expression."[5]

Reporters grilled labor leaders on whether they were behind it. "The unions had nothing to do with it," Peter Brennan said. "The men acted on their own." He was burly, with a big face, big jowls, ruddy skin, white hair, and an easy smile. An ironworker's son, Brennan had gotten his start as a painter's apprentice during the Depression. He became a journeyman and after the Second World War, where he served as a submariner in the Pacific, took up union affairs. He now led the Construction Trades Council of Greater New York. The umbrella labor group represented two hundred thousand workers in 1970. "Many of them are war veterans or have sons or relatives fighting in Vietnam," Brennan said. "They were fed up with violence by antiwar demonstrators, by those who spat at the American flag and desecrated it."[6]

The same day, the presidents of five police associations, representing different levels of NYPD ranks—by far the largest police force nationwide—accused Mayor Lindsay of hypocrisy. They said the mayor demanded police take a firm hand to workmen. But—in a veiled jab at Lindsay's liberal base—they alleged that on other occasions the police "have been ordered to stand by and overlook violations of the law by demonstrators." The police leaders added that Lindsay's "political inference" undercut confidence in a city on "the brink of anarchy."

On Tuesday in Washington, President Nixon made an unscheduled visit to the nearby AFL-CIO headquarters. Nixon met privately with labor leaders, including the AFL-CIO president, squat and jut-jawed George Meany, the grandson of Irish refugees of the Great Famine, a Bronx-born plumber, a longtime Democrat, and perhaps the most powerful American labor leader. Later, when reporters asked about the riot, Meany equivocated. "I don't like anybody beating anybody up," he said. "But I certainly feel the construction workers are no more to be blamed than the students who were resorting to violence." The next day, White House aide Tom Huston memoed Nixon's top advisors. It was time, Huston wrote, to "quit talking about the Great Silent Majority and start talking to it."[7]

In New York, the city's local CBS affiliate broadcasted a debate between NYU film student Harry Bolles and glazier Joseph Stern, who asked to be called just Joe on the air.

Joe said he had backed Humphrey in 1968. He still thought people should respect the president. He spoke most of war. His father's service in the First World War. His service in the Second World War. "I've defended that flag every way I possibly can." He conceded, however, that this was not war. "It was a gut reaction," he said. "We're fed up with the attitude that they can do whatever they want . . . like a spoiled little boy." Joe spoke of firebombed ROTC buildings. "Somebody's got to face up to it."

Harry Bolles, fresh from the antiwar protest in Washington, defended the students' "frustration." They had been "struggling" to end this war for years. He said Nixon's cavalier attitude provoked activists to burn ROTC buildings. "It's sad," he added, "but it's just what happens." He said he didn't support the flag being spat upon. But the flag had been "taken over by supporters of the Nixon government." When protestors spit on it, he added, they were "spitting on that aspect of the symbol" and "not the goodness of America."[8]

A week after the riot, more awful news. On May 14 in Mississippi, after ongoing unrest at Jackson State—the hurling of rocks and bottles, trash fires, a dump truck set ablaze—the fire department requested protection from police. Around midnight, cops came to the brick-and-concrete campus. There was no grave threat to them. Still, policemen fired some four hundred rounds. Two black students died. Campus killings by authorities were now an open-ended story. At the time, no one knew when the student bloodshed would end.

The official reports were still to come. But as the *Economist* later wrote, both shootings were at their minimum "a horrifying indictment of the abuse of lethal weapons by law enforcement."[9]

Meanwhile, marking one week since the riot, marching persisted. A thousand hardhats in midtown. Five thousand clustered downtown. They were more organized, or organizers had now come to them. A twelve-piece brass band, composed of gray-haired Italian Americans, played patriotic staples and "The Sidewalks of New York" (Al Smith's campaign song). Flag pins were now seen. Two men carried a banner that read, SILENT MAJORITY MOBILIZATION COMM. But it was mostly the (now) familiar sight. Tickertape. Hardhats denouncing peaceniks. Placards deriding Lindsay. Flags flapping in the wind.

Workmen raised the flag over the old Tweed Courthouse. The flagpole in front of the *Wall Street Journal*'s building was bare. Workmen pushed through police lines, bulled inside, and soon the flag was seen outside.

Near City Hall Park, a dozen young black people shouted antiwar slogans. Workmen glared. But they did not charge. Union leaders had instructed, "Demonstrate all you want but be careful, no violence." George Daly, the steamfitter chief and onetime boxer, attended some marches to ensure it.

The union chiefs sought to regain the media narrative. They didn't want people calling them radicals. As hardhats marched on the avenue below the US Steel Building, hundreds of workmen clanged their tools and helmets against steel beams. The wincing gong echoed across downtown.

With the spectacle, some quickly sought to co-opt the cause. In California, a Republican congressional candidate pledged to wear a hard hat every day of the primary. That first Tuesday after the riot, a 23-year-old electrical construction worker, Robert Bellow, was with the workmen near the plaza. As

A young construction worker exhorts fellow workmen. As a thousand business school students from schools such as Harvard, Wharton, and Columbia protested the war in Vietnam around Wall Street, a few thousand hardhats counterdemonstrated at the periphery. (Bettmann/Getty)

they were singing, Bellow said two men in suits with a "foreign accent, probably Italian," had "urged them to break through the barricades." He ignored them. The instigators berated these hardhats: "Leftists . . . communists . . . cowards!"[10]

In Greenwich Village, Tommy Galligan took up a collection to place a huge flag on his worksite. He had a fleshy broad face and a squinty smile. A onetime amateur boxer who believed Muhammad Ali should not have been stripped of his title (for refusing to be drafted), Galligan was a derrick driver, a father of two, an Elk who lived in the Bronx and had his car stolen more than once. He now had a police lock on his apartment door (the most fortified model: the iron bar fit into a floor socket and buttressed the door). His wife spoke "wistfully" of the suburbs. "This is where the money is. I've got to live here," he said. "You live in this country, take what it gives you, you take your chances," he added, "like everybody else." Galligan also disliked the mayor. Lindsay's recent comment that antiwar protestors were heroic "infuriated" him.[11]

Not every hardhat favored the overt patriotism. Edward Polito surveyed his fellow workmen's flag decals and said, "They should show the flag in their heart, not on their helmets." But Polito still marched with them.[12]

NBC News's Liz Trotta gave hardhats the most airtime. Ironworker Eugene Schafer recounted his scuffle with students after some "started ripping the flag up," the day before the riot. Among those she also interviewed: a guy with a cigarette behind his ear and a helmet that read K.O. JOE. "It's not a question of just construction workers," K.O. Joe said. "You see construction workers because they stand out more, [with their] dirty clothes and hats," but, he added, "it's a majority of the people that are complaining."

"I think we've run out of words," a heavyset hardhat said. "If that's the only thing that can shape them up, we'll shape them up with that, then. That's what we did in the Marine Corps."

NBC cut to the next interview. "Nobody wants violence," this hardhat said, a thin man with a genial smile. "I'm sure of that. Especially us. We're all family men. We can't afford to be violent. We have to get up and earn a living."

At times, the camera panned out. It showed the landscape of steam and steel and gravel. And for a few seconds, viewers only heard hammers hitting iron.

The NBC reporter asked another hardhat: "Some people have described this to be almost like a class struggle. Do you feel it's that way?"

"Definitely. There's nothing wrong with the working class. The working class is what built, what made us, what built this town," the construction worker said. Of the student activists: "I think if they went out and tried a little work themselves, they'd see that we have it twice as hard, as they think we have it twice as easy. It's not that easy. It's not that easy at all."[13]

◆

The Hardhat Riot left more than a hundred wounded. The NYPD recorded about seventy casualties. But its list excluded most of those treated at Trinity Church and other facilities. Protestor Drew Lynch, for example, sought treatment from a Brooklyn hospital. His expenses were paid for by a relatively new program called Medicaid. Other victims saw private doctors, such as law clerk and future federal judge Ray Randolph. Randolph's right eye had "turned blood red" and swelled shut. Soon, "my whole face was black and blue." The doctor said he "came within an inch of losing" his eye.

The typical victim was a 22-year-old white male collegian. One in four of the wounded, from the NYPD's list, were female. Seven cops were also injured. It's unclear how many hardhats were hurt. The NYPD's list counted forty young people with head wounds. The most serious injuries were to the half-dozen young men beaten unconscious.[14]

Lindsay's pledge, that there would be repercussions, was never carried out. The one hardhat arrested that day was an elevator constructor in his mid-forties. Later that month, the electrician who had scrapped with the Lehman heir was arrested for rabble-rousing at another rally.

The young lawyer knocked out for trying to stop a fight, Michael Belknap, became the lead plaintiff in a class-action suit. The ACLU called for a federal probe. Its New York branch spearheaded the litigation against the NYPD. A week after the riot, a US attorney said the federal government would determine whether protestors had been deprived of their constitutional rights on Bloody Friday. The US attorney, apparently at the urging of the ACLU, asked the FBI's Manhattan field office to carry out an investigation.

Out of political expedience, the Nixon White House might have quashed any federal investigation. On May 12, 1970, Nixon aide Tom Huston wrote Nixon's top advisors. Huston "strongly recommended" that the Justice Department not authorize the investigation because "while there may have been a lack of zealous law enforcement . . . it is questionable whether the civil rights of the protesting students were any more violated than those of countless thousands, who have previously been on the receiving end of student demonstrations. We are currently running a very large risk of alienating the Silent Majority."

If this memo had come out at the time, it would have been front-page news. Nearly a half-century later, the FBI claimed no record of an investigation. Unlike the Columbia occupation, Chicago '68, or Kent State, the Hardhat Riot was not investigated by an objective third party. Lindsay let it go, perhaps to avoid worsening relations with the cops, perhaps to avoid publicizing his city's disunity or his disengagement that day. The mayor was eyeing the presidency. Meanwhile, the litigation against the NYPD failed in federal court.[15]

In mid-August, the NYPD completed its own probe. The department was incentivized to go light on its own actions, but on other matters, such as conspiracy, it seems to have conducted itself professionally. NYPD detectives investigated for months. The intelligence division furnished investigators with lists of New Yorkers who were members of a half-dozen right-wing groups, from the John Birch Society to Cuban Power. They did not discover any relationship with the rioters. The cops eventually interviewed hundreds of witnesses and participants. There was, for the most part, a consistent criticism of police (not something cops are enthused to record, even in confidential files). But there was not a steady theme of top-down organization. The prevailing sense? Disorder. To be sure, the hardhats had loosely organized themselves. The afternoon before the riot, some men spread the word between worksites, hoping to rally construction workers to confront antiwar activists on May 8. The workmen who took on a leadership role probably did task some hardhats (like K.O. Joe) with keeping the streets clear as the bulk of hardhats paraded, a duty that at least suggests blocking and tackling. But the preponderance of the evidence, by a large length, undercut the idea of larger conspiracies. Some news outlets made one loose connection to the far right, citing the publisher of the small weekly the *New York Graphic*. The NYPD described it internally as an "ultra-rightwing periodical." Publisher Ralph Clifford and editor Jeff Smith had joined in the riot midway. The liberal *New York Post* first suggested Clifford was the riot's organizer. The *Nation* called Clifford the riot's "propagandist and instigator," and a similar theory threaded some histories thereafter. But there's no substantial evidence behind the *Graphic* theory. The confrontations with student radicals escalated over days. Film footage, numerous witness statements recounting the initial charge, and the voluminous evidence detailing the hours afterward all paint a scene of genuinely escalating tension, spontaneous outbreak, authentic rage, as well as a heartfelt revolt against lowering the flag for antiwar demonstrators. There were a few anonymous reports in the press that shop stewards paid some of the hardhats. But there's no evidence of it. The NYPD and a district attorney, according to police records, questioned both Clifford and Smith "at length." But the "investigation failed to disclose that [Clifford] has or can exert any influence on the activities of construction workers or that he planned or directed any of their activities," an NYPD internal report read. The investigators concluded: "It is more than likely that [Clifford's presence at the riot] was because of the location of his office and that he joined in after the situation began to develop."[16]

In the months after, police staked out construction sites. At the Twin Towers and other worksites, cops looked for men who matched witness accounts or photos from the riot.

Elevator constructor Joe Kelly let it slip to the *Times* that his partner, Tommy, had shimmied up a light stanchion to plant the flag. The account was roughly similar to what victims and witnesses told the cops. A detective tried to get answers at the Trade Center. In the elevator mechanics' shed, a cop found a subcontractor's book. It had fourteen Toms at the Twin Towers. The detective asked some questions of foremen but was "rebuffed."

Meanwhile, Joe Kelly was warned that the police intended to question him. Kelly fled the site. The union told Kelly to let their lawyer do the talking from now on. It was the same advice the police union gave its officers under investigation. The inquiry petered out.

In the main, scores of witnesses spoke of seeing trouble or needing help and police refusing to help. At times, several lawyers gave separate affidavits about witnessing the same incident, swearing to police indifference, but those too came to naught.[17]

Ultimately, the NYPD public report pulled punches with the hardhats. "Although there was some advance warning" of a hardhat counterdemonstration, the police wrote, it was not "readily verifiable" and the "magnitude and ebullience of the activities by them, and their hosts of supporters, could not be accurately foretold."

Internally, investigators reported that most "witnesses are unable to provide specific information to facilitate the identification of assailants or alleged police misconduct." When specific information was provided, however, no full-court press followed.[18]

Mayoral aide Kate Klein tried to obtain some justice. She named the lieutenant who had ordered subordinates to not stop a brawl. But the investigating captain decided not to push the matter. He concluded, "The security of City Hall was probably the paramount issue at the time." Thirty to forty cops had manned City Hall's steps at that moment. Could the NYPD have spared some men to stop the beatings below?[19]

"The hallmark of the professional policeman is objectivity, impartiality, fairness, adherence to the law," read a 1967 memo dictating NYPD conduct at demonstrations and ordered distributed to every cop. "The policeman has a sworn duty to uphold the law, an unmistakable obligation to preserve the peace, and a clear mandate to act when action is needed. Nothing less than full compliance with these dictums will suffice."

In their internal reports, Chiefs Taylor and Morgan wrote that their men's performance was exemplary under the "most trying of conditions," as Morgan put it. Inspector Schryver agreed. But Schryver's account to internal affairs—which was never publicly disclosed, like all internal records referenced in this book—uniquely acknowledged tension between the police and the protestors. Schryver wrote that student activism, after Cambodia and Kent State, "contributed to the hostilities between police and students which eventually reached a climax in the happenings of May 8, 1970."

In July, as a result of its inquiry, two cops faced minor charges for neglecting to render medical aid or failing to "properly investigate" and record a complaint. Ultimately, the NYPD buried most records of police malfeasance, based on the thousands of pages of NYPD and legal records that were never made public (until researching this book). For example, the police never publicized that squad cars carried flag-waving hardhats. They buried the exchange between the patrolman and the lawyer who wanted to hold K.O. Joe accountable. Internal records concluded that the young patrolman from southwest Brooklyn—who had counseled K.O. Joe, "You're gonna file a cross-complaint, right—had "urged" K.O. Joe to "present false charges." There was no disciplinary action. K.O. Joe ultimately got off scot-free too, despite at least four witnesses identifying him as an assailant (including in affidavits).

Writ large, the NYPD's probe grossly minimized the witnesses' consensus. These witnesses were not merely speaking with reporters; people commonly speak loosely with reporters. In this case, though, hundreds of witnesses gave police statements or sworn affidavits. The takeaway: police were outnumbered and overwhelmed but dozens of cops could have stopped the attacks and did not act. The NYPD's public report dodged responsibility. Instead, it blamed understaffing, the instigating students, the limited range of handheld radios, the unprecedented nature of the confrontation.[20]

The NYPD also found no evidence that labor leaders had planned the riot. Still, the assumption that they had found its way into some media accounts for decades. In part, the notion stemmed from several witnesses noting a few men in business suits rabble-rousing or trying to direct rioters. The most visible man in a suit had been atop the statue pedestal at the riot's outset, one of those men fighting at Washington's feet after the hefty man debased the flag. That man in the suit looked like a bigwig: neatly combed jet-black hair, collared shirt, Windsor-knotted tie. It turned out, though, that he had at least twelve prior arrests. His name was Richard Gauthier. He was photographed throughout the riot, applauding the hardhats from the sidelines, marching beside them. The NYPD had determined he was a "provocateur" of Bloody Friday. Film footage showed him in the area well before the hardhats arrived, while the students demonstrated, engaging activists in conversation. After the NYPD's public report came out, he was located living under an alias at a cheap hotel in the Bowery. Patrolmen Burns had also identified him, which led to his arrest. That winter, Gauthier pled guilty to attempted assault of Patrolman Burns. He was sentenced to ninety days in prison. Here was the one significant arrest for all the NYPD's work. But no one heard of it.[21]

Mayor Lindsay had, in the final measure, tasked the NYPD to investigate whether police could have protected New Yorkers. The public report's tone did not encourage an impression of impartial justice. It described the hardhats' behavior, rather euphemistically, as "ebullience." Internal documents also betrayed bias. The NYPD's records were never seen by those who bled in the riot—those most impacted, those who most cared.[22]

Media coverage noted that the police acquitted themselves. The *Journal* headline began: OWN REPORT CLEARS NEW YORK'S POLICE. The *Times* headline began: POLICE DEFEND ACTIONS. The ACLU's counsel called the report a "calculated whitewash." Lindsay ducked. He promised to give the report "intense study." Gone was his talk of "marauding" hardhats. Gone was the denunciation of police "breakdown."

Victims still cringe that the cops were never held accountable. "Policemen stood around and watched the attacks!" Michael Belknap said, clenching his teeth, his throat catching, as he struggled to find the words nearly a half-century after. "I could have been killed!" Much like Chicago '68, many of those who lived the riot's brutality were surprised no one died. "I saw some of those kids go down and I didn't think they were gonna get up," elevator mechanic Joe Kelly recounted.

Few hardhats owned up to the extent of their violence. The Monday after the riot, as hardhats stretched seven blocks, a CBS reporter pulled one aside. He had his helmet backward, wore a flannel shirt with rolled-up sleeves. His hair was dark, eyebrows wide, his sideburns trimmed at the cheekbone. The reporter asked, "How do you feel about the construction workers who attacked the demonstrators Friday?"

"Don't say attacked. Don't say attacked. They were provoked." He eyeballed the reporter. "They were provoked, man." He jabbed his right index finger forward. "We work for a living! Every day we get up!" His left hand pointed to the high skyline. "We're out there in the cold, the rain, the snow, right? We gotta have these dirty—" He clamped his mouth down and sniffed. "Forgetta 'bout it." He waved his arms, exhaled, hinted a smile. "I don't want to talk about it."[23]

Long after, the worst often went unsaid. Decades later, despite several attempts to discuss that day, K.O. Joe only said, "I did some things I'm not proud of."

"There's not a man among us who is proud of what he did," said World War Two veteran Wallace Butenhoff, a sheet metal worker who participated in the riot. "But we just couldn't stand there and take it anymore. They were waving Vietcong flags. Some of them spit on our flag. It was just a spontaneous reaction on our part." Butenhoff said the students had a "right to dissent." But, he added, "we just can't let them burn down buildings the way they do. We can't let them close down colleges. What about the kids who want to go?" He added, "Don't get me wrong. Don't think we're for war. No one is."[24]

"It was never planned to explode but it did explode," construction worker Thomas Burns recalled. "I was on Water Street and we all just headed towards Broadway. All you could hear was just shouting, senses of 'Let's get the bastards.' And, 'Let's finish this once and for all.' And there was some blood spilled," he added. "It was all in anger. All in vengeance. 'Let's get them.' And a lot of people, including myself, [were] releasing the hate and the feelings that you had. Of course, a lot of us felt [like] winners. We felt very proud. We scattered the enemy."[25]

Many of the participants prided not their brutality but what it inspired and the message it sent. They believed that privileged kids had gotten what was coming to them, that peaceniks had defamed the same country that gave them the good life. They often would concede the right to dissent. But a beat later, they would stew over how these "punks" dissented. It was not only their fury over those who preached justice while avoiding their "wartime duty," or the "brats" who had pretensions of better character as they indulged in the counterculture while securely stateside, even as others were at work or at war. It was those who justified the firebombing of public buildings (these men were builders, after all) and the New Left's tendency to get high-handed about American imperialism while not only remaining silent on the terrors of communism but also waving those red flags.

Workmen prevaricated too. There were apologists for the militant among them. When confronted with the full measure of that day, whataboutism was common. Hardhats emphasized the leftist radicals—the bombings, the arson, the seizures of public property. And, like liberal militants, they understated the harm they themselves had caused. Men noted that no one had died. No one had been paralyzed. They were a class of men who had fought wars. Their daily labor required reckoning with hazard. They were weaned in a world where young boys learned to bite their lower lip rather than admit pain, where "punch for punch" was lightweight play and tougher boys drew blood, where schoolday insults came to schoolyard blows, where the hard turns of life—dead fathers, dads out of work or with too little work—forced boys to "buck up," leave school early, and labor young. So they became men, many taking beatings along the way, and sometimes you deserved it—"You got what was coming to you." May 8 felt that way to many of them. They might not pride the brutal episodes. But all in all, to countless among them, Bloody Friday was "just deserts."

Yet the hardhats had sent that message by violating their own codes. It was more than lawlessness from those who sought law and order. Many kicked men when they were down. Scores did not "pick on someone their own size." Provocateurs were attacked, but so were innocents. It was often not a "fair fight." Some hardhats did assault unarmed students with metal tools. Workmen had "fought dirty." Countless "sucker-punched." Several hardhats had struck or harassed women. The construction workers began their protest marching for their honor, for what they honored. Yet the day they rioted, hundreds equated political opposition with the enemy. They sought to demonstrate patriotism by beating their countrymen bloody.

In the mainstream press, the riot's impact quickly exceeded its viciousness. The peaceful hardhat rallies in the days after ensured that much, as did the symbolism stirred—of old-time Democrats combatting the New Left, as well as the novelty of blue-collar demonstrations against the liberal student activists who had protested for years. "May 1970 will be remembered as the month when one segment of what President Nixon calls the Silent Majority ended its public 'silence' with a vengeance," declared the *National Observer*, a prominent weekly newspaper. Since the Hardhat Riot, reported the *Christian Science Monitor* from New York, "pro-American sentiment reached an emotional peak never seen here before." *Time* magazine reported: "Almost overnight, 'hardhats' became synonymous with white working-class conservatives." And they knew it. Joe Kelly said, "The hardhat is being used to represent all of the Silent Majority!"[26]

CHAPTER 23 | "Workers' Woodstock"

THE HARDHAT ACTIVISM culminated on May 20, twelve days after the riot. Rallies occurred in cities from Pittsburgh to San Diego. It was in Manhattan, however, that as many as 150,000 construction workers, Teamsters, and longshoremen deluged City Hall with a sea of American flags.

Shortly past noon, the national anthem played. Thousands of helmets were removed in one sweeping motion. Peter Brennan stood above the crowd, surrounded by fellow chiefs in rumpled alumicron suits. Steamfitter boss George Daly was at his side. So was Teddy Gleason, the longshoremen labor leader.

"History is being made here today," said Brennan, wearing a white hard hat with a flag decal. "We are saying to the students that maybe today we are willing to work with you. . . . We are recognizing the rights of everyone to protest, regardless of if we agree with them or not. And we are asking you to carry on the rest of this day without any violence." The crowd applauded. Brennan spoke of their "great honor" of "being the builders of this country." That they had a "responsibility that you cannot overlook by letting some-body taunt you." He reminded them, lifting his left hand and making the V-sign, that "when they give you the peace sign, all of us in World War Two used to use that as the sign of victory." And he raised his voice: "There's nothing wrong with the peace sign or the sign of victory!" He added, "Most of our men are veterans and those who served in a war know that a war is not something that you are happy about. And we want to see it ended. Now, the only difference that we may have is the procedure used to end this." He said, "America does not want to see the war in Vietnam. What it wants to see is democracy." And he reiterated, "We want the boys home." The hardhat chief asserted, "We are all against the war." But he added, "To those who are ridiculing us because we take what they call a rag," this flag is "more than just a piece of cloth. Men died for it." The throng cheered and whistled and waved their helmets.

They also booed mentions of John Lindsay. Before the rally began, several hardhats hung an effigy of the mayor on a lamppost. It was quickly removed, at the behest of police. Petitions urged Lindsay's impeachment. One sign referenced Lindsay's comment that protestors are "the guys who are heroic." It partly read: LINDSAY, BURN YOUR COMMIE CARD AND YOU TOO WILL BE A HERO. Elsewhere, workers covered a concrete mixer with flags and a sign that read, LINDSAY FOR MAYOR OF HANOI.[1]

Lindsay arrived in an unmarked car around half past twelve. He remained in his vehicle, conferring with aides. The police escort was close by. Lindsay emerged twenty minutes later and slipped inside City Hall through a rear basement door.[2]

Outside, countless signs: WE HARD HAT MEN ARE BUILDING AMERICA, NOT DESTROYING IT. NO SURRENDER. MY COUNTRY, RIGHT OR WRONG. DUMP ANARCHY. SOCK IT TO 'EM, SPIRO. HARDHATS BUILD CITIES— LINDSAY DESTROYS THEM. One sign read, perhaps aiming to goad the left, GOD BLESS THE ESTABLISHMENT. Some placards encouraged civility. BUILD, DON'T BURN read one. Another: OUR FLAG STANDS FOR A LOT AND NO 1 IS: SPEAK YOUR MIND AND LET OTHERS DO THE SAME. A large banner: LONG-SHORT HAIR, WE DON'T CARE. SUPPORT THE FLAG WE SHARE.[3]

Big Joe Kelly jutted his chin forward and waved a gold-fringed flag from the mass below. He had led a hundred of his Local No. 1 union members to the rally. Kelly was "resolutely serious-faced, rarely showing a thin smile, ignoring the pretty secretaries leaning over the police barriers," noted the *Times* man beside him. There were some clerks, businessmen, typists, and workers' family members. But it was mostly carpenters, sandhogs, laborers, elevator constructors, boilermakers, painters, plasterers, longshoremen, Teamsters, roofers, communications workers, labor secretaries, steamfitters, concrete and electrical and asbestos and sheet metal workers, bricklayers, typesetters, plumbers, lathers, ironworkers. They came from Brooklyn, Queens, Staten Island, north Jersey, upstate, the suburbs of Long Island.

"We were shocked that the streets were loaded from one end to the other," George Daly said, recalling the day vividly into his nineties. One attendee was Robert O'Malley. O'Malley, a square-jawed steamfitter from Queens with deep-set eyes, was the first Marine to receive the Medal of Honor in the Vietnam War. O'Malley remained by Daly's side all day.

Later, the *Washington Post* asked Brennan to explain this new blue-collar activism. The ruddy-faced Irishman got "close to tears" and said, "You people in the newspapers say we are bums and hoodlums. . . . But our people are decent people. They work in the church and the synagogue and the Little League and the Boys Scouts. They would tear up their union cards before they would do anything to hurt this country. We built this country. We build these beautiful buildings and churches and highways and bridges and schools. We love this country. We were afraid it was going down the drain and nobody was doing anything about it. That's why we marched."[4]

Most reporters were fair to the men this day. The *Times* would quote workmen at length. The three networks gave the rally extensive coverage.

"It's time people marched for this country instead of against it," said ironworker Joe Wright. A crane operator wearing a flag-decaled helmet, Richard Roeber, said, "It's about time something like this has been done." A 40-year-old general foreman at the Trade Center site, Robert Romano, said, "I don't think [the student protesters] are absolutely wrong" but they "are getting carried away" and have had a "silver spoon in their mouth too long." John Nash, a middle-aged newspaper printer and World War Two veteran, spoke of his boy. He was set to enter the military that winter. Nash said, "I'm proud of him. It's a chance we all had to take. It's his turn." What did the flag mean to him? "Outside of God, it's the most important thing I know," Nash answered. "I know a lot of good friends died under this." Allison Greaker marched with her family, including one-year-old Richard Nixon Greaker. "We're part of the silent majority," she said. "I have a lot of faith in the college kids," she added, but they're "heard enough, and we're answering them right now." Robert Geary, a middle-aged office worker, said the flag was "part of me. I fought for it myself two or three years in the Second World War." Why had he attended this demonstration? "I'm very proud to be an American, and I know my boy that was killed in Vietnam would be here today if he was alive, marching with us." A 25-year-old electrician from Queens, Raymond Massaro, who wore a flag-adorned hard hat, said, "I have a lot of friends that are over there being killed and I don't go for" the antiwar activism. "I should be called any day" in the draft. "I'll definitely serve this country." He said antiwar protestors "have a right to feel the way they do, especially if they have brothers or friends" in the war. But he added, "I'm for this country. These are my people. Right here."[5]

From afar, the crowd was cinematic in scope, a vast throng of primary colors. Sunlight glinted off the silver duckbill helmets and men unfurled massive flags and waved thousands of small flags. The graying musicians of the Ray Bloch Band, from *The Ed Sullivan Show*, played the "Marines'

On May 20, 1970, 150,000 construction workers, teamsters, and longshoremen demonstrated at City Hall and marched along Broadway to protest antiwar activists and Mayor John Lindsay, and express support for the troops in Vietnam. It was the largest in a series of construction worker demonstrations following the Hardhat Riot. (Spencer Jones/AP)

Hymn" from atop a flatbed truck. Men with faded war tattoos thundered along below. Countless sang the staples loud. "You're a Grand Old Flag." "Over There." "Proud of all we have done. Fighting till the battle's won," bellowed men, singing the Army's official song.

In nearby buildings, office workers leaned out their windows and again tossed fistfuls of paper shreds and tickertape. Confetti drifted through the hazy air toward the East River.

Native Americans dotted the crowd. For nearly a century, the Mohawk tribe were renowned ironworkers. Some planted roots in Brooklyn. But many Mohawks drove seven hours—sometimes it took much longer—every Friday back to the Caughnawaga Reservation along the St. Lawrence River, outside Montreal, to see their family, only to caravan back for Monday's work. A tribal spokesman, Fallen Trees, ceremonially shook his feathered war bonnet. "We're here because it's our country, even though it hasn't always treated us so well," said Ouimet, a 23-year-old who served in the military in Germany. "It's the way these men feel," said Cross, a big twentysomething. "We got tired of the punks running the country down."

A cannon fired. A flock of pigeons scattered into the pale blue sky. Near Pace, some college kids assembled behind a police line. They gave the peace sign. One student yelled, "Fascist pigs!" At that, backs went up. A barrage of insults followed—"Cowards . . . bastards . . . faggots . . . commies !" But the "prissy, self-righteous" students and the "angry and hateful" workmen yelling back, as one reporter described the scrum, did not fight. Some 3,800 cops were deployed to make sure of it. The blue helmets and the hardhats remained collegial. Some knowing smiles were exchanged. Outside that, by all accounts, the police were professional, squashing a handful of confrontations.[6]

That evening, the three networks headlined their news coverage by declaring it a massive demonstration for the Nixon administration. Tomorrow, the *Times* would describe it as a rally "supporting the Vietnam policies of President Nixon and assailing Mayor Lindsay and other opponents of the war." The *Daily News* cover line: 150,000 PARADE FOR NIXON. The *Washington Post* lede told of a "giant rally in support of the Vietnam War." The term "prowar" had littered media headlines since the onset of the blue-collar protests, as it would in headline coverage of today—from the *Wall Street Journal* to the *Washington Post* to the *New York Post*. It was the *Los Angeles Times* that found the correct note: "It was overwhelmingly an anti-antiwar protesters rally, aimed at expressing love of country and displeasure with antiwar elements, rather than unequivocal support of the Nixon Administration's conduct of the war in Vietnam and Cambodia." The *Economist* reported that most of the blue-collar "marchers deplore it"—the war, that is—even as they implored for patriotism. Later, after an *Esquire* writer spoke with dozens of hardhats, he noted, "They resent very much being simplified by the press in this fashion," as "prowar." The *Chicago Tribune* lede termed it an "unparalleled outpouring of patriotic fervor." "Probably not since the Second World War, or maybe even the First World War, has New York City seen an outburst of patriotic fervor that can match this one," ABC began its report. CBS concluded its coverage by stressing that, "in the din of counter protest," the "Silent Majority is rapidly" finding its voice. *Time* magazine declared the day "Workers' Woodstock."[7]

Some saw something else. "I'm scared," said college freshman Cliff Sloane, watching from the sidelines. "If this is what the class struggle is all about, there's something wrong."[8]

A workman holds a flag atop a lamppost on May 20, 1970, as some 150,000 workmen gather in Lower Manhattan in what *Time* magazine called "Workers' Woodstock." (Patrick A. Burns/The New York Times/Redux)

Afterward, it seemed to be snowing confetti. Tens of thousands marched down Broadway. They were sixteen to twenty abreast, parading beneath the blizzard of tickertape and streamers and paper scraps, as strangers cheered from skyscrapers. In one office, workers shredded antiwar pamphlets and tossed handfuls out the window. From the fourth floor of another building, four "office girls" held a banner: WE LOVE AMERICA AND MOST OF US ARE UNDER 30—DIG THAT! When a group of men passed a nun boutique—wimples for sale in the window—they hid their cans of Bud behind their back. Later, a "heavily-bosomed girl" leaned out a window and waved a flag. "Hey Kevin, couldn't you do with a little of that stuff right now," one man said, elbowing another. Crushed beer cans rattled off the curb. Atop a cement truck, teens and twentysomething boys reveled. One drummed the shell of the concrete mixer, booming a hollowly metallic *bang . . . bang . . . bang.* Above, a young lady wearing a red-white-and-blue boater blew kisses down at the crowd. The guys on the truck saw her and became energized. The driver blasted the air horn while riding the squealing brakes, to ensure he didn't hit anyone in the excitement, though those on foot, near the truck's cab, startled and jumped away. Elsewhere, a man in white shirtsleeves had his small son on his shoulders. The little boy held a little flag, his head swallowed by a flag-adorned hard hat. The father gripped his son's ankles and was wreathed in smiles. Nearby, a bagpipe skirled. A man in a tartan kilt and knee socks marched with an American flag. Big Joe Kelly led another contingent. When it was over, at Battery Park, a cool breeze came in from the bay. Kelly unclenched his fingers. He had carried the gold-fringed American flag for two hours. "Beautiful," one friend told him. Another, "Like a champ." Kelly hoped the day's outpouring would "wake a few people up."[9]

CHAPTER 24

"Our People Now": Nixon Sees a
Future in an Un-Silent Majority

"LAST WEEK, A group of construction workers came up Wall Street and beat the living hell out of some demonstrators who were desecrating the American flag," Pat Buchanan wrote in a confidential memo to Richard Nixon, dated one day after Workers' Woodstock. "Whether one condones this kind of violence or not, probably half the living rooms in America were in standing applause at the spectacle. Yesterday, the hardhats marched" again "in support." He added, "No union man would have done" that "ten years ago."

"The most insane suggestion I have heard about here in recent days was to the effect that we should somehow go prosecute the hardhats to win favor with the kiddies who are screaming about everything we are doing," Buchanan continued. "What have all our efforts . . . to win over the Fulbrights and the lefts—to show them we are reasonable—accomplished? With one decision in Cambodia, it went out the window."

Instead, Buchanan counseled, "it should be our focus to constantly speak to, to assure, to win, to aid, to promote the president's natural constituency—which is now the working men and women of the country, the common man, the Roosevelt New Dealer." He added, "There is a great ferment in American politics; these, quite candidly, are our people now."[1]

With more encouragement from Chuck Colson, Nixon phoned Peter Brennan and longshoreman chief Thomas Gleason that evening. Chief of Staff H. R. Haldeman wrote in his diary the same night that the president "thinks we're still too timid on mobilizing the Silent Majority." After speaking with the union bosses, Nixon immediately met with Chuck Colson. Colson was his counsel. He also occasionally liaised with labor leaders. As Colson recalled it, he first alerted Nixon to Workers' Woodstock the night before. He saw coverage of the massive rally on the news and went right in.[2]

"These people are out on the street marching in support of your policies. I think you ought to call them up," Colson said.

"I will do you one better. I would like to have them here in the White House," Nixon said, as Colson recounted it. Colson called Peter Brennan that night. He invited the union leaders to the White House and, likely, teed up the formal call with the president.[3]

"This display of emotional activity from the hardhats provides an opportunity," aide Steve Bull wrote Colson after Workers' Woodstock, "to forge a new alliance and perhaps result in the emergence of a 'new right.'" Bull continued, "The New Left has created the proper conditions" to create a "movement." "The key is to broaden the base of participation that will cut completely across racial and economic lines," he wrote. The "emphasis would be upon some of these supposedly trite mid-America values that the liberal press likes to snicker about: love of country, respect for people as individuals, the Golden Rule, etc."[4]

To Colson, Workers' Woodstock was a "seminal event in the Nixon years." In his journal, Pat Moynihan credited Colson for being "quick to spot" the political opportunity in the hardhats. Moynihan noted that Henry Kissinger was "telling the professors that if people keep taking to the streets it is them, not us, who will prevail. Power to the people means power to the hardhats and red necks." Kissinger considered the Hardhat Riot a fulcrum of Nixon's blue-collar populism. "The incident shocked some into the realization that a breakdown of civil order could backfire dangerously against the demonstrators," wrote Kissinger, Nixon's national security advisor. "But it did not slow down the pace of protest. It only encouraged Nixon in the belief that the masses of the American public were on his side." "That's where the hardhats came in. After Cambodia and Kent State," William Safire wrote, "Nixon desperately needed some expression of grassroots support."[5]

It was any campaign's dream. They could poach the other side's base. "They were clearly coming unmoored from the great FDR coalition," Pat Buchanan recalled. "These guys were alienated from an establishment, which was undermining the American war in Vietnam. They were alienated from these college kids, the revolt of the overprivileged." He added, "They were guys like the guys I grew up with."[6]

Buchanan had been born late in the Depression, the third of nine children, parochially schooled through Georgetown, and among his many causes and roles in the White House, he advocated a Catholic strategy to attract socially estranged northern Democrats.

It was coalition by common cultural foe. Nixon believed it too. Haldeman acted on the president's behalf. Four days after Bloody Friday—the same day Nixon made his unscheduled visit to AFL-CIO headquarters—Haldeman noted that the president "wants to try to implement Billy Graham's idea about a big pro-America rally, maybe on Fourth of July." It was to be called Honor America Day. It began with a conversation between Billy Graham and the president of *Reader's Digest*. A *Time* reporter wrote in his notes, after interviewing the preacher ahead of the celebration, "Graham wants it clear that Nixon had no planning or advisory function." However, the demarcation wasn't clean. Haldeman saw early plans for Honor America Day and scribbled: they needed better publicity, better crowd-building, and "a solid cornball program developer." Some aides winced at such jingoism. But not Nixon. He loved Patton, after all. A patriotic image moved him emotionally, including the day he saw a flag atop a construction crane. He relished advocating old-fashioned Americanism. "The military profession is derided in some of the 'best' circles," Nixon told Air Force Academy graduates in 1969. "Patriotism is considered by some to be a backward fetish of the uneducated and unsophisticated." It was, notably, the first major speech Buchanan authored with Nixon. Buchanan looked back on the speech's anti-elitism, along nationalistic lines that "the liberal press trashed," as a formative moment in the "New Majority . . . being born." Cultural populism had long served as American conservatism's bridge to the populous. In the first modern presidential race, 1840, Whigs tried to out-American, out-manly, basically out-Jackson Andrew Jackson, in order to defeat the candidate of the white commoner. In Nixon's day, the GOP was still considered the party of big business. A Republican aiming for the workingman was shocking. To the left, "Tricky Dick" was sneaking inside the Democratic tent and threatening a party pillar, Big Labor, and with that, the party Jackson founded.[7]

A week after Workers' Woodstock, Nixon made the courtship public. On May 26, 1970, Peter Brennan sat at Richard Nixon's right. George Daly sat beneath a portrait of Ike. They were among the two dozen labor leaders hosted at the White House. They represented more than three hundred thousand tradesmen and longshoremen. They talked about the war. Nixon said he sought to honor those "labor leaders and people from Middle America who still have character and guts and a bit of patriotism."

The president greeted each union chief with a handshake. Brennan paused at the bricklayers' boss, Mike Donovan, who wore a flag pin on his lapel and a gold star. Brennan told Nixon that Donovan's son and namesake had volunteered for Vietnam and died there.[8]

"Geez, I'm sorry to hear that," Nixon replied.

"For this country, I'd send him back again," Donovan said. "If someone would have had the courage to go into Cambodia sooner, they might have captured the bullet that took my son's life."

Nixon blinked and bit down. He spoke of his father's humble work. "We felt like we had something in common," George Daly recalled of Nixon. "Good people, they were, everybody."

In the Oval Office, the union leaders gave mementos to Nixon—a flag pin, ceremonial helmets. Brennan handed him a white helmet that read in blue, COMMANDER IN CHIEF. "We all want peace and we want to end this war in a safe and honorable way so that our men may come home," Brennan said.

George Daly had fashioned one hard hat himself. It had a flag and Nixon's name. Daly stood before the president of the United States, beaming in awe. Both men had Brylcreem hair and crinkled smiles. Daly handed the hard hat to the president. Nixon grinned and reached for it.[9]

New York Steamfitters leader George Daly hands a ceremonial hard hat, which he fashioned, to President Nixon. In the background, immediately beside Daly, is Peter Brennan, the president of the 200,000-member New York trades union council. After several weeks of high-profile actions, from the Hardhat Riot to "Workers' Woodstock," Nixon honored twenty-three union leaders on May 26, 1970. (Oliver Atkins/The Richard Nixon Presidential Library and Museum)

A T ARIZONA STATE University in Tempe, hundreds of construction workers scrapped with student activists. In Buffalo, thousands rallied in the sunlight, singing, waving flags, reciting the Pledge of Allegiance. One business-suited youth was attacked for calling workmen "warmongers." At the largest rally outside New York, in St. Louis, antiwar activists and innocent bystanders were assaulted on the sidelines as at least forty thousand construction workers marched peaceably for miles in a "Silent Majority parade." WE'D RATHER BUILD, THAN BURN read a placard. FIGHT FOR YOUR HERITAGE urged another. Countless sang patriotic song, and the St. Louis streets brimmed with the colors of helmets and flags. About a week after Workers' Woodstock, on Flag Day in Baltimore, at least ten thousand hardhats and firemen marched—singing the same songs, shouldering similar signage. There were, again, peripheral fights. A reporter wrote that the Baltimore parade had a "football game air about it." The antiwar movement's use of American symbols, none more than the flag, had catalyzed a hyperpatriotic rebuttal. Said Baltimore carpenter Clem Perke, "That's my flag they're burning."[1]

The revivalism crested on the Fourth of July, with Honor America Day. By nightfall, between 250,000 and 400,000 people gathered on the Washington Mall. Other cities echoed the theme. Bells clanged in Miami. Goodyear blimps advertised Honor America Day over New York City, Los Angeles, and Houston. Senator Edward Kennedy assured a Boston suburban crowd that "the flag is still the symbol of our unity." In Wichita Falls, Texas, someone set off the fifty air raid sirens twelve hours too early, at midnight, "sending startled residents to their telephones and into the streets, looking for catastrophe." At Central Park, a mere five hundred to two thousand showed up. The event's headliners included Mayor John Lindsay and Broadway stars, including young James Earl Jones. "We are here to honor the brave men and women who have made and kept us free," Lindsay said. "As we differ over policy, we are united by the tradition of caring deeply about the fate of America."[2]

In Washington, the beflagged masses gathered where "so many others have assembled in protest," as *Time* wrote, "to bear witness, it was their country too." Young families were everywhere. So were old ladies with parasols, old men in military uniforms, and something new—a reporter noted "husky young youths proudly wearing hard hats."[3]

Reverend Billy Graham preached from the steps of the Lincoln Memorial in the morning and Bob Hope would host in the evening. The night's entertainment would be a panoply of Middle American stars—Jack Benny, Pat Boone, Esther Phillips, Red Skelton, Vince Lombardi, Glen Campbell, Teresa Graves.

"Lately our institutions have been under attack: the Supreme Court, the Congress, the presidency, the flag, the home, the educational system, and even the church," Billy Graham preached, flanked by flags, as the temperature pushed 90 degrees. "But we are here to say, with loud voices, that in spite of their faults and failures, we believe in these institutions." He had long been America's most famous preacher, this farmer's son with a high forehead and a strong jawline and blue eyes. His wavy blond hair was now wintering white. But his voice was resonant as ever.

While Graham spoke, three hundred antiwar activists waded into the thigh-high reflecting pool, intent on offending the saccharine masses. Some students stripped nude, frolicking for cameramen. The hippies shouted, a reporter noted, "Graham's name in an obscene chant." In the crowd, a tall older man glowered beneath his hard hat. Several Marines, on leave and in civvies, invited some peaceniks to come ashore near them. The peaceniks scurried away, muttering, "You shits." The crowd rallied and drowned out the activists. Graham urged the masses, "Stop all this polarization before it is too late."[4]

"I think it's terrible that they're taking our day away from us," said Mary Ellen Fredo, a young housewife from Maryland.

The protestors came from as far as Texas and California to dissent on America's birthday. It was deemed a "smoke-in." They trickled in with knapsacks, bedrolls, backpacks. Some had gas masks and helmets. The night before, July 3, America's most famous preacher bumped into hippies beneath

In one of the many cultural clashes of the day, a young man smokes marijuana in front of a pair of middle-aged women. Between 250,000 to 400,000 people gathered on the Washington Mall on July 4, 1970, for "Honor America Day." Five to fifteen thousand antiwar activists and radicals assembled in counterdemonstration. (David Fenton/Getty)

the Washington Monument. Marijuana was offered to Billy Graham. The preacher declined. A youth gave him the peace sign. Graham lifted an index finger, a gesture for Christ as the "one way." By 1970, every tribe had hand gestures.[5]

The young activists were led by, among others, Rennie Davis of Chicago '68. As Honor America Day was being planned, Davis formed the Emergency Committee to Prevent a July Fourth Fistfight. He proceeded to provoke one. Davis told reporters that Abbie Hoffman and Allen Ginsberg should be given time onstage, the Washington Monument should be painted in psychedelic colors, and Vietcong flags should be displayed. Wrote Garry Wills, "The privileged children of the upper middle classes more and more devoted themselves, in the name of helping the oppressed, to outraging the people in between."

The Middle Americans had arranged for flag-bearing runners. Boy Scouts began from places of colonial lore, such as Valley Forge, and finished in Washington. Davis tried to arrange alternative runners from Kent State and the site of a race riot in Augusta, Georgia.

If Middle Americans assembled to recall America's best, activists would remind the nation of its worst. About a half-mile upslope from the plain people, at the Washington Monument, the Movement encampment swelled to between five and fifteen thousand. A sign read, HONOR AMERICA FOR WHAT? KILLING? MURDER? NAPALM? There were the peace flags, anarchist black flags, Vietcong flags. Peaceniks chanted, "Off the pigs! . . . Fuck Nixon! . . . Free Bobby Seale!" Someone yelled, "Free Charlie Manson!" That did not elicit a chant. Washington "is the head of the snake," said an 18-year-old girl named Sherry. "If you're going to kill it, here is where you're going to have to do it."

The young revolutionaries also "necked," sucked on popsicles, drank sweet wine from green gallon jugs and wineskins, and puffed red-white-and-blue joints. "Marijuana was rolled in the stars and stripes," read the last line in a *Washington Post* article. Some activists painted the Stars and Stripes on their bare chest. Some wore Old Glory as shirts. Others stitched flags to the butt of their pants. The flower children had come to prod the herd's sacred cows.[6]

Sometimes Middle Americans took it in stride. One bystander watched the hippies in the reflecting pool and chuckled, "It's the first bath they've had."

Near midday, with protestors still rabble-rousing in the water, rockets boomed over the Lincoln Memorial, clouding the air overhead. The Middle Americans cheered. Protestors stared up in awe, and some applauded. Later, a torrent of wind-driven rain broke the heat. Countless ran for shelter. But many protestors savored the downpour, and for the briefest moment, as Middle Americans watched the hippies, perhaps some could see what was beautiful in them.

The sun returned glassy and hot and the humidity with it. Marble memorials shimmered. At the Ellipse, thousands planted miniature flags "until they waved like poppies, spelling U.S.A." On Constitution Avenue, flagbearers led a procession. As Boy Scouts paraded in their shorts and shirtsleeves and neckerchiefs, college-age protestors chanted from the sidewalk against the "fuckin' war!"

In the afternoon, activists raided two Pepsi trucks. They flipped a huge spotlight into the reflecting pool. Scores ransacked several concession stands—"liberating" hot dogs, ice cream, bags of popcorn, and boxes of Cracker Jack from food vendors. No one chanted about power to the people. The police fired a few canisters of teargas but kept back.

It was now Bishop Fulton Sheen's turn to speak. He had deep-set blue eyes and a halting voice. "We have no rights in this country without corresponding duties," he said. Sheen was born in 1895. He ascended from country boy to archbishop. Some thirty million followed his Catholic sermons on radio and television. He had risked that prominence by advocating a pullout from Vietnam before most Americans agreed. He congenially retired on Moratorium Day. Still, the peaceniks gave him no quarter. As the archbishop urged prayer and concord, several hundred activists clustered again in the reflecting pool and chanted profanely and splashed toward the speakers' platform.[7]

Mounted police spun and formed a line. A corps of crewcut young men formed a second line. The protestors yelled but halted their advance. The crewcuts chanted "U—S—A" back at the longhairs. The longhairs retreated into the water. The crowd cheered.

"My God," said one hippie, "they would like to see my head cracked."

"Nonsense," a bystander assured, "just your mouth closed."[8]

Elsewhere, Boy Scout first-aid teams rushed to heatstroke victims, reportedly "paying little attention to amorous teenagers under the trees."[9]

And still they came. Middle Americans amassed on the soaked grass and beneath elm trees, toting chrome thermoses, folded blankets, camp stools, bags of sandwiches, small American flags. Some conservative activism came with them, including a contingent from the Young Americans for Freedom. One placard read, GOD, GUTS AND GUNPOWDER MAINTAIN LIBERTY. Read another sign, THOSE WHO CONTRIBUTE THE LEAST, COMPLAIN THE MOST— GOD BLESS OUR MEN IN VIETNAM.[10]

Bob Hope emceed apolitically, as was his wont. Of the president, he said, "Nixon came from a humble background. He was born in Whittier, California, in a log cabin which *he* helped his parents build." Nixon said in a prerecorded message: "Let us all look back today, so that we will be reminded of what great sacrifices have been made to make this day possible." Jeannie Riley sang Merle Haggard's anthem "The Fightin' Side of Me." Otherwise, performers stayed on the softer patriotic script. Though, by now, patriotism was political, and the Middle Americans came to protest that fact too. Kate Smith sang "God Bless America." Dinah Shore sang "America the Beautiful." A group of clean-cut high schoolers also sang, wearing hard hats.

Bob Hope's commentary hinted solemn. "America is one big family," he said. "Every family has problems, you know, but they fix 'em up. Some you have to work on. Some a little harder than others." He added, "But that deep love, that deep loyalty for the family never wavers." And yet, the day showed how it might, or already had.

That evening, CBS aired an hour of the variety show. ABC and NBC did not broadcast any of it. "It would be interesting to speculate what the networks' reaction would have been had four hundred thousand yippies and friends converged on the capital to celebrate July Fourth," noted critic James Bawden in Canada's *Globe and Mail*.[11]

A two-disc album of the show was produced. Actor Jimmy Stewart narrated. At the beginning, he intoned: "You are about to relive a very important day in the life of the United States—July 4, 1970." The recording offered the performance without protestors. Only, in Jimmy Stewart's words, the "warm nostalgia."

During the evening performances, activists roiled the outskirts of the crowd. At one point, short-haired conservative boys wedged between the hippies and the Middle Americans. As the longhairs neared, they carried a young man holding a Vietcong flag. The crewcuts pushed in, threw fists, and toppled the Vietcong flag waver.

"Cool it," one hippie said. "We're not hurting you."

"If that's your goddam country, then why don't you go there," a crewcut yelled back, eyeing the Vietcong flag. A canister of teargas landed in the scrum.[12]

As the daylight waned, the crowd extended to the floodlit Washington Monument. Activists intermittently pelted cops with green glass bottles, rocks, and cans.

The police remained calm. Cops with white helmets batted away the missiles with their black batons. Elsewhere, though, some policemen were injured. One cop was struck in the head and keeled over. Onstage, someone sang, "This Is My Country."

A few dozen were arrested over the bombardment. Bystanders cheered as cops corralled six activists into a paddy wagon. The New Christy Minstrels sang, "This land is your land, this land is my land," as a black protestor was placed in a paddy wagon.

Protestors were now a hundred yards from the stage. They booed, whooped, shouted. Went one chant, "Bob Hope smokes dope!" At the edge of the crowd, activists set fire to dollar bills and shouted, "Fuck the buck!" Other hippies burned American flags.

As the Navy Band started "The Star-Spangled Banner," demonstrators marched into the reflecting pool once more. They banged bongo drums and chucked fireworks near the crowd. One firework exploded between two cops, injuring them. Another cherry bomb reportedly struck a baby and a mother. "I'll never forget that woman's screams," said a bystander from Staten Island. With that came the teargas. The smoke stirred a stampede of hippies over acres of families gathered on picnic blankets.

The police had misjudged the wind. Acrid smoke blew back over some of the crowd. Toddlers cried. Parents pulled their kids into their arms and rushed out. One pregnant mother went into "hysterics," beating her husband's back, shouting, "Henry, get me out of here, I'm sick." Nearby, as the white mist dissipated into the balmy darkness, three children kneaded their bloodshot eyes. A hippie walked over and said, "Don't rub, brother," as he pulled a small boy's hands away from his tears. Nearby, police carried away a young woman who had been hit on the head with a bottle. A policeman had also been hit. He waited for treatment at a first-aid station, as blood streamed down his arm. Where the teargas was still thick, two little boys were carried out sobbing. A mother picked up a girl, about 8, as she cried out, "Mommy! Mommy!"[13]

The next day, the *Washington Post* headlined: SILENT MAJORITY WATCHES PROTESTORS IN QUIET DISBELIEF. Among them were two busloads from Great Neck, Long Island, a suburb of New York City. They had left for Washington "buoyed" with anticipation to celebrate Independence Day in the capital. They returned "a somber group, angered, shocked, and frustrated." A high school student "couldn't believe" that the "police did nothing." Most were families. One father, Otto Paulsen, was a veteran who had spent three years in a Nazi prison camp. Paulsen said, "What we needed down here was a New York construction gang."[14]

| CHAPTER 26 | "Born with a Potmetal Spoon": Nixon Launches the GOP's Blue-Collar Strategy |

RICHARD NIXON HAD long pressed Republicans to welcome the working-class world that weaned him. He was not the first Republican to try. Dwight Eisenhower had won them. But Ike didn't need populism. He was so popular that Democrats also recruited him. He won in a landslide. A majority of blue-collar whites backed him. Nearly half of the white southern vote did as well. In 1956, Ike won the Catholic vote too. Eisenhower, a moderate, personified postwar "consensus" America. Nixon became president in the late sixties, the dawn of modern polarization. And he did it, in no small part, not as a hero but as a grunt. Nixon was, as William Safire put it, a "man born with a potmetal spoon in his mouth fighting a Rockefeller for the nomination and a Kennedy for the presidency."[1]

Richard Nixon's boyhood was hard. He was not impoverished. But his family struggled. He lost two brothers to illness. His mother swore he tried to be all her sons after that. That drive, she also said, came from his father. Frank Nixon was a factory hand, a trolley conductor, an oil roustabout. He cut and sold firewood, started a land clearing business, farmed and failed at it too, but he kept at it. "Few men worked harder, or were more determined, than Frank, but he had achieved little," wrote Nixon biographer Stephen Ambrose. "Still he had faith, which, it turned out, was not misplaced."

Frank Nixon found stability in Whittier, California. He opened a modest gas station and grocery. Thin tires were stacked beside the single-story facade. Vegetables were sold in wood crates. Whittier was a proud Quaker colony. It had oil and rancher money, a college as well. The Nixon grocery, though, where the family all worked, was not on a main street. It was at the edge of town. Even then, Dick Nixon was outside, looking in.

The father built a sturdy two-story frame house. The children had Sunday suits for church but their mother never got a new dress. The parents were severe and neither smoke nor drank. Frank, a boisterous Methodist, had given up dancing for his devout Quaker wife, Hannah. The father was charitable to the needy, pro-union, and prone to rant populist. He read Ida Tarbell's muckraking on John D. Rockefeller. Frank's gas pump had a sign above it that read RICHFIELD GASOLINE, not Standard Oil. But sometimes Frank Nixon swerved conspiratorial. Nixon's father, as biographer John Farrell wrote, would also rant about "big chain stores, owned by Jews," which were "out to crush small operators like the Nixons."

Richard Nixon would later deny his progressive impulses. But young Nixon admired William Jennings Bryan, Teddy Roosevelt, and Woodrow Wilson. His mother, Hannah Nixon, was stoic, a pacifist, a true Quaker. She did her nightly prayers in her closet. She was not disposed to embrace her children. Nixon recalled his father as "explosive, dynamic" but his mother as "very controlled and I became that way," or he tried to be that way.

As a student, Nixon was a grind, had an "iron butt," it was later said. In high school, he earned the opportunity to study at Harvard or Yale. But it was the Great Depression. His parents needed him. Since his mid-teens, Nixon would study late, get too little sleep, wake at four o'clock to drive to the vegetable markets in Los Angeles for the family store, then go to school. So the good son gave up his dream and stayed home. He aimed now to become a big man at the little Quaker campus. But campus wellborns tried to keep him small. Nixon was rejected by the elite student society (the Franklins, named for Quaker Ben Franklin). Nixon founded a group called the Orthogonians, "square shooters." Nixon's Orthogonians were for capable, diligent, and striving sons of nobodies, commuter kids like Dick, boys who did not put on airs. The Orthogonians wore no tie in their club photo. The Franklins wore black tie. The Orthogonian slogan: "Beans, Brawn, Brains, and Bowels."

Nixon had brains but little brawn. One classmate described him as "a rather quiet chap about campus." He was a skinny, serious boy, and ambitious. He wanted to be student body president. He ran as a schooldays populist. His issue: the Quaker institution should allow dances. The dour grocer's boy, rejected by elite Franklins, defeated a Franklin to become school president. Nixon learned to win from without. "They were the Haves and we were the Have Nots," Nixon later said of the Franklins. And Nixon understood young that there were more have-nots.[2]

In 1946, during his first congressional race, it was Dick Nixon against Horace Jeremiah Voorhis. Jerry Voorhis was handsome and highbred, prepping at Hotchkiss, matriculating at Yale. Voorhis flirted with radicalism in his twenties, moved to the Democratic mainstream in the FDR era, and became a dedicated New Dealer. It was Nixon, though, who invoked FDR's "forgotten man." He talked of the "rabbit grower," the "small contractor," butchers, housewives, "chicken men," the "grocer forced to buy mustard to get mayonnaise." "Republicans live on both sides of the tracks," he said in a Lincoln Day speech. "In America, there is no place for class hatred," as he put it on another occasion. The tepid populism was not always a natural fit. In his first speech, Nixon appeared in his officer's uniform. He was reminded that far more voters were enlisted men, and that enlisted men disliked officers. Nixon also did not stray far from Republican orthodoxy throughout the campaign. He campaigned as a veteran, a small-government conservative (albeit one who supported extending Social Security), a man who was for free enterprise and against communism. He also suggested Voorhis was a communist. That same Nixon, though, said Jim Crow racists were "as dangerous on the right as the communists [were] on the left." He became an honorary member of the local NAACP. Nixon campaigned with little money. With his wife, Pat, they invested their modest savings into the race. At least once, they had no cash to buy stamps for campaign literature. At the outset, insiders considered Voorhis nearly unbeatable. Nixon outworked his rival, kept him on his heels, including with cheap shots. The onetime political heavyweight proved "quite out of his league" against Nixon, Ambrose wrote. Nixon was also lifted by a wave. Republicans won majorities in both houses of Congress for the first time since 1928. There was high inflation, housing shortages, labor discord, rationing. Harry Truman's approval rating was in the mid-thirties. "Throughout the campaign, [Nixon] stressed lunch-bucket issues and the Truman administration's mishandling of the economy," John Farrell wrote.

"If we send back to Congress the same men who have failed this country ever since V-J Day," Nixon said in the final debate, "we will only get another helping of the same, but the American people have had enough." Nixon received his largest applause of the night for that line, biographer Irwin Gellman noted. "Had enough?" was the GOP motto nationwide. "A vote for Nixon is a vote for change," went another Nixon pitch. Still, Nixon's populism was unusual enough to stick with Voorhis. Voorhis wrote in his memoir that the contest centered on "ins" versus "outs." As historian David

Greenberg wrote, "'The forgotten man' was central to Nixon's appeals in 1946."[3]

Six years later, Nixon used everyman imagery to retain power. He was the number two on Dwight Eisenhower's ticket. Newspapers reported a secret campaign finance fund. In an unprecedented half-hour address, Nixon sat at a pine desk inside a television studio and defended himself. He spoke of the "modest circumstances" of his boyhood, his debt, his Oldsmobile, his ordinary wartime service ("I was just there when the bombs were falling"). He said the little his family had was "honestly ours." "Pat doesn't have a mink coat, but she does have a respectable Republican cloth coat." Not everyone, he explained, was like Democratic nominee Adlai Stevenson ("who inherited a fortune from his father"). After all, Nixon assured America, "a man of modest means can also run for president."

"That must be the most demeaning experience my country has ever had to bear," said pundit Walter Lippmann to a foreign newsman. It was "corny," General Lucius Clay concluded, conveying the Washington consensus. But then Clay saw the "elevator boy crying and the doorman crying and I knew then I was wrong." "This time the common man was a Republican, for a change," wrote one columnist. Nixon had "suddenly placed the burden of old-style Republican aloofness on the Democrats."[4]

◆

New York City had been the center of old-style Republicanism since Teddy Roosevelt was born on East Twentieth Street. But by 1970, the Buckleys were the new "first family of conservatism," the *Times* reported. They had a blue-blood Protestant affectation but their heritage was mostly Irish and quite Catholic. Jim Buckley was the Conservative Party candidate for RFK's Senate seat. He was a veteran and one of ten siblings (including the little brother of Bill Buckley). Jim Buckley's television ads flickered images of crime and student radicals. The ad concluded, printing across the screen: "Isn't it about time, we had a senator?" The city skyline was at his back. The half-built Twin Towers in the distance. Buckley was an oilman's son. But the ads were staged as if Buckley was standing in Brooklyn, across the waterway, where the blue collars dwelled.[5]

On election day, liberals and moderates divided. One article highlighted the conservative's unusual coalition: "What the Buckley camp calls 'his people'—white collar workers and flag carrying hardhats."

Near the close of the '70 campaign, Jim Buckley rallied thousands at Federal Hall. He was cheery, business-suited, with a crew cut, and graying at the temples. Construction workers and longshoremen chanted, "We want Buckley!"

Buckley spoke of workmen who "so movingly demonstrated last May." They were the "rank-and-file of American labor." They personified "love of country."[6]

Across the river in Bay Ridge, Brooklyn, four ironworkers chatted with a reporter. Three of them backed Buckley. They cited "law and order." Buckley said "truthful things that some people don't want to hear," one explained. He supported prosecuting the "intellectual radicals who bomb our buildings." One of them was Eugene Schafer, the husky and bespectacled ironworker who carried a flag during the Hardhat Riot. Schafer was now running for the State Assembly as a "hard hat Democrat."

Bay Ridge, at the western nub of Brooklyn, juts into a mile-wide waterway between the upper and lower bay. The neighborhood was working-class, Irish and Italian Catholic, blocks of brown and red brick homes, tiny mowed lawns on tree-lined streets.[7]

Schafer lived near cops, firemen, fellow tradesmen. His storefront campaign headquarters was located not far from the home of the cop who helped protect K.O. Joe during the riot. His headquarters was decorated with small flags and patriotic streamers. The ironworkers sat on wood crates and sipped beer. The oldest was in his early forties, side-parted hair, an unlit cigarette loose off his lips. At one point, he pointed to a newspaper photo of him punching a protestor during the riot.

"They took all they could. They just couldn't swallow any more antiwar demonstrations. Especially seeing enemy flags," Eugene Schafer said of his fellow workmen. "I sat in a foxhole for twenty-nine months while they threw shells at me in Korea, so I'd still have a free country for these punks to grow up in. The punks!" he continued. "I'm not an educated man and I'm just going by what my heart says. I was a smart-aleck punk kid. My parents did want me to go to college but my father died when I was ten years old and I grew up in the streets of New York. I was out in street gangs with tough people in tough neighborhoods." But when "we did something wrong" in school, he stressed that teachers hit them. Youth today "get away with a lot," he added. "All these kids last year at Columbia were out demonstrating half the school year, yet all graduated."

Now the street-bred boy was a man in a tie and running for office, a "hard hat Democrat" supporting the "first family of conservatism" and echoing Nixon's embrace of FDR's terms. "I think that I'm a forgotten American," he said. "Because my community is falling apart. The streets are caving in. The sanitation's lousy. The sewer system stinks. Industry's gone out of the community. Welfare's on the rise." As for the riot, the reporter asked him why he had confronted student activists that day. He replied, "I owed the flag that much."[8]

◆

In April 1970, President Nixon received a secret Department of Labor report: "The Problem of the Blue-Collar Worker." It described workers with "static" purchasing power who were now living with "economic insecurity." They were "the first to feel the effects of an increase in unemployment." It added, "These people are most exposed to the poor and the welfare recipients. Often their wages are only a notch or so above the liberal states' welfare payments." Their "work has no 'status' in the eyes of society." They felt "forgotten." In policy terms, the report advised education grants, tax relief, and subsidized housing. It also noted that the blue-collar workers "are overripe for a political response."[9]

A month later, the Hardhat Riot and activism inspired that response. Nixon's blue-collar strategy was joined with his drive to seize traditional Democratic constituencies and produce a "New Majority." In the estimation of historian Jefferson Cowie: "[Nixon's] sole domestic political goal was to disassemble the Roosevelt coalition and to rebuild the pieces into his own modern coalition. All else—the Watergate break-in, the liberal domestic policy initiatives, much of his entire domestic presidency—derived from that central principle." Those close to Nixon, however, also recall an authentic desire to represent ordinary Americans.[10]

Nixon's larger ambition was rooted in his life experience and epitomized by his November 1969 Silent Majority speech, the most successful of his presidency. The speech's momentum, though, dissipated by early 1970, as the antiwar movement also began to dissipate. That February, an aide told Haldeman, "The president noted that it seems that our Silent Majority group has lost its steam." But with the hardhats, Nixon no longer felt like a general without an army. People were taking to the streets *for* him.

The hardhats, Nixon later confided to key advisors, "were with us when some of the elitist crowd were running away from us. Thank God for the hardhats!"[11]

"Some wrote in those days that the president stood alone," Nixon also told an AFL-CIO convention. "But I was not alone. One hundred and fifty thousand American workers walked down Wall Street supporting the armed forces abroad and supporting the commander in chief at home, and I appreciated that."[12]

After the blue-collar report leaked, *Time* magazine wrote that "[Nixon] administration leaders are closely studying" the document. The *Wall Street Journal* editorial board manned the barricades for capitalism. The *Journal* found the report a "bit depressing." "If blue-collar workers may be justified in their claim to a sense of disaffection," it wrote, "it hardly seems a realistic target of government policy, and schemes designed to help the alienated carry a strong risk of escalating expectations, increasing frustration, and eventually deepening alienation."[13]

Yet the blue-collar activism had buoyed Nixon. At the end of the summer of 1970, he received more reassurance. He read Richard M. Scammon and Ben J. Wattenberg's *The Real Majority*. The book argued that Democrats were losing Middle America on social issues and that economic issues could not be relied on to solely narrow the crescive divide between liberals and the plain people. Buchanan wrote Nixon that the *Real Majority* "contains a credible and workable blueprint for our defeat in 1972." He added, "We can no longer count on our [D]emocratic friends to cooperate in their own demise." Buchanan highlighted for Nixon the book's criticism of "Big John" Lindsay for letting his reelection campaign become a referendum on social issues. He concluded from the book that the "swing voters" are "law and order Democrats, conservatives on the 'Social Issue' but 'progressive' on domestic issues." He later defined the terms for Nixon. Social issues: "drugs, demonstrations, pornography, disruptions, 'kidlash,' permissiveness, violence, riots, crime." "Domestic" issues: "Medicare, aid to cities, anti-poverty efforts, aid to education." Buchanan counseled the president, "The party that can hold this center will win the presidency."[14]

Four days after Buchanan's memo, H. R. Haldeman noted in his journal that Nixon "talked about *Real Majority* and need to get that thinking over to all our people. Wants to really ram this home and make all decisions based on it. Very impressed with Buchanan memo analyzing it. Wants to hit pornography, dope, bad kids."

Republicans must "preempt the Social Issue in order to get the Democrats on the defensive," Nixon concluded. "We should aim our strategy primarily at disaffected Democrats, at blue-collar workers, and at working-class white ethnics." On another occasion, Nixon instructed his advisors: "Emphasize anti-crime, anti-demonstrations, anti-drugs, anti-obscenity."[15]

On Labor Day 1970, the White House fêted seventy union chiefs at a formal dinner, including George Meany and Peter Brennan. The AFL-CIO's spokesman said, "No president had ever done anything like this before." Haldeman suggested that Meany's daughters receive special attention at "Mrs. Nixon's tea for the wives of labor leaders." Nixon played golf with

Meany by day and toasted labor by night. "The message of our time is that a strong, free, independent labor movement is essential to the preservation and the growth of freedom," the Republican president told union chiefs. Haldeman later told Nixon what he saw in the unionists: "A great deal of gold to be mined."[16]

Nixon was a capable prospector. He had an instinct for the everyman, though he did not easily relate to him (or most anyone). After Nixon defeated Hubert Humphrey in 1968, George Meany was invited to meet with the president-elect in his New York hotel suite. Nixon introduced Meany to his secretary and said, "She's a Catholic, too, George." "As if that was important to me!" Meany thought. "What did I care what she was?"[17]

Nixon was still a Republican. In early 1971, to combat inflation, Nixon suspended the Davis-Bacon Act, an FDR-era act that required federally funded contractors to pay the highest prevailing wage (union wages). The *Wall Street Journal* reported that the act's suspension had "undone all the administration's careful cultivation of the blue-collar vote." But labor leaders, from Meany to Brennan, were consulted. "The construction unions led the labor movement in moderating demands. And Nixon let them have their cherished Davis-Bacon back later on," William Safire wrote. Nixon rarely let policy get in the way of political expedience.[18]

Peter Brennan had felt "abandoned" by Nixon over Davis-Bacon, according to Chuck Colson. Brennan, Colson wrote, asserted that while nearly all New York tradesmen voted for Humphrey in 1968, Brennan could deliver "90 percent to our side in 1972." Though hyperbolic, Colson claimed that Nelson Rockefeller "shares this assessment." In another memo, Colson cited the 1970 Jim Buckley race and counseled Nixon: "Even in a 3-way race Buckley got almost 50 percent of the blue-collar vote in New York and heavily carried wards that Brennan 'controls.'" Colson also stressed to Haldeman that they were now on the "verge of being irreparably damaged with the 'hardhat,' even though six months ago this represented one of our most fertile fields for political gain," or, as he also wrote, their "natural 'new' constituency."[19]

Later, Colson hired Michael Balzano to court the white ethnic councils— Sons of Italy, the Polish-American League, the Latvian League. He also became a liaison to labor. Balzano was a "deep in my marrow" Democrat. There were two portraits in his childhood kitchen: one of Jesus, one of FDR. His father showed him, as a boy, the blocks of curbstone he laid with his WPA job. Balzano came up hard, had undiagnosed dyslexia, dropped out of high school, became a garbageman. He changed his life, became a Georgetown PhD. Looking back, Balzano said that Colson had an initial sense of "shock" after the hardhat activism. His impression from Colson: "Here were all these blue-collar workers supporting Nixon" and "they were all Democrats!" Colson saw "two major breakthroughs" that "changed the president's relationship with organized labor," as Balzano wrote in his book. The first was Colson's private labor consultations—Balzano highlighted a mariners union chief, Jesse Calhoon—and the "second breakthrough happened as a result of the Hard Hat Riots in 1970." To Balzano, the hardhat demonstrations were "the most significant event in the birth of the New Majority because it created the initial bond between a Republican president and Democratic union members."[20]

In October 1970, a month before the midterm election, Colson assured Nixon that they had "effectively associated the liberals with all that is bad about permissiveness in society." He advised that they focus on "restoring order on campus," cutting drugs, and "rebuilding the moral foundation of our society." He also betrayed an assumption, in this Republican administration, that Washington should help. "We must restore" the public "faith in our ability to manage government." He urged Nixon to fill the "leadership vacuum." He told Nixon what he said Peter Brennan had told him—that despite disagreements over policy, Nixon was "winning" hardhats' "political loyalty" because "the hardhats, who are a tough breed, have come to respect you as a tough, courageous man's man." Colson continued, "The image of being strong, forceful and decisive, will have a powerful personal appeal with the alienated voter." He noted "diminishing party loyalties." If Nixon could "win" the "confidence" of the "alienated voter," he would have "an unbeatable majority."[21]

The grand talk made the midterms a letdown within Nixon's circle. With only rare exceptions, presidents' parties lose midterm races. Republicans lost twelve seats in the House—not good but not especially bad by historical standards. The GOP actually gained two Senate seats. Still, within the Nixon White House, there was disappointment. Some influential traditionalists tried to capitalize on it. Treasury's Charls Walker encouraged Nixon to cease his blue-collar silliness and "blaze away" at Big Labor. Colson argued there was no advantage in being "antagonistic" to labor "to please those Republican businessmen and bankers who still believe that being anti-labor is part and parcel of Republican orthodoxy." Looking ahead to the 1972 campaign, Colson predicted leading Democrats "will continue" to be "to the left in foreign policy"—meaning Vietnam. Among the likely Democratic candidates, Colson advised, George Meany only "could support . . . Scoop Jackson," a hawkish Democrat of the old order. It was no mean prediction. The AFL-CIO always endorsed the Democratic nominee, whoever it was. What absurdity was Colson going to predict next for 1972, that Dick Nixon would win the youth vote?[22]

Nixon did not expect reelection to come easy. He also did not stray far from his blue-collar strategy or accentuating the heartland values he associated with it, after the congressional races. Nixon wrote Haldeman in December 1970 that he wanted to "get across those fundamental decencies and virtues which the great majority of Americans like," from "hard work" to "consideration for others" to a "willingness to take the heat" when doing "what is right." The president later told top advisors, "The educated people and the leader class no longer have any character, and you can't count on them." Rather, Nixon continued, "on tough problems, the uneducated are the ones that are with us." The Republican president said that it was "vital" that "we continue to recognize and work with [blue-collar workers] and that we not attack unions which represent the organized structure of the working man." In another meeting with close aides, Nixon reminisced about the "march of the hardhats." He said his "support," when times were "tough," came from "those areas the elitists look down their noses at—from the farmers, the ethnics, from cattlemen, and so forth. But thank God for it!" He added, "We've done things labor doesn't like" but they were "supporting us" because the "real secret" of his policies was stressing the "things that united," which speechwriter Ray Price, a meeting participant, understood as Nixon's affirmation of "square values." Still, long before the 1972 campaign commenced, Nixon was unsure that it was sufficient for Middle Americans to be "against his opponents" or their values, instead of "for him." Nixon did not foresee, looking ahead to a campaign for Middle America, how easily his liberal foes would become his foil.[23]

| How America(s) Saw It

To the New Left, hardhats proved the stereotype, the domestic embodiment of brutish warmongers, like the oft-quoted US major who said of a battle in Vietnam: "It became necessary to destroy the town to save it."

Liberals struggled to abide this wave of blue-collar activism against them. "Radical chic" was indeed not extended to hardhats. As critics of protests on all sides are prone to do, there were charges of artificial grassroots. Some liberals asked: Who funded the protests? Why were the hardhats not at work? A few stories were sprinkled with anonymous allegations suggesting the hardhats were paid. Conservatives had long believed the antiwar activists were communist stooges. Now liberals declared the hardhats fascist stormtroopers.

The workmen were also frequently accused of being primarily motivated by racism. Assistant Secretary of Labor Arthur Fletcher, an affirmative action pioneer, alleged the hardhats had an "ulterior motive" of aligning with Nixon to "get inside the White House and be a formidable opponent of the Philadelphia Plan" for the racial integration of unions.

"When the hardhats beat on kids, they think they are beating on blacks," said civil rights leader James Farmer, perhaps the most prominent black official in the Nixon administration. "And the blacks know this too."

Looking back decades later, Deputy Mayor Dick Aurelio expressed the same. "The liberal movement was trying to improve integration. In this case, minority hiring in the building trades," he said. "So there was a lot of irritation in the unions against progressives like John Lindsay. It became convenient, since the progressives were against the Vietnam War, to lump the two together."[1]

It was a common conclusion—that racism inspired white hardhats to attack white antiwar protestors. Blue-collar whites became increasingly familiar with the charge over time, as one truth became the whole truth and their breakup with Democrats was blamed entirely on them, on their worst vice. It only alienated them more.

The *Village Voice* called them "payday patriots" and "grimy John Glenns and Tom Seavers" and "sacrilegious" about "dying for someone else's notion of their country." The *Nation* ran a sketch depicting the hardhats as dopey fat slobs. It reported that it was "undeniable" that the hardhats were motived by "fascism" and the "incursion of Negroes in their white union ranks." Most outlets called them "prowar." But liberal writers and leaders commonly avoided the class strain. Instead, they often described the hardhats with Neolithic qualities. Sometimes they were described as subservient to capitalists or President Nixon. There were the familiar livestock inferences— herd, sheep, pigs. At times, they were the blue-collar bourgeois—people who, ahem, thought Glenn Miller was good music (yes, that jab was made in the *Times* in 1971). Often it veered to extremes. Just as some hardhats wrongly generalized antiwar activists as commies, hardhats were deemed fascists. The *Nation* chose the broadside "Hitlerian." The general impression from the left-wing reportage: hardhats were the belligerent bigoted sort, the Nazi sort, the Charles Coughlin sort, jackbooted thugs, not real laborers, not the sons of FDR, but a rabble of boorish Willy Lomans gone mad with patriotism, in Samuel Johnson's "last refuge of scoundrels" sense—a phrase the *Village Voice* saw fit to quote directly (despite Johnson being a Tory moralist, but that's history). The *Militant,* a socialist newsweekly "published in the interest of the working people," referred to Bloody Friday as a "hooligan attack" and closed by speculating that the tradesmen were perhaps actually "cops dressed in workers' attire." The communist *Daily World* initially refused to identify the rioters as workers. In the week after the large rallies, the *Daily World* referred to hardhat protestors as alleged workers by using scare quotes ("construction workers"). It further reported that the hardhat "goon" squads "smelled like Hitler's street gangs." The *Los Angeles Times* and *New York Times* both ran a cartoon of an obese hardhat with a tiny head grabbing a skinny innocent young man giving the peace sign, with the caption, "Son . . . ! Dad . . . !" which transformed the underdiscussed class war into the comfortably familiar generation gap. The *Times* columnist Russell Baker was perplexed by hardhats' motive for "terrorizing doves" that May. The *New York Post*'s editorial board declared Bloody Friday "one of the most squalid outbursts in this city's experience," writing that the hardhats were "cold-bloodied bullies" and "brutalitarians."

When it came to the other side, the root causes were dismissed. Racist whites interpreted black riots this way. Prejudice felt vindicated by violence.

Bloody Friday was "highly organized" but "it's a little hard to say whether it was planned and organized out of the federal government or out of the mafia," said David Dellinger of Chicago '68 fame, one of the antiwar movement's leaders. "In a sense, that was the appearance of the Brownshirts on American streets," Dellinger added. "So we're really on the verge of the most serious disasters that have ever struck our country."

The conspiracy theories peaked in *Scanlan's Monthly*, a new magazine with boldfaced bylines (Hunter S. Thompson among them). *Scanlan's* published a fraudulent memo that, among many claims (there would be "no national elections in '72"), purported that the CIA was behind the Hardhat Riot ("Let's call this one 'Operation U.S.A. All the Way'").[2]

That same summer of 1970, the president of the American Psychological Association diagnosed Nixon as "authoritarian" from afar—citing his emphasis on "militarism, war, sports, and cut-throat competition" as well as Nixon's "signals to the prejudiced, the affluent, the hardhats, and the vigilantes."[3]

An impression emerged on the left: white blue-collar workers were *against* liberal progress, thus not progressive, thus regressive, thus bad, thus an antagonist to be overcome or ignored, if not demeaned, stereotyped, and othered (though this was supposedly a conservative sin alone). To add insult to psychic injury, the stereotyping came from the side claiming an "open mind" and concern for workers. Even the national labor correspondent for the *New York Times* would declare: "The typical worker, from construction craftsman to shoe clerk, has become probably the most reactionary political force in the country."

"There is no class struggle," explained Charles Reich, a doctor's son who was a professor at Yale Law School, in his counterculture megahit *The Greening of America* (1970). "There is no longer any ruling class except the machine itself." He also noted, "The exploited blue-collar worker is a chief opponent of change."[4]

After the riot, the movie *Joe* was retitled and reedited to stress backlash. It was also rushed to release. The movie featured hardhat Joe Curren (Peter Boyle), who personified the worst stereotype of average Joes. Joe Curren is a barfly simpleton who has little hair and tells others to cut their hair, a rabid "working stiff" who hates blacks and hippies, a man prone to extended rants but brief with coitus. And he's homicidal. The title tune: "Hey Joe, don't it make you want to go to war . . . once more?" "Joe Curran is the ultimate hardhat: outraged, terrified, violent and more than a little envious, lashing out blindly at threatening forces that he only dimly comprehends," *Time* magazine explained. "It is a film of Freudian anguish, biblical savagery and immense social and cinematic importance." The film, produced for $300,000, grossed $20 million. The screenplay was nominated for an Academy Award.[5]

The *Times* editorial board captured the Establishment left's disbelief at the May White House meeting with labor leaders. These same unions "have long persisted in a domestic course that has only deepened the social and economic crisis." The *Times* added, "They have been insensitive to the rightful claims of ethnic minorities. They often ignore the need for restraint on the wage front, thus sabotaging the battle against inflation. They have obstructed the road toward greater productivity through automation and other reforms." America's leading voice of the Establishment left reached for a conservative critique of wages. It advocated automation at the expense of jobs. That's the nerve Nixon's "dubious allies" struck.[6]

The nation's leading conservative editorial board weighed critical too: "Mr. Nixon's embrace included not only those who attended the rally but those who bashed heads as well." The *Journal*'s editorial added, "We think this is no time for such ambiguity."[7]

Business Week noted a high-low divide on Wall Street. "Among clerical and back-office personnel, the strong-arm approach of the hard-hatted construction crews was generally lauded," the magazine reported. But, it also reported, "management saw the workers as just more evidence that the world was in trouble." Some Wall Street grandees reached for Nazi analogies as well. The Hardhat Riot was "a matter of grave concern to me," said finance executive John Winthrop, a descendant of his puritan namesake, the colonial founder. "Like others" in the front offices, it reported, Winthrop had "noted disconcerting similarities between the fury of the workers and the Nazis." *Business Week*'s headline after the riot: THREE DAYS THAT SHOOK THE ESTABLISHMENT.[8]

◆

Americans sided with the hardhats but opposed their brutality. In the larger cultural conflict, a majority of whites "sympathized" more with the construction workers than with the student demonstrators. One-fifth of whites backed the students. When violence was specifically mentioned—alluding to the riot rather than the competing demonstrations—the margin narrowed; yet still, twice as many whites sided with the hardhats as with the students. But the public did not approve of the violence itself. When asked about beating someone up—and not to take a side in the conflict—most Americans thought the violence was wrong. Still, they ultimately sided with those who did the wrong. In the end, Americans concluded that activists had reaped what they sowed.[9]

Americans did not condone violence. Yet they were also unwilling to side with these victims. They didn't see innocent victims. The lion's share of Americans concluded the activists provoked the blue-collar cops (Chicago '68), the blue-collar guardsmen (Kent State), and the blue-collar workmen (Hardhat Riot).

Class shaped all of it. When asked where their sympathies lay (student demonstrators or hardhats), whites with no higher education sided with hardhats, 56 to 13 percent, a margin threefold larger than that seen among better-educated whites. Blue-collar white Democrats sided with hardhats by about a six-to-one ratio. Even among young white adults—treated as synonymous with liberal youth in leading outlets such as the *Times*—blue collars favored hardhats, the better-educated favored students.[10]

Class divisions deepened in the decades after, as the parties sorted and outlooks moved tectonically apart, like two landmasses violently severed and then gradually drifting out to sea, until one day it's clear that they are entirely different places, even if they are still called by one name—America.

The counterculture had won over American culture, liberalism, soon the Democratic Party. It did not create a popular "revolutionary" movement in its day, even among collegians. About two-thirds of campuses remained peaceful over this period. Cambodia and Kent State had supposedly radicalized America's youth. But even as most collegians were "more active" in "causes" than the year prior, only a tenth favored "overthrowing" the "system" or considered themselves "far left." In fact, as Seymour Lipset pointed out, only about one in ten college students consistently identified as "radical" or "revolutionary" in this era. After months of upheaval, by the autumn of 1970, the majority of collegians newly identified themselves as "middle of the road" or conservative. College students still fervently wanted out of Vietnam. But even as Cambodia sparked an historic surge in student activism, less than four in ten students favored "pulling out now" from the war zone.

The wider public was only more moderate, only more turned off by the activists by 1970. Merely one-fifth of Americans backed an "immediate" pullout of US troops. About half of American adults wanted out of Vietnam. But the plurality favored a staggered withdrawal.

To be sure, the hawks were few nationwide—not at the turn of the decade, not with the war already having claimed the lives of nearly fifty thousand American boys and counting. By early 1970, less than a tenth of Americans supported sending more soldiers into the foreign fight.

In the final measure, the antiwar movement was less popular than the Vietnam War. After 1968, most Americans deemed Vietnam a mistake. By 1971, six in ten lamented the war. That same year, roughly two-thirds of the public condemned antiwar protests. Meanwhile, in this era, only about five of every hundred Americans demonstrated against the Vietnam War. It was the vehemence and violence, the concentration of that protest at colleges—especially elite schools, especially as the mass media began its unending fixation on youth—that rocked American life.[11]

Americans were against both the war and the antiwar movement. In this sense, most hardhats were indicative of the wider public—not in their violence, but in their cause. Indeed, for those actually listening to Peter Brennan, he consistently stated he wanted the war ended.

Ultimately, most doves didn't even like the antiwar activists. Back in September 1968, after the Chicago convention, two-thirds of those who wanted to deescalate the Vietnam War backed Mayor Daley's use of police "to put down the demonstrators."[12]

Seven in ten whites, and the plurality of blacks, saw "radical troublemakers" as the cause of student unrest, rather than "deeply felt" beliefs in the "injustices in society." Even among whites who thought the Vietnam War was a "mistake," two-thirds thought "most student unrest" was caused by "radical troublemakers" rather than a belief in societal "injustices."[13]

Americans had spent too long living with the turmoil. It all blended into one Movement. To blue-collar and Middle America, the New Left seemed against the war *and* them, or at least their values, even life's hard practicalities—such as who goes to war and how you can best leave a war you don't want anymore. In turn, blue-collar whites (including doves) disrespected the antiwar movement significantly more than better-off whites.[14]

This antipathy for the antiwar movement did not stem from being "prowar." Whites with less money, less stature, were often the most against the war. It was not always that way. But one conclusion is clear after mining years of polls: in the Vietnam era, blue-collar whites were not hawks, as often reported, and they were not consistently more prowar than affluent whites.

In 1968 and 1969, polls found a similar majority of whites in all classes thought Vietnam was a "mistake."[15]

In the days after the Cambodia speech, late April 1970, upscale whites were slightly *more* in favor of escalating the war into Cambodia, compared to downscale whites.[16]

Poor and blue-collar whites were often more likely to favor withdrawing from Vietnam as well, compared to those better-off. After all, it was their people in the war zone.[17]

The Movement's more moderate wing turned off the public as well. Americans opposed the student strikes—the forced campus closures—by a five-to-one ratio. But the deeper divide was dug by militancy and its presumed enablers. The public's dislike for zealous activists was so strong that it blamed "militant student groups" for campus "unrest" far more than it blamed those who shot students at Kent State and Jackson State. In fact, more Americans blamed permissive faculty for campus unrest than the guardsmen and cops who killed students. That's how much Americans disliked campus activism and this Movement.[18]

The hardhats, meanwhile, unified to protest the kids who had protested for years, kids who seemed to have every advantage and yet dismissed that privilege as existential privation. To them, the young people who had it easy complained, while those who had it hard were more stoic—the boys who went to war, the girls who went to work instead of Woodstock. It also didn't take a college degree to know when your folkways were being belittled, to know when you were being patronized, to recognize the desecration of what you still deemed solemn.

◆

Most Americans soured on the war but not their nation or its flag. They could not conceive of detaching those colors from the soldiers who died beneath the nation's banner. They saw in the flag whatever good could be found in lost peace, lost limbs, lost lives. What else did the Stars and Stripes stand for, if not that? To desecrate the flag was to desecrate that. And if anything was still holy, if we honored any of the old things anymore, they wondered, how could we not honor that?

They saw the potency of those colors being diluted to incorporate other meanings, and by the same side that defended its desecration. Blue-collar whites were about twice as likely as college-educated whites to say there was "no more respect" for the flag and country in 1970. And later surveys showed what was obvious to any observer of the period: working-class whites were significantly more likely than well-educated whites to revere the flag and support laws prohibiting its desecration.[19]

At Northwestern University, in May 1970, a student waved an upside-down American flag, seeking to rally thousands to strike. A hefty man in work clothes reached for the flag and yelled, "That's my flag! I fought for it! You have no right to it!" Students argued with him. "To hell with your movement," the man responded. "There are millions of people like me. We're fed up with your movement. You're forcing us into it. We'll have to kill you. All I can see is a lot of kids blowing a chance I never had."[20]

To some liberal activists, the flag became a powerful means to express dissent, one more battle in the culture war. But to many Americans, it evoked real war, their pain as well as their hopes. "How can they attack the flag?" asked Peter Brennan. "It's the symbol of democracy and freedom and what brought our parents to this country."[21]

Flag desecration first earned media coverage in 1966. At Indiana's Purdue University, during an SDS recruitment meeting for a Chicago march, a speaker tore, spat, and trampled on a flag. Purdue's SDS leader said the speaker was expressing "dissent" against "all kinds of nationalism." The *Chicago Tribune* gave the story front-page treatment. In Illinois, the state legislature increased the punishment fivefold for desecrating or demonstrating contempt for the flag. Indiana increased the penalty for flag desecration from a maximum $10 fine to a $1,000 fine, plus one year in jail. (Laws punishing flag desecration were later ruled unconstitutional.) *Time* magazine smartly noticed that the flag prohibitions resembled the blasphemy statutes of the early 1900s, when one was criminally liable for religious sacrilege. As historian Robert Justin Goldstein noted, "It was no coincidence that the [flag] controversy peaked between 1967 and 1973, the years of greatest American intervention in Vietnam." Goldstein recounts another incident, a few weeks after the Purdue case. At a civil rights demonstration in Cordele, Georgia, flags were lowered at a courthouse. The American flag was ripped apart by protestors. An elderly black man, suddenly, grabbed the flag from protestors' hands. "I fought under this flag," he said. "You're not going to tear it up."[22]

In June, the *Village Voice* reported, "While growing numbers of Americans are stomping on, mutilating, defacing, tearing up, burning, mocking, desecrating, and otherwise casting contempt on their nation's colors, the streets of New York are looking more and more like a Memorial Day in Putney, Vermont." As CBS News began its report on "Workers' Woodstock": "Noontime in Lower Manhattan, but it could have been midday in Middle America."

With New Left activists characterizing flag veneration as a patriotic shibboleth, Middle Americans counterdemonstrated—they more readily flew the flag. Flag sales doubled by July 1970, compared to the year prior, even as the slim majority of Americans consistently said Vietnam was a "mistake." In that same period, the production of flag decals for vehicles exceeded fifty million, nearly half the number of vehicles on America's roads.[23]

Plenty of patriots were displeased, however. By Flag Day 1970, one Atlanta father decided not to fly Old Glory. "When I was a kid during the

Second World War, the flag stood for something decent and humanitarian," he said. "But how do you tell children about a national sickness, or about the way that symbols of one ideal can be subverted to become symbols of something entirely different?"[24]

When the city's steamfitter chief, George Daly, was young, theaters commonly began showings with the national anthem. One day, his father took him to a movie at a local theater around Fourteenth Street. A man didn't rise for the Anthem. "Stand up," Daly's father told the man. "Stand up!" The man refused. Daly's father punched the man in the mouth. "My father was always hip-hop with the American flag," Daly recalled. At that time, it was bold to sit out the anthem while most stood—a quiet expression of dissension over American foreign policy. But to Daly, you stand because it's the least you can do, considering what veterans have done for you. Daly, like so many working-class kids, was taught to respectfully fold the flag. As men, they saw the flag drape coffins and reverently folded and handed to war widows. Here is a flag for a life. Now that flag was being lowered for the kids who did not risk death, or realize death, in the nation's defense.

"I think of all the people that died for that flag," said Joe Kelly, the Twin Towers elevator constructor. "And somebody's gonna spit on it, it's like spitting on their grave."

"The flag. I can't understand why they'd want to burn it," said plumber Patrick O'Connell, a Korean War veteran. "If there's bad in the country—and it's not all good—you don't burn the flag," he added. "That's a symbol of all the good in the country."[25]

◆

Some liberals tried to save the common root. After Richard Nixon's shocking comeback, liberal activists became, like the media, more focused on workers. The hardhats' activism inspired more efforts. According to one journal, "Every large antiwar demonstration after Bloody Friday included at least a contingent of 'hard hats for peace.'"[26]

In the week after the riot, several newspapers reported that the hardhats and longshoremen did not speak for labor as a whole. Some unionists, including leaders of the municipal, hospital, and clerical workers unions, publicly chastised the hardhats. In New York, student activists from eleven colleges met with some labor leaders. Soon after the riot, one ironworker won headlines for telling a student rally that at the riot, "I didn't see Americans in action. I saw black shirts and brown shirts of Hitler's Germany." Détente, this was not.[27]

The New Left's considerate efforts—and there were some—were too little, too late. The antiwar movement was too radicalized by the seventies, the countercultural headwinds too strong. One year after the riot, the bigoted and buffoonish character of Archie Bunker premiered in the hit sitcom *All in the Family.* The social standing of blue-collar whites would erode with their prospects. That same year, the unemployment rate for construction ticked near 18 percent. American industry also crossed a threshold: the United States ran a trade deficit for the first time since 1893.

The class war over the war was itself deescalated by 1971. The college draft deferment was finally abolished. Though by then, nearly all of the Americans who would die in the war already had.

Meanwhile, John Lindsay's antiwar zeal proved part of his larger journey leftward. Less than a year after visiting Berkeley, Lindsay polled more popular with collegians than even the titans of Democratic liberalism, from Ted Kennedy to Eugene McCarthy to George McGovern. Lindsay's investment in the New Left had paid off. But what had he gained?[28]

| The End of the Beginning

B Y 1972, A onetime Republican was the most liberal candidate in the
Democratic race. John Lindsay advocated an immediate withdrawal
from Vietnam. He said he had "found no one—young or old—who thinks
that immoral war in Indochina should go on another day." He championed
amnesty for draft dodgers, school busing, national abortion rights (George
McGovern supported abortion rights but proposed leaving it to the states).
Lindsay sought to rally his "natural constituency—the young, the minorities,
the out of work, the liberal wing of the Democratic Party," the *Los Angeles
Times* reported. Lindsay inveighed against the "Pentagon's awesome power"
and against "excessive corporate power." He stressed that women "have been
victims of a social system . . . we are all victims of that war in Vietnam . . . we
are all victimized by higher prices . . . we are all victimized by crime." The
blue blood who had run for mayor with support from contributors with
names such as Whitney, Vanderbilt, Astor, Ford, and Rockefeller now
advocated policies that rivaled Europe's social democrats. Wrote Theodore
White, "Compared to John Lindsay, even George McGovern was a man of
compromise."

John Lindsay's advisors didn't think his bid for the presidency was
fantastical. New Left activists were empowered by new convention rules.
Adults ages 18 to 21 could now vote. Liberal youth admired Lindsay. So
did blacks. So did the national media. And he was famous. "You'd know
him anywhere from those hundreds of attractive photographs and those
brilliant 1,001 nights on Carson, Griffin, Frost, and Cavett," *Cosmopolitan*
reported. Cosmo's lead image: Lindsay smirking knowingly as a beautiful
and bikinied blonde embraced him. "Lindsay has immense assets to offset

his late start," the *Economist* reported. So Lindsay summoned those assets and went all in.

Lindsay placed second in an early contest in Arizona. By March, he faced his true test, the Florida primary. Aide Sid Davidoff deployed hard-edged New Yorkers to canvass the pleasant Florida suburbs. Lindsay refused to debate George McGovern. But he tried to goad George Wallace into a debate. He wore swimwear in front of the cameras. But the matinee idol strived to show that he was arthouse down deep. Lindsay sometimes stood above crowds brimming with northerners, people who had fled urban blight for blissful sun, and proceeded to detail urban blight. One day, in a conservative county, performers from Broadway's *Hair* opened for Lindsay. Onstage, Lindsay swept aside his forelock and explained how the other half lives. He spoke of New Yorkers suffering drugs and crime and loud televisions through thin tenement walls. He said that the country was divided by fear, race, and poverty, and "Wallace is running around frightening people on the question of busing." Afterward, one member of *Hair*'s cast told him: "Mayor, you've been radicalized!" Lindsay took it as a compliment.

"Here was Lindsay," Theodore White wrote, "with his furious eloquence, bringing to these green lawns and tranquil places, the nightmares of the shrill nights they had fled." Lindsay finished fifth in Florida. Wisconsin went worse. He bowed out. Looking back, one *Times* feature concluded that "what Lindsay truly lost" was his "irreplaceable mystique."[1]

Lindsay returned to a changed city. "New York City is liberalism's Vietnam. Their traditional weapons—more money, more programs, more taxes, more borrowing—didn't work here," Ken Auletta concluded. "Goaded by liberalism's compassion and ideological commitment to the redistribution of wealth, New York officials helped redistribute much of the tax base and thousands of jobs out of New York." Between 1970 and 1975, New York City would lose north of two hundred thousand manufacturing jobs alone, more than double its losses of any other industry. In the mid-seventies, America's metropolis teetered on the brink of bankruptcy. By the end of the decade, even as the national poverty rate declined, Gotham's rate increased 60 percent. Meanwhile, the city experienced its first significant population decline since 1782.[2]

"Whatever tides may be running nationally," the *Times* wrote after Lindsay's presidential bid, "New Yorkers have been manning the often-shaky piers of liberalism for almost seven years now; they are said to have found this an unnerving and expensive experience."

George McGovern initially succeeded where Lindsay failed, but ultimately repeated Lindsay's failure. He was a preacher's son, a decorated bomber pilot. And he still would be defined by the zealous youth who brought him so far.

◆

The Florida contest also offered an early lesson in the peril of primaries. Once party bosses lost their grip on nominations, as Democratic dons did in 1972, primaries empowered those most active—activists. Political activists are prone to purity tests. Some candidates vied to be purest. The purest risked losing the mainstream, and the election with it. Yet that gambit became more difficult to dismiss when the payoff might serve those who most needed one. In spring 1972, Americans were concerned about inflation, taxes, unemployment, Vietnam, and after that "racial problems," drugs, crime, welfare, pollution, "the elderly." But busing came to the fore in Florida.[3]

The issue rose in national prominence after a Virginia federal judge ordered the city of Richmond and its affluent white suburbs to merge into one "metro" district to achieve integration. Early in the 1972 primary, John Lindsay and George McGovern seized on the issue to paint their primary opponents as false liberals. Busing referenda were also on the Florida ballot. Lindsay told the Florida state legislature that busing was the "only way to integrate our schools." "Dammit, it's time for people to stand up!" Lindsay said on California TV. He added, "Busing has become a code word." Lindsay clarified the accusation: "You're for busing, you're for school integration; and if you're opposed to busing, you're against integration." George McGovern accused Senator Henry "Scoop" Jackson, a longtime supporter of civil rights, of "embracing racism" because of his opposition to mandated busing. But when McGovern faced the downside of his advocacy, McGovern downplayed it. "Busing is not even a real issue," he said. McGovern would accuse George Wallace, Nixon, Scoop Jackson, and "from time to time" Hubert Humphrey of using busing "to take people's minds off the problems which really concern them." But the issue was so explosive because it regarded people's principal concern, their children.

George Wallace said he would save the children. He was a man for the "common people," he assured voters. Sometimes he barnstormed typically populist: "You had better give tax relief to the average man in this country and put it on the filthy rich in Wall Street." "Send them a message," went a Wallace slogan. Gone was the hair pomade. His suits were now modish. But he was still George Wallace. Lindsay said Wallace was "creating mass hysteria" around busing. Yet Lindsay's and McGovern's competition to see who could be furthest left gave Wallace his wide opening—the chance to appeal to everyone who was not a leftist. The "average citizen," said Wallace, when not seeking to generate hysteria, "pays taxes, works every day, and holds the country together." But context is king. Wallace had spent a decade trying to rise in America by dividing it. He saw another chance with the "social scheming" of busing. So the pugilist returned to his familiar fight. Wallace hit the right side: "Mr. Nixon, our children are precious to us, and we want a stop to this busing." Wallace hit the left side: "These pluperfect hypocrites who live over in Maryland or Virginia and they've got their children in a private school." Wallace always could conjure resentments on all sides. "Tomorrow the chickens are coming home to roost," he said. "They gonna be sorry they bused your little children."

George Wallace won Florida, and it was not a close race.[4]

"If we handle [busing] properly, the Democrats will be stuck," Chuck Colson once wrote Richard Nixon. H. R. Haldeman noted that Democrats "lose either way." Colson counseled that Nixon should "exploit the hell out of it." Nixon did.

In February 1972, during the Democratic primary, Nixon floated a constitutional amendment forbidding "forced busing." After Wallace's "breathtaking victory" in Florida, as Michael Barone put it, Nixon cynically seized the issue. Days later, the president gave a nationally televised address on the "need" for federal "action to stop" busing.[5]

The policy, for all its virtues, was politically impossible for Democrats. Three in four Americans, sometimes more, opposed mandated busing. Eight in ten white Democrats opposed it. Blacks were divided some years, but during the '72 campaign, a bare majority favored busing and a third did not. There was no constituency galvanized by it. It wasn't difficult, however, to locate those against it.[6]

The downsides of busing fell largely on blue-collar whites. The issue was racial. But once the rhetoric was realized, the issue concerned class. There were not vast differences between downscale and upscale whites' views on busing. But the white busing advocates were upscale, and their resources often allowed them to skirt the outcome of their advocacy. The Virginia federal judge who ordered busing was an "energetic" liberal, his ruling "landmark" and "scholarly," reported the *Times*. That federal judge also had children—who attended private schools. John Lindsay didn't have kin in the game, either. All four of Lindsay's children attended private school, like their parents had. DC resident George McGovern had arranged for his daughter not to attend DC's troubled public schools. Instead, McGovern's daughter attended one of the good—and quite white—suburban Maryland schools.

The hypocrisy infuriated Scoop Jackson. He had a child in an integrated DC public school. Jackson placed third in the Florida primary. He resented McGovern's suggestion that he did it by appealing to racists. He opposed mandated busing. He also had supported every major postwar civil rights act. He seethed over what he said was a new left-wing tactic to take down the less liberal: "If you disagree with them, they call you a racist."[7]

The color of the issue sometimes cloaked the more universal issue: parents want the best for their children. In 1970, one poll asked whites how upset they would be if "it was decided to bus black children into your neighborhood schools." A third of whites said they would be very upset ("a lot," in the poll's vernacular), a response patently racist. But what about if "it was decided to bus white children into schools in black neighborhoods?" Sixty percent said they would be very upset. Both races knew black schools meant worse schools. Whites didn't want their children to have less so others could have more. They were like any other political constituency in this way— once people become accustomed to an entitlement, they feel entitled to it by custom (whether Medicare, Social Security, or the good local public school). In other words, however ugly the issue got—and ugly, it got—here was evidence that what exercised the majority of whites was not integration, it was the notion that their children might have to pay the cost. And blue collars knew it was their kids who paid America's costs.[8]

◆

Henry "Scoop" Jackson had been a Cassandra about all those electoral costs. Back in August 1971, Jackson spoke in New York. He criticized Nixon's policy toward the poor. Soon he came to the "heart of the matter," as William Safire saw it. Jackson, the son of a building contractor, was a man of gray shades—bland as that, but he also politicked like that. As a senator, he was steadfast on labor rights. He also won contracts for his state's largest employer, Boeing. He was firm on crime. He was also strong on civil rights and civil liberties (he voted against Nixon's DC crime bill because of the "no knock" and preventive detention provisions). He was a cold warrior, but opposed Red-baiting. He also made a familiar cold warrior mistake. He invested his hawkishness in Vietnam early, and never fully extricated his outlook. The New Left didn't want any more cold warriors at the wheel. So Vietnam sank Jackson too. Still he tried. "The working people are also under attack from the left fringes, by people who would like to take over the Democratic Party. If this takeover were to succeed, the Democratic Party will lose in 1972 and be in deep trouble for years thereafter," Jackson said. "There are some people in the Democratic Party, who, intentionally or not, have turned their backs on the workingman. They are either indifferent to him or downright hostile. Their cocktail parties abound with snide jokes about 'hardhats' and 'ethnics.' They mouth fashionable clichés about how workers have grown fat and conservative with affluence, and how their unions are reactionary or racist."

"We watched Jackson, who could have been a real threat to Nixon," William Safire wrote, "fail to get to first base in the Democratic nomination race; and then, to our amazement, the break came. Nixon's political, neo-majoritarian dream came true in the person of George McGovern."[9]

At the 1972 Democratic convention, delegate and playwright Arthur Miller surveyed the crowd: "The traditional [Democratic] Party no longer exists. We've been taken over." One veteran Democratic apparatchik said the Massachusetts delegation looked "like the cast of *Hair*." The Democratic platform had ninety-two mentions of "right" or "rights" and two mentions of "wrong" or "wrongs." It championed "black, brown, young, or women." It advocated preserving the ethnicities of "American Indians, the Spanish-speaking, the Asian Americans." Unnoted: Italian, Poles, Greeks, the white ethnics. The platform supported "amnesty" for those who illegally evaded the Vietnam draft. It also assured America that draft dodgers were solely motivated by "reasons of conscience." In the jobs section, it led with youth unemployment, farmers second, and returned to the vocational concerns of McGovernites—"substantial unemployment among aerospace technicians, teachers and other white-collar workers."

It was the first convention for eight out of ten delegates. They were diverse by race and sex but not class. Nearly four in ten delegates had attended graduate school, tenfold the share of graduate degrees in the electorate. The average delegate's wealth was about twice the typical American's. "There is too much hair and not enough cigars at this convention," one labor delegate told the *Times*. McGovern gave one of the best speeches of his career (near three in the morning). After watching the Democratic convention, Nixon concluded he had a "chance, not just to win the election, but to create the New Majority we had only dreamed of in 1970."[10]

Four years earlier, McGovern had chaired the committee that added quotas to ensure diverse delegations. "No one, neither Democratic party regulars nor the press, had any notion of the scope of what had been set in motion by the reform drive at the 1968 convention," Mary and Thomas Edsall wrote in *Chain Reaction*. Strategist Fred Dutton, who later became a key McGovern advisor, was on the committee as well. Dutton's 1971 book prophesied the new Democratic coalition. It advocated building a majority with, effectively, the Lindsay coalition, which became the McGovern coalition, which became the Democratic coalition. Dutton urged a "shopping list of fresh appeals" to unite a "loose Democratic coalition" of "key groups"—educated white liberals, minorities, and youth. McGovern's committee recognized that priority. With poetic justice, the reforms banished bosses such as Richard Daley. They depleted Big Labor's power. George Meany fumed. "Meany's bulging catalogue of hates" are "most sulphurous" for the "young zealots of the New Left," who "used their control to shoulder" Meany aside, the *Economist* reported. But also, as Teddy White wrote, "they were being taken for granted." The director of the AFL-CIO's political machine, Al Barkan, said during the campaign: "We aren't going to let these Harvard-Berkeley Camelots take over our party." But they couldn't stop it. Yet with the ouster of the Daleys and the Meanys, reformers also pushed out those they personified. Columnist Mike Royko counted Chicago's fifty-nine delegates in '72. Half were women. A third were black. But only one Italian. Only three Poles. Royko wrote, "Your reforms have disenfranchised Chicago's white ethnic Democrats." The *Village Voice*'s Jack Newfield, a New York convention delegate, looked back wearily. He commended efforts to correct past mistakes by giving voice to those who lacked it. But he too saw overcorrection, a "terrible new mistake." "The new Democratic Party did not make room for the white ethnic workingman," Newfield added. "The McGovern reform guidelines created quotas for women, youth, and blacks, but none for poor people, or senior citizens, or ethnic minorities—Irish, Italian, Polish." As Democratic populist Fred Harris put it in this era, the "blue-collar worker will be progressive as long as it is not progress for everyone but himself."[11]

For the first time since it was formed, the AFL-CIO did not support the Democratic nominee. The inaction was important for what it portended rather than its actual impact (polling indicates it had little impact). But it showed that union support was no longer assuredly Democratic. In the decades ahead, as Democrats further shifted their emphasis from labor issues to social issues, unionists felt less compelled to back Democrats. And on social issues, such as the antiwar movement, Meany reflected his fold. Steamfitter chief George Daly said many trade unionists had come to disdain the "likes of McGovern." They saw them as, in Daly's words, "anti-American—not anti-union—just anti-American."[12]

Nixon's surrogates sought to saddle McGovern with his extreme faithful. He was hit as the "candidate of the three A's: acid, abortion, amnesty." But McGovern also allowed it. He had become the New Left's champion.

Americans indicted moderately tempered liberals because of the radical company they kept, and because of some causes they shared. Most people agreed with McGovern about Vietnam, in the big picture. Three in four Americans wanted all the soldiers home from Vietnam in 1972. But the antiwar politician was not winning them, largely because of what also came with McGovern's views on the war. On the stump, McGovern's greatest applause line was his advocacy of amnesty for draft dodgers, despite a majority of Americans opposing it in 1972, including nearly six in ten Democrats in August. Yet McGovern's obstacles were also more nebulous. It was often not a matter of issues. In 1968, Vietnam and "law and order" dominated voters' concerns. In this general election, as one witty *Times* headline put it: POLL FINDS ISSUES NOT AN ISSUE IN '72. The campaign became a choice between two candidates and—a dynamic Democrats rued—between mainstream and extreme. The left wing loathed Nixon, but he was not disliked by enough Americans to make the race a referendum on him (six in ten independents approved of Nixon's job performance throughout the general election), while George McGovern's weaknesses allowed the election to also be about him— his othering. In this way, he became like the entire New Left, burdened with the extremes who had energized the base, brought him so far, and proved unable to take him any further.[13]

Nixon needed only to hang back and offer unity. Yet he also had a record to stand on. Nixon postured plenty. He didn't like country music but had country musicians entertain at the White House. He did little directly for Big Labor. But his presidency had helped workaday Americans, with critical assistance from the Democratic Congress. Nixon was the first president since 1849 to take office with both houses of Congress controlled by the opposition. His domestic accomplishments included the Clean Air Act, the Occupational Safety and Health Act (OSHA), the establishment of the Environmental Protection Agency (EPA), a consumer affairs office, extension of the Voting Rights Act, the first affirmative action program (Philadelphia Plan), moving the voting age to 18, a massive federal effort to combat cancer, signing Title IX to ban gender discrimination in education, the end of the college draft deferment (when the dying was mostly done), and finally the end of the draft. He did break with liberals. He showcased his opposition to "forced" busing, after all. He vetoed the Clean Water Act, a veto that Congress overrode. In the long view, Nixon was inconceivably liberal compared to the half-century of Republicans who followed him. He proposed a guaranteed annual income and large increases in federal funding for the arts. He professed Keynesianism. He used wage-and-price controls. Once Watergate brought Nixon down, it would not be conservatives who paid. Ronald Reagan realized Nixon's dreams of a New Majority with the Democrats who bore his name. Reagan's 1980 campaign plan reflected Nixon's blue-collar strategy. But Reagan's other impulse, his Goldwater outlook, benefited from Nixon's final loss. Liberals relished Nixon's downfall, but liberalism fell with him. Nixon was not quite one of them, but he had governed on liberal terms, and with him went not only some of those terms, but something more: Americans' trust that government can and should promote the common good. The left, however, could not see how they were invested in him. Years after his presidency, Nixon remained so toxic among liberals that to avoid angering their readers, both the *New York Times* and the *Washington* Post—the paragons of free speech—refused to publish ads for his presidential memoir.[14]

Nixon campaigned in 1972 for a moderate New Majority, asking Democrats "driven out" of their party to "come home." Both campaigns spotlighted blue-collar laborers, Nixon's most. There was a bumper sticker that printed a flag inside a hard hat and read, NIXON. One Nixon television ad pictured a hardhat atop the steel. It intoned against McGovern and zoomed in on the worker's creased brow, his pudgy nose, his pained stare. Across the screen: DEMOCRATS FOR NIXON. After the Democratic convention, an internal McGovern memo explained that blue collars were not prowar but the "straight-out moral condemnation still runs right against the grain of their strong sense of patriotism and respect for flag and country." Like so much, however, this realization was too late as well. "We were always subject to this pressure from the cause people," said Frank Mankiewicz, who directed McGovern's campaign. "We reacted to every threat from women, or

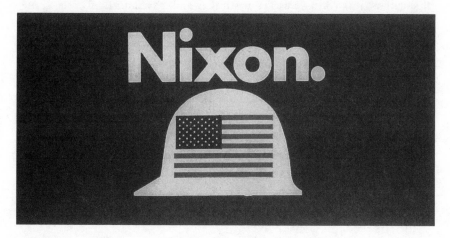

A 1972 Nixon campaign bumper sticker.

militants, or college groups. If I had to do it all over again, I'd learn when to tell them to go to hell."[15]

Nixon won a historic victory. His 61 percent of the vote essentially tied the greatest electoral feats of the twentieth century. McGovern's share of the vote was smaller than even Barry Goldwater's in 1964. The boy born with little, Frank Nixon's son, won a victory equal to FDR's. And Nixon did it with FDR's base. McGovern had written his doctoral dissertation on labor (the violent Colorado coal strike). He had a strong labor voting record. But McGovern failed to connect with the typical laborer. Remarkably, for a Republican at the time, Nixon earned the support of nearly six in ten white labor union members. About seven out of ten whites with low to middle incomes backed him. Young people turned out to vote in historic numbers— and favored Nixon. In 1960, when Nixon had faced off in a two-man race against a conventional FDR Democrat, John Kennedy, he won roughly the same share of well-educated whites as in 1972. Between JFK and McGovern, nearly all of Nixon's electoral gains were with blue-collar whites.[16]

Despite Nixon's triumph, Democrats won two Senate seats, including a narrow upset in Delaware, where 29-year-old Joe Biden became a senator. Pundits noted that Nixon's coattails proved trim. "That's how they'll piss on the whole thing," Nixon growled. But in twenty-one months, it would be Nixon who pissed it all away.

Election night, Nixon wore a light-blue checkered smoking jacket and puffed on a pipe. Haldeman sat at an antique table, mining election returns. Nixon grinned at the sight of Chuck Colson.

"Here's to you, Chuck," Nixon said, tipping his scotch and soda. "These are your votes that are pouring in—the Catholics, the union members, the blue-collars, *your* votes. It was your strategy and it's a landslide!"[17]

In the year after, the Watergate hearings signaled Richard Nixon's end. John Lindsay left City Hall on his last day alone and teary-eyed. That same year, America signed the treaty to withdraw combat forces from Vietnam, Peter Brennan became Nixon's secretary of labor, and hardhats reached the height of their heyday. Construction workers never earned again what they did in 1973. The typical American man's income peaked, roughly matching his earnings forty-five years later, as blue-collar America began its long slide, losing economically what it had already lost culturally. And few elites noticed or seemed to care, until certain candidates noticed, and then everyone cared.[18]

Afterword

NEARLY A HALF-CENTURY later, as Donald Trump pledged to "make America great again," he campaigned as a superpatriot and a New York builder. He ran against the establishment, stressed the trade deficit, vowed to revitalize manufacturing, and become an infrastructure president. He even wore a hard hat at some rallies. He stood above crowds and free-flowed the resentments that betrayed some of them. He spoke of "forgotten Americans" and the "Silent Majority," which resonated with most of them. And despite likely becoming the wealthiest president since George Washington, he came to represent a vote against elites who had disregarded or deplored them.

The American electorate would polarize to a historic degree in 2016. Though not by race or sex. Rather, by class. The votes of blue-collar whites differed from the votes of college-educated whites more than at any other time since 1964. Back then, Lyndon Johnson's landslide depended most on his blue-collar base. The electorate reversed by 2016. Trump owed his presidency to whites not of the information economy, not of the professions or coastal culture, but to those on the losing side of the postindustrial age.[1]

Yet President Trump would invest his political capital in a historic tax cut for those who did not need one. The trade deficit only widened. He pleased conservatives with judiciary appointments—a blue collar cause, it was not. He did achieve the USMCA trade agreement, which enhanced workers' protections. But when he had the power, with the GOP controlling Congress in his first years, he never truly endeavored to improve the prospects of the ordinary Americans who made him or "drain the swamp" or renovate the nation's rusting infrastructure. Still blue-collar whites stuck with him. Into Trump's bid for a second term, elites continued to be confounded by why. His fringe enthusiasts and superfans were still portrayed as prototypical. Opponents still presumed that because tens of millions chose him, they chose all of him.

Americans are not a two-party people. They are a people filed into a two-party system. Occasionally, that system is challenged. In 1992, an outlandish businessman and nationalist won nearly a fifth of voters as a third-party candidate. Ross Perot's base was more male than female, more working class than not. Two thirds of Perot's supporters were traditional Republicans. But they were disillusioned with the corporate right. Their concerns also superseded orthodoxy. Perot supported abortion rights. He opposed the first Gulf War and NAFTA. He also stressed, unlike the major parties, that "giant sucking sound" of factory jobs going to Mexico.[2]

Presidential races often are, however, reduced to that most American choice: the lesser of two evils. Factions usually do not unite over a hero, but against a common foe. Several weeks before the 2016 election, a slim majority of the white working class told pollsters that Trump lacked "decency." They saw Hillary Clinton as more civilized. But decency was not the issue of the time. After all, for many alienated whites, Trump was a middle finger to elites. As people do, they compared their present to their personal past, as well as against America's promise. For these whites, it neither mattered that the average black remained worse off or that the average Asian was better off. It was decades of their blue-collar wage stagnation. Their disappearing factory jobs. Their lost union cards. Their lost pension. Their withering communities and institutions. Their experience with automation, free trade, and downward wage pressure. Their industrial ghost towns. Their divorce or in midlife, their uniquely rising mortality rate. Their children's longer odds. Their upfront costs to be middle class—especially, exponential college costs—with less assurance on the back end. The way debt weighs down a young future and a family's wellbeing. And seismically as well, cultural alienation, depreciation, tribalization, and the ethno-racial hostility that globally rises from it. Yet also the heightened expectations once inseparable from these shores. And the friction that followed, as more people felt an impossible distance between themselves and the American Dream.

Antipathy festered, as struggling whites were told they were, in fact, "privileged" because they were white. So even their adversity was invalidated, like when the New Left was young. Yet by the dusk of the Obama era, working-class whites and nonwhites shared an economic outlook. More than four in ten of these whites said they "often don't have enough money to make ends meet," more than double the share of college-educated whites, yet only modestly less than Hispanics and blacks. Nearly six in ten blacks and working-class whites said they would find it "difficult" to pay an emergency $400 expense. Between 1989 and 2016, the share of American families who were of the white working-class decreased by about a fifth, but their portion of the nation's wealth fell by half. One cause was applauded by elites on all sides. That is, China's entrance into the WTO. It ended the livelihood of several million. It blasted open America's trade deficit. But for the most part, those losing the work or watching shops shutter along Main Street were told to move to a new city or learn a new vocation. Experts assured them: trade deficits are "good" because it allows Americans to acquire cheap goods. Economists explained, free markets flow this way, as if there was no manmade role in the severity of this unnatural disaster. Meanwhile, in this era, more than eight in ten whites without a college degree—above any other group—came to believe "elected officials in Washington lose touch with the people pretty quickly." At the same time, more working-class whites favored a path to citizenship for undocumented immigrants than did not. But an impression brewed, like many developed nations, that the corporate right and cultural left cared more for new immigrants than for their own countrymen—reminiscent of the late 1800s, when the *Times* beckoned Italian immigration and dismissed the Irish. By 2009, the worst economic crisis in seven decades exacerbated much of it. Blue collar workers constituted three in four lost jobs during the worst period of the Great Recession, and white men constituted the plurality of them. Yet no "new New Deal" came to pass. There was the auto bailout and a modest stimulus. But the portion of the stimulus focused on jobs did not focus on those losing the most jobs. It secured municipal workers (a more white-collar workforce) and state social safety nets. At the same time, into Barack Obama's reelection campaign, decades of implicit strategy cemented into consensus. The *Times* reported, "Democratic operatives for the 2012 election make it clear for the first time that the party will explicitly abandon the white working class." A few of us contested that consensus and wrote of emulating FDR's first years—his fixation on the economic crisis. But too few Democrats were listening by then. "The Democratic Party stopped being for unions, stopped being for workers, and those people in the way it had been since the 1930s," AFL-CIO political leader Michael Podhorzer told me in 2006. And, in his view, "As the Democratic Party became less credible to workers, as fewer workers were in unions to mediate all of this, the Republicans discovered and became more and more skilled at exploiting cultural issues."

The economy crashed a few years later. In time, the recovery's benefits were largely concentrated among those who least needed it. By 2016, many blue-collar whites felt slighted by a GOP establishment that championed free markets, while ignoring that most of its base—that is, them—were casualties of hyper capitalism, even as leading liberals seemed to preach sympathy for everyone but them.[3]

Trump was a rebuttal. His behavior infuriated progressives. Reporters seethed on social media. The blowback transformed even his vices into virtues. For those who shamed him had shamed them too—or held sweepingly negative views of them. This affirmed Trump's status as a no-confidence vote in the status quo. And it would help explain his election. Why Trump won about a third of the counties that Barack Obama had won. Why Trump won nearly a fourth of voters who wanted the next president to implement *more* liberal policies.

Most Republicans acted more typically. Ideological flanks can place an offense above the larger outcome and sunder coalitions. But most American voters will rarely sacrifice their entire cause for one cause, or the failings of their flawed choice (given the alternative). Bill Clinton was reelected despite a majority of voters, including about a third of liberals, saying he was *not* honest. Four years later, George W. Bush capitalized on Clinton's failings. But the Bush who first entered national politics never could have accomplished the same. Bush lost his bid for Congress in 1978. His first campaign ad showed him jogging. Noted one voter, "If a guy is jogging in" rural Texas, "somebody is after him." Bush's opponent portrayed him as a rich and immoral Yankee. By 1994, the grandson of a senator, the son of a president, ran as an evangelical family man from West Texas. And, in an upset, he won the Texas governorship. A decade later, the dean of the Washington press corps, David Broder, traveled to northern Michigan for a vacation between the party conventions. "Bush came through Traverse City, Michigan, during a political swing," Broder recalled of the 2004 campaign. "The headline across eight columns on the *Traverse City Record Eagle* the day after his visit was a quote from his speech talking about himself, and the quote was, 'a plain-spoken fella.' F-E-L-L-A. I took the paper in to see my wife—who is a yellow dog Democrat—I said if he wins this election, this is the reason."[4]

"If an educated man is not heartily American in instinct and feeling and taste and sympathy, he will amount to nothing in our public life," wrote a Phi Beta Kappa Harvard graduate with a photographic memory, Theodore Roosevelt.[5]

Perhaps it's a coincidence that the modern presidential contenders who were regularly "misunderestimated," to borrow W's phrasing, have been the same Republicans who rallied the "plain people": Nixon, Reagan, W, and Trump. Joseph Kraft's concession—"The most important organs of the press and the television are, beyond much doubt, dominated by the outlook of upper-income whites" and "are not rooted in the great mass of ordinary Americans"—was hardly less true in Trump's day than in Nixon's. The same could be argued for what *Time* magazine wrote in 1970 of elites' outlook on regular whites: "If not ignored, they have been treated with condescension." In turn, once Trump proved a contender, the prestige press "rediscovered" working-class whites, as it had after Nixon's shocking comeback.

When Ronald Reagan sought the California governorship, Democratic incumbent Pat Brown leaked damaging information on Reagan's primary opponent. Governor Brown thought Reagan's candidacy was "absurd." The Democratic campaign staff was "gleeful" that Reagan might be their opponent. It was only the first of Reagan's last laughs. "The knowledge class concluded that Reagan was stupid," Henry Allen wrote of Reagan's presidency. "Well, fine. If Reagan wasn't outsmarting them, he was outdumbing them."[6]

Ronald Reagan launched his general election campaign on Labor Day, 1980. The New York skyline and the Statue of Liberty were at his back. Flags flapped at his left and right. He stood tall and tan, his white shirt unbuttoned to the chest, and said that he was the first Republican to come to the county since 1968. "I'm here because it is the home of Democrats," Reagan continued. "There are millions of Democrats who are just as unhappy with the way things are." He talked of adding jobs and lessening taxes. "A recession is when your neighbor loses his job; a depression is when you lose yours; recovery is when Jimmy Carter loses his," went his famous line. He ennobled "American workers." "I happen to be the only president of a union ever to be a candidate for president." The conservative icon promised to always "consult" organized labor. He praised George Meany, who had died earlier that year. He mentioned the "brave workers" in Poland combatting communism. He spoke of the American dream, of a "return to spiritual and moral values," of "building" the economy. Reagan pledged: "We will make America great again."

Over the next two months, Reagan discussed joblessness in a Lithuanian neighborhood in Chicago. He spoke to an Italian society in New Haven. He toured a steel factory in Youngstown, Ohio. After he finished speaking at a Polish church in Philadelphia, the crowd burst into song. Reagan choked up and quoted an old Irish blessing, "May the wind be ever at your back." One set of campaign buttons read: COSSACKS FOR REAGAN. He pledged that he would retain labor protections and was "not antiunion," stirring a conservative "uproar." Reagan brought Michael Balzano, the Nixon liaison to white ethnics, on the road with him. He had W. J. Usery—a Navy welder who became a Nixon and Ford Labor Department leader—help direct his

Blue-Collar Working Group. Reagan's aim, as his confidential campaign plan emphasized, was the "breakup of the Democratic coalition" by working to "solidify a public impression" that he had "concern for the common man and understands the problems facing voters in their daily lives," in order to "target the populist voter" and, in part, court "urban ethnics" and "blue-collar and labor union members" by projecting "a realization that these voters are no longer solely motivated by economic concerns but by larger social issues as well."[7]

"They came to believe that Reagan was a better protector of the way of life for working people," Usery recalled. But, he later added, "Nixon opened the door to the working class. I think he did a masterful job and if there hadn't been Watergate, what would his second administration have been? Ever since, the Democrats are losing the working class. And the working class is losing too."[8]

BIBLIOGRAPHIC ESSAY

For Events Related to May 8, 1970, the Hardhat Riot

For the Hardhat Riot's chapters, the day of May 8, 1970 (Chapter 1 and Part 2 of the book), conventional notes would have been impossible, as well as byzantine and immense.

As I'll detail below, the riot narrative relies most on New York Police Department (NYPD) intelligence files from 1970. At the time I read these files, they were "unprocessed" and as they were in 1970, when the NYPD concluded its investigation. But since I saw the records, at the time this bibliography was written (October 2019), the files had been mostly "processed," drastically reorganizing what I'd seen, and are now professionally organized and systematized by an archivist.

Regarding this book, each sentence in the riot narrative, often different clauses within one sentence, derive from multiple sources (e.g., different NYPD records, legal affidavits, or two separate media accounts verifying the same fact). My goal in this bibliographic essay is to convey to readers and researchers how I created the narrative of the Hardhat Riot. I've ordered sources in terms of importance to the narrative, rather than alphabetically. I believe this best serves the reader. In the narrative itself, if prose is in quotes, it was recounted in a witness statement to the police or in an affidavit, in the fashion of a quote—or the source was a quote from a contemporaneous news account, when such a quote does not directly conflict with established facts. The narrative relies most heavily on the reports and notes from the 324 in-person interviews the NYPD conducted with participants and witnesses during its investigation of the Hardhat Riot, interviews that alone summed to seven thousand NYPD staff hours, as well as sworn affidavits given by witnesses to the riot (see details below). The NYPD's final report selectively quoted morsels from its interviews. The NYPD report also hid identifying information, and, most importantly, ignored immense amounts of material that both incriminated the NYPD and conveyed the full and more brutal story of the riot. When there are conflicts between accounts, the participants' and witnesses' comments given to police or in sworn affidavits are given pre-eminence. Witnesses or participants are more likely to be mindful of their words in statements to police or in affidavits. As any veteran reporter can tell you, people commonly speak loosely to reporters and say what they might not if they felt their words carried the weight of law.

In terms of weighting the importance of a source, here is the respective order, beginning with the most important: (1) Film footage, still and moving. Unlike, say, Chicago '68, most of the violence occurred outside the media eye. Yet when possible, I always defer to hard evidence. Most of this was found in the police files. However, even a camera lens can lie by omission—what's left outside the crop, what goes unpublished. So like all, one piece of evidence is given greater value when corroborated. (2) Witness affidavits given within roughly a week of the riot. They were given under the penalty of perjury, sealed by a notary, and often given by lawyers who witnessed the riot and would be hyperaware of the consequences of perjury. Still, even these had errors. Litigation has taught us over decades that eyewitnesses make mistakes. (3) Contemporaneous police records from the day of the riot or soon after, such as complaint reports (details ahead). (4) The in-person interviews conducted during the police investigation, which were often within several weeks of the riot, or at least within two months. These sometimes included follow-up interviews as well as maps and photographs for interviewees to confirm their account and aid memories. (5) Other police records (details ahead). (6) Other legal records (details ahead). (7) News accounts, which are not last because they are least. Writers of history owe a great debt to reporters proverbial first draft. That expressed, there were some cases of bias, such as in the *New York Post* reporting on the hardhats. The main issue, though, is that reporters are working under strict deadlines and are sometimes misled by those they quote, or can only see so much in the time they have. In this vein, I tried to avoid direct quotes from newspapers unless the quotes were essential, unique, and not contradicted by more-established facts. Sometimes I found that newspaper quotes conflicted with what that same person told police or other facts, including some serious omissions. In those cases, I defer to accounts given to police. The one exception: criticism of the NYPD that might have been omitted or skipped over during the police interviews. In those cases, I ensure the quotes in news accounts do not conflict with verifiable facts or other trustworthy sources, and depend upon them.

The legal affidavits carried the most weight in assessing police conduct. The NYPD never had the power to influence these accounts. I conducted some interviews with those at the riot that are not sourced in this book. Yet I soon realized that in-person interviews, decades later, were treacherous and often error-inducing. Eye witnesses are already error-prone and those mistakes were compounded after decades. This is also why, in the riot narrative, despite the fear it might sometimes prove repetitive to the reader, I felt compelled to weave several eyewitness's underlining a similar point, such as an incident of police malfeasance. In these cases, I felt readability had to take a hit out of my responsibility as a reporter. That said, I cut more than five thousand words from the riot chapters, and nearly every thematic pattern could be further evidenced.

I only use personal interviews when other facts corroborate the account or those perspectives logically fit the facts. Additionally, on the use of eyewitnesses decades later, there was not a great selection. Most participants in and victims of the riot, as well as those who policed it, had died before I first began to dive into the riot's history. Some living witnesses had only experienced the riot briefly, from one corner of the horde, and their memories were of little use. Some living construction workers proved difficult to locate, despite great effort, and the book's schedule also curtailed such efforts. For all these reasons, though most especially faulty memories, I relied on contemporaneous affidavits, film, and police records foremost.

Below are my sources in order of importance:

• New York Police Department Inspectional Services Bureau, Intelligence Division, Handschu Hard Hat Demonstration Files, currently stored in the New York City Municipal Archives offsite facility.

In early 2017, I initiated legal requests to multiple city agencies for the records of the NYPD's investigation into the riot via New York State's Freedom of Information Law (FOIL). The NYPD denied those requests. I filed appeals. After about a year of back-and-forth, the appeal won. The NYPD provided a partial disclosure. Meanwhile, I learned of a better route. There were more documents archived outside the NYPD's purview, untouched, and stored within New York's Municipal Archives. This was the result of a class-action settlement with the NYPD's investigative and intelligence divisions (*Handschu v. Special Services Division*, 1985). That case moved decades of files from the NYPD to the Municipal Archives. I reached out to the archive's helpful, genial, and professional staff—and one should also note, an archival staff who truly adheres to the spirit of their job, to preserve documents not for the city employees, but for the public who elects and funds municipal governance.

In 2018, I read these records in their entirety before they were reviewed by a city archivist or "processed." "Processed" broadly means examined by an archivist for information that cannot be made public, organized for researchers' ease, given a systemized order, made safe for long-term storage, and so forth. I was the first non-police officer or non-municipal official to read the Hardhat records (it's possible some city employee broadly surveyed these files in the late 1980s or early 1990s, when they left the NYPD's control). I viewed all records in full and unredacted.

At the time I saw these files, they were stuffed into large file boxes, as they were in the NYPD storage facility before being transferred to the city archives due to the *Handschu* case. In October 2019, I returned to the city archives for fact-checking. By then, they had been nearly entirely "processed" (the archivists had a few boxes left). That archival work had significantly reorganized the records. For example, numerous related police records, once stuffed into separate boxes, are now organized by subject matter or neatly in the same folder (such as concerning a single witness or participant). Even some of the news clippings the NYPD thought relevant, previously stuffed into separate boxes, have been neatly filed, which will allow researchers to efficiently consider context. Above all, the greatest improvement is the combining of one subject's records, allowing an efficient global understanding of all evidence related to him or her. All of this work means that future researchers will have a far easier time reviewing these records. This necessary archival work, however, changed the references for my research (and thus made conventional citations impossible).

It's possible that, via a FOIL appeal like mine, someone acquired some of these files via a disclosure in the half-century since the events (there's no way to verify). But since I've read everything ever written on the Hardhat Riot, I doubt anything of substance ever was seen by a non-police official before I read the documents (as a veteran city archivist explained to me as well). Since the *Handschu* case, as it was also explained to me by city archivists, most of these files (including all the Hardhat Riot and Columbia files) effectively went into storage and were forgotten about until inquiries were made, and possibly some threat of litigation regarding another portion of the intelligence files (I lacked the time to dig into this history). Consequently, the city archives officially accessioned all the Handschu boxes in 2015, where the Hardhat files were stored again for several years unread, until my inquires.

In my research of these intelligence files, I reviewed all records that were handed over by the NYPD, unredacted, and 2,382 pages of these records were critical in enabling me to construct the narrative of the Hardhat Riot, though the collection well exceeds this number. Records include: arrest reports, complaint reports, complaint reports follow-up investigations, witness/participant interview reports, interview notes, civilian complaint reports, memoranda, aided and accident cards, intelligence officer's reports, supplementary reports, summonses, grand jury subpoenas, commanding officer's reports, drafts of official police reports, official police reports, interim progress reports, progress reports, transcripts, letters, telegrams, notes, officer shield cards, call logs, telephone records, duty rosters, film, photographs, incident maps, clippings.

• New York Police Department Complaint Reports, May 1970, related to the Hardhat Riot, New York Police Department Legal Bureau. Accessed after successful FOIL appeal. Processed in 2018. They are redacted and not currently archived.

• Legal materials. *Michael Belknap et al., Plaintiffs appellees, v. Howard R. Leary, Police Commissioner of the City of New York, Inspector Harold Schryner et al., Joseph Inserra, Thomas Woodford, Robert Kesinger, Larry Tallman et al., Defendants-appellants.* Affidavits, Complaint, court rulings, preliminary memoranda. Belknap v. Leary, 1970, MS Years of Expansion, 1950–1990: Series 4: Legal Case Files, 1933–1990, Box 1231, Item 849, Mudd Library, Princeton University. American Civil Liberties Union Papers, 1912–1990. Affidavits were especially useful, and originally and graciously provided by the lead plaintiff in the case, Michael Belknap. I did not use the ACLU complaint itself as a source, because it was rushed and lacked the scope of materials I had access to, most importantly the records of the police investigation. For the events of May 7 in Wall Street's plaza, as detailed in Chapter 12, as well as activism in streets until May 20, 1970, as detailed in Chapter 22, the aforenoted police records were also utilized.

• Important author interviews related to the riot: Richard Aurelio, Sid Davidoff, A. Raymond Randolph, Michael Belknap, George Daly, Joe Guzzardi, and one unnamed hardhat who participated in the rally and would not speak for attribution.

• Major news sources: DN, NYT, NYP, WSJ, *Newsday, Staten Island Advance,* AP, UPI, WP, CT, ABC, CBS, NBC, May 5 to May 31. Threads of numerous articles in these newspaper editions were used to inform the narrative of the Hardhat Riot, and checked against other facts or accounts.

• Specific media sources that were particularly helpful: CBS, ABC, NBC, May 8, 1970 (but most of May as well, for writing about the city before and after the riot). Richard Rogin, "Joe Kelly Has Reached His Boiling Point: Why the Construction Workers Holler, 'U.S.A., All the Way!'" NYT

Magazine, June 28, 1970. Diana Lurie, "Underneath the Hard Hats: A Political Forum," NYM, November 2, 1970. Thomas Williams, "My Hard Hat Problem and Yours," *Esquire*, October 1970. "The Sudden Rising of the Hardhats," *Time*, May 25, 1970. "The Hard Hats," *Newsweek*, May 25, 1970. Fred Cook, "Hard-Hats: The Rampaging Patriots," *The Nation*, June 15, 1970. Kenneth Gross, "Life Under a Hard Hat," *Newsday*, June 6, 1970. "Three Days That Shook the Establishment," *Business Week*, May 16, 1970. *Trinity Parish Newsletter*, January–February 1968 and May–June 1970. *Pace Press*, May 15, 1970. For further context, especially on the Wall Street demonstration on May 7, 1970, and David Dellinger's thoughts on the riot, I was grateful for footage in a documentary produced by NYU film students, including riot victim Harry Bolles, and spearheaded by a (then) relatively unknown filmmaker and film instructor, Martin Scorsese. See Street Scenes, (1970; United States: New York Cinetracts Collective, Director: Martin Scorsese) Documentary.

• The John Vliet Lindsay papers at Yale were also helpful for establishing Lindsay's whereabouts daily in May 1970, for detailing his administration's actions that week, and for related records. Richard Aurelio's personal journal entry on the Hardhat Riot was also helpful, which was given to me by Aurelio.

Regarding Chapter 16, for the brief look at Nixon and his advisors during the riot's narrative, see President Richard Nixon's Daily Diary May 1, 1970–May 15, 1970," box RC-5, White House Central Files: Staff Member and Office Files: Office of Presidential Papers and Archives, NL. Henry Kissinger, *The White House Years* (Boston: Little, Brown, 1979), 509–514. Arthur M. Schlesinger Jr., *Journals, 1952–2000* (NY: Penguin, 2007), 325–326. H. R. Haldeman, *The Haldeman Diaries: Inside the Nixon White House* (NY: Berkley Books, 1994), 159–164.

A note on the riot's narrative arc (spoiler alert). I had to make hard calls that often influenced what was excluded and included. I wanted to be guided by— when in doubt, cut it out. But hundreds of witness statements, affidavits, numerous police records, and news accounts conflicted to an incalculable degree. I had to sometimes defer to the preponderance of the evidence and, as aforenoted, weight sources against one another. I created a timeline of over 250 pages alone to sort events, which became the spine of the riot narrative. I remain ambivalent about some choices. One is the initial surge up City Hall's steps that leads Chapter 17. It's possible this first and small charge up the steps was confused by some witnesses and policemen with the larger horde that stormed City Hall soon after. For example, it could be that a sliver of that larger onrush was ahead of the rest of the men, but it was all one charge. But the police public report, which excluded much that surely occurred, included an early and distinct vanguard of ten to twenty men rushing the steps. That was a key reason I kept it, absent directly contradicting evidence. Also, facts and accounts conflicted over when precisely the bulk of the violence at Pace College occurred, as it related to the seizure of City Hall. It's quite possible the worst had ended at City Hall and the flag had been raised again before the Pace turmoil commenced. In this case, because accounts conflicted, I took the liberty (for reasons of narrative flow) of placing the Pace narrative between episodes of the City Hall upheaval. In some cases, I excluded quotes or material that was the most incendiary, if such was not substantiated by other facts, including one interviewee who was certain he saw a flag burned by an antiwar activist early in the riot (I left it out because it was uncorroborated and, if it had occurred, logic dictates others would have likely recalled the incident).

ABBREVIATIONS

ABC	*ABC Evening News*
AP	Associated Press
CBS	*CBS Evening News*
CT	*Chicago Tribune*
DN	New York *Daily News*
Gallup	The Gallup Poll
GSS	General Social Survey polling
Harris	Louis Harris and Associates polling
LAT	*Los Angeles Times*
LP	John V. Lindsay Papers, Yale University
NA	National Archives at College Park, Maryland
NBC	*NBC Nightly News* or *The Huntley-Brinkley Report*, depending on date
NL	Richard Nixon Presidential Library and Museum, Yorba Linda, CA
NY	For publishers located in New York City
NYCMA	New York City Municipal Archives, Handschu NYPD Intelligence Records
NYM	*New York Magazine*
NYP	*New York Post*
NYT	*New York Times*
UPI	United Press International
USN	*US News & World Report*
WP	*Washington Post*
WSJ	*Wall Street Journal*

If a byline is absent, either there was no byline or it was a newspaper editorial. I do not distinguish between a newspaper and its sections/supplements, such as newspaper magazines; for example, NYT cites newspaper and its magazine.

Original statistical studies of about two-dozen polling datasets (the raw results of surveys) were conducted for this book with the assistance of statistician Robert Kuhn, PhD. See Notes for additional detailed results, which shed more light on the era's events and issues. The studies, exclusive to this book, are referenced by citing the poll name and the poll numbers or the date, such as in this format, "Kuhn: Harris 2055, January 1971."

NOTES

Introduction

1. E. P. Thompson, *The Making of the English Working Class* (NY: Vintage, 1963), 12–13.
2. William Safire, *Before the Fall: An Inside View of the Pre-Watergate White House* (NY: Tower Publications, 1975), 585.

Chapter 2

1. David Greenberg, *Nixon's Shadow: The History of an Image* (NY: W. W. Norton, 2003), chap. 1, Kindle.
2. Carol Kramer, "Eastern Yippies Plan for Chicago," CT, March 20, 1968. Nicholas von Hoffman, "Yippies Unveil 'Politics of Ecstasy,'" WP, March 20, 1968. "Yippie Music Theatre to Tune Up Viet Beefs During Dem's Chi Conv.," *Variety*, March 20, 1968. Norman Mailer, "The Battle of the Pentagon," *Commentary*, April 1968.
3. Nicholas von Hoffman, "Police Spoil 'Yip-in' for 3000," WP, March 24, 1968. Marty Jezer, *Abbie Hoffman: American Rebel* (New Brunswick, NJ: Rutgers University Press, 1992), 130–33. Federal Bureau of Investigation Files, Subject: Abbot H. Hoffman, File Number 176-34. Norman Mailer, *The Armies of the Night: History as a Novel, the Novel as History* (NY: Penguin Group, 1994), 122, 145, 234. Rian Dundon, "These Photos of the Radical Left Riot in Grand Central Show Yippies and Cops Squaring Off," *Medium*, August 28, 2017. James Reston, "Everyone Is a Loser," NYT, October 23, 1967.
4. "The Politics of YIP," *Time,* April 5, 1968. Jonah Raskin, *For the Hell of It: The Life and Times of Abbie Hoffman* (Berkeley: University of California Press, 1996), 134–36. Jezer, *Abbie Hoffman,* 130–33. Vincent Cannato, *The Ungovernable City: John Lindsay and His Struggle to Save New York* (NY: Basic Books, 2001),

222–23. Nicholas von Hoffman, "Police Spoil 'Yip-in' for 3000," WP, March 24, 1968. Michael Stern, "Political Activism New Hippie 'Thing,' NYT, March 24, 1968. Nat Hentoff, "Keeping the Cops From Rioting," *Village Voice,* April 4, 1968. AP, "Police Evict 3,000 Hippies From Grand Central," *The Courier-News,* March 23, 1968.

5. Mark Rudd, *Underground: My Life with the SDS and Weathermen* (NY: Harper Collins, 2009), chap. 4, Kindle. "Siege on Morningside Heights," *Time,* May 3, 1968. William Manchester, *The Glory and the Dream* (NY: Rosetta Books, 2013), chap. 33, Kindle. First Deputy Commissioner to the Police Commissioner, "Police Activity at the Columbia University Campus on April 30, 1968," New York Police Department, November 17, 1970, folder 7, box 5 Columbia University Disturbance Files, NYCMA.

6. "Columbia Closes Campus After Disorders," NYT, April 25, 1968. "Columbia Halting Work on Its Gym, Suspends Classes," NYT, April 26, 1968. "Columbia at Bay," *Newsweek,* May 6, 1968. First Deputy Commissioner to the Police Commissioner, "Police Activity at the Columbia University Campus on April 30, 1968," New York Police Department, November 17, 1970, folder 7, box 5 Columbia University Disturbance Files, NYCMA. Cannato, *The Ungovernable City,* 248–50. Mark Kurlansky, *1968: The Year That Rocked the World* (NY: Random House, 2004), chap. 11, Kindle.

7. Photograph, folder 7, Columbia University Report, box 14, Hard Hat Demonstration files, NYCMA.

8. *The Columbia Revolt* (1968; United States: Newsreel Films, Kit Parker Films) Documentary. Jezer, *Abbie Hoffman,* 142–43. Roger Kahn, *The Battle for Morningside Heights: Why Students Rebel* (NY: William Morrow, 1970), 195–96.

9. Diana Trilling, "On the Steps of Low Library: Liberalism & the Revolution of the Young," *Commentary,* November 1968. Kahn, *The Battle for Morningside Heights,* 204. Kurlansky, *1968,* chap. 11, Kindle.

10. *Crisis at Columbia: Report of the Fact-Finding Commission Appointed to Investigate the Disturbances at Columbia University in April and May 1968* (NY: Vintage, 1968), 141–42, 166, 182. "Columbia University, April 30, 1968," Police Internal Report, folder 6, Columbia Work Material, 1968, box 6, Columbia University Disturbance Files, NYCMA. First Deputy Commissioner to the Police Commissioner, "Police Activity at the Columbia University Campus on April 30, 1968," NYPD, November 17, 1970, folder 7, box 5, Columbia University Disturbance Files, NYCMA.

Photograph, folder 6, Columbia University Report, box 14, Hard Hat Demonstration files, NYCMA. "Columbia University Report 3," box 14, Hard Hat Demonstration files, NYCMA (for two examples of civilian observers, see statements by June Finer, M.D., and Jack Rohan). "Civilian Complaint Review Board Final Report on Columbia," March 26, 1970, folder 499, box 367, LP. Rudd, *Underground,* chap. 5, Kindle. "Lifting a Siege," *Time,* May

10, 1968. "Report from First Deputy Commissioner John F. Walsh, to Police Commissioner Howard Leary," May 4, 1968, folder 140, box 137, LP.

The Mathematics Hall "commune" was the most radical. But for example, inside Fayerweather Hall, the police recorded: "As the police endeavored to remove the sit-ins, they were punched, kicked, scratched, spat upon, bitten and tripped by other sit-ins. In addition, the persons being carried kicked, scratched, and flailed with their arms complicating the procession. Some of the sit-ins were found to have marked themselves with a red substance resembling blood prior to police arrival." This latter NYPD alleged fact—of fake blood— was from its internal "Police Activity at the Columbia University Campus" report. It might have been reported elsewhere, but I did not recall it elsewhere and lacked the time to confirm. That's why I did not write of it in the book's narrative. The outside investigations did not dispute the other actions and at-mospherics noted above.

On media injuries, some were caused by blatant breaches of police protocol. One (not unique) example: *Times* reporter Robert Thomas Jr. was roughed up with a "hard object" by some plainclothesmen after falling down some stairs, during the police raid, only for patrolmen to further strike him with their batons as he was pushed to the doors with the student activists; the po-lice investigation confirmed this incident. Famed columnist Walter Winchell claimed to have been "slugged" by cops but the preponderance of the evidence (film footage, interviews, etc.), at least in police records, betrayed substantial holes in Winchell's claim.

11. Kahn, *The Battle for Morningside Heights*, 204. Cannato, *The Ungovernable City*, 155, 183–84, 254, 260. Jeffrey Meyers, "Lionel Trilling and the Crisis at Columbia," *The New Criterion,* January 2003. Todd Gitlin, *The Sixties: Years of Hope, Days of Rage* (NY: Random House, 1993), chaps. 12, 13, Kindle.

12. First Deputy Commissioner to the Police Commissioner, "Police Activity at the Columbia University Campus on April 30, 1968," New York Police Department, November 17, 1970, folder 7, box 5, Columbia University Disturbance Files, NYCMA. "Investigating Officer's Report," August 27, 1968, folder 7, Worksheets, 1969–1970, box 6, Columbia University Disturbance Files, NYCMA (*Crisis at Columbia* counted 692 arrests and re-ported three-fourths were Columbia students. I deferred to NYPD records— which I verified in two separate NYPD documents—because the NYPD conducted the arrests. The NYPD found that of the 696 arrests, 481 were Columbia students and of them, 390 were undergraduates). "Memorandum for: First Deputy Commissioner," March 21, 1969, folder 7, Worksheets, box 6, Columbia University Disturbance Files, NYCMA. *Crisis at Columbia: Report of the Fact-Finding Commission Appointed to Investigate the Disturbances at Columbia University in April and May 1968* (NY: Vintage, 1968), 142, 166, 182. "Civilian Complaint Review Board Final Report on Columbia," March 26, 1970, folder 499, box 367, LP (*137 complaints of police misconduct

were filed against the NYPD). Frank Kusch, *Battleground Chicago: The Police and the 1968 Democratic National Convention* (Chicago: University of Chicago Press, 2008), 38. Susan Dominus, "Disabled During '68 Columbia Melee, a Former Officer Feels Pain, Not Rage," NYT, April 25, 2008.

13. Photograph, folder 6, Columbia University Report, box 14, Hard Hat Demonstration files, NYCMA. Tom Hayden, "Two, Three, Many Columbias," *Ramparts*, June 15 1968 (On the Che Guevara "message" to "create two, three, many Vietnams," see David Deutschman, ed., *Che Guevara Reader, Writings on Politics and Revolution* (NY: Ocean Press, 2003)). "Lifting a Siege," *Time*, May 10, 1968. Jezer, *Abbie Hoffman*, 143. Kusch, *Battleground Chicago*, 38.

Tom Hayden's role in the Columbia occupation remains unclear. I deferred to the consensus of those writers who have chronicled Columbia. But Hayden reportedly also said that he was downtown when he heard about Columbia and impulsively took the subway uptown to "see what was going on." He reportedly said he "didn't attend" any of the meetings but "circulated" and "talked with" the activists. See Nicholas Von Hoffman, "Brutality by Police and the Students," *Long Island Press,* June 25, 1968.

14. Edward C. Burks, "Columbia Poll Shows Majority Opposes the Seizures," NYT, June 6, 1968. Martin Arnold, "Poll Protest Blames Students," NYT, May 9, 1968. "Lifting a Siege," *Time,* May 10, 1968. Editorial, "The Campus Militants," NYT, April 26, 1968.

In this book, I use New Left more expansively than is traditional, especially among New Left traditionalists. New Left is not treated as a synonym for militants or anarchistic radicals. It is treated more along the lines of newish liberalism, and the prevailing tides within it—the political sources predate SDS for example, and reach back, in the more mainstream, to Adlai Stevenson and others (in intellectual outlook, postwar upscale liberalism, etc.), much as the counterculture reaches back to the beat generation, but also in its militancy, this same New Left is shaped by events such as the Cuban Revolution, reverence for Mao, Che, Malcolm X (more his first public persona, before his break from Elijah Muhammad), and so forth. I specify "New Left militants" during Chicago '68, for this reason, because not all New Left allies were militants, though the prevailing New Left was becoming more ideologically rigid and leftist writ large. I consider the more-moderate activist leaders in Chicago, the marshals or many of the pacifists, part of the New Left. So SDS and Weathermen are New Left. But so are those who got "clean for Gene" and more—the volunteers and staff that empowered (spoiler alert) Eugene McCarthy's stunning challenge to LBJ in 1968, as well as the liberals who admired John Lindsay as he turned more liberal by the late sixties, and those who would most help George McGovern win the Democratic nomination in 1972. I write about the New Left as most Americans saw it, more for its commonalities than differences, whether in virtue or in vice. The semantical and factional disputes within the New Left were legion, and hardly have suffered for authorial or media neglect (SDS, Revolutionary Youth

Movement, Revolutionary Youth Movement II, yippies, Weather Underground, Black Panthers, Progressive Labor Party, Women's Liberation Caucus, New Communist Movement, even Up Against the Wall Mother Fucker, while a favorite yippie line, was also the proper name of an East Village anarchist group, and so forth). Most of the aforementioned were or veered militant, some anarchistic and terroristic. But I do not limit the Movement to its extremes, only seek to note when the extremes steward the Movement or are most visible, and thus shape the wider public impression of the Movement, of what liberalism was in that time. I think of the New Left in terms of how it impacted America outwardly, such as McGovern. To be clear, I'm not arguing this is the right way to think of the era's left. This is just the lens I chose, the phrasing I chose. Generally, I do treat New Left as the predominant force in liberalism around the turn of the decade, 1970, and as a forbearer for the liberalism that would rise in the half-century after and come to define liberal norms. In 1970, there were still some oldtime FDR supporters who considered themselves liberal. But by the end of the sixties, in the American mind, liberalism had become inseparable from what the late sixties centrally symbolized, and that includes counterculture, civil rights, and the antiwar movement, etc. Writ large, I'm talking about a fight to lead the third of America who wanted to make America more progressive (especially regarding the new culture and rights-identity-based liberalism (identity politics is far older, and long apart of American politics on all sides) as well as active state liberalism) and at least sympathized with a counterculture outlook as it became popular culture—a population not only young, but disproportionately young, not only well educated, but disproportionately well educated. In April 1970, before the tumult of Cambodia and Kent State, Gallup found that one in three Americans considered themselves liberal. Half of Americans classified themselves as conservative by 1970. But nearly half of adults in their twenties classified themselves as liberal. Gallup's data also showed more liberalism within the college educated. Liberalism was also more prevalent among the most elite collegians, as evidenced later in this book. By 1972, the Harris poll found that only about a quarter of Americans considered themselves liberal or radical, nearly half of Democrats at the time.

15. Cannato, *The Ungovernable City*, 245–46.
16. David Broder, "McCarthy, Reagan—Vital Test in Oregon," WP, May 16, 1968. Patrick J. Buchanan, *The Greatest Comeback: How Richard Nixon Rose from Defeat to Create the New Majority* (NY: Crown, 2014), 255–56.
17. Kusch, *Battleground Chicago*, 37–38.

Chapter 3

1. Eugene Kennedy, "The Year That Shook Chicago," NYT, March 5, 1978.
2. Daniel Walker, Chicago Study Team, *Rights in Conflict, Convention Week in Chicago, August 25–29, 1968* (NY: E. P. Dutton, 1968), 147–55.

3. David Farber, *Chicago '68* (Chicago: University of Chicago Press, 1988), 123. Jay Dolan, *The Irish Americans: A History* (NY: Bloomsbury Press, 2008), 287–90.

4. NBC, ABC, CBS, August 27, 1968. Walker, Chicago Study Team, *Rights in Conflict*, 187–88.

5. CBS News, August 28, 1968. Patrick Buchanan, *The Greatest Comeback: How Richard Nixon Rose from Defeat to Create the New Majority* (NY: Crown Forum, 2014), 323.

6. Norman Mailer, *Miami and the Siege of Chicago* (NY: Random House, 2016), 156–59. Daniel Walker, Chicago Study Team, *Rights in Conflict*, 198–203. "Eccentric View," *Time*, September 9, 1968.

7. ABC News, August 26, 1968. Lucinda Franks and Thomas Powers, "Story of Diana, the Making of a Terrorist," UPI, September 14, 1970. Walker, Chicago Study Team, *Rights in Conflict*, 206–12. Harvey Araton, *When the Garden Was Eden: Clyde, the Captain, Dollar Bill, and the Glory Days of the New York Knicks* (NY: Harper Collins, 2011), chap. 4, Kindle.

8. CBS News, August 28, 1968. Chana Gazit, *American Experience: Chicago 1968*, PBS, November 13, 1995. Todd Gitlin, *The Sixties: Years of Hope, Days of Rage.* (NY: Random House, 1993), chap. 14, Kindle.

9. Paul O'Neil, "The Party Almost Came Down Around Their Ears," *Life,* September 6, 1968. Gitlin, *The Sixties*, chap. 14, Kindle.

10. Mailer, *Miami and the Siege of Chicago*, 159. Melinda Henneberger, "On Campus Torn by the 60's, Agonizing over the Path," NYT, June 21, 2000. Gitlin, *The Sixties*, chap. 14, Kindle. Walker, Chicago Study Team, *Rights in Conflict*, 257, 354–57. Ellen Willis, *Beginning to See the Light: Sex, Hope, and Rock-and-Roll* (Minneapolis: University of Minnesota Press, 1981), 130. "Battle of Chicago," USN, September 9, 1968. Chana Gazit, *American Experience: Chicago 1968*, PBS, November 13, 1995.

11. NBC, ABC, CBS News, August 29, 1968. "The Man Who Would Recapture Youth," *Time,* September 9, 1968. Mark Kurlansky, *1968: The Year That Rocked the World* (NY: Random House, 2004), chap. 16, Kindle. "Senator Abraham Ribicoff Speaks in Support of George McGovern," Getty Images, 2019, https://www.gettyimages.com/detail/video/senator-abraham-ribicoff-speaks-in-support-of-george-news-footage/450012058. Mike Royko, *Boss: Richard J. Daley of Chicago* (NY: E.P. Dutton, 1971), 189–90.

On Daley's expletives: No one is certain what he said. For example, Mike Royko left it an open question in his biography of Daley. Daley's foes claimed he said "kike" instead of "Jew." One crony claimed he said "faker" instead of "fucker." It's too vague to place quotes around any of it.

12. Paul O'Neil, "The Party Almost Came Down Around Their Ears," *Life,* September 6, 1968. "Battle of Chicago and the Consequences," USN, September 9, 1968. "Who Were the Protesters?," *Time*, September 6, 1968. Mailer, *Miami and the Siege of Chicago*, 182. John Schultz, "The Siege of '68,"

Chicago Reader, September 8, 1988. Daniel Walker, Chicago Study Team, *Rights in Conflict*, 8. Gitlin, *The Sixties*, chap. 12, Kindle.

13. Kurlansky, *1968*, chap. 11, Kindle. Chana Gazit, *American Experience: Chicago 1968*, PBS, November 13, 1995. Tom Wicker, "In the Nation: The Question of Chicago," NYT, September 1, 1968.

14. Kuhn: Harris 1875, September 1968. Kuhn: Gallup, 767, late August, 1968 (which is the source of breakouts, from class to party ID, among whites). The "used police against demonstrators" in the "right" way question comes from the Harris Poll. The question regarding only police conduct, the "way the Chicago police dealt with the young people," comes from Gallup. Two-thirds of the public also disagreed with the statement "anti-Vietnam demonstrators in Chicago had their rights to protest taken away," according to Harris. When Gallup asked directly about police conduct, 56 percent approved of the "way the Chicago police dealt with the young people," as did a majority of white Democrats. Notably, a majority of all whites opposed the antiwar protestors, even as a majority of whites also thought Vietnam was a mistake. Minorities did side against the cops on the question of how "they dealt with the young people." On whether the public agreed or disagreed that "Mayor Daley of Chicago was right the way he used the police to put down the demonstrators," 68 percent of independents agreed, 67 percent of Democrats agreed, and 66 percent of Republicans agreed.

15. Margaret Blanchard, *History of the Mass Media in the United States: An Encyclopedia* (NY: Fitzroy Dearborn, 1998), 372. David Paul Kuhn, *The Neglected Voter: White Men and the Democratic Dilemma* (NY: Palgrave Macmillan, 2007), 32. Gitlin, *The Sixties*, chap. 14, Kindle. Garry Wills, *Nixon Agonistes: The Crisis of the Self-Made Man* (NY: Open Road Media, 2017), chap. 2, Kindle.

16. Kuhn: Gallup 765, 766, 767, mid-July to late August 1968. Kuhn: Harris 1875, September 1968. On candidate support, data from the last Gallup poll before both conventions (Gallup 765), the poll between (766), and first poll after (767).

    Nixon actually lost modest support after Chicago (those voters likely moved to George Wallace, if only briefly). Nixon had a 5-point bounce after his convention, the average for conventions between 1964 and 2004. But that bounce leveled off after Chicago. Only 37 percent of the public agreed that "the way they ran their convention, the Democrats proved they can't govern America," despite overwhelmingly siding against the demonstrators. The convention's dramatics probably cost Humphrey a modest uptick in support, however fleeting. For the statement "the way they ran their convention, the Democrats proved they can't govern America," 37 percent agreed, 47 percent disagreed, 17 percent unsure (from Harris 1875).

17. Robert B. Semple Jr., "400,000 Welcome Nixon During a Tour of Chicago," NYT, September 5, 1968.

18. "The Man Who Would Recapture Youth," *Time*, September 6, 1968. Hubert H. Humphrey, *The Education of a Public Man: My Life and Politics* (Minneapolis: University of Minnesota Press, 1991), 297.

Abbie Hoffman also predicted that Nixon would "end the war in Vietnam" and would have a "better chance" than Humphrey or McCarthy at a "solution," though it's unclear if he was making a standard wartime calculation (i.e., a hawk's liberty to make peace) or if he was compensating for how he believed Chicago '68 helped elect Nixon. See Abbie Hoffman, *Revolution for the Hell of It: The Book That Earned Abbie Hoffman a Five-Year Prison Term at the Chicago Conspiracy Trial* (NY: Thunder's Mouth Press, 2005), 186.

19. Richard Nixon, "1968 Campaign and Election," *RN: The Memoirs of Richard Nixon* (NY: Simon & Schuster, 2013), Kindle. Evan Thomas, *Being Nixon: A Man Divided* (NY: Random House, 2015), chap. 11, Kindle.

20. "Survival in the Stockyards," *Time*, September 9, 1968. "The Man Who Would Recapture Youth," *Time,* September 9, 1968.

Chapter 4

1. Terrance Wills, "Wide Support Surprises Organizers of Nation-wide U.S. War Protests," *Globe and Mail,* October 15, 1969. AP, "National," *The Baltimore Sun*, October 16, 1969. Wires, "Peace Rally Across U.S.," CT, October 16, 1969. "Oct. 15: A Day to Remember," *Newsweek*, October 27, 1969. "The Meaning of the Moratorium," *Newsweek*, October 27, 1969. "Anti-War Offensive," USN, October 27, 1968. Joseph Albright, Fred Bruning, "Anti-War Protest Stirs Anti-Protest," *Newsday,* October 16, 1969. Homer Bigart, "Massive Protest on Vietnam War Expected Today," NYT, October 15, 1969. John Herbers, "Vietnam Moratorium Observed Nationwide by Foes of the War," NYT, October 16, 1969. Homer Bigart, "Rallies Here Crowded, Orderly," NYT, October 16, 1969. Crocker Snow Jr., "McGovern, Kennedy Ask for Groundtroop Pullout Within a Year," *Boston Globe,* October 16, 1970. UPI, "Muskie Warns Protestors," CT, October 16, 1970. Tim Ferris, "Lindsay, Marchi Clash Over Protest," NYP, October 15, 1969. ABC, CBS, NBC, October 15, 1969. Richard Nixon, "1969," *RN: The Memoirs of Richard Nixon* (NY: Simon & Schuster, 2013), Kindle. Vincent Cannato, *Ungovernable City: John Lindsay and His Struggle to Save New York* (NY: Basic Books, 2001), 423–24. Michael Kranish, "With Antiwar Role, High Visibility," *Boston Globe,* June 6, 2003. Michael Kelly, David Johnston, "The Vietnam War; Campaign Focus on Vietnam Reviving Debates of the 60's," NYT, October 9, 1992. Mark Rudd, *Underground: My Life with the SDS and Weathermen* (NY: Harper Collins, 2009), chap. 10, Kindle. John Kifner, "300 in S.D.S. Clash with Chicago Police," NYT, October 8, 1969.

2. Vincent Butler, "New York Divided over Protest," CT, October 16, 1969. John Herbers, "Opponents React," NYT, October 16, 1969. Robert Sales,

"Opponents Noisy . . . Few," *Boston Globe,* October 16, 1969. Robert Asher, "Moratorium, Mets Stir New Yorkers," WP, October 16, 1969. Wires, "Peace Rally Across U.S.," CT, October 16, 1969. Arthur Everett, "Moratorium Day Gets Early Start," *Atlanta Constitution,* October 15, 1969. Joseph Kiernan, "B'klyn College Pros, Antis Clash," DN, October 16, 1969. Patrick Brasley, "The Other Side," *Newsday,* October 15, 1969. Joseph Albright, Fred Bruning, "Anti-War Protest Stirs Anti-Protest," *Newsday,* October 16, 1969. Jay Maeder, "Coming from Behind, the Mayor and the Mets," DN, June 10, 2001. "The Meaning of the Moratorium," *Newsweek,* October 27, 1969. Editorial, "A Lesson in Civics for Mayor Lindsay," CT, October 16, 1969. Terrance Wills, "Wide Support Surprises Organizers of Nation-wide U.S. War Protests," *Globe and Mail,* October 15, 1969. Stuart Loory, "Reagan Hits Protests as Aid to Reds," LAT, October 15, 1969.

3. NBC broadcast, World Series, Game Four, October 15, 1969. William Federici, "Mostly, the Flag Comes Out on Top," DN, October 16, 1969. Vincent Butler, "New York Divided over Protest," CT, October 16, 1969. Editorial, "A Lesson in Civics for Mayor Lindsay," CT, October 16, 1969. James Tuite, "War Casualties Demand Full-Staff at Shea," NYT, October 16, 1969. Robert Asher, "Moratorium, Mets Stir New Yorkers," WP, October 16, 1969.

4. David Paul Kuhn, "Big Government and Its Discontents," RealClearPolitics, April 20, 2010. George Gallup, "President and Dissenters," NYT, October 19, 1969. UPI, "M-Day Frowned Upon by Majority in Survey," LAT, October 18, 1969.

5. "America Gathers Under a Sign of Peace," *Life,* October 24, 1969. "3,000 Crowd Civic Center Peace Vigil," CT, October 16, 1969. Rob Kirkpatrick, *1969: The Year Everything Changed* (NY: Skyhorse Publishing, 2009), 269.

Chapter 5

1. H. R. Haldeman, *The Haldeman Diaries: Inside the Nixon White House* (NY: Berkley Books, 1994), 120. Richard Nixon, "1969," *RN: The Memoirs of Richard Nixon* (NY: Simon & Schuster, 2013), Kindle.

2. "Career's End," *Time,* November 16, 1962. Kevin Phillips, *The Emerging Republican Majority* (New Rochelle, NY: Arlington House, 1969), 92. As many histories and reporters of the time noted, Humphrey did tighten the race in the final stretch. Nixon only won 43.4 percent of the vote, Humphrey won 42.7 percent. The suggestion by some: Nixon had no mandate. Or perhaps more precisely, there was no larger message against Democrats. But is that right? Critically, George Wallace won 13.5 percent. And from polling, we know the Wallace vote would have split about 70 to 30 in Nixon's favor. Thus, the close margin between Nixon and Humphrey obscures the larger historical point: four years after LBJ's historic landslide, a pinnacle in liberal governance,

the engine for the Great Society, the majority of Americans turned against liberalism and Democrats.

3. "Memo to RN," Buchanan to Nixon, August 31, 1968, copy provided to author from Patrick J. Buchanan personal files.

4. David Espar, Geoffrey C. Ward, *American Experience: The Presidents, Richard M. Nixon*, PBS, October 8, 1990. Will and Ariel Durant, *The Lessons of History* (Blackstone Audio, 2004), extratextual recording of Will Durant interview.

5. Steven R. Weisman, *Daniel Patrick Moynihan, A Portrait in Letters of an American Visionary* (NY: Public Affairs, 2010), 169–70.

6. Barry Gottehrer, *New York City in Crisis* (NY: WCC Books, 1965). Sean Deveney, *Fun City: John Lindsay, Joe Namath, and How Sports Saved New York in the 1960s* (NY: Sports Publishing, 2015), chap. 2, Kindle. Vincent Cannato, *The Ungovernable City: John Lindsay and His Struggle to Save New York* (NY: Basic Books, 2001), 1–10, 20, 41–45.

7. "The New Mayor of New York," *Time*, November 12, 1965. "New York: The Breakdown of the City," *Time*, November 1, 1968.

8. "Historical Census Statistics on Population Totals by Race, 1790 to 1990, and by Hispanic Origin, 1970 to 1990, for Large Cities and Other Urban Places in the United States," United States Census Bureau, last modified 2005, https://www.census.gov/population/www/documentation/twps0076/twps0076.pdf. Langston Hughes, *The Collected Poems of Langston Hughes*, ed. Arnold Rampersad (NY: Vintage, 1994), 361. Joseph P. Viteritti, ed., *Summer in the City: Lindsay, New York, and the American Dream* (Baltimore: Johns Hopkins University Press, 2014), 85–86. Isabel Wilkerson, "The Great Migration, 1915–1970," in *The Warmth of Other Suns: The Epic Story of America's Great Migration* (NY: Vintage Books, 2010), Kindle. Nicholas Lemann, *The Promised Land: The Great Black Migration* (NY: Vintage Books, 1992), 6–7. Census.gov, "We, the American Blacks," US Census Bureau, 1993, https://www.census.gov/prod/cen1990/wepeople/we-1.pdf. White population excludes Hispanics. The city's non-Hispanic white population is roughly estimated because the census included whites of Hispanic origin in its overall population totals at this time, while conducting smaller surveys to calculate the Spanish-speaking population.

9. Viteritti, ed., *Summer in the City*, 175.

10. Joshua Freeman, *Working-Class New York* (NY: The New Press, 2000), chap. 1, http://www.nytimes.com/books/first/f/freeman-newyork.html. John Darnton, "Slum-to-Suburb Commuting for High Pay Has Its Perils," *NYT*, July 19, 1970. Ken Auletta, *The Streets Were Paved with Gold* (NY: Vintage Books, 1980), chap. 2, Kindle. Viteritti, ed., *Summer in the City*, 83–84, 168. Gottehrer, *New York City in Crisis*, 196.

11. Brian Reinbold, Yi Wen, "Historical U.S. Trade Deficits," *Economic Synopses*, No. 13, 2019. Edwin L. Dale Jr., "U.S. Trade Deficit First Since 1888," *NYT*, January 26, 1972, "500 Percent Rise in Emphysema Mortality Rate in Last

Decade Reported for City," NYT, March 12, 1970. Jim Dwyer, "Remembering a City Where the Smog Could Kill," NYT, March 1, 2017.

12. "New York City," USN, November 4, 1968. Emanuel Perlmutter, "Token Lines Make Thousands Late," NYT, January 6, 1970. Edward Hudson, "Finding Cool Subway Cars Is a Tricky Job," NYT, August 3, 1970.

13. Kuhn: Harris Poll, August 1968. Kuhn: Gallup 768, late September 1968 (safe at night). George Gallup, *The Gallup Poll: 1959–1971*, vol. 3 (Princeton, NJ: Gallup Poll), 2108 (courts), 2107 (crime), 2164 (notes same stat for "safe at night"). When asked if they were "afraid to walk at night" within one mile of their home, 51 percent of women said yes, 19 percent of men said yes (and the findings held constant among whites only, or the entire public).

14. "1968 Democratic Party Platform," The American Presidency Project, August 26, 1968. Ramsey Clark, *Crime in America* (NY: Pocket Books, 1971), 34. Heather Ann Thompson, *Blood in the Water: The Attica Prison Uprising of 1971 and Its Legacy* (NY: Vintage Books, 2017), chap. 2, Kindle. U.S. Department of Justice, Bureau of Justice Statistics, "Violent Crime," Selected Findings, April 1994. A. Joan Klebba, "Homicide Trends in the United States, 1900–74," Public Health Reports, National Center for Health Statistics, 1975. Klebba reported the homicide rate reached 9.8 deaths per 100,000 in 1973, surpassing the 1933 rate of 9.7 deaths per 100,000. The rate would reach a new high by 1980.

   The tendency to understate the crime problem of this period is also visible in the trendy romanticization of NYC in the 1970s. For an excellent critique of such sentimentalism, see Mark Jacobson, "What Everyone Gets Wrong About '70s New York," *New York*, September 29, 2015.

15. "Uniform Crime Reporting Statistics," Federal Bureau of Investigation.

16. Gottehrer, *New York City in Crisis*, 160. Deveney, *Fun City*, chap. 9, Kindle.

17. Peter Kihss, "Tripled Murder Rate Here Puts Big Burden on Detective Force," NYT, June 30, 1971. Steven Pinker, The Better Angels of Our Nature: Why Violence Has Declined (NY: Penguin Books, 2011), 115 (*between 1962 and 1979, Pinker reported, the likelihood that a crime would lead to imprisonment fell nationally from 0.10 to 0.02). Cannato, *The Ungovernable City*, 525–26. As Vincent Cannato reported, New York City's crime increased before Lindsay, between 1955 and 1965: murders increased 123 percent, robberies 25 percent, assaults 88 percent. On Lindsay's watch, 1966 to 1973, murders increased 137 percent (second highest increase among big cities), robberies 209 percent (seventh), assaults 64 percent (seventh).

18. Cannato, *The Ungovernable City*, 454, 526, 532–34. Edward Burks, "Subways' Colored Tile Gets Cover-Up Job," NYT, February 21, 1970.

19. "The Cities Lock Up," *Life*, November 19, 1971.

20. Kuhn: Gallup, 768, late September 1968. Some of the noted findings can also be found here: Gallup, *The Gallup Poll*, 2164. Regarding whether Americans were "afraid to walk at night" within one mile of their home: Among whites

who lived in an urban area, 45 percent were afraid, but only a third of whites in small towns were afraid and only a quarter of whites in rural areas were afraid. Still, it's remarkable that even one in four rural whites was afraid to walk alone at night near their home in 1968.

21. Richard Bernstein, "Irving Howe, 72, Critic, Editor and Socialist, Dies," NYT, May 6, 1993.

22. "Soho," *New Yorker*, June 6, 1970.

23. Homer Bigart, "Derelicts and Hippies Are Making Washington Square a Nightmare Area," NYT, August 9, 1968. Nat Hentoff, "Disrespect for the Police: Causes and Cures," *Cosmopolitan*, December 1968. "Greenwich Village: Help!" *Newsweek*, August 16, 1971.

24. Edmund White, *City Boy: My Life in New York During the 1960s and '70s* (NY: Bloomsbury Publishing, 2009), chaps. 5, 8, Kindle.

25. Craig Claiborne, "Bleecker Street Has Lost Its Pushcarts but Not Its Pungency," NYT, June 1, 1967. Cannato, *The Ungovernable City*, 141–42, 537–38. For a sample of vintage pictures of Times Square in this era: https://allthatsinteresting.com/vintage-times-square-pictures. Clive Barnes, "Theater: Futz!" NYT, June 14, 1968. William Manchester, *The Glory and the Dream* (NY: Rosetta Books, 2013), chap. 32, Kindle.

26. Bernard Weintraub, "Police Review Panel Killed by Large Majority in City," NYT, November 9, 1966. "Mayor Campaigns for Review Board," NYT, October 9, 1966. Cannato, *The Ungovernable City*, 466.

27. Brad O'Hearn, Jerry Parker, "Cops Quell Spanish Harlem Mob," *Newsday*, July 24, 1967. AP, "Riot Hits Harlem, 2nd Night," *Boston Globe*, July 24, 1967. Homer Bigart, "Disorders Erupt in East Harlem—Mobs Dispersed," NYT, July 24, 1967. Brad O'Hearn, Edward Smith, "2 Dead in E. Harlem Disorders," *Newsday*, July 25, 1967. Linda Charlton, "Fifth Avenue Looters 'Got What They Want,'" *Newsday*, July 28, 1967.

Chapter 6

1. Kuhn: Harris 1875, September 1968. When asked who would be better at maintaining "law and order," 42 percent of Americans chose Nixon, 33 percent chose Wallace, and 25 percent chose Humphrey.

2. Richard M. Scammon, Ben J. Wattenberg, *The Real Majority: The Classic Examination of the American Electorate* (NY: Coward-McCann, 1992), 167–68.

3. On liberal and black activists' fury over "blaming the victim," see the controversy over the Moynihan report on black families in the sixties or the emerging role of feminism within liberalism, such as stressing that just because a woman dressed a certain way, didn't mean she should ever be treated the wrong way. For a larger look at the meaning of John Lindsay's outlook on crime and civil unrest, and mainstream liberalism with it (in the politesse of government), see the Kerner Report (from LBJ's commission on civil unrest

that Lindsay helped run, and the report he shaped perhaps more than any other member). The intro: "Our nation is moving toward two societies, one black, one white—separate and unequal." Or read the entire report. It noted, "White society is deeply implicated in the ghetto. White institutions created it, white institutions maintain it, and white society condones it." It warned that an "apartheid" state would come if massive new social welfare policies were not undertaken. Critics charged that the report on rioting across America shifted culpability from rioters to American society. The *Chicago Tribune* editorial board wrote that the report was "awash in tears for the poor oppressed rioters." Later, historian Gareth Davies noted that the Kerner Commission didn't interview any shopkeepers whose stores were looted during the riots and argued a "fear of appearing racist frequently deterred its members from balanced analysis."

4. John A. Farrell, *Richard Nixon: The Life* (NY: Knopf Doubleday, 2017), chap. 19, Kindle. "Man and Woman of the Year: The Middle Americans," *Time*, January 5, 1970. "Black Ruin? A Survey of Mr. Nixon's America," *Economist*, May 10, 1969. Vincent Cannato, *The Ungovernable City: John Lindsay and His Struggle to Save New York* (NY: Basic Books, 2001), 527. Carolyn Rebecca Block, "Homicides in Chicago, 1965–1981," Inter-university Consortium for Political and Social Research, Fall 1988. Carolyn Rebecca Block, "Specification of Patterns over Time in Chicago Homicide: Increases and Decreases, 1965–1981," Illinois Criminal Justice Information Authority, October 1985. Alexia Cooper, Erica L. Smith, "Homicide Trends in the United States, 1980–2008," U.S. Department of Justice Office of Justice Programs Bureau of Justice Statistics, November 2011 (*The homicide victimization rate for blacks was 27.8 per 100,000, and for whites it was 4.5 per 100,000. The homicide offending rate for blacks was 34.4 per 100,000, and for whites it was 4.5 per 100,000). Brendan O'Flaherty, Rajiv Sethi, "Homicide in Black and White," *Journal of Urban Economics*, November 2010, 215–30. Cannato, *The Ungovernable City*, 527. George Gallup, *The Gallup Poll: 1959–1971*, vol. 3 (Princeton, NJ: Gallup Poll), 2164.

5. Thomas A. Johnson, "Scattered Violence Occurs in Harlem and Brooklyn," NYT, April 5, 1968. David Andelman, David Zinman, Joseph Treen, "New York: Looting, Vandalism in Ghetto," *Newsday,* April 5, 1968. "Harlem, Brooklyn Hit by Scattered Violence," LAT, April 6, 1968. "N.Y. Reaction to Slaying," *Christian Science Monitor*, April 5, 1968. Rich Schapiro, "NYC Remained Calm Amid Nation's Violent Reaction to Martin Luther King Jr. Fatal Shooting," DN, April 3, 2018. Alistair Cooke, "New York–Chicago Split on Way to Tackle Looters," *The Guardian*, April 9, 1968.

6. Martin Gansberg, "Damage Here Since Slaying of Dr. King is Near '64 Riot Level," NYT, April 10, 1968. Editorial, "Nonviolent City," NYT, April 12, 1968.

7. After Chicago '68, when the mainstream left took disorder more seriously, Lindsay seemed to as well (he was also eyeing reelection in '69). Lindsay highlighted that he added four thousand cops to the NYPD rolls and spoke of "communities gripped by fear." But he also qualified hawkish statements, such as stressing that crime was increasing in the fifties as well. He cited a magazine that called the crime rate "shocking" a century ago. He warned that we must not move toward "repression," which read nice enough, unless you already felt repressed by unsafe streets and didn't quite see your repressor as repressed (assailant as victim). See Lindsay's essay in *Life* magazine, September 27, 1968. As previously noted, see the Kerner Report controversy for the larger debate that Lindsay personified on crime and civil unrest.

8. Ted Lewis, "Life, Hope Flickered Out as the Hours Passed," DN, June 6, 1968. "Statement on the Death of Martin Luther King, Jr., April 4, 1968," audio recording, John F. Kennedy Presidential Library & Museum, [online] available at: https://www.jfklibrary.org/asset-viewer/statement-on-the-death-of-martin-luther-king-jr-april4-1968. "Robert F. Kennedy's Martin Luther King Jr. Assassination Speech," Youtube video, 5:01, Frankie Warren, November 23, 2010, https://www.youtube.com/watch?v=BCrx_u3825g. Kuhn: Gallup 762, May 1968 (for data on RFK's demographic support). Jack Newfield, *RFK: A Memoir* (NY: Thunder's Mouth Press/Nation Books, 2003), 8–9.

9. Kuhn: Harris 2055, 1971 (data on racial views of crime, save subsequent 1968 reference). Kuhn: Gallup, 768, late September 1968 (for "afraid to walk at night"; see below for breakout). For "rehabilitate" polling, see 1980, Roper, March 29–April 5, 1980 (53 percent prison to "rehabilitate"); LAT, September 25–28, 1993 (25 percent prison to "rehabilitation"). Robert J. Sampson, Janet L. Lauritsen, "Racial and Ethnic Disparities in Crime and Criminal Justice in the United States," *Crime and Justice* 21 (1997): 311–74.

More detail on black and white views on "law and order" issue: Two-thirds of blacks and seven in ten whites said they believed "law and order" had "broken down." Two-thirds of whites and a majority of blacks agreed that a "major cause of the breakdown of law and order" was "lenient sentences for criminals." About six in ten blacks *and* whites also agreed that "poverty conditions which breed crime" were also a "major cause." Seven in ten blacks *and* whites thought a "lack of parental discipline of children" was also a "major cause." Six in ten blacks and more than four in ten whites—a majority of white women and a third of white men—were "personally worried" about their "safety" when walking on their neighborhood streets at night. In 1968, white city residents registered about the same level of concern, if not slightly more, as minorities when asked if they were "afraid to walk at night" alone near their home. In January 1971, seven in ten whites thought "law and order" had "broken down" as well.

On fear of crime and class: In general, blue-collar white women registered levels of concern about crime similar to blacks. Another example of the class gap on crime: a third of better-off whites disagreed that society was in a state of disorder, but only a fifth of working-class or poor whites thought the same. Only a third of upscale whites were worried when walking their streets at night, while a majority of working-class and poor whites were worried about walking their streets at night. The polling also indicated that while more than seven in ten whites who were Democrats or Republicans thought "law and order" had "broken down" in 1971, the class gap on views within their party was about twice as large among Democrats as among Republicans, hinting at greater class friction on the left. An additional example: three in four white Democrats with no more than a high school degree thought there was societal disorder, compared to 62 percent of whites with a post-high-school education. For Republicans, it was a 76 to 71 percent margin.

Regarding being "afraid to walk at night" alone near their home: White city residents held equivalent views as all blacks nationally and all minorities (combining blacks with other nonwhites). Because of sample size, it's impossible to compare urban blacks to urban whites. The comparison of white urbanites to blacks is roughly instructive, however, because by 1970, 58 percent of blacks lived in central cities compared to 28 percent of whites (see the 1970 Census, General Population Characteristics). In 1968, when asked if they were "afraid to walk at night" alone near their home, 35 percent of all whites said yes, but 45 percent of white city residents said yes, as did four in ten of all blacks (from anywhere), and four in ten of all minorities.

On racial views and policing: There was a modest race gap on policing—six in ten whites thought "lack of support for local police" was a "major" cause of breakdown in "law and order," while a plurality of blacks agreed (45 percent of blacks said it was a "major cause," about a fifth of blacks said it was a "minor cause," and another fifth said it was "hardly a cause"). A majority of blacks also believed "black militants" contributed to the breakdown in "law and order," though whites' antipathy for militancy was stronger, a point I'll return to later.

Another example of the correlation between crime and hawkish views on criminal prosecution: With crime plaguing cities still in 1992, Gallup found that 83 percent of Americans thought the "criminal justice system" was "not tough enough," a figure that fell to 45 percent by 2016, corresponding with the drastic decline in the violent crime rate from the early 1990s to the 2010s.

10. J. Skelly Wright, "The Courts Have Failed the Poor," NYT, March 9, 1969.
11. Kenneth T. Jackson, *Crabgrass Frontier: The Suburbanization of the United States* (NY: Oxford University Press, 1985), 201–2. Walter Waggoner, "Flight to Suburbs Hurts Newark," NYT, March 18, 1969. Fox Butterfield, "Newark Transforms Once-White Suburbs," NYT, September 27, 1971. Terry Golway, "Port Newark's Place in History," NYT, March 5, 1970. AP, "Pollution Hurting Fishing off Jersey," NYT, March 2, 1970. Fox Butterfield, "Newark Held an Angry and Anguished City," NYT, April 12, 1971. "Historical

Census Statistics on Population Totals by Race, 1790 to 1990, and by Hispanic Origin, 1970 to 1990, for Large Cities and Other Urban Places in the United States," United States Census Bureau, last modified 2005, https://www.census. gov/population/www/documentation/twps0076/twps0076.pdf.

12. Theodore H. White, *The Making of the President 1972* (NY: Harper Collins, 2011), chap. 2, Kindle.

13. Welfare spending also rose 150 percent in Lindsay's first term (from $400 million to $1 billion), while spending on higher education (which was low, but hardly vital) increased at threefold the rate of spending increases on police, fire, and public schools (where disarray was pervasive). By 1970, total public assistance for the poor consumed 28 percent of the entire city budget.

14. Joseph P. Viteritti, ed., *Summer in the City, Lindsay, New York, and the American Dream* (Baltimore: Johns Hopkins University Press, 2014), 88–91, 166–67. Michael Oreskess, "Census Traces Radical Shifts in New York's Population," NYT, September 20, 1982. Edward C. Burke, "White Population in City Fell by 617,127 in 60's," NYT, December 30, 1971. Ken Auletta, *The Streets Were Paved with Gold* (NY: Vintage Books, 1980), chap. 2, Kindle. Vincent Cannato, *The Ungovernable City*, 539, 550, 552. Andrew Hacker, "The City's Comings, Goings," NYT, December 2, 1973. Francis X. Clines, "Rise in Welfare Slowed Sharply in State in 1969," NYT, January 16, 1970. Edward B. Fiske, "After 8 Years of Open Admissions City College Still Debates Effect," NYT, June 19, 1978. The city lost 44,500 factory jobs between 1966 and 1971 alone, one study found, which it would have retained under a lighter tax burden.

15. Auletta, *The Streets Were Paved with Gold*, chaps. 2, 9, Kindle. Richard Phalon, Michael Stern, "The Changing City: A Financial Paradox," NYT, June 1, 1969.

16. Andrew Hacker, "The City's Comings, Goings," NYT, December 2, 1973.

17. Martin Waldron, "White Pupils' Rolls Drop as Families Flee the Cities," NYT, November 26, 1972. Gus Tyler, "White Worker—Blue Mood," *Dissent*, Winter 1972. Wornie L. Reed, ed., *African-Americans, Essential Perspectives* (Westport, CT: Auburn House, 1993), 10. For the statement "White suburbanites were wealthier and better educated than whites in more urban and more rural areas," source is Kuhn: Harris 2052, August 1970. Barry Gottehrer, *New York City in Crisis* (NY: WCC Books, 1965), 196.

A slim majority of suburban whites earned upper middle-class to high incomes, at least twice the ratio of whites in small and large cities (the contrast is true for suburban whites compared to more rural whites as well, but the margin appears smaller than when compared to city vs. suburb). In 1970, whites in suburbs were also roughly twice as likely to have some tertiary education as whites in more urban and more rural areas.

Chapter 7

1. "The Lindsay Style," *Life*, May 24, 1968. Nick Thimmesch, "Lindsay for President," *New York*, May 27, 1968.

2. Author interview, Buchanan. Patrick J. Buchanan, *The Greatest Comeback: How Richard Nixon Rose from Defeat to Create the New Majority* (NY: Crown, 2014), 302–3. John A. Farrell, *Richard Nixon: The Life* (NY: Knopf Doubleday, 2017), notes, Kindle. Vincent Cannato, *The Ungovernable City: John Lindsay and His Struggle to Save New York* (NY: Basic Books, 2001), 381–82. Theodore H. White, *The Making of the President 1968* (NY: Harper-Collins, 2010), chap. 8, Kindle.

3. Garry Wills, *Nixon Agonistes: The Crisis of the Self-Made Man* (NY: Open Road Media, 2017), chap. 1, Kindle.

4. Joseph Kraft, "Press Is Biased Toward the New," *Boston Globe*, September 4, 1968.

5. Rick Perlstein, *Nixonland: The Rise of a President and the Fracturing of America* (NY: Scribner, 2008), 366.

6. "The Fear Campaign," *Time*, October 4, 1968.

7. Richard Goodwin, "Sources of Public Unhappiness," *The New Yorker*, January 4, 1969.

8. Cannato, *The Ungovernable City*, 395–97, 431.

9. Jimmy Breslin to John Lindsay, September 28, 1969 (forwarded cover letter by Jeff Greenfield, October 3, 1969), series XI, box 227, folder 227-40, "City Hall Staff Memorandum," LP. Breslin also wrote Lindsay pondering how he "could help." Jimmy Breslin, "The City Politic," *New York,* June 16, 1969. Breslin expressed that he was struggling "everytime [*sic*] I try to write a set speech for John Lindsay, and I have tried for days now." Breslin encouraged Lindsay to face his detractors directly and added, "I will arrange with your staff to fill a dock in Brooklyn with people who will yell about blacks, but remain in their seats and not fight or get unruly. I then will work on the anecdotes and straight lines."

10. Peter Goldmark to Jay Kriegel and Jeff Greenfield, "Draft Memo, The Middle Class and All That," March 17, 1969, series VII, box 161, folder 531, "Middle Class," LP.

11. Nixon Presidential Materials, NA (Staff; White House Special Files; Staff Member and Office Files; President's Office Files; President's Handwriting), May 1969. David Paul Kuhn, *The Neglected Voter: White Men and the Democratic Dilemma* (NY: Palgrave Macmillan, 2007), 52. Robert Mason, *Richard Nixon and the Quest for a New Majority* (Chapel Hill: University of North Carolina Press, 2004), 46.

12. Ralph McGill, "George Wallace Tradition of Demagoguery," LAT, December 17, 1967. Matthew Cooper, "Legacy of a Healed Hater, George Wallace, 1918–1998," *Newsweek*, September 28, 1998. Kuhn, *The Neglected Voter*, 28.

13. Brendan Sexton, "Middle-Class Workers and the New Politics," *Dissent*, June 1969,

14. Peter Schrag, "The Forgotten Americans," *Harper's*, August 1, 1969.

15. Carl Tinstman, "The Lindsay Campaign and the White Lower/Middle Class," September 1969, series VII, box 161, folder 532, LP.

16. Richard Harwood, "'Working Americans' Are Rediscovered," WP, September 28, 1968. Karl Fleming, TK.

17. "The Square American Speaks Out," *Newsweek*, October 6, 1969. "Hot Under the Blue Collar," *Newsweek,* October 6, 1969. "In Politics, It's the New Populism," *Newsweek*, October 6, 1969.

18. Richard Polenberg, *One Nation Divisible: Class, Race, and Ethnicity in the United States Since 1938* (NY: Penguin Books, 1980), 231. "Twenty-Five and Under, Man of the Year," *Time*, January 6, 1967. "Youth: The Hippies," *Time*, July 7, 1967. "The Message of History's Biggest Happening," *Time*, August 8, 1969. "Man and Woman of the Year: The Middle Americans," *Time*, January 5, 1970.

19. David S. Reynolds, "Complex Marriage, to Say the Least," NYT, October 24, 1993. William Manchester, *The Glory and the Dream* (NY: Rosetta Books, 2013), chap. 32, Kindle. For Joseph Smith, early Mormons, and "plural marriage," see Todd M. Compton, *In Sacred Loneliness: The Plural Wives of Joseph Smith* (Salt Lake City, UT: Signature Books, 1997).

In Western culture, even in the centuries immediately preceding the nineteenth, there's evidence of dramatic changes in copulation rates. In England in 1650, about 1 percent of all births were to unmarried women. By 1800, a quarter of all first children were illegitimate and almost four in ten brides arrived at the altar pregnant. See Faramerz Dabhoiwala, *The Origins of Sex* (NY: Penguin Group, 2012), 204–5.

20. Lon Strauss, "Social Conflict and Control, Protest and Repression," *International Encyclopedia of the First World War*, no. 1 (October 8, 2014), DOI: 10.15463/ie1418.10281. Howard Zinn, Anthony Arnove, *Voices of a People's History of the United States* (NY: Seven Story Press, 2004), 296. Erick Trickey, "When America's Most Prominent Socialist Was Jailed for Speaking Out Against World War I," Smithsonian.com, June 15, 2018, https://www.smithsonianmag.com/history/fiery-socialist-challenged-nations-role-wwi-180969386. Richard Hofstadter, Michael Wallace, *American Violence: A Documentary History* (NY: Knopf, 1973), 19.

21. Wills, *Nixon Agonistes*, chap. 6, Kindle. Kuhn: Harris 2037, August 1970. In fact, some polling of the era showed non-southern blue-collar whites as less racist then their upper-class counterparts, as Richard F. Hamilton wrote in *Dissent* in 1972. He compared whites with blue-collar and white-collar jobs, but isolated his study to whites outside the South.

In 1970, when asked to rate activism as "harmful," "helpful," or neither—24 percent of whites said "Mexican-Americans, Indians and other minorities who agitate for more equal treatment" were "harmful"; 42 percent of whites thought "blacks who demonstrate for civil rights" were "harmful." By comparison, a majority of whites, 53 percent, thought "people who picket against the Vietnam war" were "harmful," and roughly the same share, 56 percent, thought "student demonstrators who engage in protest activities" were "harmful" (four in ten nonwhites also saw student demonstrators as "harmful," while only a fifth saw them as "helpful"). Kuhn: Harris 2037, August 1970.

22. In response to a 1963 poll asking if "Negroes should have as good a chance as white people to get any kind of job," 71 percent of white collars said yes, but so did 87 percent of blue collars. When the same question was asked in '68, more than eight in ten of both groups supported black rights, though slightly more blue collars were affirmative. Similar views were found in the two classes on open housing. When the analysis drilled down to neighborhoods, though, the pattern did not hold, perhaps unsurprisingly, as downscale urban whites lived in areas beside blacks. In 1968, when asked if whites should "have a right to keep Negroes out of their neighborhoods," only 45 percent of manual workers disagreed, compared to six in ten nonmanual workers. See Richard F. Hamilton, "Liberal Intelligentsia and White Backlash," *Dissent*, Winter 1972.

23. Kuhn: Harris 2055, January 1971. For war hawk/dove comparison by age, see George Gallup, *The Gallup Poll: 1959–1971*, vol. 3 (Princeton, NJ: Gallup Poll), 2223.

Regarding the appeal of explicit sex in film or otherwise: 66 percent of whites said it makes sex "less attractive" and 21 percent said "makes no difference"; 50 percent of blacks said "less attractive," and 35 percent responded "no difference." More on those who responded "less attractive": 70 percent of women, 57 percent of men, 68 percent of whites with no more than a high school education, 62 percent of whites with some tertiary education.

More on the exaggerated generation gap and the war: among whites, and contrary to conventional wisdom, whites over age 50 were *more* likely to call Vietnam a "mistake" than younger whites in January 1971 (Kuhn: Harris 2055).

24. Kuhn: Harris 2055, January 1971. A minority of whites disliked hippie fashion but of those who disapproved, the sentiment was strongest among blue collars. One obvious factor: the counterculture derived from rarified milieus—from college campuses to the young and urban avant-garde. Still, among whites with no more than a high school education, only about a fifth were bothered "a lot" by hippies, compared to about a tenth of better educated whites. Based on five income brackets, only 23 percent of the poorest whites were bothered "a lot" by young people's hair, dress, and talk (though wealthier whites were even less likely to disapprove of hippie fashion).

25. Jeff Greenfield, "Hail and Farewell," NYT, July 29, 1973.

26. "New York's Little Man," *The Economist*, September 13, 1969.

27. Alan Palmer, "Listen to the Stories! Narrative, Cognition and Country and Western Music," in *The Oxford Handbook of Cognitive Literary Studies*, ed. Lisa Zunshine (NY: Oxford University Press, 2015), 149.

Chapter 8

1. Leonard Klady, "Jimmy Stewart, Legendary Actor, Dies at 89," *Variety*, July 3, 1997. "Clark Gable Dies at 59," LAT, November 17, 1960. "Douglas Fairbanks Jr., Film Star, TV Producer and Good-Will Ambassador, Dies at 90," NYT, May 8, 2000. Deane McGowen, "Joe Louis, 66, Heavyweight King Who Reigned for 12 Years, Is Dead," NYT, April 13, 1981. "Hank Greenberg, First $100,000 Player, Dies," LAT, September 5, 1986. Bart Barnes, "American Icon Joe DiMaggio Dies at 84," WP, March 8, 1999. Franklin Roosevelt Jr., 74, Ex-Congressman, Dies," John T. McQuiston, August, 18, 1988. Dennis Hevesi, "Elliott Roosevelt, General and Author, Dies at 80." NYT, October 28, 1990. "Two Roosevelt Sons in Normandy Graves," NYT, June 8, 1984. Mark Shields, "When Heroes Were Ordinary Men," WP, August 3, 1998. Richard Goldstein, "John Eisenhower, Military Historian and Son of the President, Dies at 91," NYT, December 22, 2013. Nancy Gibbs, "The Kennedys Face Death: The Agony of Grieving in Public," *Time*, August 28, 2009.

2. Nat Hentoff, *A Political Life: The Education of John V. Lindsay* (NY: Alfred A Knopf, 1969), 54. For St. Paul's World War Two and Vietnam alum, see https://www.sps.edu/news-detail?pk=689251 and http://www.ohrstromblog. com/spsarchives/st-pauls-school-archives-exhibits. For Harvard alum deaths in World War Two, see https://memorialchurch.harvard.edu/world-war-ii-memorial. "Abolish the 2-S," *Harvard Crimson*, May 17, 1969. James Fallows, "Low-Class Conclusions," *Atlantic Monthly*, April 1993.

3. Kuhn: Harris 792801, November 1979. These findings—like any findings with the poll source noted and numbered in this format, which are exclusive to this book—derive from what is likely the best statistically representative dataset on Vietnam veterans ever collected, which was a large poll and robust study commissioned by the Veterans Administration and overseen by Lou Harris, noted as Harris 792801. Working with this and many raw Harris datasets allowed additional breakouts for the purposes of this book, such as to isolate the study of class to whites to control for the influence of race. The Harris poll was, of course, only conducted among those who survived the war; thus the sample itself skewed against the downscale, who were more likely to die in combat. In this book, for some general population age and characteristic comparisons, such as education, the census is utilized for more accuracy (e.g., that the Vietnam high school dropout rate was almost three times the national rate—12 percent of Americans ages 14 to 24 in 1969 were dropouts—or "38 percent of all college-age whites were enrolled in college"). See U.S. Bureau of the Census, Current Population Reports, Series P-23, No.

34, "Characteristics of American Youth: 1970," 1971. While the large Harris study for the VA did not parse out whites by class, and other cross-tabulations studied in this book, you can read the 1980 report on the study here: *A Study of Attitudes Toward Vietnam Era Veterans* (Washington, DC: United States Congress, Senate Committee on Veterans Affairs, United States Veterans Administration, 1980). Among all Vietnam veterans who were 25 to 34 years of age at the time of the 1979 poll, thus young servicemen during the war, 4.3 percent were college graduates compared to, in this poll, 28.4 percent of the same generation in the general population (the "6.5 times" difference in the body of the book; and when the "confidence limits" are tested, a statistical check to assure accuracy, that ratio ranges between fourfold and tenfold; either way, the point held true, that college students drastically underserved and dodged the war far more than those Americans with less education). Among the young generation, boys with less than a high school education were 24 percent of Vietnam veterans and 10 percent of civilians (the "twofold" difference). Perhaps the most influential study to deny the Vietnam class divide was a well-publicized and methodologically flawed 1992 MIT study that was still being cited in the *Washington Post* in 2017 to argue the class divide was a "myth." For that example, see Lan Cao, "Five Myths, the Vietnam War," WP, October 1, 2017. For the MIT study, see Arnold Barnett, Timothy Stanley, Michael Shore, "America's Vietnam Casualties: Victims of a Class War?" *Operations Research* 40, no. 5 (1992). For an example of the MIT study's flaws, see the smart and skillfully clearheaded takedown James Fallows wrote soon after the study received wide and uncritical mainstream media publicity: James Fallows, "Low-Class Conclusions," *Atlantic Monthly,* April 1993. A 1995 research paper also refuted other flawed research denying that Vietnam was a "class war," see Thomas C. Wilson, "Vietnam-era Military Service: A Test of the Class-Bias Thesis," *Armed Forces & Society: An Interdisciplinary Journal* 21, no. 3 (1995): 46.

4. Kuhn: Harris 792801, November 1979. I compare the fifth of white Vietnam vets who were dropouts to the 15.7 percent of whites 18 to 24 years old who were high school dropouts in 1969; see previously cited, "Characteristics of American Youth: 1970" census study. One example of the divide between information economy workers and industrial workers: 38 percent of Vietnam veterans were whites from a union household (union membership largely meant blue-collar workers at this time) and 35 percent of all veterans were from a union household, above the general population (28 percent of the general population was from a union household in this survey, which is corroborated by 1970 union household membership in the US calculated here: Steve Maas, "New Evidence that Unions Raise Wages for Less-Skilled Workers," The National Bureau of Economic Research, September 2018).

Other studies have come to roughly the same conclusion on the class divide. John Helmer's large Vietnam study reported that 96 percent of the subjects (servicemen of all races) came from families who lived "below affluence" and that a third hailed from "a severely deprived environment." Helmer also offered a chart in his book, based on VA data, that states from 1966 to 1971 eight in ten men who served in Vietnam—at the time of their "separation from the Armed Forces"—had no more than a high school education, see John Helmer, *Bringing the War Home: The American Soldier in Vietnam and After* (NY: Free Press, 1974), 60, 303. Helmer's book was the basis for Christian Appy writing in *Working-Class War* that "roughly 80 percent came from working-class and poor backgrounds," see Christian Appy, *Working-Class War: American Combat Soldiers and Vietnam* (Chapel Hill: University of North Carolina Press, 1993), 6, 25–26. This modestly overstates the point. For one, even based on Helmer's data, six in ten servicemen had completed twelve years of education. At this time, a high school degree was enough to sometimes reach the middle class, though often lower middle class. More likely, based on statistical runs of Harris's more representative dataset of servicemen's education *before* entering the military: seven in ten Vietnam veterans, and six in ten white Vietnam vets, had no more than a high school education. About four in ten vets were white high school graduates and another fifth of vets were white high school dropouts. By comparison, a tenth of Vietnam vets were whites with white-collar jobs before entering the service. Nonwhites accounted for 14 percent of all veterans. Thus, three in four veterans were white and lacked a white-collar job before entering the service, offering one gauge of the share of veterans who were whites with a blue-collar or poorer background, but education is conventionally considered the best shorthand for class in American life. Based on education: 7 percent of vets were whites with a college degree, but another fifth of white vets had some tertiary education. Thus, it's safe to say that at least six in ten soldiers who fought in Vietnam were blue-collar or poorer whites (about four in ten vets were white high school graduates and the rest were white dropouts). Writ large, other research illustrates the same class divide. One study found that men from low-income backgrounds were about twice as likely to serve in Vietnam and see combat as men from high-income backgrounds, see Lawrence M. Baskir, William A. Strauss, *Chance and Circumstance: The Draft, the War, and the Vietnam Generation* (NY: Vintage, 1978), 9. A massive study of Vietnam vets also sponsored by the VA during the same period as the Harris study found—dividing vets social class background into four tiers using factors from household income to a father's occupation and a father's education—the boys in the upper-most tier had about half the likelihood of military service in the Vietnam era compared to those servicemen from the lower half. Notably, even with this fairly unique data on paternal background, the study affirmed the consensus view that the primary focus to define class should be on vets' pre-induction education; the study noted, "That the most important pre-military characteristic in explaining postmilitary differences [in occupations or class] is education." This study also noted that compared to race, "class differences were much more striking"—which was truer for whites than nonwhite vets, as I'll note later, which relates to why this study also found, "White veterans are slightly more likely than black veterans to be high school dropouts." But this study, while insightful due to its large scale, did not use statistically representative sampling of the national population, unlike the Harris dataset. See Arthur Egendorf, Vietnam Era Research Project, United States Veterans Administration, "Legacies of Vietnam: Comparative Adjustment of Veterans and Their Peers: a Study" (Washington, DC: U.S. Government Printing Office, 1981).

In precise military terms, marines are not soldiers. But for the purposes of this book, I use the looser and colloquial understanding of a soldier as one engaged in military service and in this book, that often means young military men risking their life in the Vietnam theater (including marines).

5. Patricia Cayo Sexton, Brendan Sexton, *Blue Collars and Hard-Hats* (NY: Random House, 1971), 99–100. Baskir, Strauss, *Chance and Circumstance*, 5–9. John Helmer, *Bringing the War Home: The American Soldier in Vietnam and After* (NY: Free Press, 1974), 4. Appy, *Working-Class War*, 18.

Egendorf, "Legacies of Vietnam," 1981, for the study concluding that white veterans were "drawn disproportionately from the working class."

6. Kuhn: Harris 2131. Kuhn: Harris 792801, November 1979. For "frequently engaged in combat," I combined soldiers who reported "most of the time" or "fairly often" being engaged in combat (e.g., in firefights, in minefields, stationed in a forward post, flew aircraft in the war zone). By "upscale background," in this case I meant college graduates and veterans with a prior white-collar job. While only about a third of white college graduates experienced frequent combat, about half of white soldiers with a blue-collar job experienced frequent combat, as did a slim majority of white high school dropouts (52 percent) and nonwhites (55 percent). Class likely related to minorities seeing more combat. For example, the previously cited "Legacies of Vietnam" study estimated that nine in ten blacks who served were from a working-class or a poorer background. It also reported that black vets were fourfold more likely than whites to come from the lowest income bracket. Still, it further noted, black veterans were "slightly better educated" than black nonveterans, likely related to higher rates of poverty among blacks and blacks struggling, per capita, more than whites with military entrance requirements. Young soldiers were the most likely to see combat, as were the least educated. Draftees were modestly more likely than enlistees. Lou Harris made the same point in his report, noting that Vietnam soldiers who were high school dropouts were three-fold more likely to have experienced "heavy combat" than college graduates.

7. James Fallows, "The Scars of Vietnam," *Boston Globe*, October 19, 1975. Excerpted from James Fallows, "What Did You Do in the Class War, Daddy?" *Washington Monthly*, October 1975.

8. George Gallup, *The Gallup Poll: 1959–1971*, vol. 3 (Princeton, NJ: Gallup Poll), 2065. Helmer, *Bringing the War Home*, 9.

9. Bill Muller, "The Life Story of Arizona's Maverick Senator McCain," *Arizona Republic*, October 3, 1999.

10. Melinda Henneberger, "On Campus Torn by the 60's, Agonizing over the Path," NYT, June 21, 2000. Ellen Nakashima, David Maraniss, "Disillusionment Deepens Amid 'Sordid Crusade,'" WP, December 31, 1999.

11. Kuhn: Harris 2131, August 1971. Kuhn: Harris 792801, November 1979. This also utilizes the findings from Louis Harris and Associates, *Myths and Realities: A Study of Attitudes Toward Vietnam Era Veterans* (Washington, DC: United States Congress, Senate Committee on Veterans Affairs, United States Veterans Administration, 1980). "Vietnam-era veterans" includes veterans who served in the war zone but also those in cold war posts, such as Germany or South Korea, during this period.

At first blush, the offense felt by Vietnam veterans could be dismissed (and has been by some critics). Only one in three white Vietnam veterans saw their homecoming as a letdown, for example, based on Harris 1971 dataset. But for a hint of the expectations gap, think of it like a professor would, if he suddenly was treated as a freshman (after all, this writer knows more than one professor who gets offended merely if students forget the "Dr." before her or his name). On the same note, only a fifth of veterans thought the antiwar movement personally blamed Vietnam's ills on soldiers. But it was again a matter of context, and the loss of the station that soldiering once ensured. For example, only 46 percent of white Vietnam veterans agreed strongly that they were respected for having served the country; a fifth disagreed altogether, and the rest had misgivings. Almost three-quarters of veterans of earlier wars felt their peers gave them a "very friendly" homecoming. Slightly less than half of white Vietnam veterans said the same. In 1971, a majority of veterans of the Vietnam era also said they were treated "worse today" than "servicemen returning from earlier wars." Notably, half of all Vietnam-era veterans had a high sense of alienation from society after the war, compared to about a third of the public or civilian peers with a similar education. That alienation was twice as prevalent among boys who never exceeded a high school education, compared to college graduates. And while most soldiers didn't feel personally blamed by the antiwar movement, polling showed that veterans viewed the movement coldly. As the VA also reported on the Harris data in 1980, when Vietnam-era veterans were asked to rate groups on a ten-point scale of 1 (coldest) to 10 (warmest), the median score for people who left the country to avoid the draft was 2.2; antiwar demonstrators, 3.9; congressmen and senators, 5.1; journalists; 5.5; military leaders, 6.7; doctors, 8.1; veterans of World War Two or Korea, 9.5; those who served in Vietnam, 10.

Among Vietnam-era veterans, when it came to perceptions of draft dodgers, the class gap exceeded the race gap, with veterans having no more than a high school education differing more from college graduates than whites did from blacks. The same showed in data hinting of the lost status. Soldiers from poor backgrounds were the most likely to say their homecoming was "worse" than expected (31 percent), compared to lower- and middle-class soldiers (21 percent) and affluent soldiers (13 percent). Here too, the top-bottom class divide was more than double the divide among blacks and whites on the same question, expressing once more how economic circumstances trumped even racial distinctions. About six in ten veterans who had a high school education or less felt alienated after the war, compared to about a third of veterans with a college degree.

For cases of activists spitting on soldiers or police: Chapter Two, on the Columbia occupation. James Reston, "Everyone Is a Loser," NYT, October 23, 1967. Carl Bernstein, "Area Student Protests Range from Solemnity to Violence," WP, May 7, 1970.

12. Murray Polner, *No Victory Parades: The Return of the Vietnam Veteran* (NY: Holt, Rinehart and Winston, 1971), 27–29.

13. David Broder, "Vietnam Vets: An Unpopular War Rubs Off," WP, February 13, 1973.

14. Kuhn: Harris 792801, November 1979.

15. Kuhn: Harris 792801, November 1979. Theodore H. White, *The Making of the President 1972* (NY: Harper Collins, 2011), chap. 2, Kindle. When asked to rate groups on a ten-point scale of from 1 (coldest) to 10 (warmest), more than twice as many Vietnam veterans gave antiwar demonstrators their coldest rating of 1 (39 percent) as they did congressmen (14 percent), though a majority rated both coldly (between 1 and 3). Setting aside draft dodgers, only oil executives were viewed as coldly as antiwar protestors (and this poll was taken after the energy crises of the seventies). By comparison, only 8 percent rated military leaders a 1. A majority of veterans gave draft dodgers their coldest rating, and seven in ten rated them coldly. For draft dodging, see Harris 2051.

Blue-collar whites more uniformly condemned evading conscription than upscale whites. Young people were three times more likely to consider draft dodging "healthy" as older generations, but even a majority of twentysomethings disapproved of draft dodging. Among whites, 82 percent of blue collars disapproved of dodging the draft, compared to 64 percent of those who were more upscale. At least six in ten of every age thought draft dodging was bad. But more young people approved. Three in ten Americans ages 16 to 20 thought avoiding conscription was "healthy," compared to a tenth of Americans middle-aged or older. Another poll (Kuhn: Harris 2037, August 1970) asked how you would react to a son avoiding the draft. Those who said "throw him out" of the house were higher in the East (9 percent) than the Midwest (5 percent). A plurality of all Americans said they would "offer help" with advice or a lawyer, though those likely to be upscale were more likely to "offer help" (38 to 45 percent, respectively). Among both classes, the number of those who would "argue" with their son or "toss him out" nearly equaled the number who would "help" him avoid the draft.

16. David S. Surrey, *Choice of Conscience: Vietnam Era Military and Draft Resisters in Canada* (NY: Praeger, 1982), 36. Appy, *Working-Class War*, 35. Baskir, Strauss, *Chance and Circumstance*, 69, 71, 82.

17. Mary McGrory, "Triple Amputee Doesn't Think War Mistake," *Orlando Sentinel*, February 1, 1970. David Broder, "Vietnam Vets: An Unpopular War Rubs Off," WP, February 13, 1973. Rick Badie, "Hugh Cleland, 95: Father of Former US Senator Max Cleland," *Atlanta Journal-Constitution*, May 13, 2010. Neal Thompson, "A Survivor's Story," *The Baltimore Sun*, October 24, 1999.

18. David Paul Kuhn, "The 60s and Why We Still Fight," RealClearPolitics, May 27, 2010. Penny Lewis, *Hardhats, Hippies, and Hawks: The Vietnam Antiwar Movement as Myth and Memory* (Ithaca, NY: ILR Press, 2013), 22. Richard Harwood, "Flag's Defenders: Hard Hats March for a Way of Life," WP, May 31, 1970.

While self-interest obviously influenced the antiwar movement's vehemence, a study by Columbia's Robert Erickson and Berkeley's Laura Stoker confirmed it. Their conclusion: "Those who were arbitrarily, albeit randomly, handed an adverse draft number tended to turn against the war and against the new draft policy's champion, President Richard Nixon, both in their political activity and in the votes they cast in 1972. They came to express more left-leaning policy views and ideological affiliations." Lottery status also outstripped partisanship "in accounting for the political views draft eligible men came to hold by their mid-twenties." And these views had a "permanence." Robert Erikson, Laura Stoker, "Caught in the Draft: The Effects of Vietnam Draft Lottery Status on Political Attitudes," *American Political Science Review* 105, no. 2 (2011): 221–37.

19. Kuhn: Harris 792801, November 1979. Kenneth Heineman, "The Silent Majority Speaks: Antiwar Protest and Backlash, 1965–1972," *Peace & Change* 17, no. 4 (October 1992): 33. David Paul Kuhn, *The Neglected Voter* (NY: St. Martin's Press, 2007), 33–34. Appy, *Working-Class War*, 6. Richard M. Scammon and Ben J. Wattenberg, *The Real Majority: The Classic Examination of the American Electorate* (NY: Coward-McCann, 1992), 223–24.

20. Christopher Wren, "Veterans Bid City Meet Their Needs," NYT, March 15, 1973. Egendorf, "Legacies of Vietnam" (which reports: "About 54 percent of all blue collar white veterans are crafts workers"). Author interview, George Daly.

21. Kuhn: Harris 792801, November 1979. James E. Westheider, *Fighting in Vietnam: The Experiences of the U.S. Soldier* (Mechanicsburg, PA: Stackpole Books, 2011), 141. Studs Terkel, *American Dreams Lost and Found* (NY: Pantheon, 1980), 255–56. Chuck Hagel, "Chuck Hagel: Serving in Vietnam with My Brother," NYT, December 28, 2007. "William Abood," Library of Congress, Veterans History Project.

22. Richard Harwood, "Flag's Defenders: Hard Hats March for a Way of Life," WP, May 31, 1970.

23. Author interview, James Lapham.

24. Appy, *Working-Class War*, 26. Robert Semple, "Nixon Abolishes Draft Deferment for Fatherhood," NYT, April 24, 1970. David Paul Kuhn, "The 60s and Why We Still Fight," RealClearPolitics, May 27, 2010.

25. James P. Sterba, "In the Field: Grunts, Groans and Jokes," NYT, May 5, 1970. "Big Base Area Discovered," NYT, May 5, 1970.

26. "Voices of a Wounded Generation," WP, May 25, 1980.

27. Nick Anderson, "Cheney's Draft Deferments Not Outside the Norm," LAT, September 16, 2004. "Clinton's Draft Deferment," CNN, 1997. Roberto Suro, "Candidate's Record; Clinton Asked Senator's Help on Draft, His Aides Confirm," NYT, September 19, 1992. Randall Chase, "Biden Deferred, Disqualified from Vietnam Duty," AP, September 1, 2008. Steve Eder, Dave Philipps, "Donald Trump's Draft Deferments: Four for College, One for Bad Feet," NYT, August 1, 2016. Amy J. Rutenberg, "What Trump's Draft Deferments Reveal," *Atlantic Monthly*, January 2, 2019. Larry Cohler-Esses, Bob Port, "Bloomberg and His Vietnam War Story," DN, August 19, 2001. Maryalice Parks, "Bernie Sanders Applied for 'Conscientious Objector' Status During Vietnam, Campaign Confirms," ABC News, August 31, 2015. Jill Abramson, James Harmon, "40 Years After Vietnam, Rudy's Got Some Explaining to Do," DN, January 23, 2008. Bill Sammon, "Giuliani Says He Would Have Gone to Vietnam," March 1, 2007. Rebecca Walsh, "Did Karl Rove Dodge the Draft?" *Salt Lake Tribune*, September 18, 2004. "Top Republicans Found Many Ways to Avoid Vietnam," WSJ, September 10, 1992. Angie Drobnic Holan, "Fact Sheet: Who Was in Military?" PolitiFact, December 21, 2007.

28. Kuhn: GSS 1973. Census.gov (1999). The 1973 GSS question was "Have you ever taken part in" an "anti-war demonstration?" The results showed that 87 percent of Americans who attended an antiwar demonstration at some point in their lives had at least one year of higher education. One year of education allowed current collegians to be included. Amy J. Rutenberg, "What Trump's Draft Deferments Reveal," *Atlantic Monthly*, January 2, 2019. Chris Bergeron, "Abbie Hoffman Exhibit Takes Framingham Brother Jack Back in Time," *MetroWest Daily News*, February 11, 2007.

29. Jonathan Eig, "Small Ohio Town, Hurt Deeply by War, Still Produces Soldiers," WSJ, March 12, 2003. Mike Wagner, "Beallsville's Loss of Vietnam War Soldiers Still Felt," *Columbus Dispatch*, April 26, 2015. Douglas E. Kneeland, "Ohio Town That Lost 7 Men in Vietnam Now Worries More About Economy," NYT, April 4, 1975. Appy, *Working-Class War*, 14. John Weiss, "Johnsburg Man Re-creates Story of Man Who Died in Vietnam," *Post-Bulletin* (Rochester, MN), July 9, 2009.

    As Christian Appy also noted, the rural study found that 8 percent of soldiers who died in Vietnam came from towns of fewer than a thousand people, though only about 2 percent of Americans lived in them.

Chapter 9

1. Abigail Thernstrom, Stephan Thernstrom, "Black Progress: How Far We've Come, and How Far We Have to Go," Brookings Institution, March 1, 1998. Jack Rosenthal, "Poor in Nation Rise by 5 Percent, Reversing 10-Year Trend," NYT, May 8, 1971. "The A.P.A. Ruling on Homosexuality," NYT, December 23, 1973. Michael Knight, "Yale's First Full Class of Women, About to Graduate, Looks Back With Pride and Hope," NYT, June 3, 1973. Suzanne McGee, Heidi Moore, "Women's Rights and Their Money," Guardian, August 11, 2014. Vincent Cannato, *The Ungovernable City: John Lindsay and His Struggle to Save New York* (NY: Basic Books, 2001), 204–8. Lyndon B. Johnson, Remarks in Memorial Hall, Akron University, provided by Gerhard Peters, John T. Woolley, The American Presidency Project, https://www.presidency. ucsb.edu/node/242136. Hubert Humphrey, *The Education of a Public Man* (NY: Doubleday, 1976), 320–25. Editorial, "The Nixon Doctrine," LAT, November 1, 1970. Rick Perlstein, *Nixonland: The Rise of a President and The Fracturing of America* (NY: Scribner, 2008), 158. David Espar, Geoffrey C. Ward, *American Experience: The Presidents, Richard M. Nixon*, PBS, October 8, 1990. Robert Mason, *Richard Nixon and the Quest for a New Majority* (Chapel Hill: University of North Carolina Press, 2004), 44. Benjamin Welles, "G.O.P. Chiefs Say War is Johnson's," NYT, September 20, 1966 (LAT article, same day, verifies locale of pledge). Charles L. Garrettson, *Hubert H. Humphrey: The Politics of Joy* (New Brunswick, NJ: Transaction, 1993), 323–26.

Nixon also pledged he wanted peace with honor. He had long postured patriotic (and on no battle more publicly than his triumph over the pundits and liberals in the Alger Hiss case). But at the dusk of the 1968 campaign, Nixon was warned that LBJ was making peace overtures and "will accept almost any arrangement" because the "White Housers still think they can pull the election out for" Humphrey. Nixon told H. R. Haldeman to throw a "monkey wrench" in LBJ's efforts. Nixon denied it throughout his lifetime. Nixon could have wanted to stop a bad peace deal, a peace that gave up allies, as his defenders later noted. But Nixon did not make that point to LBJ. LBJ found out before election day and spoke with Nixon. Nixon denied his efforts. LBJ was unsparing in a conversation with the GOP minority leader, Senator Everett Dirksen. Johnson said, "This is treason." Dirksen replied, "I know." (The historical consensus regarding this infamous Nixon episode, commonly called the Chennault Affair, is that peace was not at hand, and thus whatever Nixon's motivations—and they likely were un-American for placing his electoral concerns before what could have been best for his nation—they also likely did not change the war's trajectory.) H. R. Haldeman notes, October 22, 1968, https://assets.documentcloud.org/documents/3248783/H-R-Haldeman-s-Notes-from-Oct-22-1968.pdf. For Nixon defense and notes on "accept almost any arrangement" memo, see "Nixon Biographer Farrell

Misinterprets a Word and Draws the Wrong Conclusion," https://www. nixonfoundation.org/2017/06/misunderstanding-a-monkey-wrench. LBJ's conversations on the Chennault Affair, http://www.lbjlibrary.org/mediakits/ chennault/telephoneconversations.html.

2. Edmund White, *City Boy: My Life in New York During the 1960s and '70s* (NY: Bloomsbury Publishing, 2009). Chap. 4, Kindle. Another example of how times had changed is visible in the views of blacks. When asked in 1970 "if things for most black people like yourself" are getting "better" or "worse" or were the "same," two-thirds of blacks said "better." A plurality of blacks, 44 percent, said they "live about the same as the whites . . . around here," compared to 31 percent who said they live "worse" and 13 percent who said they live "better." See *The Harris Survey Yearbook of Public Opinion 1970* (NY: Louis Harris and Associates, 1971), 233–34.

3. Richard Reeves, "Marchi Defeats Lindsay in G.O.P. Primary," NYT, June 18, 1969. Peter Kihss, "Ethnic Division in Vote Is Noted," NYT, June 19, 1969. Editorial, "A Lesson in Civics for Mayor Lindsay," CT, October 16, 1969. Vincent Cannato, *The Ungovernable City: John Lindsay and His Struggle to Save New York* (NY: Basic Books, 2001), 409. Joseph P. Viteritti, *Summer in the City: John Lindsay, New York, and the American Dream* (Baltimore: The Johns Hopkins University Press, 2014), 49.

4. Steve Fraser, *The Limousine Liberal: How an Incendiary Image United the Right and Fractured America* (NY: Basic Books, 2016), chap. 1, Kindle. Maria Lizzi, "My Heart Is as Black as Yours: White Backlash, Racial Identity, and Italian American Stereotypes in New York City's 1969 Mayoral Campaign," *Journal of American Ethnic History* 27, no. 3 (2008): 43–80.

5. Andy Logan, "Mayoral Follies, The 1969 Edition," NYT, January 25, 1998. Sewell Chan, "25 Years Ago, Subways and Buses Stopped Running," NYT, April 4, 2005. Joseph P. Viteritti, *Summer in the City: John Lindsay, New York, and the American Dream* (Baltimore: The Johns Hopkins University Press, 2014), 88–89. Sean Deveney, *Fun City: John Lindsay, Joe Namath, and How Sports Saved New York in the 1960s* (NY: Sports Publishing, 2015), chap. 7, Kindle.

6. "New York's Little Man?" *Economist*, September 13, 1969. "Lindsay and the Fight for New York," *Newsweek*, November 3, 1969. "Homestretch, See John Run," *Newsweek*, November 3, 1969.

7. Tom Casciato, Rob Issen, *Fun City Revisited: The Lindsay Years*, PBS, 2010. Vincent Cannato, *The Ungovernable City: John Lindsay and His Struggle to Save New York* (NY: Basic Books, 2001), 433. Jack Newfield, "The Downs and Ups of John Lindsay," *Life*, November 14, 1969. Richard M. Scammon, Ben J. Wattenberg, *The Real Majority: The Classic Examination of the American Electorate* (NY: Coward-McCann, 1992), 240–45. Peter Kihss, "Poor and Rich, Not Middle-Class, The Key to Lindsay Re-Election," NYT, November 6, 1969.

8. "Lindsay and the Fight for New York," *Newsweek*, November 3, 1969. Lawrence Van Gelder, "Mario A. Procaccino, 83, Who Lost to Lindsay in 1969, Dies," NYT, December 21, 1995. Andy Logan, "Around City Hall," *The New Yorker*, September 13, 1969. Nathan Glazer, Daniel P. Moynihan, "How the Catholics Lost Out to the Jews in New York Politics," NYM, August 10, 1970. Steve Fraser, *The Limousine Liberal: How an Incendiary Image United the Right and Fractured America* (NY: Basic Books, 2016), chap. 1, Kindle. Maria Lizzi, "My Heart Is as Black as Yours: White Backlash, Racial Identity, and Italian American Stereotypes in New York City's 1969 Mayoral Campaign," *Journal of American Ethnic History* 27, no. 3 (2008): 43–80. Vincent Cannato, *The Ungovernable City: John Lindsay and His Struggle to Save New York* (NY: Basic Books, 2001), 403–4. "New York's Little Man?" *Economist*, September 13, 1969.

9. Milton Himmelfarb, *The Jews of Modernity* (NY: Basic Books, 1973), 111.

10. Ellen Willis, *Beginning to See the Light: Sex, Hope, and Rock-and-Roll* (Hanover, NH: Wesleyan University Press, 1992), 138–49. (See also Ellen Willis, "Lessons of Chicago," *New American Review* 6 [1969]). Jonathan Rieder, *Canarsie: The Jews and Italians of Brooklyn Against Liberalism* (Cambridge, MA: Harvard University Press, 1985), 262. Michael Lerner, "Respectable Bigotry," *The New Journal at Yale*, April 12, 1969. John Welch, "New Left Knots," in Pat Walker, ed., *Between Labor and Capital* (Boston: South End Press, 1979), 184–86.

11. Vincent Cannato, *The Ungovernable City: John Lindsay and His Struggle to Save New York* (NY: Basic Books, 2001), 392–93. Douglas Schoen, *The Nixon Effect: How Richard Nixon's Presidency Fundamentally Changed American Politics* (NY: Encounter Books, 2016), 179. Patricia Cayo Sexton, Brendan Sexton, *Blue Collars and Hard-Hats* (NY: Random House, 1971), 286.

12. UPI, "Reagan Greets Lindsay as 'Occupant' of State," NYT, April 3, 1970.

13. Steven V. Roberts, "Lindsay Assails Nixon on Rights," NYT, April 3, 1970. Gloria Steinem, "Lindsay's Urban Strategy: The Opening Scenes," *New York*, May 11, 1970.

14. Steven Roberts, "Lindsay Assails Nixon on Rights," NYT, April 3, 1970. Editorial, "Lindsay in Reaganland," NYT, April 5, 1970.

15. UPI, "Lindsay Can Win Democratic Bid in '72, Goodell Says," CT, November 30, 1970. Chesly Manly, "Only Issue in N.Y. Race Is Lindsay," CT, October 29, 1969. Jack Newfield, "The Downs and Ups of John Lindsay," *Life*, November 14, 1969. "Lindsay: A Switch in Time?" Newsweek, August 23, 1971. Gloria Steinem, "Lindsay's Urban Strategy: The Opening Scenes," *New York*, May 11, 1970. Vincent Cannato, *The Ungovernable City: John Lindsay and His Struggle to Save New York* (NY: Basic Books, 2001), 445.

16. Ellen Willis, *Beginning to See the Light: Sex, Hope, and Rock-and-Roll* (Minneapolis: University of Minnesota Press, 1981), 132. Vincent Cannato, *The Ungovernable City: John Lindsay and His Struggle to Save New York* (NY: Basic

Books, 2001), 218–19. Richard Reeves, "Mayor Urges Youths to Aid War Resistance," NYT, March 20, 1968.

17. Vincent Cannato, *The Ungovernable City: John Lindsay and His Struggle to Save New York* (NY: Basic Books, 2001), 223–24. Rick Perlstein, *Nixonland: The Rise of a President and the Fracturing of America* (NY: Scribner, 2008), 290. Marty Jezer, *Abbie Hoffman: American Rebel* (New Brunswick, NJ: Rutgers University Press, 1992), 92.

18. Tom Hayden, "A Special Supplement: The Occupation of Newark," *New York Review of Books*, August 24, 1967.

19. Mike Marqusee and Bill Harris, eds., *New York, An Anthology* (NY: Barnes and Noble, 1985), 325.

20. Charlotte Curtis, "Black Panther Philosophy Is Debated at the Bernsteins," NYT, January 15, 1970. Editorial, "False Note on Black Panthers," NYT, January 16, 1970. Vincent Cannato, *The Ungovernable City: John Lindsay and His Struggle to Save New York* (NY: Basic Books, 2001), 448. Tom Wolfe, "Radical Chic: That Party at Lenny's," NYM, June 8, 1970.

Chapter 10

1. Shannon McCaffrey, "Ironworkers Who Built Twin Towers Are Cleaning Up Site," AP, October 15, 2001. James Glanz, Eric Lipton, *City in the Sky: The Rise and Fall of the World Trade Center* (NY: Times Books, Henry Holt and Company, 2013), chap. 7, Kindle.

2. Ada Louise Huxtable, "A New City Is Emerging Downtown," NYT, March 29, 1970. Ada Louise Huxtable, "Architecture: How Not to Build a City," NYT, November 22, 1970. Anthony W. Robins, *The World Trade Center* (NY: Thompson and Columbus, 2011), chap. 1, Kindle. "Statement by Minoru Yamasaki of Minoru Yamasaki and Associates," December 1964, Architects and Architecture, Anthony W. Robins World Trade Center archive.

3. Fact Sheet The World Trade Center in Port Authority of New York–New Jersey," June 1984, Chronologies and "Fact Sheets," Anthony W. Robins World Trade Center archive. Jerry Cheslow, "A New Neighborhood Along the Hudson," NYT, December 26, 1993. Edith Iglauer, "The Biggest Foundation," *New Yorker*, November 4, 1972.

4. Glanz, Lipton, *City in the Sky*, chap. 4, Kindle.

5. "Telegram to the Editorial Page of the New York Times from Richard Roth, Emery Roth & Sons, February 14, 1964," Architects and Architecture, Anthony W. Robins World Trade Center archive. James Barron, "Flaming Horror on the 79th Floor; 50 Years Ago Today, in the Fog, a Plane Hit the World's Tallest Building," NYT, July 28, 1995. "The Mountain Comes to Manhattan," NYT, advertisement, May 2, 1968 (see page 38).

6. Eric Nalder, "Twin Towers Engineered to Withstand Jet Collision," *Seattle Times*, February 27, 1993. James Glanz, "In Collapsing Towers, a Cascade of Failures," NYT, November 11, 2001. Glanz, Lipton, *City in the Sky*, chap. 5, Kindle. "New Sears Building in Chicago Planned as the World's Tallest," NYT, July 28, 1970. "The Building and Fire Safety Investigation into the World Trade Center Collapse," October 26, 2005, National Institute of Standards and Technology, U.S. Department of Commerce.

7. Ada Louise Huxtable, "Big but Not So Bold, Trade Center Towers Are Tallest, but Architecture Is Smaller Scale," NYT, April 5, 1973. Richard Bernstein, "Stories of Trade Center, Now Suddenly Obituaries," NYT, September 24, 2001.

8. Jay P. Dolan, *The Irish Americans: A History* (NY: Bloomsbury Press, 2008), chaps. 3, 4, Kindle. Melvyn Dubofsky, Joseph McCartin, *Labor in America: A History* (Wheeling, WV: Harlan Davidson, 2004), 109–13. Thomas Maier, *The Kennedys: America's Emerald Kings: A Five-Generation History of the Ultimate Irish Catholic Family* (NY: Basic Books, 2003), 30–31. Andrew Kolin, *Political Economy of Labor Repression in the United States* (NY: Lexington Books, 2017), 70–77. Robert Bartholomew, Anja Reumschussel, *American Intolerance: Our Dark History of Demonizing Immigrants* (NY: Prometheus Books, 2018), chap. 1, Kindle. Tyler Anbinder, *City of Dreams: The 400-Year Epic History of Immigrant New York* (Boston: Houghton Mifflin, 2016), 160. Barnet Schecter, *The Devil's Own Work: The Civil War Draft Riots and the Fight to Reconstruct America* (NY: Walker & Company, 2005), 78.

9. Richard Krickus, *Pursuing the American Dream: White Ethnics and the New Populism* (Bloomington: Indiana University Press, 1976), 45–49. "Map No. 2, City of New York, Showing the Distribution of the Principal Nationalities by Sanitary Districts," 1895 (based on 1890 census), Library of Congress. Erik Kirshbaum, "Whatever Happened to German America?" NYT, September 23, 2015. Jennifer Ludden, "In Rural Wisconsin, German Reigned for Decades," NPR, April 1, 2009. James McPherson, *Battle Cry of Freedom: The Civil War Era* (NY: Oxford University Press, 1988), 35–36, 40.

10. McPherson, *Battle Cry of Freedom*, 30–33, 40, 136–37. Sean Wilentz, *The Rise of American Democracy: Jefferson to Lincoln* (NY: W. W. Norton, 2005), 682–85. John R. Mulkern, *The Know-Nothing Party in Massachusetts: The Rise and Fall of a People's Movement* (Boston: Northeastern University Press, 1990), 85–86. John H. Aldrich, *Why Parties? The Origin and Transformation of Political Parties in America* (Chicago: University of Chicago Press, 1995), 150. Dolan, *The Irish Americans*, chap. 4, Kindle. Richard Krickus, *Pursuing the American Dream: White Ethnics and the New Populism* (Bloomington: Indiana University Press, 1976), 45–50, 54. Charles H. Hubbard, ed., *Lincoln, the Law, and Presidential Leadership* (Carbondale: Southern Illinois University Press, 2015), 35.

11. Dolan, *The Irish Americans*, chap. 4, Kindle. Davy Crockett, *Life of David Crockett: The Original Humorist and Irrepressible Backwoodsman* (NY: A. L. Burt

and Company, 1902), 185. McPherson, *Battle Cry of Freedom*, 40, 137. For annual wages, see Bureau of Labor Statistics, "History of Wages in the United States from Colonial Times to 1928," 1934.

The relationship between blacks and Irish Americans was not uniformly acrimonious. In New York's Five Points, "black and white, white and black, all hugemsnug together," read Davy Crockett's ghostwritten account, an impression Charles Dickens corroborated. But Irish-black tension had also predated the Civil War. In New York State, a unified Irish electorate helped defeat an 1846 referendum to extend the right to vote to blacks.

12. Ulysses S. Grant, *The Papers of Ulysses S. Grant: 1875*, ed. John Y. Simon (Carbondale: Southern Illinois University Press, 2003), 343.

13. Dolan, *The Irish Americans*, chaps. 3, 4, Kindle. Dubofsky, McCartin, *Labor in America*, 109–13; Kolin, *Political Economy of Labor Repression in the United States*, 70–77.

14. Anbinder, *City of Dreams*, 304. Andy McCarthy, "A Brief Passage in U.S. Immigration History," New York Public Library, July 1, 2016, https://www.nypl.org/blog/2016/07/01/us-immigration-history. Mary Elizabeth Brown, "The Italians of the South Village," Greenwich Village Society for Historic Preservation, October 2007.

The 1890 population percentages are from census counts. See "Map No. 2, City of New York, Showing the Distribution of the Principal Nationalities by Sanitary Districts," 1895 (based on 1890 census), Library of Congress. "Table 12. Population of the 100 Largest Urban Places: 1890," U.S. Bureau of the Census.

15. Tyler Anbinder, *Five Points: The Nineteenth-Century New York City Neighborhood That Invented Tap Dance, Stole Elections, and Became the World's Most Notorious Slum* (NY: Free Press, 2010), 375. Paul Good, "The Bricks and Mortar of Racism," NYT, May 21, 1972. Editorial, "Italian Workmen," NYT, June 25, 1874. Dolan, *The Irish Americans*, chap. 9, Kindle. Rosario Iaconis, "An Overdue Apology to Italian-Americans," WSJ, April 8, 2019. AP, "New Orleans to Apologize for Worst Mass Lynching in America's History," *Guardian*, March 31, 2015.

16. "Map No. 2, City of New York, Showing the Distribution of the Principal Nationalities by Sanitary Districts," 1895 (based on 1890 census), Library of Congress. Helen Moore, "Tenement Neighborhood Idea—University Settlement, in The Literature of Philanthropy," in *The Literature of Philanthropy*, ed. Frances A. Goodale (NY: Harper & Brothers, 1893), 36–48. McPherson, *Battle Cry of Freedom,* 23, 33. "Early Tenements," *History of Poverty and Homelessness in NYC*, Institute for Children, Poverty and Homelessness, http://povertyhistory.org/era/nineteenth#tenement-houses. "1830–1889," "Tenements," History.com, April 22, 2010. Louis Heaton Pink, *Old Tenements and the New Law* (NY: Fred F. French, 1932), 3–6. Joseph P. Viteritti, *Summer in the City: John Lindsay, New York, and the American Dream* (Baltimore: Johns Hopkins University Press, 2014), 81. Sean Wilentz, *Chants*

Democratic: New York City and the Rise of the American Working Class, 1788–1850 (NY: Oxford University Press, 1984), 109, 118, 405. David Von Drehle, *Triangle: The Fire That Changed America* (NY: Grove Press, 2003), 42.

In total, between mid-1891 and 1910, 12.5 million immigrants arrived in the United States. Nearly two-thirds of that wave hailed from southern and eastern Europe, compared to only 16 percent between 1881 and 1891, and less than half that share the decade prior. More than four million Italians alone came between 1880 and 1924. Meanwhile, while there were already some Sephardic and German Jews in the country—such as a Jewish girl who wrote of "tired masses yearning to breathe free"—decades of massacres of Jews in Russia helped spur about 2.6 million Jewish immigrants between 1881 to 1925. By the turn of the century, there were also some two million Poles in the country.

17. Richard Krickus, *Pursuing the American Dream: White Ethnics and the New Populism* (Bloomington: Indiana University Press, 1976), 42, 57–58. After Reconstruction, Jim Crow laws kept black men disenfranchised in the South until the mid-1960s. Native American male enfranchisement was not fully realized until the early twentieth century.

18. Robert A. Orsi, ed., *Gods of the City: Religion and the American Urban Landscape* (Bloomington: Indiana University Press, 1999), 253. Michael N. Dobkowski, "American Anti-Semitism: A Reinterpretation," *American Quarterly* 29, no. 2 (Summer 1977): 166–81. Richard Krickus, *Pursuing the American Dream: White Ethnics and the New Populism* (Bloomington: Indiana University Press, 1976), 50–51. "The Immigration Act of 1924," United States House of Representatives, Office of Art and Archives, Office of the Clerk.

19. Woodrow Wilson, *A History of the American People* (NY: Harper & Brothers, 1902), 60–63, 212–14. Sarah Churchwell, "American Immigration: A Century of Racism," *New York Review of Books*, September 26, 2019.

20. Richard Krickus, *Pursuing the American Dream: White Ethnics and the New Populism* (Bloomington: Indiana University Press, 1976), 176–77. David Paul Kuhn, *The Neglected Voter: White Men and the Democratic Dilemma* (NY: Palgrave Macmillan, 2007), 47–49. William Manchester, *The Glory and the Dream* (NY: Rosetta Books, 2013), chap. 5. Kindle.

South Carolina governor Strom Thurmond's 1948 defection from the Democrats is said to be the beginning of the "southern flip," when the South was said to have left Democrats over civil rights. But "States' Rights Strom" and his Dixiecrats only won four Deep South states, including Alabama and Mississippi. The first GOP inroads were, again, in 1928, when Democrats and Republicans did not champion black equality, and Democrats effectively had a Faustian bargain with the Jim Crow South. In 1968, only about a fifth of Nixon's electoral votes (57 of 301) came from the South and, tellingly, they came from the peripheral South. George Wallace locked down the Deep South in 1968 along racist lines, under the euphemistic guise of "state's rights."

On Al Smith's strong ethnic white support: In New York in 1928, eight in ten Irish backed Smith, compared to six in ten supporting Democrats in 1924. Italian support for Democrats increased from about half to three-quarters over the same time span.

21. Richard Hofstadter, *The Age of Reform* (NY: Vintage Books, 1955), 77–82. Michael N. Dobkowski, "American Anti-Semitism: A Reinterpretation," *American Quarterly* 29, no. 2 (Summer 1977): 166–81. Rafael Medoff, "What FDR Said About Jews in Private," LAT, April 7, 2013. Dirk Johnson, "Yale's Limit on Jewish Enrollment Lasted Until Early 1960s, Book Says," NYT, March 4, 1986.

There is ongoing debate over antisemitism within the populist movement. Democratic populist William Jennings Bryan, according to biographer Michael Kazin, opposed some flagrant anti-Semitism. For instance, Kazin writes that Bryan "attacked Henry Ford for reprinting the anti-Semitic fraud The Protocols of the Elders of Zion," (see Michael Kazin, *Godly Hero: The Life of William Jennings Bryan* (NY: Alfred A. Knopf, 2006), 273). But Bryan also spoke of Shakespeare's Shylock—"flesh" as collateral—on the House floor, and arguably mingled conspiracies of bankers and Christ's crucifixion in his most famous speech as the Democratic presidential nominee—"You shall not crucify mankind upon a cross of gold"—at a time when it remained common to blame Jews for deicide (killing Jesus, the Christian God). During Bryan's "cross of gold" speech, Paolo Coletta wrote, some convention delegates shouted back, "Down with gold! Down with the hook-nosed Shylocks of Wall Street! Down with the Christ-killing gold bugs!" Richard Hofstadter argued it was "chiefly populist writers" who utilized imagery of Jewish usury and the "international gold ring." "The omnipresent symbol of the Shylock can hardly be taken in itself as evidence of antisemitism," Hofstadter continued, "but the frequent references to the House of Rotshchild make it clear that for many silverites the Jew was an organic part of the conspiracy theory of history." Recent scholarship has generally dismissed or depreciated the antisemitism within the populist movement. University of Nebraska historian William C. Pratt pushed back against this new consensus in 2009, noting that while Hofstadter "overstated" his case, "over the last twenty or twenty-five years there has been a virtual conspiracy of silence on the topic of antisemitism by populist historians." One telling example Pratt notes comes from a South Dakota populist newspaper the year before Bryan's famed speech. It too mingles Christ's crucifixion with conspiracy theories about Jewish banking: "We are opposed to permitting the Jews through Baron Rothchilds [*sic*] to continue crucifying Christ by oppressing His people." See William Jennings Bryan, "The Gold Bond Contract: Speech in the House of Representatives," February 14, 1895. Paolo E. Coletta, *William Jennings Bryan: Political Evangelist, 1860–1908* (Lincoln: University of Nebraska Press, 1964), 141. "The Populist Vision: A

Roundtable Discussion," *Kansas History: A Journal of the Central Plains* 32 (Spring 2009): 33.

22. William Manchester, *The Glory and the Dream* (NY: Rosetta Books, 2013), chap. 1, Kindle. Dolan, *The Irish Americans*, chap. 9, Kindle. Rafael Medoff, "What FDR Said About Jews in Private," LAT, April 7, 2013. Andy McCarthy, "A Brief Passage in U.S. Immigration History," New York Public Library, July 1, 2016, https://www.nypl.org/blog/2016/07/01/us-immigration-history.

23. Jynnah Radford, Luis Noe-Bustamante, "Facts on U.S. Immigrants, 2017," Pew Research Center, Washington D.C., June 3, 2019. Patricia Cayo Sexton, Brendan Sexton, *Blue Collars and Hard-Hats* (NY: Random House, 1971), 222 (in this case, I'm defining "affluent" as at least $14,000 in annual household earnings). Irving M. Levine and Judith Herman, "The Life of White Ethnics," *Dissent*, Winter 1972. Diana Nelson Jones, "Appalachia's War," *Pittsburgh Post-Gazette*, November 26, 2000. Ben A. Franklin, "In Appalachia: Vast Aid, Scant Relief," NYT, November 29, 1970.

24. Irving M. Levine and Judith Herman, "The Life of White Ethnics," *Dissent*, Winter 1972. Peter Schrag, "The Forgotten American," *Harper's Magazine*, August 1, 1969. Gus Tyler, "White Worker—Blue Mood," *Dissent*, Winter 1972. Michael Harrington, "Old Working Class, New Working Class," *Dissent*, Winter 1972. "Hot Under the Blue Collar," *Newsweek*, October 6, 1969. Vincent Cannato, *The Ungovernable City: John Lindsay and His Struggle to Save New York* (NY: Basic Books, 2001), 550. Michael Harrington, "Old Working Class, New Working Class," *Dissent*, Winter 1972.

Between 1947 and 1968, the median family income rose about 75 percent after controlling for inflation. Still, as the 1970s dawned, about half of New York City's whites earned between $5,000 and $10,000 annually, though the Bureau of Labor Statistics reported that a family of four in a city (not even a city as costly as NYC) must earn at least $9,500 to maintain a "modest but adequate" standard of living.

25. Author interview, George Daly. Walter Bernstein, "Hit Him on the Horn Georgie," *New Yorker*, September 16, 1950.

26. Rick Perlstein, *Before the Storm* (NY: Nation Books, 2009), 236.

27. Joshua B. Freeman, "Hardhats: Construction Workers, Manliness, and the 1970 Pro-War Demonstrations," *Journal of Social History* 26, no. 4 (Summer 1993): 725–44. "News Summary and Index," NYT, April 12, 1970.

28. Jill Lepore, *New York Burning: Liberty, Slavery and Conspiracy in Eighteenth-Century New York* (NY: Alfred A. Knopf, 2005), 235-39. Gus Tyler, "White Worker—Blue Mood," *Dissent*, Winter 1972.

29. "Labor Letter: A Special News Report on People and Their Jobs in Offices, Fields and Factories," WSJ, May 19, 1970. Antonio Flores, "2015, Hispanic Population in the United States Statistical Portrait," Pew Research Center, Washington, DC, September 18, 2017. Brendan Sexton, "Unions and the

Black Power Broker," *Dissent*, February 1972. Patricia Cayo Sexton, Brendan Sexton, *Blue Collars and Hard-Hats* (NY: Random House, 1971), 258, 269.

Racial minorities were also more likely to be in the lower-paying trades than whites, which by the 1950s was—like all of this—some combination of discrimination and the reality that the higher-paying trades had the highest barriers, whether in training or mere supply, and were the most desired for their pay scale.

30. Robert Mason, *Richard Nixon and the Quest for a New Majority* (Chapel Hill: University of North Carolina Press, 2004), 53–54. Editorial, "Who's in the Rank and File," WP, October 15, 1970. Pat Buchanan, *Nixon's White House Wars: The Battles That Made and Broke a President and Divided America Forever* (NY: Crown Forum, 2017), 86.

31. Kenneth Gross, "Life Under a Hard Hat," *Newsday*, June 6, 1970

32. Richard Harwood, " 'Working Americans' Are Rediscovered," WP, September 28, 1969.

33. A. H. Raskin, "Labor and Blacks," NYT, September 9, 1969. Editorial, "Who's in the Rank and File," WP, October 15, 1970. Carl Gershman, "Reform Currents in the Building Trades," *Dissent*, July–August 1970. Marc Linder, *Wars of Attrition: Vietnam, the Business Roundtable, and the Decline of Construction Unions* (Iowa City: University of Iowa Press, 2000), 234.

34. Unemployment extracted and calculated from Unemployment Rate, All Industries, Labor Force Statistics from the Current Population Survey, 1948–2017, U.S. Bureau of Labor Statistics. Viteritti, *Summer in the City*, 166. Richard Rogin, "Joe Kelly Has Reached His Boiling Point: Why the Construction Workers Holler USA All the Way!" NYT Magazine, June 28, 1970. James Glanz, Eric Lipton, *City in the Sky*, chap. 7, Kindle.

Chapter 11

1. Russell Freeburg, "Nixon's Viet Nam Optimism Seems to Be Backed by Facts," CT, April 21, 1970. Linda Charlton, "Big Rallies Are Planned," NYT, May 2, 1970.

2. Federal Bureau of Investigation, Kent State files. ABC, NBC, CBS, May 4–5, 1970. Howard Means, *67 Shots: Kent State and the End of American Innocence* (Boston: Da Capo Press, 2016), chap. 2, Kindle. " 'Not Going to Get Hurt,' He Said," DN, May 6, 1970. Ottavio M. Casale, Louis Paskoff, eds., *The Kent Affair: Documents and Interpretations* (Boston: Houghton Mifflin, 1971), 11.

3. Combined: CT, LAT, WP, DN, NYP, NYT, AP, ABC, NBC, CBS, May 4–7, 1970. Additional relevant articles include: Terry Robards, "War and Economy Spur Stock Drops," NYT, May 5, 1970. Tribune Wire Service, "Reagan Asks College to Close," CT, May 7, 1970. Michael Kaufman, "Campus Unrest over War Spreads with Strike Calls," NYT, May 4, 1970. J. W. Stillman, "Guard Kills 4 at Kent," *Harvard Crimson*, May 5, 1970. "Students Across the

Nation Vent Their Rage and Grief," DN, May 6, 1970. Mel Greene, William Neugebauer, William McFadden, "In Wake of Kent: Sleep-ins & Fires," DN, May 7, 1970. Charles DeBenedetti, *An American Ordeal: The Antiwar Movement of the Vietnam Era* (NY: Syracuse University Press, 1990), 284. "At War with War," *Time*, May 18, 1970. "Who Owns the Stars and Stripes," *Time*, July 6, 1970. For moving and still film footage, see Kent State Shootings: Digital Archive, Kent State University, https://omeka.library.kent.edu/special-collections/kent-state-shootings-digital-archive. Anna Bowers, Jonathan Halperin, *The Day the '60s Died*, PBS, April 28, 2015. "Witnessed: The Killings at Kent State," CNN, May 4, 2014.

4. Sanford Ungar, "Gas Routs AU Students," WP, May 7, 1970. Carl Bernstein, "Area Student Protests Range from Solemnity to Violence," WP, May 7, 1970.

5. Combined: DN, NYP, NYT, ABC, CBS, NBC, May 5–8, 1970. Additional relevant articles include: Andy Soltis, "NYU Computer 'Kidnap' Ends," NYP, May 7, 1970. Hugh Wyatt, "Avert Computer Bombing, Rout Students," DN, May 8, 1970. Pete Hamill, "On the March," NYP, May 6. Sandor M. Polster, "Protests Are Peaceful," NYP, May 6, 1970. Linda Charlton, "City to Shut Schools Today, to Honor Kent State Dead, Spock Delivers Eulogy," NYT, May 8, 1970. Mel Greene, William Neugebauer, William McFadden, "In Wake of Kent: Sleep-ins & Fires," DN, May 7, 1970. Joseph Lelyveld, "Protests on Cambodia and Kent State Are Joined by Many Local Schools," NYT, May 6, 1970.

6. "Report of the President's Commission on Campus Unrest," President's Commission on Campus Unrest, Washington, DC (New York: Commerce Clearing House, 1970), 17–18 (for data behind sentences on student strikes increasing "exponentially"). J. Hoberman, "Off the Hippies: 'Joe' and the Chaotic Summer of '70," NYT, July 30, 2000. AP, "Nixon Makes Offer to Meet Protesters: Student Protests Multiply," *Atlanta Constitution*, May 9, 1970. Combined Services, "Classes Boycotted Across the Nation," DN, May 7, 1970. Joseph Lelyveld, "Protests on Cambodia and Kent State Are Joined by Many Local Schools," NYT, May 6, 1970. Robert D. McFadden, "College Strife Spreads," NYT, May 7, 1970.

7. "Talk of the Town," *New Yorker*, May 16, 1970.

8. John A. Farrell, *Richard Nixon: The Life* (NY: Knopf Doubleday, 2017), chap. 21, Kindle. David C. Taylor, dir., *Nixon: A Presidency Revealed*, The History Channel, February 15, 2007.

9. "History of Bombings Before 'Village' Explosion," NYT, March 13, 1970. Joseph Modzelewski, "Explosions & Fire Destroy Village Townhouse, 1 Dead," DN, March 7, 1970. Wade Greene, "The Militants Who Play with Dynamite," NYT, October 25, 1970. Mark Rudd, *Underground: My Life with the SDS and Weathermen* (NY: Harper Collins, 2009), chap. 11, Kindle. Lucinda Franks, Thomas Powers, "Story of Diana, The Making of a Terrorist," UPI, September 14, 1970.

10. Census statistics on education: Chart No. 263, "Educational Attainment, by Race and Hispanic Origin: 1960 to 1998," United States Census Bureau, 269, https://www.census.gov/prod/99pubs/99statab/sec04.pdf. US Bureau of the Census, "Characteristics of American Youth: 1970," Current Population Reports, series P-23, no. 34, Department of Commerce, Washington, DC, 1971. "Why Those Students Are Protesting," *Time*, May 3, 1968. Polling on views of a college degree, Kuhn: Harris 2037, August 1970. For info on liberal and far-left ideology of college students, see *The Harris Survey Yearbook of Public Opinion 1970* (NY: Louis Harris and Associates, 1971), 286, 305–6. On *Fortune* college poll and "forerunner" views, see Rick Perlstein, *Nixonland: The Rise of a President and the Fracturing of America* (NY: Scribner, 2008), 378–80. "Americans Are Better Educated," USN, June 1, 1970. Author interview, Buchanan.

Only a third of students in the lowest tier, after that dramatic May 1970, thought "most" students supported the antiwar demonstrations, while half of students at the better schools did. When students were asked if they would "accept the draft call and serve," 47 percent of those in the lowest tier of schools said yes, about 20 percentage points higher than students in the better schools. Regarding the propensity of students at elite schools to become more liberal: The Harris poll not only asked students their current ideological outlook but also asked students their outlook when they entered college. Regarding the increase of liberal and far-left outlooks between entering college and the present: At the best third of schools, students became 27 percentage points more liberal (40 to 67 percent), the middle third became 18 points more liberal (35 to 53 percent), and the bottom third, 22 points more liberal (22 to 44 percent). Equally notable, the data indicates, the most elite schools admitted students who were significantly more liberal at the outset compared to their peers elsewhere. See *The Harris Survey Yearbook*, 1970, 286–87 (combined "liberal" and "far left" to mean "liberal" for this comparison).

11. Godfrey Hodgson, *America in Our Time: From World War II to Nixon* (Princeton, NJ: Princeton University Press, 2005), 394–95. Perlstein, *Nixonland*, 387. Michael Harrington, "Old Working Class, New Working Class," *Dissent*, Winter 1972.

12. Charles W. Colson, *Born Again* (Old Tappan, NJ: Chosen Books, 1976), 39–40.

13. Richard Nixon, *RN: The Memoirs of Richard Nixon* (NY: Simon & Schuster, 2013), chap. "1970," Kindle.. Farrell, *Richard Nixon*, chap. 21, Kindle.

14. "New Dimensions for Dissents," *Economist*, May 16, 1970, 41.

15. CBS News, May 4–5, 1970. Robert B. Semple Jr., "Nixon Says Violence Invites Tragedy," NYT, May 5, 1970. H. R. Haldeman, *The Haldeman Diaries: Inside the Nixon White House* (NY: Berkley Books, 1994), 159–64. Henry Kissinger, *Ending the Vietnam War: A History of America's Involvement in and Extradition from the Vietnam War* (NY: Simon & Schuster, 2003), 170. Author interview, Pat Buchanan. Pat Buchanan, *Nixon's White House Wars: The Battles That Made and Broke a President and Divided America Forever* (NY: Crown Forum, 2017), 165.

Walter Pincus, "Haldeman: Reelection Drove Nixon Policy," WP, May 18, 1994. Martin Nolan, "Nixon Says Kent Deaths Show How 'Violence Invites Tragedy,'" *Boston Globe*, May 5, 1970. David Schmitz, *Richard Nixon and the Vietnam War: The End of the American Century* (NY: Rowman & Littlefield, 2014), 91–92. John Ehrlichman, *Witness to Power* (New York: Simon & Schuster, 1982), 149–50. Football anecdote: See Stephen Ambrose, *Nixon: The Triumph of a Politician, 1962–1972* (NY: Simon and Schuster, 1989), 44.

16. Nixon, *RN*, chap. "1970," Kindle.

Chapter 12

1. Author interview, Dick Aurelio.

2. For sourcing on demonstrations and incidents in NYC from May 5 to May 7, primarily from NYPD records, witness affidavits, and news accounts, see the Bibliographic Essay. Additional relevant news articles on activism and disorder in NYC: Sandor M. Polster, "Protests Are Peaceful," NYP, May 6, 1970. Pete Hamill, "On the March," NYP, May 6, 1970. Pete Hamill, "In the Heart of the Beast," NYP, May 7, 1970. Pete Hamill, "Hardhats and Cops," May 12, 1970. Linda Charlton, "Activity Stepped Up Here," NYT, May 7, 1970.

3. Author interview, Joe Guzzardi.

4. Author interviews, Sid Davidoff and Jay Kriegel. Kriegel agreed the incident likely occurred as Davidoff recalled it, but Kriegel couldn't recall it, though he had admittedly forgotten many specifics of these years; these interviews were conducted nearly a half-century after events.

5. Maurice Carroll, "V.F.W. Proclaims Mayor Unwelcome," NYT, May 1, 1970. Kuhn: Harris 2131. Some detail on the generational comparison: The fifth of young people (adults ages 18 to 29) who agreed the "real heroes of the Vietnam War are those who refused induction" was two or three times the share of older adults with that view. A fifth of those same young adults—more than three times the number in older generations—disagreed that "veterans should feel proud to have served their country in the armed forces."

6. "Talk of the Town," *New Yorker*, May 16, 1970, 33. Edward C. Burks, "Lindsay Assails War Policy," NYT, May 7, 1970.

7. John Darnton, "Factory Workers Differ on Protests," NYT, May 8, 1970. John Darnton, "Slum-to-Suburb Commuting for High Pay Has Its Perils," NYT, July 19, 1970. Nancy Isenberg, *White Trash* (NY: Penguin Publishing Group, 2016), 239.

8. Mel Greene, William Neugebauer, William McFadden, "In Wake of Kent: Sleep-ins & Fires," DN, May 7, 1970. "Nixon Makes Offer to Meet Protesters: Student Protests Multiply," *Atlanta Constitution*, May 9, 1970. "Workers and War Critics Clash," CT, May 9, 1970. Bert Shanas, Joseph Modzelewski, "Collegians Drop Scheme to Plug City's Arteries," DN, May 7, 1970.

9. Arlene Eisenberg, Howard Eisenberg, "Dear Dr. Spock," *Baltimore Sun,* March 2, 1969. "On Being an American Parent," *Time,* December 15, 1967. Nan Robertson, "Columbia Rebels Find Disruption Pays," NYT, June 10, 1968.

10. Richard Oliver, "3,000 Bid L.I. Kent Victim Farewell," DN, May 8, 1970. Anthony Burton, "The Kids, Quiet Now, Grieve for Jeff," DN, May 8, 1970. Ron Hollander, "Tears, Hope, Mark Rites," NYP, May 7, 1970. Michael T. Kaufman, "Marcher Felt She 'Had to Do Something,'" NYT, May 8, 1970. Linda Charlton, "City to Shut Schools Today, to Honor Kent State Dead, Spock Delivers Eulogy," May 8, 1970, NYT. "Talk of the Town," *New Yorker,* May 16, 1970.

11. Edward Larson, *The Return of George Washington* (NY: William Morrow, 2014), chap. 9, Kindle. Ron Chernow, *Washington* (NY: Penguin, 2010), chap. 46, Kindle.

12. Richard Neustadt, *Presidential Power and the Modern Presidents: The Politics of Leadership from Roosevelt to Reagan* (NY: Free Press, 1991), 198.

13. For citations in this section, see the Bibliographic Essay.

Chapter 14

1. In every case, unless proven in a court of law or confessed, I've decided to withhold the surname of those I described doing something illegal, such as assault or worse. If they are in the narrative, I'm confident it happened. This is a narrative built on thousands of pages of records—hundreds of witness statements, police complaints, cop notes, internal investigation reports, numerous legal affidavits, other legal records, countless photographs and film footage, media reports, and so forth. If witness statements conflict (and they commonly do—including, not uncommonly, media reports, as I discovered plenty of errors in news accounts), I use other facts to arrive at an accurate account of history, as best one can. But I'm wary of asserting myself as judge and jury. So while it hinders the storytelling and reads as more awkward, for those who specifically commit crimes that they were not sentenced for, or even arrested for, I'm only referring to them by their first names or other generalities. This includes specific cases of police malfeasance, as well as some victims/provocateur names, for example in a subsequent case of mental illness. With the distance of history, in my view, what matters most is what happened, far more than the specific name of the fella who did it. The statute of limitations does not make legal action possible. But these are people who have died and/or are not in the spotlight (whereas a police commander, union boss, or power broker is a public figure). For all these reasons, I'm wary of writing an individual's guilt conclusively, short of conviction or an assertion already in the readily accessible public domain. Still, I realize other authors have named folks in histories of other riots or the like, even if they were never convicted. I'm not sure I made the right choice. But I'd rather be wrong this way than the other way.

2. The hefty man who defaced the flag was a mentally ill veteran and, at least in part, angry at America for being involuntarily committed. He did speak briefly with some reporters after this incident, and it was clear he was mentally unwell. Later internal police records, such as information from his brother and subsequent institutionalization, evidences his state of mind and background. I've withheld his name because he was not of sound mind, and while he seemed to have admitted what he did, I still hesitate to name him for the reasons mentioned in the preceding note.

3. Chief Taylor later, in internal NYPD documents, denied Fleischmann's account. Taylor reported that he "suddenly heard a loud uproar from the crowd whose attention seemed to be directed to the statue of George Washington." He said he was behind the statue and "was unable to see what was taking place." But that he "immediately made his way to the location." There he "observed a prostrate figure lying on the ground in front of the statue." He "promptly" directed a "cordon of police" to surround the man and "protect him from the construction workers."

   Yet film footage shows a sustained period where the hardhats were on the pedestal, elevated above the multitude, trying to get at the hefty man. Taylor's attention could have been directed at the horde. But many cops faced the fight. Richard Fleischmann wondered why "no action was taken by police" to protect the man before he was knocked flat. The clash escalated "within clear view of the police," another attorney, Lawrence Grosberg, swore in his affidavit. Still another lawyer, Allan Sperling, also witnessed the confrontation worsening with cops nearby. He too swore cops made "no apparent effort" to interfere with the men grabbing at the hefty man. The violence that followed, Grosberg added, "occurred within full view of several police officers and patrolmen, many of whom were no further than five feet from the scene of the attack. However, no arrests were made despite the efforts of several bystanders to convince police officers." Fleischmann, who also gave a sworn statement, was one of those bystanders. He "demanded" that several "witnessing police officers" arrest the lead attacker. Said it was a felony. Yet he was "refused." Fleischmann stood there shaking his head, watching as the attacker was "permitted to escape into the crowd."

Chapter 15

1. "Legal observers" generally were law students meant to witness improper policing and offer legal advice to demonstrators.

Chapter 16

1. All three attorneys gave these accounts in affidavits. Witness-sworn statements cited in this book are technically all "affidavits," as they are all sealed by a notary and were given under the penalty of perjury. The affidavits were largely taken within a fortnight of the riot.

Chapter 19

1. This comment was later reported to the mayor's staff. The sergeant was questioned internally. The sergeant alleged that he was trying to protect the kids. A Pace employee was using a long board to break the remaining shards of glass. "The glass was hanging and it was a dangerous condition," the sergeant stated. "It was making a lot of noise," he added. "I was afraid it would attract the construction workers who were over in City Hall Park and they would return."

   He was asked about the "slaughter" comment. He said a student told him, "You must let us in. If you don't let us in, they are going to slaughter us."

   "We are not going to let you in," the sergeant said he replied. "And if you don't leave, they will slaughter you."

Chapter 21

1. Frank Deford, "In for Two Plus the Title," *Sports Illustrated*, May 18, 1970.
2. ABC Sports telecast of Game Seven, May 8, 1970. *NBA Dynasty Series: New York Knicks: The Complete History*, Warner Home Video, November 8, 2005.
3. *NBA Dynasty Series: New York Knicks: The Complete History*, Warner Home Video, November 8, 2005.
4. Harvey Araton, *When the Garden Was Eden: Clyde, the Captain, Dollar Bill, and the Glory Days of the New York Knicks* (NY: Harper Collins, 2011), chap. 9, Kindle.
5. Author interviews, Aurelio and Davidoff.
6. Dave Anderson, "When Willis Reed's 4 Points Won a Title," NYT, May 6, 1990.
7. Frank Deford, "In for Two Plus the Title," *Sports Illustrated*, May 18, 1970.
8. Jon Mooallem, "History of the High Five," ESPN, July 28, 2011.
9. ABC Sports telecast of Game Seven, May 8, 1970.
10. Leonard Sloan, "Nostalgia for Extinct Pop Culture Creates Industry," NYT, March 22, 1970. William Manchester, *The Glory and the Dream* (NY: Rosetta Books, 2013), chap. 36, Kindle.
11. Leonard Koppett, "Knicks Take First Title," NYT, May 9, 1970. Araton, *When the Garden Was Eden*, chap. 10, Kindle. "The Open Man," *Kirkus Reviews*, October 15, 1970. "Lindsay Salutes Knicks for a 'Feast of Victory," NYT, May 9, 1970.
12. Richard Nixon, *RN: The Memoirs of Richard Nixon* (NY: Simon & Schuster, 2013), chap. "1970," Kindle. David Greenberg, *Nixon's Shadow: The History of an Image* (NY: W. W. Norton, 2003), chap. 6, Kindle. H. R. Haldeman, *The Haldeman Diaries: Inside the Nixon White House* (NY: Berkley Books, 1994), 163. Evan Thomas, *Being Nixon: A Man Divided* (NY: Random House, 2015), chap. 16, Kindle.
13. Charles W. Colson, *Born Again* (Old Tappan, NJ: Chosen Books, 1976), 39. Thomas, *Being Nixon*, chap. 15, Kindle. Autor interview, Patrick J. Buchanan. Patrick J. Buchanan, *Nixon's White House Wars: The Battles*

That Made and Broke a President and Divided America Forever (NY: Crown Forum, 2017), 166.

14. This quote has been rendered somewhat differently over the years. Nixon's dialogue is based on Nixon's version of events, which he dictated on audiotape several days after the encounter.

15. "President Richard Nixon's Daily Diary May 1, 1970–May 15, 1970," box RC-5, White House Central Files: Staff Member & Office Files: Office of Presidential Papers and Archives, NL. Though it conflicts with some important books on the Nixon era, I rely on the Nixon Daily Diary as the source for Nixon's conversations into the predawn hours of May 9, 1970. Henry Kissinger, *Ending the Vietnam War: A History of America's Involvement in and Extradition from the Vietnam War* (NY: Simon & Schuster, 2003), 170. William Safire, *Before the Fall* (NY: Tower Publications, 1975), 209–12. Nancy Dickerson, *Among Those Present: A Reporter's View of Twenty-Five Years in Washington* (NY: Random House, 1976), 134. Raymond Price, *With Nixon* (New York: Viking Press, 1977), 170–74. Haldeman, *The Haldeman Diaries*, 159–64. Jerry Greene, "Nixon Woos Students but Gets in Some Zingers," DN, May 9, 1970. Jerome Cahill, "Nixon Beards Kids in Predawn Visit," DN, May 10, 1970. Robert B. Semple Jr., "Nixon, in Pre-Dawn Tour, Talks to War Protesters," NYT, May 10, 1970. "New Nixon Tapes Reveal Details of Meeting with Anti-War Activists," PBS, November 25, 2011. John A. Farrell, *Richard Nixon: The Life* (NY: Knopf Doubleday, 2017), chap. 21, Kindle. Richard Reeves, *President Nixon: Alone in the White House* (NY: Simon & Schuster, 2001), 219–22.

16. ABC, CBS, NBC, May 9, 1970. John Herbers, "Big Capital Rally Asks U.S. Pullout in Southeast Asia," NYT, May 10, 1970. Robert D. McFadden, "Nationwide College Protest Continues," NYT, May 10, 1970.

17. "Gallup Poll Finds 57 Percent Support President on Cambodian Policy," NYT, 1970. Only a plurality thought "shooting at rioting students" was "justified." Most upper-class whites said it was "unjustified." Still, considering that four unarmed students were killed, it was telling that the plurality of Americans defended the guardsmen and the majority blamed those certain they were victims—the students.

18. *The Day the '60s Died*, PBS, writers Anna Bowers, Jonathan Halperin, April 28, 2015. Haldeman, *The Haldeman Diaries*, 163–64.

Chapter 22

1. "Statement by Mayor John V. Lindsay," May 9, 1970, group 592, series VIII, folder 124, box 175, LP. William Federici, Frank Faso, Henry Lee, "Lindsay Says Police Did Not Do Their Job," DN, May 10, 1970. Cy Egan, "Mayor Calls Police Brass on the Carpet," NYP, May 9, 1970.

2. Accounts of activism and incidents in NYC from May 9 to May 20 are primarily from NYPD records, witness affidavits, and news accounts. See the Bibliographic Essay. Additional relevant news sources in this section: James Antone, "Pro-Nixon Workers Parade from Wall St. to City Hall," *Women's Wear Daily*, May 21, 1970. Homer Bigart, "Thousands Assail Lindsay in 2d Protest by Workers," NYT, May 12, 1970. Emanuel Perlmutter, "Head of Building Trades Unions Here Says Response Favors Friday's Action," NYT, May 12, 1970.

3. Prudence Brown, "Cops Keep Hard Hats from Student Rally," *Newsday*, May 13, 1970. Homer Bigart, "2 Protest Groups Meet on Wall St.," NYT, May 13, 1970. UPI, "1,000 Attack Lindsay for Liberalism," *Hartford Courant*, May 13, 1970. Author interview, James Lapham.

4. Combined: DN, NYP, NYT, ABC, NBC, CBS, May 11–12, 1970. Author interview, James Lapham. Additional relevant articles include: UPI, "1,000 Attack Lindsay for Liberalism," *Hartford Courant*, May 13, 1970. Homer Bigart, "2 Protest Groups Meet on Wall St.," NYT, May 13, 1970. AP, "2,000 Workmen March in N.Y.," *Atlanta Constitution*, May 12, 1970. Karl E. Meyer, "N.Y. Workers Demonstrate Peacefully," WP, May 12, 1970. Reuters, "Construction Workers Fill Wall St. Again," *Boston Globe*, May 12, 1970. Kenneth Gross, "Life Under a Hard Hat," *Newsday*, June 6, 1970. "Three Days That Shook the Establishment," *Business Week*, May 16, 1970.

5. Editorial, "Violence on the Right," NYT, May 9, 1970. Mail and telegrams also flooded City Hall. Some supported the hardhats and the cops. Some were aghast. One telegram came from Democratic state senate candidate George Spitz— energetic, sinewy, a budding gadfly of Gotham politics. Spitz was riled over the "shameless conduct of the construction workers." He pressed Lindsay for a "temporary halt on all commercial construction" and a "crash survey to determine" the extent to which "pre-fabrication or industrial" methods might replace the hardhats.

6. Emanuel Perlmutter, "Head of Building Trades Unions Here Says Response Favors Friday's Action," NYT, May 12, 1970. Brennan biography, Office of the White House Press Secretary, November 29, 1972, White House Press Release Unit Files or the Presidential Personnel Office Files at the Gerald R. Ford Presidential Library. Robert D. McFadden, "Peter Brennan, 78, Union Head and Nixon's Labor Chief," NYT, October 4, 1996.

7. Robert Mason, *Richard Nixon and the Quest for a New Majority* (Chapel Hill: University of North Carolina Press, 2004), 71, 248. Huston to Harlow, Dent, Nofziger, Chotiner, Haldeman, and Ehrlichman, May 13, 1970, Haldeman Files, NL.

8. WCBS-TV transcript excerpted in "The Hard Hat and the Student," *National Observer*, June 1, 1970.

9. "Postmortems," *Economist*, October 10, 1970, 54.

10. See the Bibliographic Essay.

11. Thomas Williams, "My Hard Hat Problem—and Yours," *Esquire,* October 1970.

12. "Who Owns the Stars and Stripes," *Time,* July 6, 1970.

13. NBC, May 15, 1970.

14. Of the seventy injuries recorded by the NYPD, the median age of the injured was 22; the average was 25. The ages of four of those injured were unknown.

15. Huston to Ehrlichman, Haldeman, Dent, and Colson, May 12, 1970, folder New York Construction Workers—Building and Construction Trades Council, box 89, White House Special Files: Staff Member and Office Files: Charles W. Colson, NL.

16. Richard Schwartz, "Man in Gray & Violence," NYP, May 12, 1970. Fred Cook, "Hard-Hats: The Rampaging Patriots," *The Nation,* June 15, 1970. Based on the plaintiff's records, the ACLU witnesses were interviewed by the police investigators (this writer reviewed the ACLU legal records as well).

Some larger conspiracy theories have lingered in left-leaning articles and books in the decades after. Of course, as any veteran political reporter will tell you, one side is always saying the other side's mass activism or riot is artificial and insincere. Still, though the allegations were rooted in the *New York Post* and the *Nation,* both produced plenty of good journalism in this era. There was an anonymous quote in the *Nation*'s article that the *Graphic* produced the "Rally for America" flyers, with a large American flag. Some hardhats held those flyers, though not the workmen who initially arrived at Wall Street's plaza. It's unclear if those flyers corresponded to this assemblage on Wall Street or were distributed as hardhats congregated in the plaza and used for the large picture of the flag. The *Graphic*'s office was near City Hall. Its small staff were right-wing activists. But if the *Graphic* produced the flyers, and it could have, there's no evidence those flyers served a significant role in organizing the men. Yet some hardhats might have been paid, or not docked pay, for rioting or rallying rather than working. For example, in the *Journal,* Michael Drosnin quoted one anonymous hardhat who called his fellow rioters "storm troopers" and "claimed the attack was organized by shop stewards and some contractors. He said one contractor offered his men cash bonuses to join the fray." The NYPD's sizable investigation found no evidence of it. But it's possible some were given cash to jump into the fray. Shop stewards notoriously were not happy with hippies in this era, such as on Haight Street in San Francisco. I could find nothing more than some loose talk to reporters without named attribution, which is as common as it is often wrong. But again, that doesn't mean it's wrong. I found significant errors in most press accounts of the riot, even on facts or on-the-record quotes, and thus am especially wary of ever drawing conclusions from a few anonymous quotes or anecdotes. It was also unclear if some allegations in different media came from the same source (which commonly occurs to this day—in, say, reports on the White House). Some hardhats appear to have been allowed to leave their job for hours and not lose pay during the riot. But even if they left the site for a few hours, and were not docked pay, that likely betrayed sympathy more than conspiracy. After all, construction workers are monitored by foremen, supervisors like them, men they often drink with, not developers or bigwigs in a suit. Some liberal writers have suggested the rallies themselves were synthetic—that marchers, such as on Workers' Woodstock, were paid to show up. And by implication, it's a tool to not only invalidate their protest but even invalidate their emotions. *Esquire*'s fine reporting touched on this accusation, quoting a hardhat talking about reports "which said, that all the workers who marched were on full pay." He told *Esquire*, "[Reporters/reports] told me that a few were, like shop stewards and some others [paid workers], but that most of those who marched—eighty-five to ninety percent of the men—were not paid that day." Still, the anonymous reports called for digging.

I dug for actual evidence of conspiracy and couldn't find it, including years of frustrating Freedom of Information Act back-and-forth with the FBI and the NYPD, which delayed this book and left me rushed to write it. Though the NYPD disclosures did bear fruit, via FOIA and old-fashioned reporting/research, both agencies obstructed from the outset. Once I finally saw the thousands of pages of previously confidential NYPD records from its internal investigation of the riot, I hunted for conspiracy. A reporter would love to find as much. And, dear reader, let's be candid: the surest way for an author of the first book on the Hardhat Riot to achieve media coverage, especially from the mavens of book criticism, would be to expose a right-wing conspiracy around these "seminal" events in Nixon's Silent Majority. But I couldn't find it.

Still, I ran out of time to close up every loose end, or fully dig (as I would have liked) into even the farfetched. The FBI consistently dragged its feet in response to my FOIA requests, and finally, to technically follow the law, it would release a tad here and there (though I requested full disclosure). Or it would merely give pre-released records, the oldest records, on those I inquired about in the public spotlight, such as union chiefs, again to technically comply with the law but never fulfill the full spirit of the law. There clearly is a de facto policy—even for records nearly a half-century old and not involving national security—to delay and begin with a "no." The NYPD did start from this posture as well, but the FBI should be held to a higher standard. Finally, after extended FBI foot-dragging and refusals, I acquired some new records on notables. But the documents proved not notable, like all other records I dug up and interviews I conducted, in regard to conspiracy. Nor did some new records I found on Jay Lovestone, the AFL-CIO official who was among the unionists who advised Colson (I'll return to Lovestone later). The FBI refused to acknowledge if it had any files on the *Graphic*'s publisher, Ralph Clifford, despite several appeals to multiple departments. The FBI claimed that this newspaper publisher and activist who spoke at a public rally (in an historic event) and chose to be interviewed by mainstream newspaper reporters was in fact *not* a public figure, and the FBI stuck by its boilerplate refusal throughout the appeals process, saying that any disclosure of his records, which they would not confirm existed (and may not exist), "constitute a clearly unwarranted invasion of personal privacy." As FOIA goes, once your appeals fail, your only recourse is to litigate; I lacked the time for such. Another factor: Amid evidence in the NYPD records that Clifford played no conspiratorial role, I didn't also feel like I was likely giving much up. Because of the Clifford refusal, I knew I would never receive any FBI confirmation or information, *if* it exists, on no-names such as *Graphic* editor Jeff Smith or rabble-rouser Richard Gauthier. Still, Richard Gauthier's NYPD rap sheet and the NYPD investigation give no hints of unionist ties, and he was the most visible business-suit-wearing man seen in the riot. (Certainly, I wish I had more time to further dig into Richard Gauthier, to the extent there is anything to locate, and likewise.) Writ large, however, as the NYPD records indicate, there's no evidence of actual rightist organizations directing these men. The NYPD intelligence unit knew what and whom to look for. It did document a fair bit of looking. Nonetheless, as is true of any conspiracy theory until every loose end is tied up, I'm not going to argue conspiracy is impossible. But basic logic suggests that it's almost surely not possible. The core reason: the hardhats' actions were brutal during the riot but also demonstrably sincere. The riot escalated and began spontaneously, as seen in accounts from countless witnesses and in footage. We know the riot consistently worsened over flag disputes. We know there were smaller incidents beforehand and larger rallies after. For history's sake, it's safe to say generally that this surge in blue collar activism was authentic.

In light of Watergate, though, speculation on any number of events that relate to Nixon is fair and worth checking. About a year after the riot, on May 5, 1971, a Nixon tape recorded Haldeman speaking of using hardhats to "stir up some of this Vietcong flag business as Colson's gonna do it through hard hats and Legionnaires." But it's probable any effort to co-opt hardhats was spurred by their new visibility as potential Nixon allies. In this same vein, on May 22 (after Workers' Woodstock), the memo from Steve Bull to Chuck Colson has this line: "Obviously, more of these [hardhat demonstrations] will be occurring throughout the Nation, perhaps partially as a result of your clandestine activity." But again, this is after the peak of hardhat activism. Colson's "clandestine" activity was mainly with folks such as Jesse Calhoon (who headed the Marine Engineers' Beneficial Association) and Jay Lovestone, and neither had significant ties to the NYC trade unions.

Some histories have suggested that Jay Lovestone played a conspiratorial role related to the hardhats. Even a respectable biography of Lovestone contained some unsubstantiated suggestions of some influence with the Hardhat Riot and activism. This is not only based on Lovestone's FBI files. The records of him in the Nixon Library reveal a different dynamic. On May 5, 1970, Lovestone and Colson met. The timing of this meeting has fueled some conspirators, considering it was two days before the riot. But when you read the notes and records, the influential historic event is Nixon's recent expansion of the war into Cambodia, which Lovestone cheered (Lovestone said of the Cambodia speech, according to Colson, that Nixon "was the first since Harry Truman to have real guts"). The records and communications between Colson and Lovestone have to do with communism, international affairs, and union affairs, such as later strife between auto workers and management. Lovestone was at one time a leading communist activist in the country (which gave him a big FBI file) but by the sixties he had, as they say, the zeal of the convert. He became an obsessive anti-communist. He did play a formative role in the AFL-CIO's international affairs, meant to concern trade, though it blended into Cold War politics, like so much international affairs of the era. Colson comes off in memos to Haldeman and other records, as well as in letters to Lovestone, like a typical White House staffer trying to manage the more extreme within his party's base, or activists aligned with them, in an effort to utilize that passion for his own ends. Colson demonstrably wanted to use anti-communism to get Lovestone to help them warm ties with the AFL-CIO and other unions. It's also clear that Lovestone and Colson did help smooth the ground for Nixon's unscheduled visit to the AFL-CIO the week after the riot. Collectively, the documents convey what was clear in the dynamic between AFL-CIO boss George Meany and Colson (and between Meany and Nixon): that while the hardhat activism created a "bond" with regular workmen, the White House was hoping to largely ingratiate itself with union leaders through their shared concern about communism. See Colson to Haldeman, May 5, 1970, folder Jay Lovestone—AFL-CIO [III] [4 of 4], box 73; White House Special Files: Staff Member and Office Files: Charles W. Colson, NL. Colson to Bill Timmons, May 27, 1970, folder Jay Lovestone—AFL-CIO [II] [4 of 4], box 73, White House Special Files: Staff Member and Office Files: Charles W. Colson, NL. Colson to Bud Krogh, May 28, 1970, folder Jay Lovestone—AFL-CIO [III] [4 of 4], box 73, White House Special Files: Staff Member and Office Files: Charles W. Colson, NL.

Anthony Summers's book *The Arrogance of Power* follows the typical pattern of conspiracists: it reports conjecture as facts, finds loose threads and says it's a pattern, and in the end ignores the overwhelming volume of evidence that undercuts its alleged pattern of conspiracy. It quotes Ehrlichman, long after the White House years, saying he assumed the White House had "laid on" the hardhat demonstrations. But Ehrlichman assumed many things wrongly, in and out of the White House, and no evidence supports his speculation. And the reactions of Nixon and his staff (such as Colson's "shock" that these blue-collar guys were protesting *for* them), as well as contemporaneous records, paint a scene of surprise (and plenty of records betray facts Nixon and staff wished had never come out). What else explains Nixon being near a nervous breakdown the night after the riot, or—and a few days later (once the news had spread)—Haldeman referencing the riot in his diary as giving Nixon new confidence? And, importantly, Safire, Kissinger, and others recorded the same impression, which my interview with Pat Buchanan only further reinforced.

The excellent academic Jefferson Cowie, as well as several of his research assistants, did a deep dive through this era, including a particular focus on Nixon's blue-collar strategy. Many others have too. Nothing has been found that evidenced a hardhat conspiracy (though plenty of material on other conspiracies turned up, and proved true). The pantheon of Nixon biographers has found nothing relevant either. This writer lacked the time to do a conclusive excavation of all the Nixon Library records, which I would have liked to have done. So for context, my research and reporting has been aided greatly by the shelves of biographers' and academics' work, to ensure I did not miss anything substantial. That said, I welcome future academics and reporters doing what I could not. Research and reporting are rarely a conclusive endeavor.

17. For example, white-shoe lawyers Lillian Kraemer and Mark Walker both recounted in their affidavit that they tried to get someone to guard Trinity Church but were "totally ignored" by policemen. Same with the more serious cases, such as the electrical foreman who punched the man off the Washington statue for flag desecration. Witnesses identified the foreman, who went by Richie. Four lawyers submitted affidavits affirming the account. Film footage, obtained by police, captured the entire incident, including the punch. But Richie got away with it. One witness to Richie's attack, attorney Richard Fleischmann, filed a complaint with the NYPD afterward. A detective told him that without the victim's testimony, he could not arrest Richie because he "feared a false arrest action." Fleischmann got the cops to dig more. A few visited Richie's employer. Colleagues stonewalled. Someone said Richie went on vacation to Florida. With the victim unable to be interviewed because he was "presently confided to a mental institution," the district attorney decided "prosecution was not tenable."

18. Consider attorney Howard Bushman. He saw an attack, identified the attacker, pressed cops to act. And, uniquely, he overhead the attacker's name and address after a cop read aloud the journeyman's card. In the days after the riot, amid the wave of bad press, Bushman persisted. He filed a complaint. As a result, cops visited the journeyman's Staten Island home and phoned him repeatedly. His mother slammed the phone receiver down. The journeyman got a lawyer. The attorney told the cops, "I don't know of any exploratory interview ever being helpful to clients." And this too was let go.

19. Another example of a detailed account: there was the detective who confronted a young man wearing a brown "AB" helmet. That hardhat had a "very strong resemblance" to an "AB" man photographed on Bloody Friday. The man denied the resemblance, and the cops left it at that.

20. An earlier draft of the final report "recommended that a board of impartial observers, consisting of attorneys and prominent citizens, be established" to monitor police performance at protests. The suggestion was cut from the final draft.

21. For sourcing on the NYPD investigation of the Hardhat Riot and related inquiries, such as by the ACLU, see the Bibliographic Essay.

22. An example of bias: A June 3, 1970, report on the investigation, meant for NYPD eyes only, concluded the obvious: that hardhats were the "aggressor." Yet even that determination was qualified. For example, amid the violence outside Pace, it claimed the Pace students "triggered" the workmen. Not provoked. Not incited. "Triggered," implying no agency. Frailty, thy name is ironworker? It was a risible inference on all sides. It never would have met the smell test. But it was never tested in public. The final report also downplayed the warning signs and skirmishes that preceded the riot. The report noted three warnings. Then it claimed "these messages were received" by command "well after business hours and could not be verified in any way" because offices were "closed for the day." Yet it admitted the first of those warnings came at 4:20 p.m. And then there were the warnings that morning, hours before the riot began. At 9:16: Hardhats "might cause trouble" downtown. At 10:05: "Construction workers at the Twin Towers are going to take care of the protestors on Wall Street." Yet instead of owning up to its mistakes, the NYPD ignored countervailing facts and acquitted itself. As critics expected, investigators gave fellow cops the benefit of the doubt. This was in the spring of 1970. Less than a fortnight before the riot, the *Times* had published an exposé on the graft-plagued NYPD. That exposé spurred the Knapp Commission on police corruption. The commission was made famous after Al Pacino played the courageous detective at the center of the drama, Frank Serpico. The 1st Precinct, one of the precincts most enmeshed in the riot, was so corrupt that several years later the NYPD transferred out most of its 110 cops. None of that directly involved the Hardhat Riot. But it was the context of the era—a police force overworked, understaffed, often underappreciated, and terribly ensnared by a decade of skyrocketing crime rates, but also one inundated with graft, as well as an ethos to protect its own, even when their offenses sullied the NYPD's reputation.

23. CBS, May 11, 1970.

24. "The Sudden Rising of the Hardhats," *Time*, May 25, 1970.

25. Roger Goodman, dir., *The Century: America's Time*, ABC, April 12, 1999.

26. "The Hard Hat and the Student," *National Observer*, June 1, 1970. David Holmstrom, "Worker Demonstrations Turn to Violent Tactics," *Christian Science Monitor*, May 16, 1970. "The Sudden Rising of the Hardhats," *Time*, May 25, 1970. Richard Rogin, "Joe Kelly Has Reached His Boiling Point: Why the Construction Workers Holler USA All the Way!" *NYT Magazine*, June 28, 1970.

Chapter 23

1. Homer Bigart, "Huge City Hall Rally Backs Nixon's Indochina Policies," NYT, May 21, 1970. Owen Fitzgerald, Joseph Modzelewski, "Thousands Parade in Peace to Support War," DN, May 21, 1970.

2. Homer Bigart, "Huge City Hall Rally Backs Nixon's Indochina Policies," NYT, May 21, 1970.

3. Richard Dougherty, "150,000 Flag-Waving 'Hardhats' Stage Patriotism Rally in N.Y.," LAT, May 21, 1970. UPI, "100,000 Workers in N.Y. Rally," *Boston Globe*, May 21, 1970. Patrick Brasley, "100,000 Hard Hats March to Back Nixon," *Newsday*, May 21, 1970. Francis Clines, "For the Flag and for Country, They March," NYT, May 21, 1970. "Showing the Flag," *Economist*, May 30, 1970, 40.

4. Richard Harwood, "Flag's Defenders: Hard Hats March for a Way of Life," WP, May 31, 1970.

5. Patrick Brasley, "100,000 Hard Hats March to Back Nixon," *Newsday*, May 21, 1970. Francis Clines, "For the Flag and for Country, They March," NYT, May 21, 1970.

6. Karl Meyer, "N.Y. Rally of 100,000 Backs War," WP, May 21, 1970. Chauncey Howell, "Protest," *Women's Wear Daily*, May 21, 1970. Joseph Mitchell, "The Mohawks in High Steel," *New Yorker*, September 9, 1949. Charlie Leduff, "A Mohawk Trail to the Skyline," NYT, March 16, 2001.

7. CBS, NBC, ABC, May 20, 1970. Homer Bigart, "Huge City Hall Rally Backs Nixon's Indochina Policies," NYT, May 21, 1970. Owen Fitzgerald, Joseph Modzelewski, "Thousands Parade in Peace to Support War," DN, May 21, 1970. Joseph Zullo, "Workers Rap Lindsay, Hail Nixon Policies," CT, May 21, 1970. "Construction Unions Stage Prowar Rally in Lower New York," WSJ, May 21, 1970. Karl Meyer, "N.Y. Rally of 100,000 Backs War," WP, May 21, 1970. Sandor Polster, "Pro-War Rally Draws Huge Crowd," NYP, May 20, 1970. Thomas Williams, "My Hard Hat Problem—and Yours," *Esquire,* October 1970. Richard Dougherty, "150,000 Flag-Waving 'Hardhats' Stage Patriotism Rally in N.Y.," LAT, May 21, 1970. "Showing the Flag," *Economist*, May 30, 1970, 40. "Workers' Woodstock," *Time*, June 1, 1970.

8. Homer Bigart, "Huge City Hall Rally Backs Nixon's Indochina Policies," NYT, May 21, 1970.

9. Richard Rogin, "Joe Kelly Has Reached His Boiling Point: Why the Construction Workers Holler USA All the Way!" *NYT Magazine*, June 28, 1970. Kenneth Gross, "Life Under a Hard Hat," *Newsday*, June 6, 1970. Patrick Brasley, "100,000 Hard Hats March to Back Nixon," *Newsday*, May 21, 1970.

Chapter 24

1. Buchanan to Nixon, "Media Memorandum for the President," May 21, 1970, folder [CF] FG 6-11-1/Haldeman, H. R. 1/20/69-8/31/70 [1969–1970],

box 15, White House Special Files: White House Subject Files: Confidential Files, NL.

2. "President Richard Nixon's Daily Diary May 16, 1970–May 31, 1970," box RC-5, White House Central Files: Staff Member and Office Files: Office of Presidential Papers and Archives, NL. H. R. Haldeman, *The Haldeman Diaries, Inside the Nixon White House* (NY: Berkley Books, 1994), 168.

3. Charles Colson, "The Silent Majority: Support for the President," in *Richard M. Nixon: Politician, President, Administrator*, ed. Leon Friedman, William Levantrosser (Westport, CT: Greenwood Press, 1991), 276.

Nixon's schedule only shows a meeting with Colson on May 21, 1970, the day after Workers' Woodstock, from 6:29 to 6:36 p.m., notably the first meeting after Nixon completed a phone call with Peter Brennan and another with longshoremen's union boss Thomas Gleason. The timing hints that Colson was involved in urging the calls. And it's possible Colson had an undocumented visit with Nixon the day before, as he recalled. Absent contradictory evidence, I deferred to Colson's recollection.

4. Bull to Colson, May 22, 1970, folder Hard Hats—Building and Construction Trades [2 of 2], box 65, White House Special Files: Staff Member and Office Files: Charles W. Colson, NL.

Aide Steve Bull also wrote in this memo after Workers' Woodstock: "More of these will be occurring throughout the nation, perhaps partially as a result of your clandestine activity." This is perhaps the most suggestive note of conspiracy in all Nixon records. Yet the tone of the entire memo is one of surprise ("I have been fascinated by the hard hat demonstrations"). I know of no evidence, and nothing is noted in the shelves of respected books on the Nixon era, that Bull's use of "clandestine activity" refers to anything besides Colson's periodic and private meetings with a few Washington labor leaders, such as Jesse Calhoon (of the marine engineers' union) and Jay Lovestone (an AFL-CIO official who stewarded its foreign affairs—international trade, anticommunism). These meetings reflected Colson's effort to keep a toe in the labor movement. He would not be charged with overseeing Nixon's blue-collar strategy for several more months. Neither Calhoon or Lovestone had any substantial influence with the NYC trade unions, and there's no evidence of them, or any Nixon staff, playing a role in organizing Workers' Woodstock, which there is for Honor America Day, as soon noted in the book. Considering the paper trail and audiotapes on all manner of criminal activity in the White House, I read the absence of evidence for conspiracy as exculpatory, a matter I'll return to later regarding hardhat conspiracy theories writ large.

5. Charles Colson, "The Silent Majority: Support for the President," in *Richard M. Nixon: Politician, President, Administrator*, ed. Leon Friedman and William Levantrosser (Westport, CT: Greenwood Press, 1991), 276. *Daniel Patrick Moynihan: A Portrait in Letters of an American Visionary*, ed. Steven R. Weisman (NY: Public Affairs, 2010), 315. Henry Kissinger, *White House Years*

(Boston: Little, Brown and Company, 1979), 512. William Safire, *Before the Fall* (NY: Tower Publications, 1975), 585.

6. Author interview, Buchanan.

7. Author interview, Buchanan. "Honor America Day—Take II," *Time* reporting via telex, July 2, 1970, Arthur White Collection, folder 2, box 20, Odum Library, Valdosta State University, Georgia. Nancy Gibbs, Michael Duffy, *The Preacher and the Presidents: Billy Graham in the White House* (NY: Hachette, 2007), 187–88. Pat Buchanan, *Nixon's White House Wars: The Battles That Made and Broke a President and Divided America Forever* (NY: Crown Forum, 2017), 47–49. For the anecdote on Nixon seeing the construction crane photo in the *Times*, see Michael Balzano, *Building a New Majority* (Bloomington, IN: iUniverse, 2016), chap. 1, Kindle.

8. Don Oberdorfer, "Unions Give Nixon a Hard Hat as Sign of Cambodia Support," *Boston Globe*, May 27, 1970.

9. Author interview, George Daly. (The first part of the Donovan quote—"For this country, I'd send him back again"—is from Daly.) Stuart Loory, "Nixon Gets Hard Hat as Union Gift," LAT, May 27, 1970. Richard Nixon, *RN: The Memoirs of Richard Nixon* (NY: Simon & Schuster, 2013), 1970, Kindle. Michael Hanrahan, "Hard Hats to Be Nixon's Guests," DN, May 26, 1970. Paul Healy, "Pro-War N.Y. Union Leaders Give the President a Hard Hat," DN, May 27, 1970. Aldo Beckman, "Nixon Thanks Hardhat Workers for Support on His Viet Policy," CT, May 27, 1970. Don Oberdorfer, "Nixon Meets 'Hard Hat' Supporters," WP, May 27, 1970.

Chapter 25

1. "Hard Hat Protests Stir Minor Violence," *Arizona Republic*, May 31, 1970. "Buffalo Workers Protest," NYT, May 21, 1970. "Some Violence at March Backing War," *St. Louis Post-Dispatch*, June 8, 1970. John Hanrahan, "Hard-Hat Workers Stage Flag March," WP, June 16, 1970. "Who Owns the Stars and Stripes," *Time*, July 6, 1970.

2. "Honor America Day—Take II," *Time* reporting via telex, July 2, 1970, Arthur White Collection, folder 2, box 20, Odum Library, Valdosta State University, Georgia. Martin Gansberg, "Lindsay Leads City in Marking Honor America Day," NYT, July 5, 1970. "Celebration Is Varied over U.S.," WP, July 5, 1970. John MacLean, "400,000 in Capital Join in Honor America Day," CT, July 5, 1970.

3. "Gathering in Praise of America," *Time*, July 13, 1970. Joseph Albright, Myron Waldman, "Middle America's Day a Diary of Differences," *Newsday*, July 6, 1970.

4. "Honor America Day—Saturday Updating—Take I–II," *Time* reporting via telex, July 4, 1970, Arthur White Collection, folder 2, box 20, Odum Library, Valdosta State University, Georgia. William Greider and John Hanrahan,

"Thousand Rally Here, Vow Faith in America," WP, July 5, 1970. Martin Flusser Jr., "Rally Round Trip: Anticipation to Anger," *Newsday,* July 6, 1970. Bob Hope and varied performers, *Proudly They Came to Honor America—Live 1970,* recorded July 4, 1970, issued on MP3 July 20, 2013. Paul W. Valentine, "Dissidents Clash with Police," WP, July 5, 1970. Rudy Abramson, Murray Seeger, "America Honored in Capital with Speech, Song, Symbol," LAT, July 5, 1970.

5. Nancy Gibbs, Michael Duffy, *The Preacher and the Presidents: Billy Graham in the White House* (NY: Hachette, 2007), 188.

6. "Who Owns the Stars and Stripes," *Time,* July 6, 1970. "Honor America Day— Take I," *Time* reporting via telex, July 2, 1970, Arthur White Collection, folder 2, box 20, Odum Library archives, Valdosta State University, Georgia. Garry Wills, *Nixon Agonistes: The Crisis of the Self-Made Man* (NY: Open Road Media, 2017), chap. 2, Kindle. William Greider and John Hanrahan, "Thousand Rally Here, Vow Faith in America," WP, July 5, 1970. Bruce Lambert Jr., "Extremes Come Full Circle at Rally," *Newsday,* July 6, 1970. "Gathering in Praise of America," *Time,* July 13, 1970.

7. "Honor America Day—Saturday Updating—Take I," *Time* reporting via telex, July 4, 1970, Arthur White Collection, folder 2, box 20, Odum Library, Valdosta State University, Georgia. "Gathering in Praise of America," *Time,* July 13, 1970. Joseph Albright, Myron Waldman, "Middle America's Day a Diary of Differences," *Newsday,* July 6, 1970. Rudy Abramson, Murray Seeger, "America Honored in Capital with Speech, Song, Symbol," LAT, July 5, 1970. David Boldt, Richard Cohen, "Silent Majority Watches Protesters in Quiet Disbelief," WP, July 5, 1970. Workforce statistics from David Paul Kuhn, *The Neglected Voter: White Men and the Democratic Dilemma* (NY: Palgrave Macmillan, 2007), 35. "The 20th Century Transformation of U.S. Agriculture and Farm Policy," United States Department of Agriculture (2005), 2. AP, "Bishop Sheen, 74, Retires," NYP, October 15, 1969.

8. "Honor America Day—Saturday Updating—Take I," *Time* reporting via telex, July 4, 1970, Arthur White Collection, folder 2, box 20, Odum Library, Valdosta State University, Georgia. "Gathering in Praise of America," *Time,* July 13, 1970.

9. Rudy Abramson, Murray Seeger, "America Honored in Capital with Speech, Song, Symbol," LAT, July 5, 1970.

10. "Honor America Day—Saturday Updating—Take I," *Time* reporting via telex, July 4, 1970, Arthur White Collection, folder 2, box 20, Odum Library, Valdosta State University, Georgia. "1970 Census of Population: Population and Housing Characteristics for the United States," U.S. Department of Commerce, 1972.

11. James Bawden, "Scant Coverage for Middle America's July 4 Celebration," *Globe and Mail,* July 5, 1970.

12. Jack Rosenthal, "Long-Hairs Clash with Crew-Cuts at Capital Rally," NYT, July 5, 1970.

13. "Honor America Day—Saturday Updating—Take VI–VII," *Time* reporting via telex, July 4, 1970, Arthur White Collection, folder 2, box 20, Odum Library, Valdosta State University, Georgia. William Greider and John Hanrahan, "Thousand Rally Here, Vow Faith in America," WP, July 5, 1970. Martin Flusser Jr., "Rally Round Trip: Anticipation to Anger," *Newsday,* July 6, 1970. Joseph Albright, Myron Waldman, "Middle America's Day: A Diary of Differences," *Newsday*, July 6, 1970. John MacLean, "400,000 in Capital Join in Honor America Day," CT, July 5, 1970.

On Archbishop Sheen and Vietnam, one example is "Sheen Links Racial Peace with Call to End the Viet War," *National Catholic Reporter*, August 9, 1967.

14. William Greider and John Hanrahan, "Thousand Rally Here, Vow Faith in America," WP, July 5, 1970. Martin Flusser Jr., "Rally Round Trip: Anticipation to Anger," *Newsday,* July 6, 1970. Leslie Hanscom, "The Straight People Stand Tall," *Newsday,* July 6, 1970. Bob Hope and varied performers, *Proudly They Came to Honor America—Live* 1970, recorded July 4, 1970, released as MP3 July 20, 2013. John MacLean, "400,000 in Capital Join in Honor America Day," CT, July 5, 1970.

Chapter 26

1. Kuhn: University of Michigan American National Election Studies (ANES) datasets 1948, 1952, 1956, and cumulative ANES dataset. William Safire, *Before the Fall* (NY: Tower Publications, 1975), 579. In 1952, 56 percent of whites with no education beyond high school voted for Ike (8 percentage points better than the GOP's performance in 1948).

2. Evan Thomas, *Being Nixon: A Man Divided* (NY: Random House, 2015), chap. 1, Kindle. Rick Perlstein, *Nixonland: The Rise of a President and the Fracturing of America* (NY: Scribner, 2008), 22–23.

3. Irwin F. Gellman, *The Contender: Richard Nixon: The Congress Years, 1946–1952* (New Haven, CT: Yale University Press, 2017), chaps. 1, 3, Kindle. Stephen Ambrose, *Nixon: The Triumph of a Politician, 1962–1972* (NY: Simon and Schuster, 1989), 122, 125–26. David Greenberg, *Nixon's Shadow: The History of an Image* (NY: W. W. Norton, 2003), chap. 1, Kindle.

4. "Nixon's Checkers Speech," PBS, September 23, 1952, https://www.pbs.org/wgbh/americanexperience/features/eisenhower-checkers. John A. Farrell, *Richard Nixon: The Life* (NY: Knopf Doubleday, 2017), chap. 10, Kindle. Perlstein, *Nixonland*, 41.

5. L. Clayton Dubois, "The First Family of Conservatism," NYT, August 9, 1970. "Jim Buckley for Senate, 1970," YouTube video, 1:56, posted by 8mmguy, December 27, 2011, https://www.youtube.com/watch?v=z5nsd47RyKo.

6. John Cummings, "Buckley Cheered in City," *Newsday,* September 17, 1970.

7. Gay Talese, *The Bridge: The Building of the Verrazano-Narrows Bridge* (NY: Bloomsbury, 1964), chap. 2, Kindle.

8. Diana Lurie, "Underneath the Hard Hats: A Political Symposium," *NY Magazine*, November 2, 1970. "The Blue Collar Worker's Lowdown Blues," *Time*, November 9, 1970.

9. Jerome Rosow, "The Problem of the Blue Collar Worker," US Department of Labor, April 16, 1970.

10. Jefferson Cowie, *Stayin' Alive: The 1970s and the Last Days of the Working Class* (NY: New Press, 2010), 184.

11. Tom Wells, *The War Within: America's Battle over Vietnam* (Berkeley: University of California Press, 1994), 409. William Safire, *Before the Fall* (NY: Tower Publications, 1975), 678.

12. "Remarks to the AFL-CIO Ninth Constitutional Convention in Bal Harbour, Florida," November 19, 1971, University of California American Presidency Project.

13. Editorial, "Blue-Collar Alienation," WSJ, July 17, 1970.

14. Buchanan to Nixon, August 24, 1970, "Memorandum for the President," folder 30, box 48, Contested Materials Collection, NL.

15. H. R. Haldeman, *The Haldeman Diaries, Inside the Nixon White House* (NY: Berkley Books, 1994), 191. Bruce J. Schulman, *The Seventies: The Great Shift in American Culture, Society and Politics* (Cambridge, MA: Da Capo Press, 2001), 38. Ambrose, *Nixon*, 374. Richard Reeves, *President Nixon: Alone in the White House* (NY: Touchstone, 2001), 245.

16. "Dinner Date on Labor Day," *National Journal*, January 30, 1971. Edmund F. Wehrle, *Between a River and a Mountain: The AFL-CIO and the Vietnam War* (Ann Arbor: University of Michigan Press, 2006), 162–63. Jefferson Cowie, "Nixon's Class Struggle: Romancing the New-Right Worker, 1969–1973," *Labor History* 43, no. 3 (Summer 2002).

17. Archie Robinson, *George Meany and His Times* (NY: Simon and Schuster, 1981), 279.

18. Safire, *Before the Fall*, 585.

19. Colson to Chapin, February 25, 1971, "Peter Brennan," folder "Hard Hats—Buildings and Construction Trades" [1 of 2], box 65, White House Special Files: Staff Member and Office Files: Charles W. Colson, NL. Colson to Nixon, July 2, 1971, "Meeting with Peter Brennan," NL, https://www.nixonlibrary. gov/sites/default/files/virtuallibrary/documents/jun09/070271_Colson_ President.pdf. May 5, 1971, tape also available at NL or see partial transcript here: "Excerpts from White House Tape of a Nixon-Haldeman Talk in May 1971," NYT, September 24, 1981. For these examples of Nixon's bigotry, see George Lardner Jr. and Michael Dobbs, "New Tapes Reveal Depth of Nixon's Anti-Semitism," WP, October 6, 1999. James Warren, "Nixon Looked Out for Ambitious Rumsfeld, Tape Reveals," CT, January 7, 2001. Colson to

Haldeman, May 21, 1971, "Political Strategy," folder 41, box 46, Contested Materials Collection, NL.

Nixon and his staff could mistake his hardhat support for a blank check. In the years after the Hardhat Riot, Nixon sometimes spoke of workmen as his muscle, as did some top advisors. On April 19, 1971, during a conversation between Nixon, Colson, and Haldeman in the Oval Office, Haldeman discussed how "great" it would be if hardhats set upon DC antiwar demonstrators and "bust 'em up" (see: Partial transcript of conversation between Nixon, Colson, and Haldeman, April 19, 1971, Conversation No. 482–27, NL). Nixon and his staff, like the media, frequently misconstrued hardhats' frustration with the antiwar movement as blind support for the war. Not long after that April conversation, one year after Kent State—amid the media and activists marking the anniversary—Nixon was annoyed at the sight of activists waving enemy flags in Washington. "We can't have that flag flyin' around here!" Nixon said. "That's a lovely thing to get into a fight about." Nixon ranted on, "Get the hardhats, or somebody." "Well," Colson said, "the hardhats turned out up on Pennsylvania Avenue en masse yesterday." "Yeah, anyone who would just, up and bust the bastards," Nixon said. Afterward, Nixon asked his secretary her opinion of the peaceniks. Nixon was prone to rant and careen between topics, from matters of state to his bigotry. He was Frank Nixon's son, after all, in virtue and in vice. The next day, May 5, Nixon continued to steam over antiwar activists carrying the Vietcong flag. Haldeman told Nixon they were "gonna stir up some of this Vietcong flag business as Colson's gonna do it through hard hats and Legionnaires." Nixon's staff regularly ignored the president's orders, concluding he sometimes didn't mean what he said. Nixon complained about it. But the dynamic endured (and he would not be the last president for whom this was the case, most visibly with Donald Trump).

On Richard Nixon's bigotry and his other demons: After Watergate, as the Nixon tapes gradually emerged, Nixon's ugly side took America aback, including the extensive profanity from a president. The tapes betrayed consistent paranoia and oversimplification (considering he was well read), as well as regular antisemitism ("most Jews are disloyal," to cite one example) and racism against blacks (most Africans are "basically just out of the trees," to cite another example of prejudice). Was Nixon excessively bigoted for the era? There's no way to empirically test such things. He was bigoted, and to a degree many powerful men were not by this period. Considering Nixon's good and bad civil rights record, overall it leaned significantly more strongly to the good. And Henry Kissinger, his guru on foreign affairs (Nixon's true passion), was Jewish, after all. In this way, Nixon was the opposite of Barry Goldwater. Goldwater was a member of the NAACP and hired black staff. But he also voted against the Civil Rights Act, which Nixon supported, among other hallmark legislation Nixon backed that aided blacks. Goldwater called the act federal encroachment. But Mr. Conservative, as Goldwater was called, had voted to effectively allow for institutional racism. The private Nixon was darker than the public man, though Nixon, as Watergate would prove, would let that darkness warp his entire presidency, in the end.

20. Author interview, Michael Balzano. Michael Balzano, *Building a New Majority* (Bloomington: iUniverse, 2016), chaps. 3, 11, Kindle.
21. Colson to Haldeman, October 26, 1970, "Memorandum for the President," folder Broder Articles [3 of 3], box 40, White House Subject Files: Staff Member and Office Files: Charles W. Colson, NL.
22. Safire, *Before the Fall*, 586. (It was Safire who summarized Charls Walker's outlook as "blaze away.") Jefferson Cowie, "Nixon's Class Struggle: Romancing the New-Right Worker, 1969–1973," *Labor History* 43, no. 3 (Summer 2002).
23. Nixon to Haldeman, December 4, 1970, folder 44, box 10, Contested Materials Collection, NL. Robert Mason, *Richard Nixon and the Quest for a New Majority* (Chapel Hill: University of North Carolina Press, 2004), 135. Safire, *Before the Fall*, 586. Patrick J. Buchanan, *Nixon's White House Wars: The Battles That Made and Broke a President and Divided America Forever* (NY: Crown Forum, 2017), 148–49. Raymond Price, *With Nixon* (New York: Viking Press, 1977), 120–23.

There are many more anecdotes exemplifying Nixon's blue-collar sensibility and strategy. A typical example came in September 1971, Pat Buchanan wrote a memo to Nixon about an essay he read in *Harper's*. The author was Michael Novak, a Catholic antiwar academic. "Growing up in America has been an assault upon my sense of worthiness," Novak wrote. "I am born of PIGS—those Polish, Italian, Greeks, and Slavs, those non-English-speaking immigrants numbered so heavily among the workingmen of this nation . . . —and thus privy to neither power nor status nor intellectual voice." Nixon underlined the last line of Buchanan's memo on the article: "Our political types, working the Chicano precincts and the ghettoes, and Navajo reservations for Republican converts, would do well to focus their attention upon the Holy Name Society, the Women's Sodality, and the Polish-American Union." "I totally agree," Nixon scribbled. "Let's see what we can do to aim some of our domestic programs and our scheduling toward this group."

Chapter 27

1. Author interview, Dick Aurelio.
2. Fred Cook, "Hard-Hats: The Rampaging Patriots," *The Nation*, June 15, 1970. Joe Flaherty, "Requiem for the Payday Patriots," *Village Voice,* May 21, 1970. Richard Harwood, "Flag's Defenders: Hard Hats March for a Way of Life," WP, May 31, 1970. Herman Miller, "Why Help the Blue-Collar Worker?" cartoon, WP, August 16, 1970. Gilbert Sorrentino, "No Radical Chic in Brooklyn," NYT, January 16, 1971. "New York Rightwing Attacks Bring Outraged Reactions," *The Militant*, Friday, June 5, 1970. Marc Linder, *Wars of*

Attrition: Vietnam, the Business Roundtable, and the Decline of Construction Unions (Iowa City: University of Iowa Press, 2000), 204 (its *Daily World* citations: "Goon Squads and Cops," *Daily World*, May 12, 1970. "Business Students in Wall St. Peace Rally," *Daily World*, May 13, 1970). Russell Baker, "Passions in Search of an Understanding," NYT, May 17, 1970. Conrad (LAT cartoonist), NYT, May 24, 1970. Editorial, "Hard Hats and Broken Heads," NYP, May 9, 1970. Street Scenes, 1970. (1970; United States: New York Cinetracts Collective, Director: Martin Scorsese) Documentary. *Scanlan's Monthly,* August 1970.

The next month (September 1970), *Scanlan's* caricatured hardhats in an image as fat, bug-eyed, and demonic. In this issue, *Scanlan's* also accurately reported what was no secret: that of the nearly two dozen union chiefs who attended the White House meeting the preceding May, several of the lesser known labor leaders were corrupt, and a few were associated with the mafia (this was 1970, unions, and New York City). But *Scanlan's* didn't stop at that. It called the meeting between Nixon and all the union leaders "the most extraordinary bunch of bums, gougers, and defrauders of the poor ever to gather under one roof." Hyperbole aside, several of these guys were anything but Boy Scouts. One of those at the White House meeting was Sidney Glasser of the glaziers' union. He was on the Executive Committee of the Building and Trades Council. Little more than a month before the White House meeting, on April 17, 1970, Glasser was convicted in the Southern District of New York of conspiracy, as well as two other counts that were later reversed. See *United States of America, Appellee, v. Sidney Glasser, Appellant*, 443 F.2d 994 (2d Cir. 1971). To exemplify what was long publicly known, as *Newsday* reported on March 8, 1969, Glasser was one of three glaziers union leaders who were indicted for a "racket in which businessmen who failed to deal with 'approved' glass firms found their display windows ruined by acid." Another example is Biagio Lanza, who was also on the Executive Committee and was with the plasterers union. To continue with the *Newsday* example, the newspaper produced on March 1, 1969, a large feature on the Genovese crime family. It reported Lanza's prior arrests, including for bookmaking, when he was the plasterers union business manager. *Newsday* also termed Lanza a "family soldier" tied to the Genovese clan. It is notable that officials with Biagio's and Glasser's records were allowed into the meeting, but so go the standards of the era, as well as poor staff advance work. I don't get into these matters in the book because, as much as readers would enjoy mafia drama within political drama, and especially Nixon's world, there's no evidence (and I dug within my time constraints) that the unionists who were corrupted by 1970 had any substantial connection to the Hardhat Riot or activism in May 1970, or bonds with the Nixon White House afterward. If anything, it exemplifies how unprepared both sides (NYC hardhat chiefs and Nixon's White House) were for this new dynamic—NYC tradesmen entering the national spotlight and to boot, opposing the rising Democratic base (the New Left).

3. Stuart Auerbac, "Nixon Called 'Authoritarian,'" WP, June 19, 1970. David Holmstrom, "Worker Demonstrations Turn to Violent Tactics," *Christian Science Monitor*, May 16, 1970.

4. Charles A. Reich, *The Greening of America* (NY: Random House, 1970), 310. Charles A. Reich, "The Greening of America," *New Yorker*, September 18, 1970. Andrew Levison, "The Blue-Collar Majority: Or, Shattering the 'Hard Hat' Myths," WP, September 29, 1974.

5. J. Hoberman, "Off the Hippies: 'Joe' and the Chaotic Summer of '70," NYT, July 30, 2000. "Jonah in a Hard Hat," *Time*, July 27, 1970.

6. Editorial, "The President's Allies," NYT, May 28, 1970.

7. Editorial, "No Time for Ambiguity," WSJ, May 28, 1970.

8. "Three Days That Shook the Establishment," *Business Week,* May 16, 1970, 24.

9. Kuhn: Harris 2037, August 1970. For July polling: *The Harris Survey Yearbook of Public Opinion 1970* (NY: Louis Harris and Associates, 1971), 278, 279. I especially detail these findings because this book centers on the riot and activism that followed, and like other significant public polling cited in this book, there have been many histories of the era, some by major publishers, who have misreported the public's view of the hardhat-student divide, and the riot itself.

To the data: In August, Harris asked Americans merely to choose sides in the divide between hardhats and campus activists. "Do you sympathize more with student demonstrators or hard-hat construction workers?" Whites sided with hardhats 51 to 18 percent. Blacks sided with hardhats 38 to 33 percent. White Humphrey voters sided with the hardhats 48 to 21 percent. White Nixon voters sided with the hardhats 58 to 7 percent. In fact, among whites, "white Southerners who oppose school integration" garnered more sympathy (29 percent) than "student demonstrators" (18 percent)—on integration, whites sympathized with the Supreme Court over "white Southerners" 48 to 29 percent.

In July 1970, Harris phrased the question two ways. Question 1: "Recently in New York City, construction workers who support the Vietnam War beat up students who were demonstrating against the war. Who did you sympathize more with, the construction workers or the students?" The overall public favored hardhats 40 to 24 percent; whites favored hardhats 45 to 22 percent. Now, with violence mentioned in the question, a plurality of blacks sympathized more with the students. The July poll, what we'll call Question 2, also asked the "justified" violence question, though it was leading: "Do you feel the construction workers were justified in beating up the students because they didn't show enough respect for the flag, or do you think no physical violence by one group against another can be justified?" With this phrasing, a slim majority of the public, including most union members, said the hardhats' violence was *not* justified. This phrasing took the matter outside the public view of the antiwar movement and instead framed Bloody Friday as a matter of whether it is okay to attack someone for not showing respect for the American flag, while avoiding the substantial conflict behind the symbol. I read this later question as a flawed but still telling gauge that Americans did not approve of the violence itself, because it was isolated from the hardhat-versus-student-activist dynamic by not asking about sympathies. In regard to the riot itself, Question 1 seems to be the most accurate gauge (though still modestly biased against the hardhats, as it wrongly describes them as all pro-war). When it comes to sympathies in the larger cultural polarization—the hardhat-activist divide—the August poll seems most accurate. It does not limit the question to violence, the riot, or describe hardhats as pro-war. Instead, after sustained activism on both sides, the August question captures the big picture societal divide.

10. Kuhn: Harris 2037, August 1970. Again, the question: "Do you sympathize more with student demonstrators or hard-hat construction workers?" First, on the employment divide. Whites with white-collar jobs favored hardhats 47 to 25 percent, but blue-collar whites in labor jobs favored hardhats 58 to 13 percent. (White collars were whites who identified themselves as professionals, technical workers, managers, and proprietors; blue collars were foremen, skilled laborers, and non-skilled laborers.) Whites who were working-class to lower-middle-class were the most supportive of the hardhats. Favoring hardhats over student activists: white household income under $5,000, 48 to 15 percent; white households $5,000 to $9,999, 60 to 14 percent; white households $10,000 to $14,999, 52 to 18 percent; and a narrow plurality of wealthier whites appear to have favored hardhats. Other margins on groups sympathizing more with hardhats: whites from union households, 59 to 17 percent; non-union white households, 48 to 20 percent. Whites with no more than a high school education, 56 to 13 percent; whites with some secondary education but *not* college graduates, 49 to 27 percent; for white college graduates, the margin was too close and sample size too small to be sure (based on p-value, for the statistically inclined), but it trended lower in support for hardhats than less educated whites. Hence, I highlight the subsequent margin, which is the statistically significant education indicator in this poll: whites with at least some post-high-school education favored hardhats 43 to 28 percent (thus by a margin of 15 percentage points, compared to the 43-point margin of whites with a high school education or less); whites with no more than a high school education but age 35 or under, 52 to 23 percent; whites age 35 or under with at least some secondary education, 32 to 44 percent (meaning, they favored students). By "blue-collar white Democrats sided with hardhats by about a six-to-one ratio," I'm referring to whites with no more than a high school education who identified as Democrats in the poll and sided with hardhats 59 to 9 percent, while Democrats with at least some secondary education split evenly between students and hardhats (about one-third for each)—and Republicans did not have this class gap, with both education stratums siding with hardhats at roughly the same margin as blue-collar

Democrats. When a question phrased the polarization as "pro-war protestors" versus "antiwar," the class gap sustained though—perhaps because of the term "pro-war"—the margins were narrower. A narrow plurality of blacks preferred the antiwar side, in this question, though a narrow plurality of blacks had sided with hardhats in the hardhat-student schema.

11. "Report of the President's Commission on Campus Unrest," President's Commission on Campus Unrest, Washington, DC (New York: Commerce Clearing House, 1970), 18 (by the end of May 1970, it reported, "Nearly one-third of" colleges "had experienced some kind of protest activity," hence two-thirds did not). *The Harris Survey Yearbook of Public Opinion 1970* (NY: Louis Harris and Associates, 1971), 286, 313, 317 (for collegians "overthrowing" system, share "far left," and being "more active," respectively). Seymour M. Lipset, "Polls and Protests," *Foreign Affairs*, April 1971 (campus views and "pulling out now"). Lydia Saad, "Gallup Vault: Hawks vs. Doves on Vietnam," Gallup, May 24, 2016. Lydia Saad, "Gallup Vault: 1969 College Students' Resistance to Vietnam," Gallup, March 16, 2018. "Americans' Preferred Plan for Vietnam," Roper Center (chart on Gallup 1970 data), https://ropercenter. cornell.edu/topics-glance/vietnam-war. *The Gallup Poll: 1959–1971*, vol. 3 (Princeton, NJ: Gallup Poll), 2250–53 (more on withdrawal plans). Kuhn: GSS, 1973 (5 percent said they had ever taken part in an antiwar demonstration).

By a two-to-one ratio (52 to 25 percent), one poll found that Americans believed the antiwar demonstrations *hurt* the prospects of ending the war, rather than helped. A 1969 poll found that 94 percent of Americans agreed they would "in general" like "college administrators [to] take a stronger stand on student disorders." See "Going too Far: The American Public's Attitudes Toward Protest Movements," Roper Center (views of antiwar movement, including 52 percent finding that its protests "hurt" chance at peace), https:// ropercenter.cornell.edu/going-too-far-american-publics-attitudes-toward-protest-movements. David Paul Kuhn, *The Neglected Voter: White Men and the Democratic Dilemma* (NY: Palgrave Macmillan, 2007), 62 (94 percent poll).

In three 1970 polls, including May, adults under age 30 remained divided on whether the pace of the Vietnam withdrawal was "too slow" or "about right" (*The Harris Survey Yearbook of Public Opinion 1970*, 110). And while most campuses actually remained peaceful, surveys indicate that the majority of students might have still seen protests in person (perhaps because of activism on large state campuses). Collegians also did tilt leftward more than the typical young adult. But the historic activism and violence, following Cambodia and Kent State, tempered that impulse. The share of students identifying as "middle of the road" or conservative was a minority of collegians in May; come autumn 1970, it was a slim majority. In late May 1970, weeks after Cambodia and Kent State, Gallup asked about the "most important problem facing" America today. The plurality chose "campus unrest" (27 percent), followed by the war itself (22 percent). By comparison, roughly half as many chose second-tier issues, whether "racial strife" or the "high cost of living." Meanwhile, eight in ten adults disagreed with college students "going on strike" to protest American governance. The less educated adults were, the more likely they were to oppose the student strike. Still, even seven in ten college-educated adults opposed the strike, as did a slim majority of blacks and nearly seven of every eight whites. See George Gallup, *The Gallup Poll: 1959–1971*, vol. 3 (Princeton, NJ: Gallup Poll), 2250–53 (in this poll, adults were defined as at least age 21).

12. Kuhn: Harris 1875, September 1968. In reference to Chicago '68 polling, even those who said "get out of Vietnam altogether" sided more against the Chicago demonstrators than against Mayor Daley. My phrasing of "those who wanted to deescalate the Vietnam War" includes poll respondents who wanted the war deescalated or a gradual withdrawal. This phrasing combines two answers to questions in this poll on what course the next president should take in Vietnam: "pull US troops back to the cities" and leave the rest of the fighting to South Vietnamese, and "withdraw U.S. troops gradually" but still supply the South Vietnamese. And among them, they backed Daley's use of the cops at the convention by 66 to 23 percent. Among those who said "get out of Vietnam altogether," they favored Daley's use of the cops, but the sample size was too small to draw conclusions beyond that. By comparison, among those who wanted a more hawkish course in Vietnam, 77 percent said Daley "was right, the way he used the police to put down the demonstrators."

13. Kuhn: Harris 2055, January 1971. In January 1971, a Harris poll asked: "Would you favor or oppose a congressional act which would require all US troops to be withdrawn from Vietnam by the end of 1971?" A slim majority of whites said they favored the mandated pullout. Those whites who favored withdrawal also thought, by a slim majority, that student demonstrators were a "major cause of the breakdown of law and order." And here too, two-thirds of whites who favored a mandated pullout also believed "most student unrest" was caused by "radical troublemakers."

   Among those who thought the war was a "mistake," nearly half (47 percent) also thought student protestors were a "major cause of the breakdown of law and order," while about one-third (32 percent) thought they were a "minor cause"; less than one-fifth of doves thought student protestors were "hardly a cause" of "the breakdown of law and order."

14. Kuhn: Harris 2055, January 1971. More than three in four whites with no more than a high school degree thought student protests were caused by "radical troublemakers," far above the proportion among college-educated whites. Among whites who concluded the war was a "mistake," nearly three in four with no more than a high school education concluded "most student unrest" was caused by "radical troublemakers" rather than a sincere sense of "injustices in society," about 25 to 30 points above the better-educated.

15. Kuhn: Gallup 766, mid-August 1968. George Gallup, *The Gallup Poll: 1959–1971*, vol. 3 (Princeton, NJ: Gallup Poll), 2065, 2227–28 (collegian dove-hawk), 2223 (dove-hawk for all adults by education). In mid-August 1968, 53 percent of whites with no more than a high school education thought Vietnam was a "mistake," as did 53 percent of whites with at least some secondary education (when isolated to college grads—I hedge due to small sample size—they likely were only several points more dovish). College students, like the public, became more dovish as the war worsened. In 1967, slightly more than one-third of collegians said they were doves (half were hawks). But in winter 1969, two-thirds of collegians identified as doves. But half of college students still *approved* of how "Nixon is handling the situation in Vietnam," capturing how dovish collegians also held nuanced views rarely conveyed in the prestige press. Among all adults in winter 1969: a majority of those with a college degree said they were doves, but so did a majority of high school and grade-school-educated Americans.

16. Kuhn, Gallup 806, April-May 1970. Based on four income brackets, upscale whites were slightly *more* likely to support Nixon's Cambodian incursion than downscale whites (a slim majority, at least, of affluent whites backed Nixon on Cambodia, though the plurality of whites of all income levels did as well); 58 percent of whites with at least some secondary education (and roughly the same share of college grads) supported Nixon's Cambodia decision, compared to 49 percent of less-educated whites.

17. Kuhn: Gallup 821 and Gallup 824 combined, January and February 1971 (combining the datasets allows for a larger sample size and thus more statistically accurate demographic breakouts). In early 1971, 71 percent of whites with no more than a high school education wanted Congress to "require" troops to come home by the "end of this year," compared to 59 percent of whites with at least some college (college graduates, alone, polled at 59 percent as well). Even among whites who approved of President Nixon, two-thirds of blue collars wanted Congress to "require" troops come home by the "end of this year," compared to half of better-off whites. ("Blue collar" here means those with no higher education; "Better-off" includes respondents with at least some higher education.)

In early 1971, most whites and blacks wanted Congress to mandate the troop's return. But poor and blue-collar whites felt this way more strongly than upper-class whites. Indeed, three in four poor whites backed Congress mandating that the troops come home within the year. At least seven in ten whites from poor to middle-class households agreed. But only six in ten whites from upper-middle class to wealthy backgrounds supported the measure.

Furthermore, even when blue-collar whites were sometimes modestly less inclined to deem Vietnam a "mistake" (because, in part, they were more invested in the war and didn't want to believe it was for naught), they still wanted the boys home more than upscale whites (and perhaps that related to, proportionately, fewer affluent whites having kin in combat). In January 1971, the share who thought Vietnam was a "mistake": 56 percent of blue-collar whites (whites with no more than a high school education), nearly six in ten of all whites, and about two-thirds of nonwhites and white college graduates. But as with the Gallup data cited directly prior, this poll also found that blue-collar whites were more supportive than upscale whites of mandating all US troops leave Vietnam by the end of 1971 (Kuhn: Harris 2055, January 1971).

18. Kuhn: Gallup 806, April–June 1970. Harris, *The Harris Survey Yearbook of Public Opinion 1970* (NY: Louis Harris and Associates, 1971), 272, 275. "Nixon Popularity Increases in Poll," NYT, June 6, 1970.

After the worst wave of antiwar unrest, by October 1970 three in four Americans thought "militant student groups" were a "major cause" of "unrest on colleges campuses." But when asked the same question, this time citing "shootings, such as at Kent State and Jackson State," only 45 percent agreed the shootings were a "major cause" of unrest. By comparison, the majority saw "lenient" and "permissive" college presidents as a "major cause" of unrest.

The student protestors had allies. After the Cambodia escalation, but before the tumult of May, about a quarter of the public supported protestors. That was a relative high-water mark. It likely betrayed some frustration with the president over Cambodia. About one-third of Americans disapproved of how Nixon was "handling the Cambodian situation." Of course, based on the media coverage, the average American might have thought America was up in arms over Cambodia. Still, that less approved of student activism than approved of Cambodia is also telling (Kuhn: Harris 2037, August 1970).

19. Kuhn: Harris 2037, August 1970. Kuhn: Harris, 891105, August 18, 1989. Forty-two percent of whites without a college education said there was no respect, compared to 23 percent of whites who were college graduates. Views on the flag are not strictly rooted in class or in the "warrior class," those who fight our wars. For example, I suspect the more religious an American is, the more likely he or she is to hold traditional views of the flag.

On working-class whites revering the flag: For example, in 1989, after the Supreme Court ruled that the First Amendment protected the right to burn the American flag and the issue was at the fore of the national conversation, working-class whites disagreed with the ruling by a margin of 80 to 20 percent, while college-educated whites were nearly split, disagreeing 52 to 45 percent (see Kuhn: Harris, 891105, cited above).

20. Kuhn: Harris 2037, August 1970. "At War with War," *Time*, May 18, 1970.

21. Richard Harwood, "Flag's Defenders: Hard Hats March for a Way of Life," WP, May 31, 1970.

22. Robert Justin Goldstein, *Saving Old Glory: The History of the American Flag Desecration Controversy* (Boulder, CO: Westview Press, 1996), 99–102.

23. "Who Owns the Stars and Stripes?" *Time*, July 6, 1970. CBS, July 3, 1970. Federal Highway Administration, "State Motor Vehicle Registrations, by Years, 1900–1995," https://www.fhwa.dot.gov/ohim/summary95/mv200.pdf.

24. Hal Burton, "Yes, It's a Grand Old Flag . . . But Not All That Grand," *Newsday*, May 13, 1970. "Who Owns the Stars and Stripes?" *Time*, July 6, 1970.

25. Kenneth Gross, "Life Under a Hard Hat," *Newsday*, June 6, 1970.

26. Philip Foner, "Bloody Friday," *Left Review*, Spring 1980, 19–21.

27. Pat Walker, ed., *Between Labor and Capital* (Boston: South End Press, 1979), 184–86. Damon Stetson, "Unions Differ on Indochina War," NYT, May 13, 1970. Emanuel Perlmutter, "Head of Building Trades Unions Here Says Response Favors Friday's Action," NYT, May 12, 1970.

28. "The Lindsay Talk," *Newsweek*, March 1, 1971. In this Gallup poll, released in February 1971 according to *Newsweek* (I could not readily locate the dataset), Lindsay's lead over Gene McCarthy and Ed Muskie was likely within the poll's margin of error, though such was not reported. Still, it would still have been remarkable if Lindsay merely had tied the New Left hero of '68, Gene McCarthy, and Ed Muskie (then, leading contenders for the '72 nomination). In the poll, the politicians' favorability ratings with college students were thus: John Lindsay, 81 percent; Gene McCarthy, 79 percent; Ed Muskie, 78 percent; George McGovern, 76 percent; Ted Kennedy, 75 percent; Nelson Rockefeller, 63 percent; Hubert Humphrey, 60 percent, Richard Nixon, 49 percent, Ronald Reagan, 48 percent; George Wallace, 16 percent.

Chapter 28

1. Richard Bergholz, "Lindsay Slash at Power of Pentagon," LAT, February 24, 1972. "John Comes Lately," *Economist,* January 1, 1972. Theodore H. White, *The Making of the President 1972* (NY: Harper Collins, 2011), chap. 4, Kindle. Vincent Cannato, *The Ungovernable City: John Lindsay and His Struggle to Save New York* (NY: Basic Books, 2001), 499, 515–21. Liz Smith, "John V. Lindsay: Charisma's Child," *Cosmopolitan*, February 1972.

    Polling on Lindsay in early 1972 supports much of the impression in the media and the impression I try to come to historically in this book. For simplicity, I'll quote some of Louis Harris's analysis of his own polling in April 1972 rather than break it down into further subgroups. By 58 to 18 percent, the public agreed Lindsay was "an exciting, attractive public personality." The rub for Lindsay, by a 45 to 24 percent, was that they saw him as "more glamour than a sound man to run the country." By 50 to 15 percent, half the public believed Lindsay was not afraid to "speak out, even when it is unpopular to do so." Yet by a 34 to 24 percent the public saw him as too liberal, though notably the plurality was unsure on this question, likely because Lindsay was more widely known for his political celebrity and for being outspoken than for the specifics of his views, which would have changed had he remained in the race. Finally, by 48 to 23 percent, Americans' impression of his mayoralty at this time was that Lindsay "hasn't done so bad in an impossible job"; still, by a 40 to 27 percent margin, they thought he had a "poor record." See Louis Harris, "The Public Looks at John Lindsay," *Harris Survey*, April 3, 1972.

2. Richard A. Armstrong, "The Re-Education of John Lindsay," NYT, October 8, 1972. Ken Auletta, *The Streets Were Paved with Gold* (NY: Vintage Books, 1980), chaps. 2, 9, Kindle. Joseph P. Viteritti, ed., *Summer in the City: Lindsay, New York, and the American Dream* (Baltimore: Johns Hopkins University Press, 2014), 92. Michael Oreskes, "Census Traces Radical Shift in New York City's Population," NYT, September 20, 1982.

In 1969, New York City's poverty rate was 14.5 percent; the US rate was 13.7 percent. A decade later, the national poverty rate declined to 12.4 but Gotham's rate increased to 20.2—a 60 percent increase. See Mark K. Levitan, Susan S. Wieler, "Poverty in New York City, 1969–99: The Influence of Demographic Change, Income Growth, and Income Inequality," *Federal Reserve Bank of New York Economic Policy Review*, July 2008.

3. For issues in early 1972, May 1972 Harris poll, see Louis Harris, *The Harris Survey Yearbook of Public Opinion 1972*, 131.

4. Ben A. Franklin, "Pupil Busing Plan in Richard Area Upset on Appeal," NYT, June 7, 1972. Richard Bergholz, "Lindsay Slash at Power of Pentagon," LAT, February 24, 1972. Christopher Lydon, "The 1972 Campaign," NYT, March 24, 1972. Kenneth Reich, "Lindsay Finds Florida Votes Hard to Gather," LAT, March 11, 1972. Robert G. Kaufman, *Henry M. Jackson: A Life in Politics* (Seattle: University of Washington Press, 2000), 232–33. Melvin Maddocks, "Populism, What Does It Really Mean Anyway?" *Christian Science Monitor*, May 5, 1972.

5. John A. Farrell, *Richard Nixon: The Life* (NY: Knopf Doubleday, 2017), chap. 20, Kindle. Michael Barone, *Our Country: The Shaping of America from Roosevelt to Reagan* (New York: Macmillan Free Press, 1990), 500. John Herders, "Nixon Will Move to Offset Rulings for Pupil Busing," NYT, February 15, 1972. CBS News, March 16, 1972.

6. Kuhn: Gallup 801, March 1970. Data on "height of the Democratic primary," from March and May '72 Harris polls, see Harris, *The Harris Survey Yearbook of Public Opinion 1972*, 292, 293.

More Gallup results, for the March '70 poll: 85 percent of whites opposed busing, whether having no higher education or at least some higher education, and in this poll 82 percent of white Democrats, 86 percent of white independents, 88 percent of white Republicans, and 81 percent of white liberals were against busing, while white conservatives were 88 percent against.

Regarding black views of busing, Gallup October '71 polling showed blacks statistically split (47 percent against busing, 45 percent in favor); whites were, in this poll, 79 percent opposed, 18 percent in favor. Muskie supporters were

25 percent in favor, 67 percent opposed, while only about a tenth of Nixon and Wallace supporters favored busing. As the issue became more public by 1972, it appears blacks came to modestly favor busing, as three Harris polls found in 1972, where blacks ranged from 50 to 52 percent for and 34 to 37 percent against. The October 1971 Gallup poll was reported widely, perhaps explaining why the impression endured among historians and reporters that blacks were never for busing. For a relevant news story, see George H. Gallup, "3 of 4 Object to Pupil Busing, Though Opposition Softens," *Philadelphia Inquirer*, November 1, 1971.

7. Ben A. Franklin, "A Decision That May Be a Real Blockbuster: Busing," NYT, January 16, 1972. Robert G. Kaufman, *Henry M. Jackson: A Life in Politics* (Seattle: University of Washington Press, 2000), 232–33.

8. Poll question comparison based on questions from September 1970 Harris poll, questions listed in Harris, *The Harris Survey Yearbook of Public Opinion 1970*, 223.

9. William Safire, *Before the Fall* (NY: Tower Publications, 1975), 591–92. David S. Broder, "The Controversial Candidate," WP, October 3, 1971.

10. David Paul Kuhn, *The Neglected Voter: White Men and the Democratic Dilemma* (NY: Palgrave Macmillan, 2007), 61. "Cope Unable to Cope," *Economist*, October 14, 1972. Richard Krickus, *Pursuing the American Dream: White Ethnics and the New Populism* (Bloomington: Indiana University Press, 1976), 245. Tom Wicker, "In the Nation," NYT, July 9, 1972. R. W. Apple, "M'Govern Facing Troublesome Job in Unifying Party," NYT, July 17, 1972. Dan T. Carter, *The Politics of Rage: George Wallace, the Origins of the New Conservatism, and the Transformation of American Politics* (Baton Rouge: Louisiana State University Press, 1995), 449.

11. Thomas Byrne Edsall, Mary D. Edsall, *Chain Reaction: The Impact of Race, Rights, and Taxes on American Politics* (NY: W. W. Norton, 1992), 91, 93. Frederick G. Dutton, *Changing Sources of Power: American Politics in the 1970s* (NY: McGraw-Hill, 1971), 239–40. Jules Witcover, "Kennedy Aide Bridged Gap Between Politicians," *Baltimore Sun*, June 29, 2005. "Cope Unable to Cope," *Economist*, October 14, 1972. White, *The Making of the President 1972*, chap. 2, Kindle. "Radic-Lib Takes Wry Look at Demo Convention," *Human Events,* July 29, 1972. Jonathan Rieder, "Politics and Authenticity," *Dissent*, Summer 1975.

12. "Cope Unable to Cope," *Economist*, October 14, 1972. Dan T. Carter, *The Politics of Rage: George Wallace, the Origins of the New Conservatism, and the Transformation of American Politics* (Baton Rouge: Louisiana State University Press, 1995), 449. Harris, The Harris Survey Yearbook of Public Opinion *1972*, 78. Author interview, George Daly.

    With the AFL-CIO withholding its endorsement, Old Labor had pulled a New Left. McGovern had a better record on labor issues. So why did it happen? Nixon was not vehemently antilabor and had, for years, built cultural bridges to its ranks. The economy wasn't dire. Conventional material appeals felt small beside the cultural conflicts of the day, which encompassed wartime issues. But the withheld endorsement likely had scant impact. In the Harris poll, cited above, only a tenth of Americans from union households said Meany's opposition to McGovern made them "less likely" to back McGovern. Once party bosses lost their control of nominations, endorsements became especially overrated. In this time, one example was George Wallace. He was opposed by most of the Democratic establishment, had a modest electoral machine, and far outperformed expectations. At the convention, McGovern courted Wallace to attract his voters. Wallace explained: "Even if I was to endorse you, I couldn't get them to support you."

The larger lesson, however, of this AFL-CIO episode is what it foreshadowed for the Democratic coalition. The shifting concerns of liberals contributed to, as AFL-CIO leaders stress, Democrats not stressing fundamental union concerns in the decades ahead. That included not striving to repeal the portion of the Taft-Hartley Act that empowered conservatives to pass "right to work" laws when Democrats controlled the presidency and Congress. But it was also the absence of smaller fights, such as creating far greater penalties for firing workers who try to create unions. Such policies, while controversial, would have significantly mitigated labor's collapse. Union membership gradually declined between midcentury and 1970, to be 23 percent of the workforce that year. In 2016, it was 11 percent. That drop, though, includes white- and blue-collar unions. Blue-collar unions suffered most of these losses—their unionization rate is now below a tenth. And with those unions went a force limiting the wage gap (inequality) as well as Democrats last institutional connection with blue-collar whites. See David Paul Kuhn, "Big Labor's Last Stand," RealClearPolitics, February 27, 2011. On de-unionization's relationship to Democratic white support, as well as to the wage gap, see Kuhn, *The Neglected Voter*, 215–17. The Great Recession helped stimulate a wave of fascinating studies and articles on inequality and de-unionization. A smart primer is Alana Semuels, "Fewer Unions, Lower Pay for Everybody," *Atlantic*, August 30, 2016.

13. Harris, *The Harris Survey Yearbook of Public Opinion 1972*, 180, 204. Jack Rosenthal, "Poll Finds Issues Not an Issue in '72," NYT, October 8, 1972.

14. Reagan for President Campaign Plan 1980 (not a public record, in author's files). David Paul Kuhn, "Big Government and Its Discontents," RealClearPolitics, April 20, 2010. Craig Fehrman, "All the President's Memories," NYT, November 4, 2010.

15. On McGovern memo, see Jefferson Cowie, *Stayin' Alive: The 1970s and the Last Days of the Working Class* (NY: New Press, 2010), 166. Ben J. Wattenberg, *In Search of the Real America: A Challenge to the Chaos of Failure and Guilt* (NY: G. P. Putman's Sons, 1974), 287.

In June 1972, the American public was 53 to 38 percent against amnesty for draft dodgers. With the general election effectively under way by August, the margin was 59 to 24 against. On wanting troops home from Vietnam, both Harris polls in May and August 1972 found about three in four favored bringing all the troops home from Vietnam.

The October '72 Gallup poll asked what respondents thought the top issue was. About a quarter answered Vietnam (half what it was in '68), about a quarter answered inflation and the cost of living.

16. Kuhn: 1972 National Election Day Survey, CBS News exit poll for 1972. Kuhn: University of Michigan American National Election Studies (ANES) datasets 1960, 1968, 1972, and cumulative ANES dataset. (When citing cross-tabs for voting blocs in 1972—for example, the white labor vote—I use the CBS exit poll in no small part because the exit poll has a sample size of 17,595, compared to 2,705 in ANES 1972; ANES is used for longitudinal comparisons preceding 1972.)

Nixon's blue-collar gains between 1960 and 1972 were seen whether whites with no tertiary education were compared with college-educated whites, or whites with no education beyond high school were compared to those with at least some post-high-school education. The same pattern held between 1968 and 1972. Even without a third-party candidate in the race, McGovern's support among the white and well-educated (in this era: at least some college or college-educated alone) matched Democrats' support in 1968 or possibly inched up, but the support of those whites with no more than a high school education fell from 39 percent in 1968 to 31 percent in 1972. A slim majority of voters between the ages of 18 and 29 turned out to vote in 1972, a record to this day; it was because of educated youth, as more than six in ten young voters with at least some college education voted. Nixon won the youth vote 52 to 46 percent, and he won white young adults 57 to 41 percent.

17. Charles W. Colson, *Born Again* (Old Tappan, NJ: Chosen Books, 1976), 3–4.
18. Natalie Kitroeff, "Immigrants Flooded California Construction. Worker Pay Sank. Here's Why," LAT, April 22, 2017. U.S. Bureau of the Census, "Historical Income Tables, Table P-8. Age—People, All Races, by Median Income and Sex: 1947 to 2018." By "typical," I'm referring to the median male income from 1973 to 2018, adjusted for inflation. In 1973, the median male income was $40,810. It would not reach that level again for three decades, only to decline and reach $41,615 in 2018. When adjusted for inflation, the median income for white men was also the same when Trump won the presidency as when the Watergate hearings heralded the end of Nixon's presidency. Thus, after an historically strong economic recovery following the Great Recession, the median American man still earned roughly the same as he did in 1973.

Afterword

1. David Paul Kuhn, "How FDR's 'Forgotten Man' Sunk Obama's Coalition," DN, November 9, 2016.

2. David Paul Kuhn, "Will the Political Establishment Be Trumped by The Donald?" *National Review*, August 22, 2015.

3. Kuhn: Pew Research Center's polarization polls, June 2014 (Those who said "I often don't have enough money to make ends meet": 55 percent of blacks, 51 percent of Hispanics, 43 percent of working class whites agree, 18 percent of college educated whites. On the view that "elected officials in Washington lose touch with the people pretty quickly": 83 percent of the white working class agreed, slightly above college educated whites and 8 percentage points more than blacks and Hispanics. One note, sample size on this Pew dataset was unusually large, 10,013 adults, allowing precision with demographic comparisons). Kuhn: PRRI poll, October 2016 (Those who would find it "difficult" to pay a $400 emergency expense: 22 percent of college educated whites, 57 percent of working class whites, 58 percent of blacks, and 63 percent of Hispanics). Camilo Maldonado, "Price Of College Increasing Almost 8 Times Faster Than Wages," *Forbes*, July 24, 2018 (the growth in college costs outpaced wages by at least sevenfold between 1989 and 2016). Anne Case, Angus Deaton, "Mortality and Morbidity in the 21st Century," Brookings Institution, Brookings Papers on Economic Activity (Spring 2017) (between about 2000 and 2015, the midlife mortality rate for the white working-class surpassed minority groups for the first time). William Emmons, Ana Hernández Kent, Lowell Ricketts, "Why Is the White Working Class in Decline?" St. Louis Fed, May 20, 2019 (reported that white working class share of American families declined from 55 to 42 percent from 1989 to 2016, while their share of the national wealth fell from 45 to 22 percent). Robert E. Scott, "Growth in U.S.–China Trade Deficit Between 2001 and 2015 Cost 3.4 Million Jobs," Economic Policy Institute, January 31, 2017 (Between 2001 and 2015, the Economic Policy Institute found that China's WTO entrance cost the United States 3.4 million jobs, mostly within manufacturing). David Paul Kuhn, "Obama and the Invisible Workingman," RealClearPolitics, December 22, 2009. Thomas Edsall, "The Future of the Obama Coalition," NYT, November 27, 2011. David Paul Kuhn, "The Crash, Obama and the Disappearing Dem Majority, RealClearPolitics, September 15, 2010. David Paul Kuhn, "The Jobless Gender Gap," WSJ, November 27, 2009. David Paul Kuhn, "Democrats Dare Not 'Abandon' the White Working Class, RealClearPolitics, December 5, 2011. Kuhn, *Neglected Voter,* 216 (For Podhorzer quote and regarding pensions: between 1980 and 2003, the share of the workforce with defined benefit pensions plummeted from 28 to 5 percent). Emmanuel Saez, Thomas Piketty, Gabriel Zucman, "Economic Growth in the United States: A Tale of Two Countries," The Washington

Center for Equitable Growth, December 6, 2016. For male income stagnation, for all races and whites, see the end of Chapter 28 and corresponding note.

4. David Paul Kuhn, "Sorry, Liberals. Bigotry Didn't Elect Donald Trump," NYT, December 26, 2016. Paul Farhi, "#Biased? Reporters on Twitter Don't Hold Back About Trump," WP, October 27, 2016. Dylan Byers, "The Temptations of Twitter: Why Social Media Is Still a Minefield for Journalists," NBCnews.com, October 22, 2018. Patricia Hart, "Not So Great in '78," *Texas Monthly*, May 31, 1999. David Paul Kuhn, *The Neglected Voter: White Men and the Democratic Dilemma* (NY: Palgrave Macmillan, 2007), 168, 201.

5. Theodore Roosevelt, *The Works of Theodore Roosevelt: American Ideals* (NY: P. F. Collier & Son, 1897), 75.

6. Lou Cannon, *Governor Reagan: His Rise to Power* (NY: Public Affairs, 2003), 147. Steven F. Hayward, *The Age of Reagan: The Fall of the Old Liberal Order, 1964–1980* (NY: Three Rivers Press, 2001), 99. Henry Allen, "The Real 1980s, How Life Went On," WP, November 14, 1989.

7. "Ronald Reagan's Remarks at Liberty State Park on September 1, 1980," YouTube video, 20:56, posted by Reagan Library, June 25, 2018, https://www.youtube.com/watch?v=BVGlxqowmKA. Rachelle Patterson, "The Stretch Drive, Reagan Goes After Blue-Collar Voters," *Boston Globe,* September 2, 1980. Douglas E. Kneeland, "Reagan Hits Chicago Streets with a Visit to Lithuanians," NYT, September 9, 1980. Rachelle Patterson, "Reagan Has a Way with Ethnic Groups," *Boston Globe*, October 10, 1980. Howell Raines, "In Move to the Center, Reagan Plans to Alter 2 Antiunion Positions," NYT, October 9, 1980. David Paul Kuhn, *The Neglected Voter: White Men and the Democratic Dilemma* (NY: Palgrave Macmillan, 2007), 105. Reagan for President Campaign Plan 1980, author's files.

8. Author interview, W. J. Usery. David Paul Kuhn, *The Neglected Voter: White Men and the Democratic Dilemma* (NY: Palgrave Macmillan, 2007), 64.

INDEX

For the benefit of digital users, indexed terms that span two pages (e.g., 52–53) may, on occasion, appear on only one of those pages.

Bleecker Street, 45

Bloody Friday. *See* Hardhat Riot

Bloomberg, Michael, 78

blue-collar Americans. *See also* hardhats
activism and, 66–67, 117, 123
busing and, 284–85
college education and, 115–16
decline of, 3, 280, 290
Democratic Party and, 2, 62, 285–87, 289–90, 295–96
discontents of, 61–65, 231, 235
Fallows on, 71–72
flag desecration and, 277–79
Goodwin on, 60
Hamill on, 61–62
Kennedy (Robert) and, 51–53, 90–91
Kennedy (Ted) on, 63
New Left and, 3, 88–89, 273–74, 276, 280
police ties of, 155–56
Reagan and, 294–96
Republican Party and, 252, 294–96
trade union integration and, 106–8
Trump and, 291–95
Vietnam War service and, 70–71, 72, 75, 76–79, 327n3

Boland, Martin, 178

Bolles, Harry, 157–58, 173, 232–33

bombings in response to Kent State, 114–15, 124, 227, 241

Boone, Pat, 255

Boston, 29–30, 34

Boyle, Peter, 273–74

Brachfeld, Nancy, 128, 130

Bradley, Bill, 31, 219, 222–23

Brennan, Jack, 118

Brennan, Peter
on ending Vietnam War, 76, 276
on flag desecration, 278
military service of, 155
Nixon and, 250–51, 252–53, 253*f*, 267–68, 269, 359n3

as secretary of labor, 290
on union men in Hardhat Riot, 231–32
Workers' Woodstock and, 243–44, 245

Breslin, Jimmy, 49–50, 61, 66–67, 85–86, 323n9

Brewster, Kingman, 214–15

Broder, David, 73, 292

Brooklyn College, 34

Brown, H. Rap, 12

Brown, Pat, 295

Bryan, William Jennings, 262, 340n20

Bryant Park, 31

Buchanan, Pat
on affirmative action, 107
on days following Kent State, 223–24
Democratic National Convention protest and, 23
draft evasion by, 78
on Lindsay, 83
on Nixon, 58–59, 118, 352n16
Nixon's blue-collar strategy and, 250, 251, 365n23
on Reagan, 34, 57–58
Silent Majority and, 38
student demonstrations and, 19–20, 116
on swing voters, 267

Buckley, Jim, 264–65, 268

Buckleys, 261

Bull, Steve, 223–24, 251, 352n16, 359n4

Bunche, Ralph, 60

Burkhardt, Karen, 200

Burns, John, 148, 149, 152, 215–16, 239

Burns, Thomas, 241

Burroughs, William, 23

Bush, George H. W., 39, 69

Bush, George W., 78, 292, 294–95

Bush, Nancy, 39

crime and crime rates (*cont.*)
  New York City and, 42, 43–47, 49,
    317n13, 317n16
  Newark and, 53
  poverty and, 52–53
  in the sixties, 27, 43
Cronkite, Walter, 36, 227
Cuba and Cuban Revolution,
    14, 310n14
Curtis, Charlotte, 95

Daily News
  on Hardhat Riot, 228–29
  on Moratorium Day, 33
  on Worker's Woodstock, 247
Daley, Richard
  1968 Democratic National
    Convention and, 21, 22, 23, 25–
    27, 28, 312n11
  King assassination and, 51
  police deployment by, 25–27,
    276, 313n14
  on press and television, 59
  public opinion of, 370n12
Daly, George
  on American flag, 279
  Democratic Party and, 286–87
  on draft, 75
  military service of, 155
  Nixon and, 252–53, 253*f*
  on police, 156
  steamfitters' union and, 105
  on violence at hardhat
    demonstrations, 233
  Workers' Woodstock and, 243–44
Dartmouth, 230–31
Daub, Robert, 172, 176
Davidoff, Sid
  on Columbia occupation, 15
  Hardhat Riot and, 121, 197, 199,
    220–21, 346n4
  on Kent State memorial actions, 8

King assassination and, 49–50
Lindsay's presidential campaign
    and, 282
Davies, Gareth, 318–19n3
Davis, Rennie, 13, 26, 112,
    116–17, 256
Davis-Bacon Act (1931), 268
de Chaves, Joseph, 181
Death Wish (film), 43
Debs, Eugene, 66
DeBusschere, Dave, 31, 221, 222–23
deferments. *See* draft
deindustrialization of cities, 41–
    42, 56. *See also* factories and
    manufacturing
Dellinger, Dave, 13, 24, 116–17, 273
Democratic National Convention
    (Chicago, 1968)
  Columbia occupation and, 14
  demonstrations during, 21–27, 31,
    40–41, 53, 313n14, 370n12
  impact of, 27, 87–88, 276,
    313n16, 320n7
  media coverage of, 22–23, 26, 27
  police brutality and, 24, 25, 26
Democratic Party. *See also* Democratic
    National Convention
  1968 presidential election and,
    315–16n2
  1972 elections and, 286–90
  2016 elections and, 2
  Chicago convention protest
    and, 29, 38
  counterculture and, 275
  hardhats and, 272
  Jackson on, 285–86
  law in order in platform of, 42–43,
    48, 320n9
  Lindsay and, 92–93, 281
  Middle America and, 267
  New Left and, 286, 310n14
  in the South, 103, 340n19

Humphrey and, 27–28
ideology of, 16, 27–28,
  285–86, 310n14
Kerry and, 130
liberal accomplishments and, 82–83
Lindsay and, 83, 90, 91–95, 121,
  280, 281–82, 310n14
McGovern and, 287–88, 310n14
police and, 16–17, 18, 24
New Majority, 266, 268–69,
  286, 288–90
New York City
  1970 elections in, 264–66
  as blue-collar city, 3, 41, 104–5, 342n23
  crime in, 42, 43–47, 49,
    317n13, 317n16
  factories and manufacturing in,
    41–42, 322n14
  federal policy impacting, 40
  Great Migration and, 40–41
  Honor America Day in, 254–55
  immigrant populations in, 101–2,
    105, 265
  Kent State shooting protests
    in, 119–31
  King assassination and, 49–51
  Lindsay and, 39–40, 45–47, 54–55,
    57–58, 84–85
  Moratorium Day and, 31, 32f, 34
  pollution in, 41–42
  poverty and, 282, 374n2
  prostitution in, 46
  Spanish Harlem riot in, 46–47
  transit strike in, 84
  white/corporate flight from, 54, 55–56
  Workers' Woodstock in, 243–49
  World War Two victory celebrations
    in, 154–55
  yuppiedom and, 44–45
New York City Municipal Archives,
  299–300
New York Graphic, 182,
  236–37, 352n16

New York Police Department
  (NYPD). *See also* New York Police
  Department (NYPD) in Hardhat
  Riot; police
  ACLU class-action suit against,
    236, 301
  Columbia occupation and, 15–18,
    112–13, 308n10, 309–10n12
  Hardhat Riot investigation by, 236–
    40, 351n2, 352n16, 356–57n22
  intelligence files of, 297–301
  Irish immigrants and, 18
  Italian immigrants and, 18
  Lindsay and, 46–47, 228–29, 232,
    234–35, 236, 239–40
  media on hardhat investigation
    of, 240
New York Police Department (NYPD)
  in Hardhat Riot
  all-clear reported by, 169
  City Hall defense by, 175–83, 177f,
    198–201, 203, 238
  crowd control units deployed,
    168, 173
  dispersal efforts of, 213
  flag desecration and, 348n3
  hardhat arrests by, 214, 230
  hardhat support from, 148–49,
    173, 174, 183, 187, 189,
    199–200, 206
  hardhats breaking through line of,
    139, 141–44
  inaction of, 189, 190, 191, 192,
    194, 195, 196–97, 201, 203, 212,
    239, 356n17
  K.O. Joe and, 170–71
  Leary on, 228
  Pace College attacks and, 195–97,
    203, 214–15, 349n1
  student demonstrations and, 130,
    131, 135, 136, 138–39, 196
  students injured by, 167, 195, 211
  underreporting by, 168